NAFTA'S IMPACT
ON
NORTH AMERICA

Significant Issues Series
Timely books presenting current CSIS research and analysis of interest to the
academic, business, government, and policy communities.
Managing editor: Roberta L. Howard

For four decades, the **Center for Strategic and International Studies (CSIS)** has been
dedicated to providing world leaders with strategic insights on—and policy solutions
to—current and emerging global issues.

CSIS is led by John J. Hamre, formerly deputy secretary of defense, who has been
president and CEO since April 2000. It is guided by a board of trustees chaired by
former senator Sam Nunn and consisting of prominent individuals from both the
public and private sectors.

The CSIS staff of 190 researchers and support staff focus primarily on three subject
areas. First, CSIS addresses the full spectrum of new challenges to national and
international security. Second, it maintains resident experts on all of the world's major
geographical regions. Third, it is committed to helping to develop new methods of
governance for the global age; to this end, CSIS has programs on technology and
public policy, international trade and finance, and energy.

Headquartered in Washington, D.C., CSIS is private, bipartisan, and tax-exempt.
CSIS does not take specific policy positions; accordingly, all views expressed herein
should be understood to be solely those of the author(s).

The CSIS Press
Center for Strategic and International Studies
1800 K Street, N.W., Washington, D.C. 20006
Telephone: (202) 887-0200 Fax: (202) 775-3199
E-mail: books@csis.org Web: www.csis.org

NAFTA'S IMPACT
ON
NORTH AMERICA

THE FIRST DECADE

EDITED BY SIDNEY WEINTRAUB

FOREWORD BY CARLA A. HILLS

THE CSIS PRESS

Center for Strategic
and International Studies
Washington, D.C.

Significant Issues Series, Volume 26, Number 5
Cover design by Robert L. Wiser
Cover photograph: © Corbis

08 07 06 05 04   5 4 3 2 1

ISSN 0736-7136
ISBN 0-89206-451-X

Library of Congress Cataloging-in-Publication Data

NAFTA's impact on North America : the first decade / edited by Sidney Weintraub ;
foreword by Carla A. Hills
    p. cm. — (CSIS significant issues series ; v. 26, no. 5)
    Includes bibliographical references and index.
    ISBN 0-89206-451-X (pb : alk. paper)
1. Free trade—North America. 2. Canada. Treaties, etc. 1992 Oct. 7. 3. North
America—Economic conditions. 4. North America—Economic integration. 5. United
States—Foreign relations—Mexico. 6. Mexico—Foreign relations—United States.
I. Weintraub, Sidney, 1922– II. Center for Strategic and International Studies
(Washington, D.C.). III. Title. IV. Series.
    HF1746.N34 2004
    382'.917–dc22   2004016450

CONTENTS

Foreword   vii

Preface   xi

Acknowledgments   xxiii

PART I. ECONOMICS AND BUSINESS

1. **Trade, Investment, and Economic Growth**
Sidney Weintraub   3

2. **The New Regionalism and Foreign Direct Investment in the Americas**
Lorraine Eden and Dan Li   21

3. **Prospects for North American Monetary Cooperation in the Next Decade**
Rogelio Ramírez de la O   69

PART II. LABOR AND THE ENVIRONMENT

4. **Mixing Environment and Trade Policies under NAFTA**
Jan Gilbreath and Janine Ferretti   93

5. **Labor Regulations and Trade Union Convergence in North America**
Graciela Bensusán   123

PART III. GOVERNMENTAL AND PRIVATE LINKS

6. The Functioning of NAFTA and Its Impact on
   Mexican–U.S. Relations
   Rafael Fernández de Castro   159

7. Civil Society Organizations, Freedom of Information,
   and Transparency in Mexico's Agenda in the
   Context of NAFTA: A Normative Approach
   Ernesto Villanueva   187

PART IV. SECURITY

8. Mexican Policy against Drugs:
   From Deterring to Embracing the United States
   María Celia Toro   209

9. Security Imperatives of North American Integration:
   Back to a Future of Hub and Spokes
   John Bailey   235

PART V. SOCIAL ISSUES

10. NAFTA and Mexican Migration to the United States
    Frank D. Bean and B. Lindsay Lowell   263

11. NAFTA and Mexican Higher Education
    Carlos Ornelas   285

12. Poverty and Inequality
    John Scott   307

PART VI. POLITICAL ISSUES

13. NAFTA and Sovereignty
    James Robinson   341

14. Democracy in Mexico
    José Woldenberg Karakowsky   371

15. North American Integration:
    A Spontaneous Process or a Driven Enterprise?
    Jesús F. Reyes-Heroles   391

    Index   411

    About the Authors   437

FOREWORD

Carla A. Hills

Very early in the morning of August 12, 1992, exactly 14 months after formal negotiations were launched in Toronto, the trade ministers of Canada, Mexico, and the United States shook hands, advised their respective prime minister and presidents, and announced publicly that they had reached agreement on the terms of the North American Free Trade Agreement (NAFTA).

Although Presidents Bush and Salinas and Prime Minister Mulroney signed NAFTA in December 1992, it was only after a lengthy and acrimonious debate that Congress finally approved the agreement in November 1993. Ten years later, NAFTA continues to generate sharp controversy.

The political backlash against the ratification of NAFTA contributed to the unwillingness of the U.S. Congress for the succeeding eight years to renew the president's trade-negotiating authority. In 2002 President Bush secured that authority by a bare three-vote margin in the House of Representatives.

Ironically, as the economic benefits and opportunities generated by NAFTA have accumulated, public support throughout North America for open markets has waned. A large number of citizens in all three countries, but especially in the United States, are skeptical about whether they benefit from trade agreements. Many believe that all trade agreements, but particularly NAFTA, cost more jobs than they create.

NAFTA has served as a convenient scapegoat for the problems connected to our recent economic slowdown. "No more NAFTAs" is a familiar rallying cry for those protesting against trade. For the past half-decade,

Carla A. Hills, formerly the U.S. trade representative, is chair and CEO of Hills & Company, International Consultants.

antitrade protests have been a feature of every meeting of the World Trade Organization, the International Monetary Fund, and the World Bank. Fifty thousand protesters marched on Cancun last summer. We can agree with the protesters that economic liberalization is not a panacea for the region's ills. Trade and investment alone do not educate children or eradicate disease. That requires the public and private sectors to be willing to use some of the gains derived from trade and investment for those purposes.

But it is indisputable that broad trade agreements, like NAFTA, that lock in existing liberalization and encourage future reform help to create the resources necessary to deal with tough social problems. In addition, broad trade agreements promote the rule of law, transparency, and respect for property that encourage political reform.

NAFTA is a broad trade agreement, the product of an unusual negotiation. Apart from very few exempted sectors, the three participants agreed at the outset that their objective was free trade. Although hard bargaining took place over the scope of the exemptions and about the time that each would take to eliminate restrictions—particularly those that were politically sensitive—we were partners in the effort to find ways to overcome the obstacles to achieving the agreed result, free trade within the North America region.

As a result, NAFTA was the most comprehensive trade agreement ever concluded. Its broad market-opening provisions still serve as a benchmark for ongoing trade negotiations. For example:

- It eliminated, not just reduced, tariffs on all industrial goods in periods of less than 15 years;

- it guaranteed unrestricted agricultural trade within 15 years between Mexico and and the United States—the first trade agreement to remove all such barriers;

- it opened a broad range of services, including financial services;

- it provided the highest standard of protection for intellectual property;

- it established clear rules to protect investors; and

- most important, it created a framework that encourages transparency, respect for property, and adherence to rule of law increasing predictability in commercial dealings.

As a direct result of its market-opening provisions, trade among the three participants has grown more than twice as fast as their trade with the rest of the world. Last year trade among the three hit a record of $625 billion. In the 10 years since the adoption of NAFTA, Mexico's exports have climbed more than 200 percent. More than 80 percent of Mexico and Canada's exports come to the United States, pulled by the large U.S. market, lower cost of transport, and high degree of related-party production. Less frequently noted is the huge value of U.S. exports to its two neighbors: combined, they exceed U.S. exports to all of Europe and are nearly equal to U.S. exports to all of Asia.

In addition, foreign direct investment within the region has soared, as NAFTA partners have substantially increased investment in each other's markets. Also, NAFTA has stimulated increased investment from countries outside the region. North America now accounts for a quarter of global inward investment.

By reducing trade barriers and restrictions on investment, NAFTA has enabled industries—like automotive, electronic, chemical, and textile, and apparel—to integrate production across the entire North American market, which has substantially strengthened their competitive positions not only in the region but also globally.

Importantly, NAFTA did more than stimulate trade and competition throughout the region. It demonstrated that nations of different cultural backgrounds, different languages, and very different levels of development could negotiate a means to enlarge economic opportunities that would benefit all of the participants.

The 1994 ratification of the agreement by the U.S. Congress affected policy thinking worldwide:

- It encouraged leaders at the Asia-Pacific Economic Cooperation forum a few days following ratification to agree to open trade and investment throughout the Pacific Rim;
- it breathed new life into then-stalled global multilateral trade negotiations—a few months later the Uruguay Round was concluded, and the World Trade Organization was created; and
- it persuaded the 34 hemispheric leaders at the Miami Summit to agree, just one year later, to negotiate a Free Trade Area of the Americas.

Also, the increased commercial interaction among the citizens of the two developed democracies in the North with citizens in Mexico had significant nontrade effects. Many believe that the spotlight placed on Mexico as a result of NAFTA contributed significantly to the advance of democratic reforms. President Zedillo's election in 1994 was considered the cleanest in years, with 78 percent of registered voters participating.

President Zedillo sponsored reforms to share governmental power with Congress, the judiciary, and the states, reversing a tradition of placing absolute control in the hands of the president.

Mexico's legislative elections in 1997, deemed fair by international observers, caused the ruling party (the PRI) to lose control of Congress for the first time in 69 years. Contrary to predictions, the executive and legislative branches managed to work together, most notably in passing the 1998 budget in a timely fashion. With the smooth transition following the election of 2000 when Vicente Fox, a member of an opposition party, was elected president, Mexico demonstrated continued progress toward becoming a multiparty democracy.

Sidney Weintraub, a career diplomat, professor, and scholar of Latin America who currently holds the William E. Simon Chair in Political Economy at CSIS and directs the CSIS Americas Program, provides in *NAFTA's Impact on North America: The First Decade* a thorough evaluation of NAFTA in all of its ramifications. He has assembled 16 specialists: 4 from the United States (with Sidney as an author as well as editor), 2 from Canada, and 10 from Mexico. Their careful analyses cover not only the economic outcomes, but also issues involving labor and the environment, institutional development, security, social concerns, and political development.

Weintraub has done a masterful job. His study will be extremely useful not only to those interested in the economic, trade, social, political, and security effects of NAFTA, but also to those interested in the likely consequences of other broad regional trade agreements. The 34 democratically elected governments of the Western Hemisphere are currently engaged in negotiating a Free Trade Area of the Americas. *NAFTA's Impact on North America: The First Decade* provides a useful checklist of the policy outcomes that should and should not be expected from a comprehensive market opening agreement in this hemisphere.

PREFACE

Sidney Weintraub

The entry into force on January 1, 1994, of the North American Free Trade Agreement (NAFTA) was a significant event in North American relations and for global trade policy. For the three countries of North America—Canada, Mexico, and the United States—it presaged a new trade and investment relationship, buttressed by preferential treatment.[1] As a consequence, trade among the three countries soared beyond the substantial level that had previously existed. The proportions of intra-NAFTA exports relative to total exports for the three countries in 2002 were Canada, 87 percent; Mexico, 90 percent; and the United States, 36 percent.

Free trade agreements (FTAs) have proliferated in the Western Hemisphere during the past 15 years. NAFTA is not only the most important in economic terms, but is the gold-plated model because of the many disciplines it encompasses. Most other hemispheric economic integration agreements, whether they are FTAs or customs unions, fall far short of NAFTA in their obligations—and, hence, their benefits—for the signatory nations.[2]

NAFTA'S PERFORMANCE

NAFTA was born in conflict in each of the three countries because the opening of markets impinges both favorably and negatively on different interests. Companies able to compete effectively in export markets welcome the opportunity an FTA offers; those subject to competition from lower-cost foreign suppliers lobby hard to retain their protection. Free trade brings winners and losers. Whether free trade is beneficial to a country therefore requires some assessment that there are more winners than losers among producers of goods and services and their employees. The original insight on how to determine the desirability of an economic integration agreement was to measure whether it created more trade for the world than existed earlier, or whether it merely diverted trade from outsiders to insiders in the integration arrangement.[3] By any measure, whether the calculation is static or dynamic, NAFTA as devised was overwhelmingly trade creating.

Nationals of countries as consumers clearly benefit from free trade because they enjoy access to more goods and services at lower prices than when they are taxed indirectly by tariffs on imports. This greater consumer choice is abundantly evident to anybody who now shops in Mexican supermarkets and department stores and compares the selection with what existed pre-NAFTA. Free trade is about competition, and this is the key to consumer benefits. Thus, although the evidence is overwhelmingly positive that the general population of all three NAFTA countries benefited from NAFTA, the measures taken to compensate the losers—particularly workers who lost their jobs—have not been adequate in any of them. Workers who lose jobs for any reason—from trade, technological change, fashion changes, or whatever—must largely fend for themselves in Mexico and the United States.

The benefits of NAFTA affected the various regions of countries differently. In Mexico, for example, the north and the Valley of Mexico saw considerable job creation while the south was largely unaffected. Consequently, economic and social disparities widened between regions. These regional disparities have long existed in Mexico; NAFTA did not create them.

Most analyses of NAFTA deal with the trade and economic consequences of the agreement, and this is done explicitly in chapter 1; but that is not the book's main purpose because these matters have been much discussed in all three countries during the past 10 years. The focus of this book is on the noneconomic outcomes of NAFTA. As noted in chapter 1, President George H.W. Bush responded affirmatively to the proposal made by President Carlos Salinas de Gortari of Mexico to enter into free trade negotiations because he was convinced this would narrow the political distance between the two countries.[4] In an earlier situation, President George H.W. Bush had reacted similarly earlier when the Canadian prime minister, Brian Mulroney, proposed the negotiation of an FTA between the two countries.

The chapters of this book demonstrate, in my view, that the positive fallout from NAFTA in its totality has been more important than even the significant trade and investment growth. Before NAFTA, there was a definite coolness, a formality that stifled friendship, in Mexican–U.S. relations. Governmental relations between the two countries today are less stilted, in fact highly informal at the working level, more open to give-and-take, and more productive than had existed for a century or more before NAFTA.

Intergovernmental problems still arise between the NAFTA countries—as they do between all countries, no matter how friendly they are—but they are now discussed and, for the most part, have become more amenable to satisfactory compromise. This is true for such thorny issues as environmental protection and drug trafficking, and perhaps soon for migration—and all these subjects are dealt with in separate chapters in the book. Mexico has become a more democratic country over the past decade, mostly due to an internal clamor over many years, but the deeper contact with the United States stemming from NAFTA may have accelerated this process. Nongovernmental organizations now cooperate across the border more deeply than was the case before NAFTA. This is true for the environment and labor, and to protect human rights. A North American community akin to what has happened in Western Europe in the post–World War II period does not exist, but it is no longer an impossible dream.

Canada and Mexico, in effect, discovered each other as a result of NAFTA. Mexico was able to emerge from its serious financial and economic crisis of 1995 within a year partly because of its more favorable access to the U.S. market after NAFTA—combined with the U.S.-led financial support package—whereas the emergence from Mexico's debt crisis in 1982 took six years. When the Liberal Party took over the government of Canada, it shifted its position and strongly supported the Canada–U.S. Free Trade Agreement (CUFTA) and then NAFTA, whereas the party leadership vehemently opposed free trade with the United States in the election in 1987 in which CUFTA was the main issue.

NAFTA has not been a panacea. It has not cured all internal ills in the three countries, nor led to the resolution of all problems that exist among them. Trade has flourished, but this has not abolished trade disputes; it may even have increased these disputes because there is so much more trade. NAFTA has not stemmed the rise in unemployment in the United States since 2000, nor was it responsible for the full employment in the United States during much of the 1990s. NAFTA was not sufficient in and of itself to foster high economic growth rates in any of the three countries, but it contributed to this growth to the extent that increased trade can do this.

NAFTA must be assessed for what it is. It is a trade and investment agreement that succeeded in its central purpose. And, in the process, it brought the three countries together in a variety of noneconomic areas in a most salutary fashion.

CONTENTS OF THE BOOK

The book has 15 chapters. Americans wrote or contributed to 4 of them, Mexicans to 10, and Canadians to 2. There is much more emphasis on United States–Mexico relations, and internal Mexican developments, than on United States–Canada relations. This is because the U.S.-Canada relationship was less conflicted than the United States–Mexico relationship before NAFTA. Even on free trade, CUFTA preceded NAFTA by six years, and Canada thus had an opportunity to assess the benefits and costs to it of free trade. Indeed, Canadians who had participated in the CUFTA negotiations were brought in to advise Mexicans on how to deal with Americans in a trade negotiation. Canada and the United States are both high-income countries, and Mexico is not. Indeed, when put into place, NAFTA was a more severe experiment than existed elsewhere—including in the then-enlarged European Economic Community, which included Ireland, Greece, Portugal, and Spain—on the effect of free trade between less-developed and more-developed countries.

Part I of the book considers economic and business issues. In chapter 1, "Trade, Investment, and Economic Growth," Sidney Weintraub explains why each of the three countries agreed to join in NAFTA, making clear that for the United States the main motive may have been noneconomic—namely, to bring Mexico and the United States closer politically. For Canada and Mexico, the main motive was economic—to stimulate and secure exports to the United States and to attract more foreign direct investment.

With respect to augmenting trade and investment, which are the explicit objectives spelled out in the agreement, NAFTA achieved its intent. The bulk of intra-NAFTA trade moves expeditiously, even agricultural trade where disputes between Mexico and the United States abound and have been hard to resolve. The big disappointment for Mexico has been its lackluster growth in the years since NAFTA went into effect, but this stems from broad macroeconomic and structural policy deficiencies. NAFTA may have helped to maintain Mexico's economic growth by the expanding the country's external sector, but the agreement could not be a panacea for all of Mexico's problems.

In chapter 2, "The New Regionalism and Foreign Direct Investment in the Americas," Lorraine Eden and Dan Li provide a comprehensive discussion of the literature and what is happening in the "new regionalism" in the Americas—which they define at one point as a movement from shallow integration (old regionalism) to deep integration. Considerable data are provided on investment flows. Just as trade stemming from an economic integration agreement can be trade creating or trade diverting, so too can foreign direct investment (FDI) be investment creating (i.e., more investment is added than would have existed without the regional integration) or investment diverting (i.e., a shift in investment going to outside countries and directing it instead to inside countries).

The empirical literature is not clear whether regional integration stimulates more horizontal FDI, where the production the investment generates is mainly for the domestic market, or vertical FDI, which links the value chain of the investing multinational corporation. The chapter closes with a discussion of the integration options in the Americas.

In chapter 3, "Prospects for North American Monetary Cooperation in the Next Decade," Rogelio Ramírez de la O notes that the peso devaluation in December 1994 stimulated much debate in Mexico on monetary policy and the exchange rate regime. The United States and Canada favored floating exchange rates, and the peso was allowed to float after the devaluation. NAFTA did not address monetary issues, but the economic integration agreement set the stage for subsequent integrating steps.

The chapter discusses various exchange rate options for Mexico, including continued floating, a fixed peso peg with the dollar, a nominal target range, and dollarization. The conclusion reached is that a floating exchange rate is the only feasible option for Mexico for now, as long as this is coupled with sound macroeconomic policy.

Part II considers issues of labor and the environment. In chapter 4, "Mixing Environment and Trade Policies under NAFTA," Jan Gilbreath and Janine Ferretti point out that the pioneering step of including a side agreement on the environment in NAFTA—prompted mainly by nongovernmental environmental groups—has since led to making environmental protection a continental issue. Since then, much of the progress on this issue in Mexico has been stimulated by environmental nongovernmental organizations (NGOs) empowered by NAFTA. These homegrown NGOs are abetted by North American environmental institutions, such as the trilateral Environmental Cooperation Commission and the binational (United States and Mexico) Border Environmental Cooperation Commission.

Much policy convergence in the three NAFTA countries is now evident in such areas as the reduced use of toxic chemicals and support for biodiversity. However, the enforcement of environmental laws and regulations remains a problem in all three countries. Most of the investor-state disputes under chapter 11 of NAFTA deal with environmental issues; the nature of these disputes is summarized in the chapter. Some formidable challenges remain, such as water quality and usage in the Mexico–U.S. border area and deforestation in Mexico.

In chapter 5, "Labor Regulations and Trade Union Convergence in North America," Graciela Bensusán states that opportunities for labor have been less than expected under NAFTA. She points out that there has been no coordinated effort to harmonize labor rights in the three countries, which she attributes to protection of sovereignty. Nevertheless, she believes that NAFTA has opened space for greater union cooperation among the three countries. A key aspect of her presentation is that building labor strength, especially in Mexico, depends on the growth of the internal market in that companies involved in exports employ only a small proportion of the country's workers. Mexican wages have not gone up in line with productivity increases; indeed, real wages went down over much of the NAFTA period.

The NAFTA side accord contains the seeds for sanctions for violations of the terms of the agreement, but this has not really functioned. The number of complaints of violations, in fact, has decreased over time because of loss of interest. The chapter provides much detail on the nature and outcome of these violations. It also provides material on the changes in labor unions in the three countries, especially Mexico, in recent years. She notes the protectionist stance of the large labor confederations in the United States and Canada and the reality that the large Mexican labor confederation when NAFTA was born was under the political control of the governing party. The chapter contains a recommendation in favor of a migrant worker agreement to provide greater protection for Mexican workers in the United States.

Part III considers issues of intergovernmental relations and nongovernmental organizations. In chapter 6, "The Functioning of NAFTA and

Its Impact on Mexican–U.S. Relations," Rafael Fernández de Castro focuses on two themes: the effectiveness of NAFTA's institutional arrangements and the effects of the agreement on Mexican policy toward the United States. NAFTA's framework is quite sparse, certainly as compared with that in Europe. One reason was the reluctance of each of the countries to give up too much sovereignty. This is evident in the U.S. insistence that each country retain its own antidumping and countervailing duty laws. NAFTA is referred to in the chapter as a "gentleman's agreement" among three countries, and, as a consequence, it lacks the intrinsic capacity for deepening the relationship. Nevertheless, the many committees and working groups that have been formed serve as an effective channel of communication.

Mexico altered its passive pre-NAFTA official behavior in the United States to a highly active one as the agreement went through its approval process in the U.S. Congress. Mexico now hires lobbying firms in the United States and more fully staffs its embassy with professionals from many cabinet agencies. There are annual meetings of a cabinet-level Binational Commission, which sets up working groups on key issues, such as fighting drug trafficking and dealing with migration. Despite these meetings, the lack of an institutional prod to move the agreement into new ventures has led to a waning of interest in the agreement in both Mexico and the United States.

In chapter 7, "Civil Society Organizations, Freedom of Information, and Transparency in Mexico's Agenda in the Context of NAFTA: A Normative Approach," Ernesto Villanueva traces the evolution of nongovernmental organizations (NGOs) in Mexico during the past two decades. The idea of civic associations was contemplated in the constitution, but the limited number of NGOs that existed before the 1980s had little agenda-setting function; that was left to the government and the government party, the Institutional Revolutionary Party (Partido Revolucionario Institucional, or PRI). Between 1983 and 1988, as the PRI began to democratize its procedures, 53 new thematic NGOs appeared, the most important of which was the Mexican Academy of Human Rights.

NAFTA says nothing in its text about civic organizations, but the agreement's emphasis on transparency carried over into this field. NAFTA also encouraged Mexican NGOs to collaborate with and learn from U.S. and Canadian counterparts. It is estimated that more than 50 percent of existing NGOs were born during the past 10 years. One of the more important is the umbrella group, the Civic Alliance, which focuses on politics and human rights. One element of conflict in the functioning of Mexico's NGOs is whether they should be intermediaries between the government and the governed or exercise political power themselves.

Part IV deals with security issues. In chapter 8, "Mexican Policy against Drugs: From Deterring to Embracing the United States," María Celia Toro provides substantial detail on how Mexico altered its stance of resisting U.S. efforts to influence its antinarcotics policy to embracing a cooperative policy with the United States. One motivation for this transformation was the reality that dealing with drug trafficking became the most important source of United States–Mexico conflict in the 1980s. Mexico, during the 1980s and 1990s, restructured its antinarcotics machinery, accepted the stationing of agents from the U.S. Drug Enforcement Administration (DEA) in Mexico, militarized the antidrug effort, and broke precedent by extraditing Mexican nationals to face the U.S. justice system.

There were a number of high profile incidents over this period, such as the murder of DEA agent Enrique Camarena in February 1985 and the U.S. Supreme Court decision in 1992 to permit the judicial proceedings against Alvarez Machain to take place in the United States after he was kidnapped in Mexico. The change to bilateral cooperation in the antinarcotics effort was not the direct result of NAFTA—the process started long before NAFTA was a gleam in the eye of either official Mexico City or Washington—but NAFTA did add a general sense of cooperation between the two countries that affected antidrug trafficking efforts.

In chapter 9, "Security Imperatives of North American Integration: Back to a Future of Hub and Spokes," John Bailey anticipates that security cooperation will be more intense with Canada from the U.S. hub than with Mexico. The discussion in the chapter is from a U.S. perspective. The chapter defines what is meant by national and pubic security and argues that NAFTA is not seen by the publics of the three countries as relevant to national security concerns—except to the extent that there is fear that security measures could slow the movement of goods and people across the northern and southern borders into the United States.

For many years, the U.S. assurance to Mexico was that as long as Mexico pledged support on key issues, Mexico was free to pursue an independent foreign policy. There have been strains in this understanding, especially since September 11, 2001, when Mexico was slow to react and then gave qualified support to U.S. measures against Al Qaeda, the Taliban, and later Iraq. Canada's support, similarly, was lukewarm. However, the development of "smart border" agreements was more detailed with Canada than with Mexico and was more aggressive in its implementation.

Part V considers important social issues. In chapter 10, "NAFTA and Mexican Migration to the United States," Frank D. Bean and B. Lindsay Lowell begin their discussion by noting the change in thinking of the United States after September 11, 2002, from contemplating more open access for Mexican migrants to an emphasis on tightening border controls. The stagnation of the U.S. economy starting in 2000 further dampened U.S. receptivity to a more open immigration policy.

The chapter traces the history of Mexican migration to the United States and U.S. efforts to control unauthorized Mexican migration. The authors speculate that despite the decline in Mexican birth rates, migration from there to the United States is unlikely to slow because of the family and village networks that have been established and the large wage and income disparities between the two countries.

In chapter 11, "NAFTA and Mexican Higher Education," Carlos Ornelas argues that the main effect of NAFTA on education in Mexico, especially higher education, was to speed up trends already under way. Trilateral discussions toned up accreditation mechanisms in Mexico, promoted regional mobility of students and faculty, and led to considerable collaborative and parallel research with American and other foreign scholars. President Carlos Salinas, who firmly believed in the need to upgrade skills in Mexico, stimulated these developments. He pushed measures to improve the educational structure at all levels as being necessary for the country to move ahead technically and economically.

During the Salinas *sexenio* (six-year term of office), the educational structure was decentralized; Ernesto Zedillo, who succeeded Salinas as president, was the education secretary when this was done. Traditional university autonomy was altered, especially in the public universities, to make them more accountable. A frantic pace of peer evaluations was carried out under guidance of respected international bodies. The chapter provides much detail about this regional cooperation in education.

In chapter 12, "Poverty and Inequality," John Scott points out the disappointing reality that there has been no convergence in incomes since

NAFTA, either within the three countries or between them. In Mexico, distributive inequality antedates NAFTA and has worsened over the past 10 years, as have regional inequalities. The chapter argues that when income returns to education are high, as they are in Mexico, this tends to widen income disparities between those with access to education and those lacking this access.

The focus of the chapter is on Mexico's inadequate educational system. The argument is that the lack of educational opportunities is the most important factor limiting the poor from benefiting from free trade. There is much discussion of the substantial rural poverty in Mexico. The chapter is replete with data documenting the positions taken. The main point of the paper is that improving opportunities for education is the most important policy prescription for reducing poverty in Mexico.

Part VI considers political issues. In chapter 13, "NAFTA and Sovereignty," James Robinson comments that trade agreements elicit casual indifference, but passions run high when a link to sovereignty is raised. Sovereignty as used in the chapter includes the right to enter into international agreements. Sovereignty refers to internal self-determination, but not independent from international law. Hence there are legal limits to what sovereign states can choose as policy; sovereign rights are not absolute.

The chapter discusses the "constitutional" sovereignty of the United States and the defensive "national" sovereignty of Mexico—a defensiveness that can be traced to its history. Canada was concerned about its "cultural" sovereignty when it entered NAFTA. Although it is a trade agreement, NAFTA unleashed forces for political and social change, and this, in turn, led to the birth and strengthening of NGOs in such fields as human rights and democracy.

In chapter 14, "Democracy in Mexico," José Woldenberg Karakowsky cites the series of changes during the past decade, following earlier changes that gradually transformed Mexico from an authoritarian regime to a democracy. These changes found their expression in the 2000 elections when an opposition candidate won the presidency. Before that, elections did not reflect the true political situation. The chapter calls attention to the 1988 presidential election and the lack of public confidence in the recount that gave the victory to Carlos Salinas over Cuahtémoc Cárdenas.

The major reform law was enacted in 1996, giving authority to an independent Federal Electoral Commission and an electoral tribunal.

This provided the necessary legal basis and accompanying regulations, and set up a solid institutional structure. The chapter closes with a discussion of five issues: setting up a state of laws; culturally motivating the citizenry to take responsibility for democracy; developing responsible political parties; the importance of media; and the imperative of effective governments.

In chapter 15, "North American Integration: A Spontaneous Process or a Driven Enterprise?" Jesús F. Reyes-Heroles argues that over the past 10 years the words North America have become more than a geographical reference, but also include a sense of growing integration. Although the roots for integration have long existed, NAFTA provides a framework. Yet, the integration discussion today lacks a sense of purpose. Real transformation leads and governments follow. The chapter is replete with data on trade, investment, energy, and demography.

There are notable omissions in the NAFTA text, such as on the movement of people and the development of regional labor markets, oil as this relates to Mexico and the United States, and funds for the development of backward regions. On the plus side, there is a contested correlation between market opening and the development of democracy. In looking ahead, the chapter notes possibilities for further integration in the traditional areas of trade, investment, and migration, but also in other areas such as e-commerce, tax cooperation, resource transfers for development, social safety nets, security cooperation, and, perhaps one day, even perimeter security.

Notes

1. The preferential aspect between the United States and Canada came into effect earlier in 1988 under the Canada–U.S. Free Trade Agreement. This agreement was subsumed, and its contents amplified, in NAFTA.

2. For those uninitiated in trade parlance, an FTA is an arrangement under which the member countries are committed to reach zero import tariffs on substantially all goods in their trade with each other, but are able to retain their individual external tariffs on imports from nonmembers. A customs union requires a common external tariff as well as internal free trade.

3. Jacob Viner, *The Customs Union Issue* (Washington, D.C.: Carnegie Endowment for International Peace, 1950).

4. The words used come from the best-selling book by Alan Riding, *Distant Neighbors: A Portrait of the Mexicans* (New York: Alfred A. Knopf, 1984).

ACKNOWLEDGMENTS

This book was in gestation for longer than it takes to produce a human child. One reason for this was to obtain the collaboration of a balanced group of authors from the three NAFTA nations who were either expert in their specific fields or had experience that was broad enough to permit them to speculate about future substantive developments within and among the countries. The book was designed not to replicate the standard analyses of NAFTA's economic effects, but to examine as well other significant issues that were simultaneously in play. These other issues are important, as can be seen from a quick look at the chapter themes. I do want to thank the individual authors. Judgments on the quality of individual chapters are best left to readers.

This book was part of collaboration between the Wilson Center for International Scholars, especially its Latin American Program under the direction of Joseph Tulchin. The Wilson Center was the site for a remarkable meeting, held December 9–10, 2002, that highlighted presentations by the three heads of government when NAFTA was conceived and negotiations began: President George H.W. Bush of the United States, Prime Minister Brian Mulroney of Canada, and President Carlos Salinas de Gortari of Mexico. The Wilson Center, under the direction of Lee Hamilton, took the lead for that event, and CSIS took responsibility for producing this book. I wish also to thank Kent Hughes and Andrew Selee of the Wilson Center for their help during this collaboration.

In addition to funds from CSIS itself, support for this work came from the Rockefeller Foundation. Ruben Puentes who directs the foundation office in Mexico City provided guidance on the content of the book. The Inter-American Development Bank gave financial support to the project, as did the Embassy of Canada in the United States. The consulting firm Public Strategies Incorporated (PSI) also contributed funds to carry out the project.

Many individuals helped me identify authors and others made suggestions about the content, format, and the preparation of the book. These included Donna Spitler and James Dunton of the CSIS publications office. Donna devoted long hours to getting editing things right. We were fortunate to have an excellent and perceptive editor, Alfred Imhoff. Many of the Mexican authors wrote their papers in Spanish, and Manuel Bandrés prepared initial translations into English. Rafael Fernández de Castro of the Instituto Technólogico Autónomo de México, in addition to preparing a chapter, helped me identify a number of the Mexican chapter authors. I received help on particular issues concerning Mexico from Armand Peschard-Sverdrup, director of the Mexico Project at CSIS, as well as from M. Delal Baer, also of CSIS, before her untimely death. She was originally slated to prepare a chapter for the book, but her poor health precluded this. The idea for the book came from Chris Sands, then director of the Canada project at CSIS, and now a senior associate, in the course of a conversation about possible future activities of the Americas Program.

I was immensely gratified by the immediate and gracious willingness of Carla Hills to prepare the foreword to the book.

I most especially want to single out Veronica Prado, research associate in the office of the William E. Simon Chair in political economy at CSIS, for her dedication in getting out this book. Veronica was the principal prodder—of me to get moving, of delinquent authors to get their chapters in, of handling the long-distance editing problems, particularly in getting Spanish speakers to react to the English versions of their chapters. The long gestation period would have been much, much longer without her dedicated attention to getting the job done.

S.W.

ECONOMICS AND BUSINESS

CHAPTER ONE

TRADE, INVESTMENT, AND ECONOMIC GROWTH

Sidney Weintraub

The North American Free Trade Agreement (NAFTA) is a trade pact. Or, if one wishes to label it more expansively, it is a trade and investment pact. Yet its consequences have been far more substantial for each of the three member countries—Canada, Mexico, and the United States—in that the agreement represented an important change in policy direction for all of them. For Canada, the policy shift came a few years earlier, when it entered into a free trade agreement (FTA) with the United States in 1988 after a century of flirting with this step but never before taking it. For Mexico, NAFTA was an embrace of the United States (and Canada to boot) after almost a century and a half of keeping its distance, both politically and economically. For the United States, the FTA with Canada was a major step into preferential bilateralism after half a century of near exclusive reliance on multilateralism in trade matters.[1]

Canada's concern over free trade with the United States was political, that it would lose its sovereignty if it took this step. Indeed, in the electoral campaign in 1987 that determined entry into the Canada–U.S. Free Trade Agreement (CUFTA), the main thrust of the Liberal Party opposition was that free trade would inevitably lead to political integration and that Canada would sacrifice its sovereignty. CUFTA came into existence after the Conservatives won that election.[2]

President George H.W. Bush agreed to the proposal of Mexican president Carlos Salinas de Gortari for an FTA largely because the request meant that much of the antipathy toward closer relations with the United States—indeed, much of the anti-Americanism of Mexican domestic and foreign policy—would be dissipated. Trade between the two countries has boomed since NAFTA came into existence, as will be shown below, but the original U.S. motivation dealt with an entire bilateral relationship and not just trade.

Finally, the biggest gamble was the one that Mexico took, because it stood to lose the most if the FTA wiped out its still nascent industrial development. Salinas's motivation for this action, as he has stated frequently, was to encourage foreign direct investment. He realized that Europe's attention at that moment—just after the fall of the Berlin Wall—would be focused on Eastern Europe and the Soviet Union, and he felt he had no alternative but to turn to the United States.[3] NAFTA, in my view, was the most important agreement that Mexico signed with the United States since the Treaty of Guadalupe Hidalgo of 1848, under which huge chunks of Mexico were ceded to the United States after the Mexican War.

NAFTA is taken for granted now, whether one approves of it or not. The remembrance of the opposition that existed 10 years ago (16 years ago in Canada, dating from CUFTA) takes the form of slogans: Ross Perot's sucking sound of jobs moving to Mexico; the sacrifice of sovereignty on which John Turner based the Liberal Party campaign; and the subservience to the United States that opponents of President Salinas stressed. If NAFTA were to disappear today, the dream that those who supported the idea would not reach its full fruition, but it is unlikely that any of the three countries would revert to pre-NAFTA trade policies toward each other. Their economies are too intertwined. Yet it took courage by leaders in all three countries to push NAFTA to fruition.

This opening chapter deals primarily with the economic changes that NAFTA has wrought and could still bring in the years ahead. Integration agreements like NAFTA are barely in their infancy at 10 years of age—as witness the European Union, which already has 50 years of transition to what it might eventually become. The purpose of this chapter is to look at the changes at 10 years and to speculate what they might be at 20.

The rest of this book covers many of the political, social, and nontrade changes that have accompanied NAFTA during the past ten years. To repeat, the focus of this chapter is economics, largely trade and investment and their contribution to economic growth.

NAFTA AND TRADE

There are many ways to look at the trade effects of an economic integration agreement. These include the growth of internal trade among the member countries, the extent of intraindustry specialization that the integration spawns, the sectoral composition of this trade, the product diversification it brings about, the ability to quickly resolve trade disputes, and how trade with nonmember countries is affected. Bilateral trade can also grow rapidly between countries not joined in an economic integration agreement—witness the recent growth in trade between China and the United States—and the question relevant in analyzing the NAFTA experience is whether the agreement itself contributed strongly to the trade growth.

A simple way to measure the growth in intra-NAFTA trade since the agreement went into effect on January 1, 1994, is to compare this growth with the growth of trade of the three NAFTA countries with the rest of the world. As tables 1.1 and 1.2 and figures 1.1, 1.2, and 1.3 show quite vividly, the growth of internal trade among the three NAFTA countries flourished after the agreement went into effect.[4]

As table 1.3 shows, Mexican and Canadian exports are more highly concentrated in the United States than when NAFTA went into effect. In the heyday years of high U.S. economic growth in the 1990s, this growing concentration benefited the other two NAFTA countries as the U.S. economy sucked in imports. By contrast, the two other NAFTA countries suffered when U.S. economic and import growth slowed starting in 2000. This great vulnerability to the state of the U.S economy has long troubled both Canada and Mexico, and each has sought and continues to seek greater market diversification. Neither has succeeded thus far, as table 1.3 shows. On the whole, however, the two countries have benefited greatly from the dynamism and openness of the U.S. economy, coupled with their preferential situation in the U.S. market. It is by no means clear that either Canada or Mexico would have been better off during the past three years if their markets had been more diversified, because global trade also suffered from the sluggishness of the economies of the industrial countries generally. Indeed, even during the bad years thus far in this century, the U.S. economy still has had more growth than the economies of Western Europe and Japan.

Intraindustry Trade

Nevertheless, the United States alone among the three NAFTA countries can be considered a world trader. For Canada and Mexico, as the data in the figures and tables show, the export market is almost completely the United States and not the world. The two smaller countries,

Table 1.1. Absolute Level of Merchandise Exports, 1993 and 2002 (millions of dollars)

Source or Total	Destination	1993	2002
U.S. exports to	Canada	100,444	160,922
	Mexico	41,580	97,470
Canadian exports to	United States	116,740	219,985
	Mexico	638	1,539
Mexican exports to	United States	42,850	143,047
	Canada	1,568	2,806
Total Intra-NAFTA		303,823	625,771
NAFTA with rest of world		535,682	761,510

Sources: U.S. Census Bureau, Foreign Trade Division; Secretaria de Economía de México; Banco de México; and Statistics Canada.

Table 1.2. Absolute Level of Total Merchandise Trade, 1993 and 2002 (millions of dollars)

Trade	1993	2002	Percentage Growth
Intra-NAFTA	303,823	625,771	106
NAFTA with rest of world	535,682	761,510	42

Sources: U.S. Census Bureau, Foreign Trade Division; Secretaria de Economía de México; Banco de México; and Statistics Canada.

Figure 1.1. U.S. Merchandise Exports to Canada and Mexico and to the Rest of the World, 1993–2002 (millions of dollars)

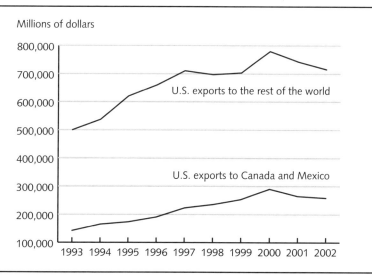

Source: U.S. Bureau of the Census.

Figure 1.2. Canadian Merchandise Exports to the United States and Mexico and to the Rest of the World, 1993–2002 (millions of dollars)

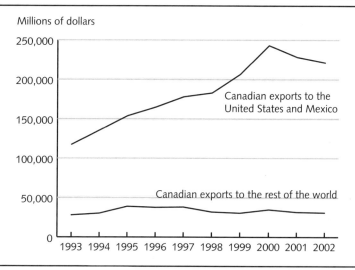

Source: U.S. Bureau of the Census.

Figure 1.3. Mexican Merchandise Exports to the United States and Canada and to the Rest of the World, 1993–2002 (millions of dollars)

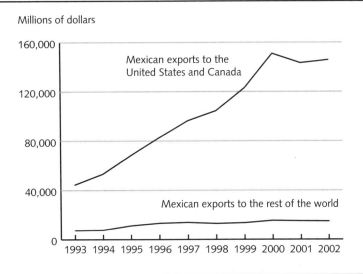

Source: U.S. Bureau of the Census.

Table 1.3. Internal versus External Growth of Merchandise Exports of NAFTA Member Countries, 1993–2002 (annual average percentage)

Exports from/to	Canada	Mexico	United States	Rest of World
Canada	—	11.1	7.2	1.1
Mexico	7.0	—	14.3	8.1
United States	5.4	9.9	—	4.0

Sources: U.S. Census Bureau, Foreign Trade Division; Secretaria de Economía de México; Banco de México; and Statistics Canada.

one industrialized and the other best described as having an emerging economy, have been able to upgrade their industrial structures to higher value-added products under NAFTA, thanks to the openness of the U.S. market and the development of intraindustry exchanges. The best example of this is the automotive industry, in which each of the two smaller countries has become an important trader thanks to the existence of this intraindustry trade—or refined further, thanks to intrafirm trade.[5] Each of the three NAFTA countries sells more automotive goods to the other two than products in any other sector, but the products are differentiated. As a general proposition, Mexico produces smaller cars, the United States intermediate and specialty vehicles, and Canada larger autos and light trucks. Different parts are produced in the three countries for shipment between the other two and the United States for final assembly. This has proceeded to such as extent that the large automakers in the northern United States can order the necessary parts for their assembly plants from Canada only hours before they are needed. This just-in-time inventory system works on a tight schedule, sometimes with as little as a 15-minute tolerance in crossing the bridge from Windsor, Ontario, directly to the assembly line in Detroit. This is an important competitive feature. The just-in-time inventory feature has not reached this degree of sophistication in United States–Mexico automotive trade.

The intraindustry model of economic integration also has been an important feature of trade growth and production upgrading for other industries in NAFTA, such as electrical machinery, optical, and other equipment. The maquiladora plants that sprouted in Mexico near the U.S. border were attractive to U.S. investors well before NAFTA came into existence because more capital-intensive parts of products could be produced in the United States, then be shipped to Mexico for the more labor-intensive operations, and then be shipped back to the United States for final sales. The early product development of the maquiladora was in apparel and computers, but it also included automotive products. The maquiladora industry has declined in recent years in Mexico because there are alternative locations where labor is even cheaper than in Mexico, such as China and Central America.[6] However, Mexico still retains an advantage of location and low transportation costs for co-production for the U.S. market. In order to survive, the maquiladora plants will themselves have to upgrade their product output, and this will require more skilled workers and deeper technology.

However, there is an important difference between maquiladora and other manufacturing in that maquiladora producers obtain only a small amount of their product inputs from Mexico itself, whereas manufacturing for intraindustry trade in general is more integrated into the Mexican production structure.

Today, about 89 percent of Mexico's exports are manufactured goods. In the early 1980s, before Mexico abandoned its import-substitution development model, oil exports made up about 75 percent of total exports; in 2002, oil exports were only 8 percent of the total.[7] The shift to manufactures started before NAFTA but received its greatest impetus from the agreement. For Canada, NAFTA facilitated the growth of high-value-added manufacturing, adding to the natural resource products that Canada had traditionally exported (Schwanen 1997).

The growth in intraindustry trade has long been considered an important feature of economic integration in that it facilitates specialization across countries. Politicians often argue for economic integration with countries with which there is little product competition because this does not bring the unpleasant side effect of job loss from plant relocation and import competition. But if there is no product competition, there is little reason to integrate economically in the first place. The benefits from integration come from the stimulus of meeting competitive pressures through specialization and cost saving, such as the just-in-time inventory techniques that exist in the combined U.S.–Canadian automotive industry.[8]

Agricultural Trade

Trade in agricultural products has long been the neglected stepchild of international negotiations to lower trade barriers. This has been the case from the outset of the General Agreement on Tariffs and Trade, which came into existence just after World War II, to the current Doha Round of trade negotiations in the World Trade Organization (WTO). Indeed, the inability to reach agreement on the producer and export subsidies of industrial countries (the United States, the European Union, and Japan, in particular) in a WTO ministerial meeting in Cancún, Mexico, in September 2003 was the underlying cause of the failure of that meeting, jeopardizing the completion of the Doha Round as a whole. The treatment of agriculture is a central issue as well in the negotiations for concluding a Free Trade Area of the Americas (FTAA).

There were separate agreements on agriculture in NAFTA, one involving the United States and Mexico, in which no agricultural products were excluded; and the second between these two countries and Canada, in which there were considerable agricultural exclusions.[9] The Mexican negotiators have since had to endure severe internal attacks for giving away the agricultural store in NAFTA, and this has led to calls from leading Mexican figures, including the president of the country, for a renegotiation of the agricultural provisions of NAFTA. This will not happen, unless NAFTA itself is discarded—but the proponents of renegotiation omit this reality.

To be fair to the Mexican NAFTA negotiators, one should keep in mind their conviction that Mexico's agricultural problem could not be solved in the *campo*, but required job creation in urban areas across the country. This is because millions of *campesinos* live in poverty and have little opportunity for economic advancement if they remain where they are in rural areas. The central government budgets of poor countries cannot endure long-term subsidies to millions of people who live in rural areas to provide them with a decent existence. There are already too many small farms (*minifundos*) in areas in Mexico that lack irrigation for further land distribution to work. Today, some 25 million Mexicans, 25 percent of the total population, live in rural areas, and agricultural products generate only 6 percent of national income. The hope of the NAFTA negotiators was that Mexican gross domestic product (GDP) would grow at perhaps 6 percent a year over NAFTA's 15-year transition before zero import duties were reached for sensitive agricultural products and that this growth would create enough jobs for *campesinos* to migrate to a better life. The calculations were wrong. In the nine-year period as a whole from 1994, when NAFTA went into effect, through 2002, real GDP in Mexico has grown by about 3 percent a year—about half of what was needed for the necessary job creation.

The problem of rural poverty cannot be attributed to NAFTA but must be attacked in the very structure of Mexico's agricultural sector. In fact, Mexico's agricultural exports, including processed foods, within NAFTA grew by 9.4 percent a year between 1994 and 2001, whereas agro-food imports grew by a lower amount of 6.9 percent a year. The composition of the export and import growth has not had the same effect on different products and on the various regions of the country where the products are grown and cultivated; some regions have benefited, others have suffered.[10]

Thus, while agriculture was included in the Mexican–U.S. NAFTA agreements, and while the trade has grown in both directions, this has not eliminated disputes in this sector. The most serious conflict deals with sugar, and this is aligned, in Mexican minds, with high-fructose corn syrup (HFCS). If the reader will bear with me, I will provide a simplified discussion of the problem. Two tracks were spelled out in NAFTA for Mexico's access to the U.S. sugar market: Tier I was based on a tariff rate quota, which would be removed if Mexico became a net sugar exporter; Tier II, or over-quota imports, had an import tariff scheduled to decline gradually to zero by 2008. A side-letter subsequently modified the terms of the underlying agreement by putting a limit on Tier I imports by the United States, but there is disagreement to this day on whether Mexico consented to the provisions of the side-letter.

There are several linkages between the sugar agreement and developments in the HFCS market. Mexico consumes a large quantity of soft drinks, and HFCS can replace sugar in that industry. Consequently, the U.S. corn-milling industry geared up its capacity to supply Mexico with large amounts of HFCS to replace the sugar equivalent of Mexico's projected sugar exports to the United States. When Mexico appeared to be developing a surplus that would permit it to export sugar under Tier I, the United States sought to rewrite the agreement to exclude the sugar equivalent made available by HFCS imports from the calculation of the surplus. Mexico saw this as a U.S. denial of what it had been promised in the text of NAFTA stemming from pressure exerted on the U.S. government by sugar producers. The Mexican authorities also anticipate that protectionist pressure will develop to modify the Tier II understanding as 2008 approaches and over-quota duties are scheduled to be fully removed.

Mexico dealt with U.S. actions on sugar by imposing antidumping duties of 20 percent on imports of HFCS from the United States. In a sense, Mexico conflated the sugar and HFCS issues, just as the United States tried to do by using HFCS imports to alter the Tier I agreement. Mexico's antidumping duties were found invalid by dispute-settlement panels in both NAFTA and the WTO. Mexico responded to these decisions in January 2002 by imposing a 20 percent consumption tax on HFCS use in the soft drink industry. This has shut off all HFCS exports to Mexico from the United States, to the benefit of sugar producers in both countries. Discussions between the private interests and the two governments are taking place as this is written to find some solution to the sweetener fiasco.

Figure 1.4. Foreign Direct Investment in Mexico, 1980–2002 (millions of dollars)

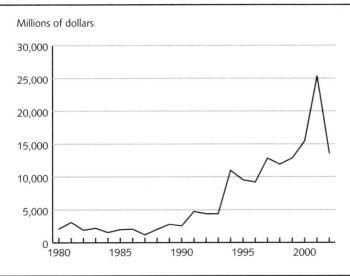

Source: IMF, *International Financial Statistics.*

INVESTMENT

As indicated earlier in the chapter, NAFTA can be described as a trade and investment agreement. Indeed, the two elements are inseparable. Much of the U.S. direct investment in Mexico is designed to produce goods and services for export back to the United States. This pattern is the essence of the maquiladora, but it also holds true across the entire productive sector of Mexico. The preferential treatment provided Mexican goods in the United States under NAFTA was intended, as well, to stimulate investment by Mexican entrepreneurs to take advantage of the large market next door. All this is happening, including many joint ventures between Mexican and U.S. firms. The business-to-business relationships that have developed between the two countries are analyzed in chapter 2.

Figure 1.4 shows vividly how foreign direct investment (FDI) in Mexico took off once it was clear that NAFTA would come into existence. Between 1980 and 1993, FDI in Mexico was more or less constant at between $3 and $5 billion a year. The average level of FDI from 1994 through 2002, by contrast, was $13 billion a year. The spurt in investment in 2001 that can be seen in the figure is explained by the purchase by Citibank of Banco Nacional de México (Banamex) for $12.5 billion.

Between 1994 and 2002, the United States supplied 63 percent of the total FDI into Mexico.

NAFTA AND ECONOMIC DEVELOPMENT

The ultimate objective of NAFTA is to increase trade and investment in the three countries, not as an end in itself, but rather as a spur to economic growth. This was particularly true for Mexico in that the other two member countries were already industrialized. President Salinas of Mexico sold the agreement to his compatriots on precisely this basis. In many respects, he oversold it in that Mexicans generally looked on the agreement as a panacea for many of the country's economic ills. The selling technique in the United States focused on the jobs that NAFTA would create from increased exports, and that in Canada on the agreement's potential to upgrade the value added in Canada's exports.

As one looks back, only the Canadian expectation was achieved— more or less achieved, because the change in the composition of the country's exports might have occurred in any event. However, putting aside this counterfactual possibility, Canada obtained what it sought from NAFTA, save for the elimination of U.S. antidumping and countervailing duty procedures.[12] The job-creation objective so dear to U.S. politicians was always a political rather than an economic argument in that the U.S. economy is large enough on its own to use domestic macroeconomic policy to achieve full employment.[13] In fact, the United States did have full employment from 1994 to 2000. The subsequent decline in employment was unrelated to trade policy.

The particularly interesting case of the three is Mexico. Its trade did boom as a result of NAFTA, as did the inflow of FDI.[14] Yet sustained economic growth did not follow. Most recently, since 2000, real GDP per capita has declined, but so have exports. Figure 1.5 shows annual percentage changes in real GDP in Mexico from 1980 through 2002. The growth rates have not been impressive. The average annual change in GDP over this period was only 1.2 percent (Lederman, Maloney, and Serven 2003). In per capita terms, real GDP has declined since 2000, but so have exports.

In the slogan "export-led growth," which was used in Mexico after NAFTA, the key qualifier is in the phrase "export-*led*." Put differently, a successful trade policy cannot overcome deficient macroeconomic, structural, and social policies. In 1995—the second year after NAFTA came into being—the Mexican economy collapsed as a result of faulty

Figure 1.5. Mexico's Real GDP Growth, 1980–2002 (annual average percentage change)

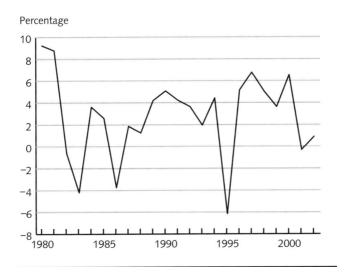

Percentage

Source: World Bank, *World Development Indicators.*

monetary and exchange rate policies. Fiscal policy in the year before the depression of 1995 was looser than advertised because of off-budget expenditures of about 3 percent of GDP through official development banks. Tax collections in Mexico are now about 11 percent of GDP, low even by Latin American standards, forcing the government to use substantial funds from Petróleos Mexicanos (Pemex) to meet budget needs, thereby starving Pemex of resources for exploration and exploitation. The shortage of public funds for such social needs as education and health care has not permitted the necessary updating of these vital areas. The reduction of poverty requires sustained high growth rates; hence, poverty reduction has not been possible since NAFTA has come into effect. Electricity shortages loom in Mexico, and despite large natural gas resources, the country has become a net importer of this product. The benefits of NAFTA were felt largely in northern Mexico and in the Valley of Mexico, widening the development gap between these two regions and southern Mexico.

Many in Mexico have blamed the country's recent pedestrian growth performance on NAFTA—even though the agreement delivered what was intended in trade and investment. Coincidence in time has been transformed in many minds into causation: NAFTA was born;

there has been inadequate economic growth since then; ergo, NAFTA is to blame. In addition, NAFTA has brought little benefit to the population of Mexico's southern states, and they have little reason to feel warmly about the agreement.

During the past several years, as the maquiladora sector has declined, economic hardships have been felt in northern Mexico as well. The constant drumbeat against NAFTA's agricultural provisions surely has made the agreement anathema in many rural communities, and probably in urban areas as well. Failures of the Mexican government—in macroeconomic and regional policies, in dealing with burning social issues—have been morphed into NAFTA failures. Here the counterfactual may have some validity: If NAFTA had not come into existence, is there any basis for believing that Mexicans would be better off today than they are? Would the economic situation be better if Mexico had not become an exporting powerhouse? Surely not.

LOOKING AHEAD

Much of Mexico's trade success since NAFTA can be attributed to low wages. Mexico is a convenient location for industrial co-production, but this natural advantage was enhanced by the country's low wages. Mexican hourly compensation costs for production workers in manufacturing are still low, about 11 percent of those in the United States, but they are lower in other places—China and Central America, for example (BLS 2003). To retain competitiveness in the face of cheaper wages elsewhere, Mexico must augment the level of technology in its production processes. This is not only my view, but also that of the Consejo Nacional de Ciencia y Tecnología (CONACYT), Mexico's science and technology institute.[15] This will require more skilled personnel and this, in turn, demands improved educational facilities at all levels. This, obviously, cannot be accomplished in the short term, but is surely necessary both to make NAFTA more effective in the future and to achieve Mexico's economic growth goals.

Mexico has thus far enjoyed a 10-year run of near unique preferential access to the U.S. market, but this is eroding as the United States signs free trade agreements with other countries, such as Chile and Central America. If the FTAA comes into existence, this sharing of preferences in the U.S. market will become even more widespread. Mexico cannot logically object to what the United States is doing because Mexico has been one of the champions of signing FTAs with almost any and all comers despite its membership in NAFTA. This inevitable sharing of privileged access to the U.S. market requires Mexico to upgrade its competitive position and reinforces the CONACYT objective of technological advances.

The sophistication of the just-in-time inventory system for co-production by Canada and the United States has been noted above. This is a critical aspect of meeting foreign competition, especially in the automotive industry. Indeed, there was something approaching panic in Canada after the terrorist attacks of September 11, 2001, when the United States slowed down the entry of goods at the border as a security measure. The 30-point (now 30 plus) "Smart Border" agreement was a consequence of the new security demands, namely, how to meet U.S. security needs and still keep the goods moving across the border to meet the just-in-time production processes. A similar border agreement exists between Mexico and the United States, but delays in the movement of goods are substantially greater at that border. To meet foreign competition, even as wage costs in Mexico rise, the movement of goods between the two countries must be accelerated. This is a NAFTA requirement, just as it is a development necessity for Mexico. Customs clearance procedures in Mexico are still more cumbersome than they need be, and these can be improved. In trade language, trade facilitation measures are needed.

NAFTA will not function optimally if disputes are not resolved expeditiously. Indeed, the agreement itself falls into general disrepute when either country cuts off agricultural and fishery imports ostensibly on fair trade, sanitary, or environmental grounds, but really to protect domestic producers. The United States has been guilty of this (e.g., for tomatoes, avocados, and tuna), but Mexico is the more aggressive offender at the moment for agricultural products. The sweetener dispute is being dealt with by reciprocal name calling and import restrictions, whereas what is needed is negotiation and a mutual compromise that does not seek to exempt every entrenched interest.

On a more technical level, the joint setting of product and parts standards that is an essential component of co-production or, when this is not feasible, mutual recognition of each other's standards, has by no means gone far enough. This was a critical aspect of the European Union's reforms during the 1990s, just as it should be of NAFTA's reforms.

The central economic task facing Mexico is not dealing with NAFTA per se but how to best take advantage of export and investment increases in order to grow the economy at a higher rate and on a more sustained basis. NAFTA, in other words, must be an adjunct to more comprehensive internal development policies of the nature discussed above, and it must not be made a scapegoat for internal policy failures.

Vicente Fox came into office seeking something called NAFTA-Plus. The "plus" was mostly a comprehensive migration agreement to regularize the millions of undocumented Mexicans already living in the United States and to increase the number of Mexicans legally able to enter and work in the United States. The objectives were understandable, but were not attainable—certainly not in their entirety.

If Mexico were able to achieve sustained high rates of GDP growth on the order of 6 percent a year for at least 10 to 15 years, this, coupled with the already declining birthrates, would largely eliminate the unauthorized migration issue because Mexicans could find opportunities at home. This is not a new observation; the same reasoning was contained in the *Binational Study: Migration between Mexico and the United States* completed in 1997; and emigration from Mexico has only seen increases since then.[16] The reason for the earlier miscalculation was the failure of Mexico to grow economically at a satisfactory pace.

It is impossible to state with any assurance that the policy alterations recommended here and by many Mexican officials and scholars will come to pass in the next 10 years and beyond. Many of them must come, because their failure would increase discontent in Mexico enough to force changes. It would be better if they came from deliberate reforms, rather than being forced on the system in the aftermath of future crises.

Notes

1. The United States entered into an FTA with Israel in 1996, but this was largely a political agreement with modest trade content. The FTA with Canada, by contrast, was with the largest U.S. trading partner.

2. Stairs (1996, 1–38) concludes that this fear dissipated once the FTA went into effect.

3. This is stated most directly in Salinas de Gortari (2000, 39–63).

4. The growth in Canadian trade with the United States after NAFTA went into effect is a continuation of the trade-enhancing effect of CUFTA, which came into being on January 1, 1988.

5. The big-three U.S. automobile-manufacturing companies produce in all three countries, as do producers of many other products, and this is the basis for intra-firm trade. Indeed, more than half of Canada's and Mexico's manufactured exports to the United States is related-party trade, i.e., trade not conducted at arm's length. According to Hart (1994, 20), about 70 percent of Canada's trade is of this nature. The statement about Mexico comes from my own calculations.

6. For a good discussion of the current status of maquiladora plants, see GAO (2003).

7. The 1982 figure for oil exports as a percent of total Mexican exports was 78 percent and comes from the Banco de México, *Indicadores económicos*; the 2002 figure is from the Instituto Nacional de Estadística, Geografía e Informática.

8. Preusse (forthcoming, 138–50) argues quite forcefully that an intraindustry trade strategy has not served Mercosur well because of the limited size of the internal market combined with the lack of attention in augmenting external trade competitiveness.

9. In the Canada–United States negotiation, Canada excluded dairy, poultry, eggs, and margarine; and the United States excluded dairy, peanuts, peanut butter, sugar and sugar products, and cotton. In the Canada–Mexico negotiation, Canada excluded dairy, eggs, poultry, and sugar products; and Mexico excluded the same. For a description of these negotiations, see Espinal (2002).

10. For a more detailed discussion of how NAFTA has affected Mexican agriculture, see Sarmiento (2003).

11. I owe a debt of gratitude to Robert Johnson of Cargill, who helped me understand the thinking of a large private U.S. agricultural company.

12. This was foreordained because Canada was unable to change these procedures in the negotiations for its free trade agreement with the United States.

13. The argument supporting this statement can be found in Weintraub (1997, 11–15).

14. The counterfactual argument that these developments might have occurred without NAFTA is difficult, I think impossible, to sustain. It is being made, largely by assertion, by NAFTA opponents in Mexico.

15. This was stated in a presentation by Jaime Parada Ávila of CONACYT, "Toward Science and Technology Cooperation in NAFTA," in July 2003.

16. This report was issued by the Mexican Ministry of Foreign Affairs and U.S. Commission on Immigration Reform (1998). See pp. 167–69.

References

BLS (Bureau of Labor Statistics, U.S. Department of Labor). 2003. *International Comparisons of Hourly Compensation Costs for Production Workers in Manufacturing, 2002.* Washington, D.C.: BLS. Available at www.bls.gov/fls.

Espinal, Carlos. 2002. La negociación agrícola en el ALCA: Análisis de la experiencia de México en el NAFTA. Serie Informe ALCA, Agricultura—informe 1. Bogotá: Latin American Trade Network.

GAO (U.S. General Accounting Office). 2003. *International Trade: Mexico's Maquiladora Decline Affects U.S.–Mexico Border Communities; Recovery Depends in Part on Mexico's Actions.* Report GAO-03-891. Washington, D.C.: GAO.

Hart, Michael. 1994. *What's Next: Canada, the Global Economy and the New Trade Policy.* Ottawa: Center for Trade Policy and Law.

Lederman, Daniel, William F. Maloney, and Luis Serven. 2003. *Lessons from NAFTA for Latin America and the Caribbean Countries: A Summary of Research Findings.* Washington, D.C.: World Bank.

Mexican Ministry of Foreign Affairs and U.S. Commission on Immigration Reform. 1998. *Binational Study: Migration between Mexico and the United States.* Mexico City and Washington, D.C.: Mexican Ministry of Foreign Affairs and U.S. Commission on Immigration Reform.

Preusse, Heinz G. Forthcoming. *The New American Regionalism.* Northampton, Mass.: Edward Elgar.

Salinas de Gortari, Carlos. 2000. *México: Un paso difícil a la modernidad.* Barcelona: Plaza & Janés.

Sarmiento, Sergio. 2003. Mexico Alert: NAFTA and Mexico's Agriculture. *Hemisphere Focus* (Center for Strategic and International Studies) 11, no. 8 (March 4).

Schwanen, Daniel. 1997. *Trading Up: The Impact of Increased Continental Integration on Trade, Investment, and Jobs in Canada.* Toronto: C. D. Howe Institute.

Stairs, Denis. 1996. The Canadian Dilemma in North America. In *NAFTA and Sovereignty: Trade-Offs for Canada, Mexico, and the United States,* ed. Joyce Hoebing, Sidney Weintraub, and M. Delal Baer. Washington, D.C.: Center for Strategic and International Studies.

Weintraub, Sidney. 1997. *NAFTA at Three: A Progress Report.* Washington, D.C.: CSIS.

CHAPTER TWO

THE NEW REGIONALISM AND FOREIGN DIRECT INVESTMENT IN THE AMERICAS

Lorraine Eden and Dan Li

Regional integration is an excellent example of the pendulum theory. Regional trade agreements (RTAs), which were popular in the 1950s and 1960s, fell out of favor in the 1970s and 1980s, only to see a resurgence in the late 1980s. The 1990s were unparalleled in terms of interest in regional integration. Between 1995 and 2002, 125 new agreements were notified to the World Trade Organization (WTO), bringing the total to 250 RTAs (WTO 2002). The explosion of RTAs has been most notable in the Americas. The new agreements are so different that policymakers now distinguish between the "old regionalism" and "new regionalism" (Devlin and Estevadeordal 2001; IDB 2002; Iglesias 2002).

Table 2.1 lists the RTAs that have been signed or are under negotiation in the Americas, as of May 2003, showing the rapid expansion in the number of agreements and their geographic breadth. There are now an amazing 45 regional trade agreements in the hemisphere (28 signed and 17 under negotiation). Most RTAs are free trade agreements (FTAs), which eliminate internal tariffs but allow countries to maintain their own external tariffs against nonmember countries, such as the 1989 Canada–U.S. Free Trade Agreement (CUSFTA) and the North American Free Trade Agreement (NAFTA). A few RTAs are customs unions (e.g., Mercosur and the Andean Pact), where a common external tariff replaces national tariffs on nonmember countries.

An earlier version of this chapter was presented at the Canada–United States Business Conference, Indiana University, Bloomington, April 11–12, 2003. The authors thank Masataka Fujita, George von Furstenburg, Kishore Gawande, Steve Globerman, Maureen Molot, Miguel Perez-Ludena, Enrique Dussel Peters, Someshwar Rao, Alan Rugman, Karl Sauvant, Aaron Sydor, Doug Thomas, and Sidney Weintraub for helpful discussions and assistance, while retaining full responsibility for the contents.

Table 2.1. Regional Trade Agreements (RTAs) in the Americas: How Many? How Broad?

Part I: Signed Regional Trade Agreements

North–North or South–South RTAs	Year	North–South RTAs	Year
Central American Common Market (CACM): El Salvador, Guatemala, Honduras, Nicaragua, Costa Rica	1960[a]	NAFTA: Canada, United States, Mexico	1992
Andean Community (AC): Bolivia, Colombia, Ecuador, Peru, Venezuela	1969[a]	Chile–Canada	1996
Caribbean Community (CARICOM): Antigua and Barbuda, Barbados, Jamaica, St. Kitts and Nevis, Trinidad and Tobago, Belize, Dominica, Grenada, Monserrat, St. Lucia, St. Vincent and the Grenadines, Bahamas	1973[a]	Mexico– European Union	1999
Canada–United States (CUSFTA)	1988	Mexico–European Free Trade Area (EFTA)	2000
Southern Cone Common Market (Mercosur): Argentina, Brazil, Paraguay, Uruguay	1991	Mexico–Israel	2000
Chile–Venezuela	1993	Costa Rica– Canada	2001[b]
Colombia–Chile	1994	Chile–European Union	2002
Costa Rica–Mexico	1994	Chile–United States	2002[b]
Group of Three (G-3): Mexico, Colombia,Venezuela	1994		
Bolivia–Mexico	1994		
Chile–Mercosur	1996		
Bolivia–Mercosur	1996		
Mexico–Nicaragua	1997		

Table 2.1. *(continued)*

Dominican Republic–CACM	1998[b]
Chile–Peru	1998
Chile–CACM	1999
Chile–Mexico	1999
Mexico–Northern Triangle (Guatemala, Honduras, El Salvador)	2000
CARICOM–Dominican Republic	2000
Costa Rica–Trinidad and Tobago	2002[b]
El Salvador–Panama	2002[b]

Part II: Regional Trade Agreements under Negotiation

South–South RTAs	North–South RTAs
Mercosur–Andean Community	CACM–United States
Costa Rica–Panama	CARICOM–European Union
Mexico–Panama	Central America-4–Canada
Mexico–Peru	Chile–EFTA
Mexico–Ecuador	Chile–South Korea
Mexico–Trinidad and Tobago	Free Trade Area of the Americas (FTAA)
Brazil–China	Mercosur–European Union
Brazil–Russia	Mexico–Japan
	Uruguay–United States

Source: Updated version of IDB (2002, 26).

[a] Relaunched in the 1990s.
[b] Awaiting ratification.

An important issue surrounding RTAs is their impacts on the level and direction of foreign direct investment (FDI). Politicians, policy-makers, academic researchers, and the public can and do have different opinions about the economic impacts. Economists traditionally have been optimistic in their appraisals of regional integration (Rugman 1990; Globerman and Shapiro 2001; Weintraub 1993). Conversely, Canadian nationalists voiced strong warnings about the likelihood of multinational corporations (MNCs) shutting down plants and reopening them in the United States in response to CUSFTA. In the United States, politicians like Ross Perot warned of "NAFTA's giant sucking sound" that would pull U.S. investment capital and jobs to the ostensibly more profitable climes of Mexico.

The polls show similar concerns. In 1990, 57 percent of Canadians said they supported CUSFTA; in 2000, the same percentage said that they had "little or no confidence in NAFTA" (Nevitte, Anderson, and Brym 2002, 187). Warf and Kull (2002, 213), in their review of U.S. polls on free trade, found only "modest support" for NAFTA among the American public. A 2001 poll in Mexico found that, while 56 percent believed entering NAFTA was the right decision for Mexico, only 44 percent thought that the results had been good for Mexicans (Moreno 2002).

In this chapter, we examine the economic relationships between the new regionalism and FDI in the Americas, focusing on NAFTA. How have RTAs, particularly NAFTA, affected the location patterns of FDI throughout the hemisphere? Has creating two major trade agreements in the 1990s, NAFTA and Mercosur, encouraged capital inflows into member countries at the expense of nonmembers? Have the reactions of "insider MNCs" headquartered within an RTA been different from those of "outsider MNCs"? We outline the key differences between the old and new regionalisms, review the economic literature on FDI and the locational responses of multinationals to RTAs, and examine recent empirical research findings about the Americas. We end with some policy choices for deepening the relationship between FDI and regional integration in the Americas.

THE NEW REGIONALISM

In Latin America, NAFTA and Mercosur—the two subregional trade groups—dominate the field of RTAs, but they are different types of agreements. NAFTA is an FTA using rules of origin to control duty-free access to national markets. Mercosur, conversely, is a customs union with a common external tariff. Each RTA has a regional hegemon (or economic hub) at its center. Both hegemons—Brazil and the United States—are the current cochairs of the Free Trade Area of the Americas (FTAA) negotiations, which are designed to create a hemispheric-wide RTA starting in 2005.

In North America, the old regionalism was mostly about one event: sectoral free trade for U.S. and Canadian producers under the 1965 Auto Pact, which removed cross-border trade barriers in automobiles and auto parts. The new regionalism starts with the 1989 CUSFTA, which extended the integration process to goods, business services, and investments in almost all sectors of both economies. In 1990, Mexico approached the United States about a bilateral free trade accord, which subsequently became NAFTA in 1994. Whereas the CUSFTA was a North–North agreement, adding Mexico created the first North–South RTA in the hemisphere. Canada–United States merchandise trade has been practically tariff free since January 1, 1998. The final round of tariff cuts for United States–Mexico and Canada–Mexico trade were applied on January 1, 2003, with some exceptions for agricultural products until 2008 (Canada 2003, 33, 48).

In Latin America, the old regionalism was import-substitution industrialization (ISI) "writ large." Latin American economists and policymakers, in the 1960s and 1970s, believed the growth prospects of natural resources were limited by the secular decline in the terms of trade for primary products and resource-exploiting FDI. Economic development was expected from an ISI strategy, which required protecting infant industries from import competition, strong state-owned enterprises, and controls on inward FDI. Regional integration was a complement to ISI strategies, enabling Latin American countries to lessen trade and FDI barriers among themselves while keeping (or raising) them against outsiders. Thus, the old regionalism was a substitute for taking part in the multilateral trading system (Ethier 2001).

Because of the protectionist, inward-looking motivations behind the old regionalism, the results of early RTAs in Latin America—such as the Central American Common Market, the Latin American Free Trade Area, the Andean Group, and the Caribbean Community— were limited. The underlying policies of protectionism, state intervention, and bureaucratic authoritarianism meant that governments only halfheartedly engaged in region building. Tariffs were lowered only where domestic firms were weak or nonexistent, while nontariff barriers such as licenses and quotas exploded.

The new regionalism in Latin America (Ethier 2001; Iglesias 2002) has several characteristics that distinguish it from the first wave of

RTAs.[1] First, the new regionalism arose out of crisis and was accompanied (and often preceded) by unilateral domestic policy reforms. Vernon (1994) has argued that all meaningful trade liberalization has been born from crisis. In the early 1980s, the debt crisis in Latin America caused the region's economic collapse. The subsequent entry of the International Monetary Fund and the World Bank precipitated structural adjustment policies designed to open Latin America to the world economy. Major economic reforms—liberalization, deregulation, and privatization—and democratic reforms swept through the region. Elsewhere, the rapid growth of the East Asian tigers demonstrated a successful alternative to ISI, while the collapse of the Soviet Union at the end of the 1980s meant the competition for inward FDI would become much more aggressive. This combination of world events precipitated the second wave of regional integration programs in Latin America.

Another notable difference between the old and new regionalisms is the shift from North–North and South–South agreements to North–South agreements. Historically, North–South agreements were in the form of preferential access for southern products in northern markets, often on an ex-colonial basis (e.g., the Lomé Convention between the European Community and the African, Caribbean, and Pacific countries) or organized under the General Agreement on Tariffs and Trade (GATT; e.g., the Generalized System of Preferences). NAFTA, bringing Mexico into an expanded Canada–United States FTA, was the first of the new North–South RTAs in the Americas.

NAFTA also signaled a third change: The new regionalism typically has one or more small countries linking with a large-country neighbor (Ethier 2001). Eden and Molot (1992) argued economic linkages within in North America were best pictured as two dyads, a northern United States–Canada dyad and a southern United States–Mexico dyad, because Canada–Mexico trade and FDI linkages were (and remain) so small. In Mercosur, Uruguay and Paraguay are in a similar situation vis-à-vis Argentina and Brazil.

A fourth notable change is the shift from *shallow integration* (elimination of tariff barriers among the RTA partners) to *deep integration* (the added reduction in, or harmonization of, nontariff barriers to trade and investment within the RTA). Led by the example of the European Community's EC 1992 program, which focused on internal barriers, many RTAs now liberalize trade in goods, services, investments, and technology. The motivation for deep integration is the belief that liberalizing trade and investment policies is seen as the best way to en-courage productive investment and long-run national competitiveness (Eden 1996a).

Table 2.2 provides some evidence on "how deep" are the current RTAs in the Americas by outlining the key components of each agreement. On the basis of a simple count of the possible commitments that could be made in the agreements, NAFTA and the just released U.S.–Chile FTA[2] are the deepest agreements (with 15 commitments), followed by the Group of Three (Colombia, Mexico, and Venezuela) and the Mexi-co–Nicaragua FTAs (13). Although economists traditionally think of customs unions as being deeper than FTAs, in fact, Mercosur is shallow-er than NAFTA in its provisions. The notable differences are in sanitary and phyto-sanitary measures, government procurement, and labor and environmental commitments.[3]

The new regionalism is not the only widespread policy change liber-alizing trade and FDI flows. Since the late 1980s, there has been enor-mous growth in bilateral arrangements linking countries: bilateral investment treaties (BITs), bilateral tax treaties (BTTs), and transna-tional arbitration treaties (TATs). Besides signaling an "open door" policy for FDI, these two-way FDI accords are helping to create an in-ternational investment regime that extends the GATT norm of nation-al treatment (i.e., foreign activities performed within a country's borders receive the same treatment as activities of nationals) to foreign invest-ment, services, and intellectual property (Eden 1996a). Thus, RTAs are occurring along with multilateral commitments, helping to solidify (and acting as a backstop to) domestic policy reforms in Latin America. The key impact of these BITs, BTTs, TATs, and RTAs is not just an explo-sion of acronyms but also an explosion of multiple overlapping trade and investment agreements of differing degrees of breadth and depth throughout the Western Hemisphere.

RTAs AND FDI: THEORY

The literature on the effects of RTAs on FDI is considerably smaller than that on the trade effects. Research by international economists has mostly been in the form of country-level (macroeconomic) analyses, which look at the economic impacts of RTAs on trade flows and national welfare, and in which FDI is a secondary consideration. Some studies have been done at the industry (meso) level of analysis, particularly for sensitive sectors such as automobiles and agriculture. International

Table 2.2. Provisions in Selected Regional Trade Agreements in the Americas: How Deep?

Provisions	Mercosur, 1991 and 1995	NAFTA, 1994	G-3, 1994	Bolivia-Mercosur, 1996
Agriculture separate chapter	X	X	X	0
Antidumping / countervailing duties	0	X	0	X
Competition policy	0	0	0	0
General dispute settlement	X	X	X	X
Government procurement	0	X	X	0
Intellectual property	X	X	X	0
Investment	X	X	X	0
Investor-state dispute settlement	X	X	X	0
Labor/environment	0	SA	0	0
Rules of origin (HS or ALADI)	X	X	X	X
Sanitary and phyto-sanitary measures	0	X	X	X
Services	X	X	X	BE
Special and differential treatment	0	0	0	X
Special rules for auto sector	X	X	X	0
Tariff elimination	X	X	X	X
Technical barriers to trade	X	X	X	0
Temporary entry of business persons	0	X	X	0
Sum of commitments[b]	10	15	13	6

Source: IDB (2002, 65), updated to include provisions in Mercosur using OAS (1996; www.sice.oas.org/) and the United States–Chile FTA (www.mac.doc.gov/chileFTA/FTAtext.html).

Note: CARICOM = Caribbean Community; SA = side agreement; BE = best endeavor to define in the future: the parties shall explicitly seek to develop disciplines in these areas in the future; HS = harmonization system; ALADI = Latin American Integration Association (Argentina, Bolivia, Brazil, Chile, Colombia, Cuba, Ecuador, Mexico, Paraguay, Peru, Uruguay, and Venezuela).

[a] The parties agreed to a reciprocal exemption from the application of anti-dumping.
[b] Does not include "best endeavors to define in the future."

Table 2.2. *(continued)*

Chile-Mercosur, 1996	Canada-Chile, 1996	Mexico-Nicaragua, 1997	Chile-Central America, 1999	Mexico-North Triangle, 2000	CARICOM-Dominican Republic, 2000	Chile-United States, 2003
0	0	X	0	X	X	X
X	X[a]	X	X	X	X	X
0	X	0	X	0	0	0
X	X	X	X	X	X	X
0	0	X	X	0	BE	X
X	0	X	0	X	X	X
X	X	X	X	X	X	X
0	X	X	0	X	0	X
0	SA	0	0	0	0	X
X	X	X	X	X	X	X
X	0	X	X	X	X	X
X	X	X	X	X	X	X
X	0	0	0	0	X	0
X	X	0	0	0	0	X
X	X	X	X	X	X	X
0	0	X	X	X	X	X
0	X	X	X	X	X	X
10	10	13	11	12	12	15

Figure 2.1. Impact of Regional Trade Agreement Formation on Foreign Direct Investment (FDI)—The Country-Level Perspective

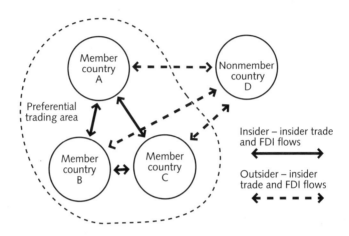

business scholars, conversely, have focused specifically on firm-level (microeconomic) effects of regional integration on the production and FDI strategies of domestic and foreign firms.

Country-Level Analysis

International trade economists have long studied the welfare impacts of RTAs, generally focusing on the customs union case, where the member countries reduce internal tariffs to zero and erect a common external tariff (Baldwin and Wyplosz 2003; Bhagwati, Greenaway, and Panagariya 1998; Bhagwati and Panagariya 1996; Lipsey 1960). The general model assumes that two or three countries (members or insiders) form an RTA, leaving out the remaining countries (nonmembers or outsiders), as in figure 2.1.

The economic effects of RTAs can be separated into short-term and long-term effects (Eden 2002). First are the short-run welfare gains that come from improved specialization of resources and greater opportunities for exchange within the region. These are known as the *static gains from trade*, and they are broken into trade creation and trade diversion effects. *Trade creation* occurs when reducing trade barriers within the RTA shifts trade patterns in favor of the lowest-cost producers, improving economic efficiency within the region. Trade creation requires that the RTA include lower-cost producers; then, the fall in internal trade barriers benefits the lower-cost members at the expense of higher cost members. *Trade diversion*, conversely, occurs when the RTA causes a shift to higher-cost internal producers from lower-cost external producers because the products of the external producers have become uncompetitive in the internal market.

At the same time, there are also short-term *transitional costs or losses* that fall on inefficient sectors and immobile factors as firms rationalize and reallocate their activities throughout the region as they respond to regional integration. These income-redistributional effects are the "Janus face" of the static gains from trade.

Because trade creation and trade diversion effects will vary by product and industry, the net impact of forming an RTA on the welfare of member and nonmember countries depends on many factors. To the extent that the member countries share similar endowments and demand conditions, economists believe that an RTA causes intraindustry trade (trade in differentiated products, e.g., small and medium-sized cars) to expand much faster than interindustry trade (trade in dissimilar products, e.g., corn and wheat) within the region. The general presumption is the more trade expands between two countries after forming an RTA and the less the negative impact on trade with nonmember countries, the more likely that trade creation effects have dominated trade diversion effects. However, Bhagwati, Greenaway, and Panagariya (1998, 1130) argue that "trade diversion is not necessarily a negligible phenomenon in current PTAs." Several empirical studies have found significant estimates of trade diversion. In addition, PTAs can lead to endogenous trade diversion as member countries raise trade barriers against nonmembers.[4]

RTAs also have long-run effects. They create welfare gains, the so-called *dynamic gains from trade*, that come from exploiting region-based economies of scale and scope, attracting FDI inflows and technology transfers, and greater competition among firms in national markets. In the long run, *greater economic interdependence* within the region is also likely to occur in response to rising interregional linkages created by trade and investment flows. Greater interdependence means more sensitivity and vulnerability to instabilities within the region (e.g., exchange rate shocks like the 1994–95 Mexican peso crisis), but it also creates added potential gains from the multiplier effects of economic linkages with other member countries.

It is this second set of effects, the dynamic impacts, that directly link RTAs to FDI. *Investment creation* occurs when the fall in trade barriers within the RTA causes a shift from lower-profitability investments to higher-profitability investments within the region.[5] In addition, investment creation occurs when the now-larger regional market attracts more FDI from outside the region as firms that had previously exported to individual countries within the region shift from exports to FDI.

Investment diversion occurs when the RTA causes a shift away from higher-profitability external investments to lower-profitability internal investments because the investments outside the region have become uncompetitive in the internal market. In other words, if investments are diverted into the region that would have been made or were previously made in a nonmember country, because of creating the RTA, this is investment diversion; a recent example is the movement of cut-and-sew garment firms from the Caribbean to Mexico after NAFTA was formed because Mexico would have preferential access to the U.S. market.

Transport costs and economies of scale at the plant level become more important as tariff barriers disappear on intraregional trade. To the extent that investments by firms in one member country were originally made in another member country for tariff-jumping reasons, their reason for existence disappears once an RTA is formed; as result, disinvestments can occur. Unless other locational attractions are more important than avoiding tariffs, the combination of initially high internal trade barriers that fall to zero coupled with large plant-level economies of scale could result in lower FDI flows, and higher trade flows, within the region (Eaton, Curtis, and Safarian 1994b). Agglomeration economies can also lead to clustering in some locations and disagglomerations in others (Dunning 2002; Eaton, Curtis, and Safarian 1994a).

Sometimes (see table 2.1 for examples), the RTA contains an investment chapter with specific rules designed to encourage FDI flows into and within the region. These investment chapters typically offer national treatment, most-favored-nation, transparency, dispute-resolution procedures, and so on (Eden and Molot 1996; Rugman and Gestrin 1993a; UNCTAD 1998). Regional agreements with investment chapters should, ceteris paribus, have stronger FDI impacts than agreements without such chapters because they offer more protection and reduce policy risks for foreign investments and investors. Because developing countries typically have weaker FDI protections than countries that belong to the Organization for Economic Cooperation and Development (OECD), one might therefore expect South–South and South–North RTAs to generate larger FDI flows to the less developed member countries if the RTAs have investment chapters (assuming that multinational enterprises, or MNEs, see the commitments as binding and enforceable).

Economists believe static effects are short run, small, and swamped by the dynamic effects. The overall size of these four effects depends on several factors, the most important of which are the scope of the RTA in number of member countries, industries, and products covered; the degree of liberalization of tariff and nontariff barriers among the members; and the current and potential economic complementarity of member relative to nonmember countries. The relative impact on the member countries is primarily driven by size; small countries are expected to suffer most of the adjustment costs but reap most of the gains as they adjust to prices set by the larger members. Overall, whether RTAs lead to increased or decreased FDI flows probably depends on the same factors that influence general economic impacts (that is, the scope of the RTA, the degree of liberalization, and the complementarity of member relative to nonmember countries), with one additional factor: whether trade and FDI are substitutes or complements.

Industry-Level and Firm-Level Analyses

International business scholars look at the formation of an RTA as a policy shock that affects decisionmaking by multinational and domestic firms, both inside and outside the RTA (Buckley 2002; Eden 1994, 2002; Narula 2003; Rugman 1990, 1994; Rugman and Gestrin 1993b; Vernon 1994; Levy Yeyati, Stein, and Daude 2002a). The details of the agreement, the breadth and depth of preexisting trade and FDI linkages between member countries, and country-level and region-level locational advantages are key environmental and policy reasons that determine the attractiveness of the RTA to MNCs.

How a firm is likely to respond to the RTA depends on its motivation for investment, its particular value-adding activities, and whether the firm is an insider MNC, outsider MNC, or domestic. Firms are assumed to have four main motivations for FDI: market seeking, resource seeking, efficiency seeking, and strategic asset seeking (Dunning 1993). Each firm must decide which activity to move, how the activity is linked with the rest of the MNC's activities, where to put the activity, and how to structure its ownership (mode of entry). Three possible types of intrafirm trade can occur with the establishment of FDI: horizontal integration in homogeneous products, horizontal integration in differentiated products, or vertical integration. The location question can be analyzed from the perspective of either macroregions (the national level) or microregions (agglomeration or clustering within regions); see Dunning (2002) and Eden (2002). Figure 2.2 outlines the theoretical framework used by most international business scholars to explore the impacts of RTAs on FDI.

International trade economists have begun to contribute to this literature, building on Dunning's eclectic paradigm of ownership, internalization, and location advantages as explanations for FDI (Dunning 1993). Their models assume product differentiation, economies of scale, and one factor that behaves as a public input (typically, technology). The MNE is assumed to consist of a headquarters and one or more production plants. Vertical specialization involves positioning specific activities in the MNC's value chain in geographically separated affiliates (Helpman 1984; Helpman and Krugman 1985). *Vertical FDI* is assumed to be resource or efficiency seeking, whereby MNEs separate their production processes so as to take advantage of factor price differentials across countries. Horizontal specialization typically involves rationalizing production across affiliates so individual affiliates have the responsibility for producing and exporting specific products. *Horizontal FDI* is assumed to be motivated by market seeking, possibly to exploit the firm's knowledge-based assets (Markusen 1994; Markusen and Venables 1998). The key difference between horizontal and vertical FDI is that, under vertical FDI, production in each affiliate is not only for the local/domestic market but also driven by the need to integrate the MNE's value chain across countries. The implementation of RTAs removes trade barriers, thus dramatically reducing the transaction costs of vertical and horizontal FDI within the region, while enlarging the overall size of the market.

The type of firm is also an important factor in predicting the impact of regional integration on FDI. Three categories of firms can be identified that are likely to have different responses to regional integration (Eden and Molot 1993; Vernon 1994). *Insiders* refer to the well-established multinationals located inside a free trade area with significant investments in the partner countries before the agreement. *Outsiders*

Figure 2.2. The Impact of Regional Trade Agreement (RTA) Formation on Foreign Direct Investment (FDI)—The Firm-Level Perspective

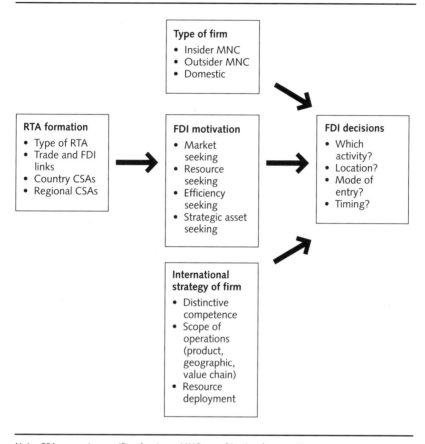

Note: CSA = country specific advantage; MNC = multinational corporation.

are foreign firms outside the area, which may have been exporting into the area or may have investments inside the area. *Domestics* refer to the local firms inside the area that are mostly focused on their national market (or a subunit within that market) without significant investments in the other partner countries; they may or may not already be exporting to these countries.

Insiders should see benefits from lower intraregional barriers and then respond by rationalizing product lines (horizontal integration) and/or production processes (vertical integration) to better exploit economies of scale and scope across the region. There is both a short-run response as MNCs engage in locational reshufflings in response to the falling trade barriers, and a long-run response where insiders locate, close, and/or expand their plants with the whole regional market in mind. Buckley and Casson (1998) break the insiders' FDI strategies into two categories: *reorganization investment* by insider firms that reorganize production within the integrated area based on regional comparative advantage; and *rationalization investment* by insiders to take advantage of the newly created returns-to-scale possibilities in the integrated area.

Outsiders are likely to also expand and rationalize their investments to take advantage of the larger market size. If rules of origin are tightened to meet North American content, transplants may be forced to upgrade production and source more inputs locally. Thus, parts plants may be induced to follow distributors and assembly plants. Outsiders that are exporting to North America may shift to FDI. They are likely to be drawn to the larger market or hub, the U.S. market, unless cost differentials make location in the smaller countries (Canada and Mexico) more attractive and/or interregional barriers are completely eliminated. Buckley and Casson (1998) call the investment reaction by outsider MNEs *defensive import-substituting investment* based on the new balance of locational advantages between the rest of the world and the region. They also discuss a fourth investment strategy called *offensive import substitution*, which is undertaken by both insiders and outsiders to take advantage of the growing intraregional market.

For domestics, firms without established links to other potential NAFTA members, a free trade area will be seen as both an opportunity (i.e., new markets, access to lower cost inputs) and a threat (i.e., more competition). Such firms, with encouragement, may start or increase their exports within North America and possibly open up distributors or offshore plants where market size or costs warrant. They will, however, have to face the difficult task of breaking into established distribution networks of domestics and MNCs in the North American markets. The key question is whether to "go regional" and branch outside the home country into other parts of North America or to stay at home and most likely be acquired by a NAFTA multinational.

In summary, the key effects of RTAs on FDI are expected to depend on the (1) the type of firm (insider MNC, outsider MNC, trader, or domestic), (2) the firm's motivation for entry, and (3) the components of the firm's international strategy (its distinctive competence, scope of operations, and current resource deployment). The typical decisions to be made are the "who, what, where, when, why, and how" questions; that is, which activity(ies) should be moved and where, the mode of entry choice, and timing issues. "Locational shufflings" are expected as MNCs allocate production and sales on a regional basis, taking advantage of the larger, barrier-free market to achieve economies of scale and scope (efficiency-seeking FDI).

Caveats and Problems

Before we turn to the empirical work on RTAs and FDI in the Americas, it is important to spell out several caveats that should be applied to the results of these empirical studies. These include timing issues, confounding events, the spaghetti bowl effect, and data sources and problems.

Timing Issues. First, when analyzing the economic effects of RTAs, it is important to distinguish between de jure and de facto liberalization. RTA negotiations often take several years. Some firms will react to the RTA in advance of the starting date, seeking first-mover advantages to preempt the competition. Conversely, when a new RTA is announced, gains are expected quickly. However, reductions in trade barriers tend to be phased in during a transition period to give local firms time to adjust (e.g., NAFTA was phased in mostly over 10 years), many nontariff barriers are grandfathered, and some sectors (usually the most controversial, like agriculture) are excluded. In addition, RTAs sometimes resort to positive lists of products to be liberalized rather than negative lists of exceptions; negative lists are more trade promoting because they eliminate tariffs on unlisted products. Thus, the effects can be complicated.

Confounding Events. Second, confounding factors make it difficult to separate out the impacts of regional integration from other macroeconomic and policy changes. For example, the 1994 peso shock and Mexico's 1993 liberalizing FDI law are difficult to disentangle from the adoption of NAFTA. However, most scholars agree NAFTA did encourage FDI in Mexico (Globerman 2002; Krueger 2000; Levy Yeyati, Stein, and Daude 2002a). More recently, exchange rate depreciations in Brazil in 1999 and Argentina in 2002 have strained economic relationships within Mercosur. Currency devaluations lower export prices and raise import prices, causing large trade adjustments that can induce FDI reshufflings within the region. Devaluations can also provoke more direct forms of protectionism; for example, Mexico reacted to its peso devaluation by raising tariffs against non-NAFTA countries, whereas Argentina responded to its own peso crisis by raising tariffs against Brazil. Because exchange rate swings can often be several magnitudes larger than tariff reductions, the increased trade and investment interdependencies encouraged by RTAs leave the member countries more exposed to each other's poor monetary and fiscal policies.

The Spaghetti Bowl Effect. Third, empirical work on regional integration typically focuses on one RTA at a time. However, one of the features of the new regionalism is the proliferation of bilateral accords. This considerably complicates the economic analysis of RTAs. For example, when the U.S. Congress failed to extend fast-track authority to President Bill Clinton in 1995, leaving Chile out in the cold, the U.S. withdrawal left the regional integration field wide open to other countries. Chile and other small Latin American countries responded by signing multiple RTAs. Mexico, for example, has signed bilateral RTAs with Chile, Bolivia, Costa Rica, the European Union, Nicaragua, and Israel, among others. Chile has bilateral RTAs with Canada, Mexico, the United States, Colombia, Ecuador, and associate member status within Mercosur.

Although most of these agreements have been within the region, others have not (e.g., with the European Union). This ad hoc proliferation of RTAs has been likened to a "spaghetti bowl" mixture of bilateral, trilateral, and multilateral RTAs. These political hub-and-spoke arrangements create "who is whose" problems that increase protectionism and reduce the overall welfare gains from RTAs (Bhagwati, Greenaway, and Panagariya 1998; IDB 2002; Wonnacott 1996).

In the simplest hub-and-spoke pattern, one country (the hub) has bilateral RTAs with two other countries (the spokes). Trade barriers are eliminated within each RTA but not between RTAs. Comparisons between two hub-and-spoke RTAs and one trilateral RTA demonstrate that potential static and dynamic benefits are higher under the trilateral RTA. Two bilaterals leave trade barriers in place between the spokes, whereas one trilateral eliminates these barriers.

At the same time, administrative and transport costs are higher in a hub-and-spoke system because of its greater complexity, potential for rent-seeking behavior, and inconsistencies. Instead of one tariff rate for imports, tariff schedules vary depending on which RTA applies. Different rules of origin for the same product encourage "forum shopping" for the lowest rates, raising the cost of administering these agreements. To the extent that rules of origin are seen as transaction costs for firms, they can influence not only trade flows but also investment decisions.

The distribution of (albeit smaller) gains differs also, with the gains being distributed more unevenly in a hub-and-spoke system. The hub gains at the expense of the spokes because the hub benefits from preferences in both spoke markets and only firms in the hub can buy duty-free inputs from each spoke. The spokes, conversely, lose because they do not have duty-free access to the other spokes, face more competition in the hub market from the spokes, and are less competitive relative to hub firms because their input costs are higher.

Data Sources and Problems. The last problem that plagues empirical work on regional integration and FDI in the Americas is data availability and comparability. Most governments report their FDI data to the OECD, the UN Conference on Trade and Development (UNCTAD), and the IMF.[6] Data are reported in both flow and stock formats. UNCTAD's *World Investment Report* and the Economic Commission for Latin America and the Caribbean's *Foreign Investment in Latin America and the Caribbean* are the two annual publications with the most thorough and detailed analyses of FDI in the Western Hemisphere. Both provide extensive access to FDI studies and/or statistics on their Web sites.[7]

In the three NAFTA countries, FDI transactions (balance of payments) or flow data, both inward and outward, are reported as the sum of direct investment income (income on equity plus retained earnings plus income on debt) and direct investment financial flows (equity capital plus other capital). FDI transactions data for Mexico, however, are only available from 1994 on; before 1994, the data reflect only notifications to the Mexican government, not actual FDI. In addition, Mexican FDI flow data are only available for inward FDI because there is minimal outward FDI.

International investment position (FDI stock) data are reported as the sum of equity capital, reinvested earnings, and other capital in Canada and the United States. In Mexico, FDI position data are not reported, either for inward or outward FDI stock. For Canada, FDI position data are measured at book value, whereas in the United States, FDI position data are reported at market value (in aggregate) and at book value (historical cost) for detailed data by country and by industry. Differences between book and market value are caused by the following factors:[8] valuation adjustments between historical cost and market value, exchange rate fluctuations, corporate reorganizations, migration of principal owners, and shifts between FDI and foreign portfolio investment where nonresidents increase their ownership to 10 percent or more of voting interest (or decrease it to less than 10 percent).

If a researcher wants to study the impact of NAFTA on FDI, he or she can use either flow or stock data, and either in aggregate (to or from all other countries) or bilateral (between pairs of countries) form. The theoretical macro and micro models we have outlined above suggest that the impact of RTAs on FDI is best studied by examining both total and bilateral FDI patterns, particularly member–member FDI and member–nonmember FDI patterns. To examine the impact of NAFTA on FDI, for example, one would need to aggregate FDI data for the three member countries, either on a stock or flow basis. There are clear problems with both approaches.

Suppose one attempts to amalgamate FDI flow data for the three countries. Bilateral FDI data by country are available in both stocks and flows for the United States (inward only), flows for Mexico, and stocks and (very limited) flows for Canada. Therefore, while Mexico and the United States publish country-level FDI flow data, Canada publishes detailed country-level data only for stocks, not for flows (Statistics Canada does this for confidentiality reasons, although why it is not a problem in Mexico and the United States but is a problem in Canada is not clear). At the flow level for Canada, only FDI flow data with the United States, the United Kingdom, and Japan are available.

Alternatively, one could amalgamate FDI stock data for the three countries. Whereas the U.S. and Canadian bilateral stock data are quite detailed, Mexican stock data before 1994 are based on notifications to the Mexican government, not on actual investments. In addition, the pre-1994 stock data for Mexico are recorded at market value, the U.S. data are at historical cost, and the Canadian data are at book value. After 1994, no stock data for Mexico are available, period. Thus, the Mexican FDI series breaks at 1994, and the pre-1994 data are not consistent with the U.S. and Canadian data.[9]

As a result, the researcher who wants to analyze the impacts of RTAs on FDI patterns are "betwixed the devil and the deep blue sea," with either approach. Most FDI researchers, but not all, are sensitive to these problems. However, one still regularly sees empirical work that ignores the data problems associated with analyzing FDI patterns in the Americas. With these caveats and problems in mind, we now turn to exploring empirical work on RTAs and FDI in the Americas.

RTAs AND FDI: EMPIRICAL WORK

In this section, we review the recent empirical studies exploring the economic effects of RTAs on FDI in the Americas, focusing primarily on CUSFTA and NAFTA, with some attention to Mercosur. We limit our review to papers published from 1998 on; readers interested in earlier work on this topic are directed to Eden (2002) and Hejazi and Safarian (1999). We start with recent statistics on FDI.

Recent FDI Patterns

Figure 2.3 shows the changing shares of intraregional and interregional outward FDI stocks between 1986 and 1999 in what Rugman and Brain (2003, 19) refer to as the "broad Triad." The enormous growth in FDI stocks in North America, Asia, and the European Union is evident. Intraregional FDI as a share of all North American FDI fell from 30.3 percent in 1986 to 18.2 percent in 1999, while the intraregional FDI share rose in both Asia and the European Union.

Table 2.3 (on pages 44 and 45) provides a long-rum view of intraregional FDI flows, focusing specifically on NAFTA. Gross FDI flows into the three NAFTA member countries declined over the 1988–93 period, from $67.5 billion in 1988 to a low of $32.0 billion in 1992, but almost doubled in 1993 and 1994. Because Mexican FDI statistics switched from reporting FDI notifications to recording actual FDI expenditures, the country's FDI data before and after 1994 are not directly comparable. However, NAFTA's FDI gains appear to come primarily from FDI into the United States, not Canada or Mexico. Since 1994, gross inflows to NAFTA have increased rapidly, peaking at $383.0 billion in 2000, before falling back to $177.2 billion in 2001. The U.S. share of inward FDI into NAFTA rose from 70.5 percent in 1994 to peak at 88.4 percent in 1999, before falling back to 70.2 percent in 2001.

Although FDI inflows rose enormously during the 1990s, that growth came to a sudden halt in 2001. FDI inflows into OECD countries and worldwide dropped precipitously in 2001. When NAFTA FDI is considered as a percentage of gross FDI inflows for all OECD countries, or worldwide, the pattern is similar. NAFTA's share fell from 48.8 percent of all OECD inflows in 1988 to a low of 25.1 percent in 1992, recovering to 41.1 percent in 1993, before falling again to a low of 33.1 percent in 1995. From 1996 on, NAFTA's share rose to 42 percent of all OECD FDI, before jumping to 46.7 percent in 1999. The share gains in

Figure 2.3. Interregional and Intraregional Outward Stocks of Foreign Direct Investment (FDI), 1986 and 1999 (billions of dollars)

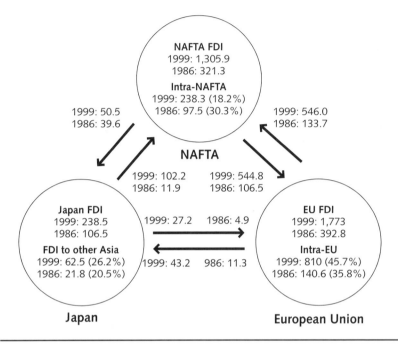

Source: Adapted from Rugman (2001, 116, 120); used with permission.

the second half of the 1990s clearly reflect trends in U.S. inward FDI because Canada's share of world FDI has been stuck in the 4 percent range since 1995, while Mexico's share fell steadily after NAFTA was introduced to slightly less than 2 percent of OECD FDI flows in 1999. The collapse of world FDI inflows in 2001 affected Canada and the United States the most; only Mexico increased its share, rebounding from 1 to 3.4 percent of worldwide FDI inflows in 2001. More recent numbers (Evans 2002; ECLAC 2003) suggest that all three countries suffered further declines in inward FDI in 2002. These data provide the context for our presentation of empirical studies of FDI and regional integration.

Country-Level Effects

The typical model of the economic impacts of forming an RTA is based on a gravity model equation originally developed to explain bilateral trade patterns.[10] The gravity model explicitly includes income and distance measures:

$$FDI_{IJ} = GDP_I + GDP_J + DISTANCE_{IJ} + TRADE_{IJ} + RTA + Z$$

The embedded assumption is that trade between countries I and J should be positively related to their gross domestic products (GDPs) (and/or their per capita GDPs) and negatively to the distance between them (DISTANCE). FDI is assumed to be either a substitute or complement to trade patterns (TRADE). The impact of the formation of the regional trade agreement is tested by adding a dummy variable (RTA). Z is a vector of control variables that could also potentially explain FDI patterns, such as industry mix, exchange rates, and real interest rates. The gravity model can be seen in many FDI studies, such as Krueger (2000); Levy Yeyati (2001); Levy Yeyati, Stein, and Daude (2002b); Stein and Daude (2001); Mauro (2000); Harrigan (2001); and Frankel and Rose (2000).

It is well documented in the literature that FDI is strongly attracted to countries characterized by relatively large domestic economies and by increasing levels of real per capita income (Globerman and Shapiro 2002). Levy Yeyati, Stein, and Daude (2002a) also indicate that the gains may be smaller for countries that are less developed, closed to international trade, and altogether unattractive for foreign investors. Virtually overall studies of FDI flows stress the dominating importance of the size and income level of the host country (Graham 1999). Implementing regional integration creates a common boundary for member countries (as shown in figure 2.1). The new regional economy competes with nonmember countries, and an increase in FDI into the region is expected once the RTA is launched. MacDermott (2002), for example, applies both the traditional gravity model and the knowledge-capital model to analyze the bilateral OECD FDI data from 1980 to 1997, and finds that implementing NAFTA led to an increase in FDI into member countries. This is particularly evident for Mexico, which is not surprising because NAFTA was mainly about adding Mexico to the preexisting Canada–U.S. FTA.

One difficulty in assessing the role of RTAs on FDI—particularly for a specific country's FDI—is that there are many channels through which RTAs could potentially have impacts on FDI flows (Levy Yeyati, Stein, and Daude 2002a). The impact of RTAs will depend on characteristics

Table 2.3. Gross Inward Foreign Direct Investment (FDI) Flows, 1988–2001 (millions of dollars)

Host	Pre-CUSFTA	Post-CUSFTA				
	1988	1989	1990	1991	1992	1993
Canada	6,124.9	6,010.2	7,582.5	2,881.2	4,722.4	4,730.8
Mexico	2,800.8	3,881.5	3,373.7	5,704.7	8,093.7	6,715.0
U.S.	58,571.0	69,010.0	48,422.0	22,799.0	19,222.0	50,663.0
NAFTA	67,496.7	78,901.7	59,378.2	31,384.9	32,038.1	62,108.8
OECD	138,327.0	171,376.0	178,687.0	124,931.0	118,052.0	151,079.0
World	n.a.	200,612.0	203,812.0	157,773.0	175,841.0	219,421.0

As Percentage of FDI Flows into NAFTA

Host						
Canada	9.1	7.6	12.8	9.2	14.7	7.6
Mexico	4.1	4.9	5.7	18.2	25.3	10.8
U.S.	86.8	87.5	81.5	72.6	60.0	81.6

As Percentage of FDI Flows into OECD

Host						
Canada	4.4	3.5	4.2	2.3	4.0	3.1
Mexico	2.0	2.3	1.9	4.6	6.9	4.4
U.S.	42.3	40.3	27.1	18.2	16.3	33.5
NAFTA	48.8	46.0	33.2	25.1	27.1	41.1

As percentage of World FDI Inflows

Host						
Canada		3.0	3.7	1.8	2.7	2.2
Mexico		1.9	1.7	3.6	4.6	3.1
U.S.		34.4	23.8	14.5	10.9	23.1
NAFTA		39.3	29.1	19.9	18.2	28.3

Percentage Change Year over Year

Host						
Canada		−1.9	26.2	−62.0	63.9	0.2
Mexico		38.6	−13.1	69.1	41.9	−17.0
U.S.		17.8	−29.8	−52.9	−15.7	163.6
NAFTA		16.9	−24.7	−47.1	2.1	93.9
OECD		23.9	4.3	−30.1	−5.5	28.0

Source: Author's calculations using FDI data from appendices in UNCTAD (2001, 2002). Mexican data for 1994–2001 are from Mexican Government FDI Statistics.

Note: CUSFTA = U.S.-Canada Free Trade Agreement; NAFTA = North American Free Trade Agreement; OECD = Organization for Economic Cooperation and Development; n.a. = not available.

Table 2.3. *(continued)*

			Post-NAFTA				
1994	1995	1996	1997	1998	1999	2000	2001
8,205.7	9,255.8	9,635.0	11,525.2	22,804.1	24,436.5	66,621.3	27,458.7
10,639.8	8,324.8	7,703.6	12,125.8	8,126.9	12,856.0	15,484.4	25,334.4
45,095.0	58,772.0	84,455.0	103,398.0	174,434.0	283,376.0	300,912.0	124,435.0
63,940.5	76,352.6	101,793.6	127,049.0	205,365.0	320,668.5	383,017.7	177,228.1
164,971.0	230,846.0	248,882.0	299,004.0	509,313.0	683,744.0	n.a.	n.a.
255,988.0	331,844.0	386,140.0	478,082.0	694,457.0	1,088,263.0	1,491,934.0	735,146.0
12.8	12.1	9.5	9.1	11.1	7.6	17.4	15.5
16.6	10.9	7.6	9.5	4.0	4.0	4.0	14.3
70.5	77.0	83.0	81.4	84.9	88.4	78.6	70.2
5.0	4.0	3.9	3.9	4.5	3.6	n.a.	n.a.
6.4	3.6	3.1	4.1	1.6	1.9	n.a.	n.a.
27.3	25.5	33.9	34.6	34.2	41.4	n.a.	n.a.
38.8	33.1	40.9	42.5	40.3	46.9	n.a.	n.a.
3.2	2.8	2.5	2.4	3.3	2.2	4.5	3.7
4.2	2.5	2.0	2.5	1.2	1.2	1.0	3.4
17.6	17.7	21.9	21.6	25.1	26.0	20.2	16.9
25.0	23.0	26.4	26.6	29.6	29.5	25.7	24.1
73.5	12.8	4.1	19.6	97.9	7.2	172.6	−58.8
n.a.	−21.8	−7.5	57.4	−33.0	58.2	20.4	63.6
−11.0	30.3	43.7	22.4	68.7	62.5	6.2	−58.6
2.9	19.4	33.3	24.8	61.6	56.1	19.4	−53.7
9.2	39.9	7.8	20.1	70.3	34.2	n.a.	n.a.

of the host countries that make them more or less attractive than their RTA partners as a potential location of foreign investment (IDB 2002). It is therefore critical to take other potential explanations into account by including them as control variables in the gravity model in order to isolate the impact of the RTA on FDI patterns.

For example, *domestic economic reforms* can confound the analysis. Graham and Wada (2000) find that investment into Mexico began to speed up following the onset of policy reform in Mexico in the later 1980s, which was well before NAFTA. They cite two possible causes: bilateral trade agreements between the United States and Mexico during the period 1985–89, and policy reforms implemented unilaterally by Mexico. They infer the first explanation is not consistent with U.S. FDI patterns, but the second explanation does fit the facts. Therefore, Graham and argue that it is probable, even if not provable, that NAFTA kept FDI flows into Mexico from falling after domestic reforms had been fully implemented.

Globerman and Shapiro (2001) provide another example of the importance of domestic policies. They identify two domestic explanations for Canada's declining share of inward FDI in North America: (1) higher taxes in Canada discouraged investment by domestic and foreign investors; and (2) Canada's declining capacity to innovate and support "new economy" activities discouraged FDI inflows. Further, Blomstrom and Kokko (1997) claim both economic reforms and macroeconomic factors affect FDI. Their paper shows that the most positive impacts on FDI when regional integration coincides with domestic liberalization and macroeconomic stabilization.

Another factor that can influence FDI patterns is *factor costs and availability*. Love and Lage-Hidalgo (1999) conclude that U.S. FDI into Mexico is systematically influenced by relative Canadian–Mexican wage rates and demand differentials in both the short and long runs. However, there is no evidence of similar influences at work on U.S. investment into Canada. The U.S. FDI pattern in Mexico and Canada is due to the different industrial composition of U.S. FDI in these two partners. They conclude that Canadian concerns about the extent to which Canada competes with Mexico may be overstated. Also, market size serves as an important consideration of investment location (e.g., Bertrand and Madariaga 2002).

Finally, *exchange rate changes* can also influence FDI patterns. Buckley and others (2003) find the acceleration of changes in the exchange rate fostered U.S. FDI into Canada. In contrast, Mauro's (2000) empirical study of worldwide FDI patterns shows that exchange rate variability does not appear to have affected firms' decisions to invest abroad, except during the turbulent 1980s when FDI represented a means of reducing exchange rate risk.

Trade–FDI Linkages

The net impact of the trade-creating and trade-diverting effects of RTAs is typically measured by looking at the resulting changes in intraregional compared with interregional trade patterns. Table 2.4 shows estimates by the Asian Development Bank (ADB 2002) of intraregional export shares in five-year periods from 1980 to 2000. The three NAFTA member countries, for example, saw intraregional exports grow from 41.3 to 58.8 percent of their total exports. The bigger the RTA, the larger intraregional shares tend to be.

Trade intensity indices (TIIs) are better measures of relative growth than export growth rates. The TII is the ratio of the RTA's intraregional trade share divided by the RTA's share of all world trade. If the ratio is close to one, the regional agreement is seen as having a neutral impact on world trade; indexes well above (or below) 1 are associated with net trade diversion (creation). Table 2.4 shows that TIIs for NAFTA and the European Union are quite low relative to Mercosur and the Andean Pact, for example. This suggests that NAFTA has been a trade-creating RTA, whereas the impacts of Mercosur have been primarily trade diverting. North American intraregional exports of goods and services now stand at 55.7 percent of North American exports, up from 33.6 percent in 1980 and 49.19 percent in 1996 (Rugman and Brain 2003, 5, 16); similar growth patterns can be seen in the interregional export shares in table 2.4. This accords with Krueger (2000), who finds that for the United States, the impact of NAFTA has been relatively small, and that for Mexico, the results do not give much support to the view that NAFTA might be seriously trade diverting.

Eden and Molot (1992) argue that NAFTA increased the dependence of Canada and Mexico on the U.S. market. In the late 1980s, three-quarters of Canadian and Mexican trade and FDI flows were with the United States. By 2003, the U.S. share of both countries' exports had risen above 85 percent, significantly increasing their economic dependence on the United States (Rugman and Brain 2003). A similar pattern

Table 2.4. Changing Trade Patterns within Regional Trade Agreements, 1980-2000

Regional Trade Agreement	1980–1984	1985–1989	1990–1994	1995–1999	2000
Intraregional export shares					
NAFTA	41.3	46.7	48.2	53.2	58.8
Mercosur	9.9	8.5	15.9	24.8	22.3
Andean Community	5.0	4.8	9.1	13.2	10.8
European Union	62.0	65.1	66.5	65.1	66.9
European Free Trade Area	16.5	16.4	13.7	12.6	11.8
Asia-Pacific Economic Cooperation	66.3	72.2	73.1	74.3	75.2
Asian Free Trade Area (ASEAN)	20.8	18.9	22.5	24.8	24.5
CER (Australia-New Zealand)	8.0	8.4	9.1	10.7	9.3
Trade intensity indexes					
NAFTA	1.8	1.8	2.0	2.2	2.2
Mercosur	5.6	7.5	11.7	13.2	14.3
Andean Community	3.6	5.4	10.9	15.7	16.6
European Union	1.5	1.5	1.6	1.7	1.7
European Free Trade Area	2.3	2.1	2.0	2.1	2.2
Asia Pacific Economic Cooperation)	1.6	1.6	1.6	1.5	1.5
Asian Free Trade Area (ASEAN)	4.2	4.8	3.8	3.7	4.0
CER (Australia-New Zealand)	4.1	4.6	5.8	7.1	6.8

Source: ADB (2002, 185-86).

Note: ASEAN = Association of Southeast Asian Nations. CER = Australia–New Zealand Closer Economic Relations Trade Agreement.

of increasing dependence holds for Canadian and Mexican imports from the United States.

The same pattern, however, is not true for the United States. In 1980, 17 percent of U.S. exports went to Canada and 7 percent to Mexico; by the end of the 1980s, Canada's share had risen to 20 percent, while Mexico's share of U.S. exports was unchanged. The averages for the period 1996–2001 were remarkably similar to those in 1980: 19 percent for Canada and 9 percent for Mexico (Globerman 2002, 31). The same pattern holds for the share of U.S. imports from Canada: In comparison with the late 1980s, there has been minimal change (from 17 to 18 percent). Conversely, Mexico's share in U.S. imports has increased, albeit from a low base, from 5 to 8 percent of all U.S. imports.

Whether international trade and FDI are substitutes or complements is a critical link in assessing the impacts of regional integration on FDI. The empirical evidence in the literature suggests that trade and FDI are complements, although the evidence is not definitive (Bloningen 1999; McMorriston 2000). For example, Hejazi and Safarian (2001) establish that trade and FDI are complements, using trade and FDI stock data on bilateral basis between the United States and 51 other countries over 1982–94. Specifically, U.S. outward FDI is found to have a larger predicted impact on U.S. exports than does inward FDI. Conversely, U.S. inward FDI predicts U.S. imports better than does outward FDI. An exploration of sector differences indicates that U.S. outward FDI in manufacturing has a large predicted impact on both exports and imports, whereas U.S. outward FDI in services has a large predicted impact on U.S. exports but little or no predicted impact on imports.

In the same vein, Mauro (2000), in his study of worldwide FDI patterns, finds that FDI stocks and exports are complementary at the aggregate level; a 10 percent increase in exports causes an increase in a country's FDI stock of more than 10 percent. Tariffs have no impact on FDI, implying that the "tariff-jumping" argument is not supported by empirical analysis. One possible explanation is that tariff barriers have been falling worldwide, so they can erode as an RTA mechanism. Yet Mauro finds that nontariff barriers did discourage FDI, and that a requirement for FDI to respond positively to the formation of an RTA is that internal barriers fall.

In contrast, Globerman (2002) argues that changes in intraregional trade intensity need not be mirrored by changes in intraregional FDI intensity because RTAs encourage both intraregional trade and extraregional FDI. This is particularly so in the case of Mexico's outward FDI flows to the United States, which are quite small over the 1980–98 period (Globerman 2002). At the regional level, Feinberg, Keane, and

Bognanno (1998) find that U.S. FDI in Canada, as proxied by the employment and assets of U.S. MNC affiliates in Canada, rose as Canadian tariff rates fell over the 1990s.

Specific circumstances surrounding the integration process are also important. For example, in reviewing other empirical studies, Fontagne (1999) notes that FDI into developing countries tends to have a much higher export multiplier associated with it than does FDI into industrial countries. This is because FDI into OECD member countries is more likely to be motivated by the goal of serving high-income consumers. In addition, there is likely to be greater local capability in terms of support, both in infrastructure and services, in industrial countries.

The observed variation in the trade intensity–FDI intensity relationship might also be caused by different levels of aggregation of the studies. For example, Bloningen (1999) examines product-level data and finds substantial evidence for both a substitution and a complementary effect between affiliate production and exports with Japanese auto parts for the U.S. market. He emphasizes the importance of vertical specialization as a critical determinant of the trade–FDI relationship.

Intraregional Differences in FDI Patterns

The introduction of an RTA is expected to increase FDI inflows into the region. To the extent that this occurs, the FDI statistics should show a structural break around the time that the RTA comes into force. Andresen and Pereira (2002) test this hypothesis for 63 countries using the Vogelsang SupWald test. They find clear evidence of structural breaks for Canada and the United States in 1992, and for Mexico in 1993. Both the levels of FDI (Canada, 797 percent; United States, 760 percent; Mexico 866 percent) and the ratios of inward FDI to GDP (Canada, 547 percent; United States, 505 percent; Mexico, 579 percent) rose after the structural break. The authors conclude that "regional integration is positively related to FDI levels" and that smaller countries had larger structural breaks (p. 12).

However, not all countries need benefit equally from the introduction of an RTA. Figure 2.2 shows that the intra-NAFTA FDI as a share of all outward FDI stocks fell from 30.3 percent in 1986 to 18.2 percent in 1999. The declining intra-NAFTA FDI share is one of the puzzles economists have sought to explain in their empirical work. A key explanation has been Canada's decreasing FDI intensity with the United States since the signing of CUSFTA (Eden and Monteils 2000; Globerman 2002). Both FDI flow and stock data point to the growth of inward FDI in the United States relative to Canada during the past few decades (see Buckley et al., forthcoming; Globerman and Shapiro 2001). Rugman and Brain (2003) found that the share of U.S. outward FDI stock in Canada fell from 20.9 percent in 1982, to 16.7 percent in 1989, and to 10.2 percent in 2000 (see also Hejazi and Safarian 2001; Safarian and Hejazi 2001). They argue that NAFTA caused MNEs to close plants in Canada and use U.S. exports to supply the Canadian market.

Eden and Monteils (2000) also note that Canadian share of world FDI inflow fell from 8.55 percent in 1985 to 3.97 percent in 1997 and that the U.S. share also fell from 24.40 percent in 1985 to 20.86 percent in 1997, even though for both countries the absolute amount of FDI increased. Only Mexico maintained its share (approximately 2.5 percent) of world FDI inflows. Overall, the region's share of world FDI fell from 35.43 to 27.34 percent between 1985 and 1997. Thus, NAFTA became a less attractive region, in a relative sense, for world FDI. This may reflect the reduced attractiveness of NAFTA as an investment location or, more likely, the increased attractiveness of other regions. Similar reports can be found in Swimmer (2000) and other studies. Eden and Monteils also find that the same patterns hold for NAFTA's share—and for the individual country's share—of outward FDI.

Globerman (2002) observed that European investors almost disappeared as a source of inward FDI to Canada in the latter part of the 1990s. Investors based in the "NAFTA zone," essentially U.S. investors, became increasingly dominant sources of inward FDI for Canada in the 1990s. Meanwhile, European investors became the dominant investors in the United States. According to Globerman (2002), one possible reason for Canada's declining attractiveness to European FDI was that favored "new economy" acquisition targets were more heavily represented in the United States.[11]

Horizontal and Vertical FDI

The key difference between horizontal and vertical FDI is that, under vertical FDI, the production in each affiliate is linked through the value chain to MNC affiliates in other countries; but horizontal integration is primarily driven by domestic market seeking. Whether regional integration primarily stimulates vertical or horizontal FDI is not clear from the literature.

One of the major advantages of regional integration is the economies of scale gains that come from replacing small, national markets with a larger, regional market; this suggests that horizontal FDI (locational shufflings for efficiency reasons) should be the primary response to RTAs. Empirical analysis of FDI patterns worldwide suggests that horizontal FDI is the primary explanation (Markusen and Maskus 1999). Mauro (2000), in analyzing the impacts of tariff and nontariff barrier reductions on bilateral FDI patterns in 1988, 1993, and 1996, finds that FDI is primarily market seeking.

However, Levy Yeyati, Stein, and Daude (2002b), examine bilateral FDI patterns between 20 OECD countries and 60 host countries from 1982 through 1998, finding that RTAs tend to promote vertical over horizontal FDI. They find that vertical FDI for differentiated products does not substitute for trade, while the conclusion on horizontal FDI is not definitive. Waldkirch (2001) also finds that vertical integration is the likely explanation for the large increase in Mexico's FDI from Canada and the United States after NAFTA. Similar results are reported by other studies (e.g., Aizenman and Marion 2001; Hanson, Mataloni, and Slaughter 2001).

Moreover, MNCs display strategy preference patterns according to their origins, which affects the linkages between RTAs and FDI. For instance, Makhija and Williamson (2000) argue that U.S. industries are mostly multidomestic in comparison to other nations. That is, U.S. firms tend to duplicate production activities across the different countries in which they operate and to be less vertically specialized than MNCs from other OECD countries. This, according to Makhija and Williamson, implies the NAFTA experience might differ from that of the European Union.

When interpreting intraregional FDI data, differences in sectoral performance should also be taken into account (Rugman and Brain 2003). However, there are few econometric studies focusing on individual sectors and regional integration, probably because of FDI data limitations. The most important sector in terms of bilateral trade flows within NAFTA is automobiles and auto parts, which represents between one-third and one-half of NAFTA trade, depending on how broadly the sector is defined (Eden and Molot 1992, 1993; Hunter, Markusen, and Rutherford 1995a, 1995b; Molot 1993). The Canadian and U.S. auto industries were not expected to see major MNE location shifts after CUSFTA and NAFTA because of bilateral producer free trade since the 1965 Auto Pact. NAFTA, in terms of autos and auto parts, was primarily about the opening and integration of the Mexican auto industry into an already deeply integrated North American auto sector (Weintraub and Sands 1998).[12]

Insiders versus Outsiders

A body of empirical work on the impact of RTAs on FDI inflows finds that RTAs benefit member countries (insiders) and have no impact or negative effects on nonmember countries (outsiders), as the executors of RTAs expected. Bertrand and Madariaga (2002) use the panel data on U.S. FDI in NAFTA and Mercosur from 1989 to 1998 and find that economic integration certainly plays a major role in U.S. firms' location patterns. The U.S. position regarding the two agreements—an insider in NAFTA, an outsider in Mercosur—seems to matter. Their regression results indicate significant positive relationship between U.S. (insider) FDI and NAFTA dummy variables, while no relationship is detected between U.S. (outsider) FDI and Mercosur dummies.

Monge-Naranjo (2002) compares the effect of NAFTA on flows of FDI received by Mexico (an insider) and the countries in the region excluded from NAFTA (outsiders). He finds that, with the exception of Costa Rica, all other Central American countries lagged behind Mexico after 1994. The most severe bias occurred in textile and apparel sectors, which represented most of the FDI flows in Honduras, El Salvador, and Guatemala, but not Costa Rica. For Costa Rica, what attracts FDI was the production of electronic components, medical equipment, and so on. Unlike other outsiders, Costa Rica, after the launching of NAFTA, still remained its attractiveness for FDI inflows. The "secret" lies in its production of electronic components, medical equipment, and so on.

The Bottom Line: Empirical Studies of Regional Integration and FDI in the Americas

In this section, we have reviewed dozens of empirical studies, done over the past five years, which have analyzed the relationships between regional integration and foreign investment. The gravity model has been the preferred method of analysis, more recently supplemented by variables that distinguish between horizontal and vertical integration, and between insider and outsider investments. Although there have been many studies, the one *definitive* study of the impacts of regional integration on FDI in the Americas has not yet been done. In addition, most of the empirical work focuses on NAFTA, with little attention to the rest of the hemisphere.

The implications of RTAs for policymakers, as a result, are not obvious. Though there is a clear presumption that regional integration benefits member economies, a solid economic explanation for why some members lose FDI (e.g., Canada in NAFTA) and how this can be prevented is still in its infancy. Linking the micro-level locational strategies of individual firms to the macro-level shifts in FDI flows and stocks in response to regional integration also remains a challenge. Statistical agencies in the Americas are clearly one culprit here. Until FDI flow and stock data, at the bilateral and industry level, are harmonized in terms of definitions and collection practices, and the data are made freely available to researchers, the empirical studies of FDI and regional integration will continue to be piecemeal and problematic. We view this as an essential prerequisite to better econometric work on hemispheric issues.

POLICY OPTIONS

The new regionalism in the Americas is very much at a crossroads. The renewal of fast-track authority in the United States in the fall of 2002 gave the U.S. president a key precondition for the executive branch's successful negotiation of new trade accords. President Bush has announced U.S. interest in pursuing bilateral (e.g., Chile and Singapore), plurilateral (Central America), regional (FTAA), and multilateral (WTO) agreements. At the same time, the long recession in the Americas, depression in stock prices, collapse of FDI flows and unstable currency markets could hardly provide a less propitious time to be negotiating these accords. Worldwide FDI flows dropped in both 2001 and 2002, with predictions of similar declines in 2003; FDI inflows into North America, Latin America, and the Caribbean experienced similar declines (Evans 2002; ECLAC 2003).

Still, the question of how and where to deepen regional integration is important if the momentum for RTAs is to continue, and thoughtful suggestions for new policy directions continue to be made (Harris 2001; Dobson 2002). Here, we explore a few options linking regional integration in the Americas to foreign direct investment.

Our first option is *deepening the current agreements*. For shallow RTAs, this primarily involves the removal of remaining internal tariff barriers and the dismantling or harmonization of nontariff barriers such as quotas. Most Latin American customs unions, including Mercosur, are incomplete. Tariffs are not zero among members, and differences exist in the level and variety of barriers against nonmembers. This creates exactly the type of costs that RTAs were expected to eliminate.

For already deep agreements like NAFTA, further deepening would involve greater liberalization of services, devising consistent regulatory provisions, harmonizing policies that affect trade and FDI flows, opening up grandfathered sectors (e.g., agriculture), and strengthening regional institutions. For example, the Inter-American Development Bank (IDB 2002, 81) estimates that mean agricultural tariff rates within NAFTA were still quite high in 2000 (Mexico, 23.3 percent; Canada, 20.8 percent; and the United States, 11.4 percent), although median rates were lower (Mexico, 15.0 percent; Canada, 3.0 percent; and the United States, 3.7 percent). These rates suggest there is considerable room for reducing internal barriers to agricultural trade.

Tariff reductions, however, may not be politically feasible given the (externally perceived) aggressive subsidies in the 2002 U.S. Farm Bill, recent protests against NAFTA by Mexican farmers, and the new trade dispute over U.S. tariffs on Canadian wheat exports (Canada 2003; Morton 2003; Rosenberg 2003; Taylor 2003). At least the 1998 Canada–U.S. Record of Understanding provides an institutional forum for exchange of information and discussing the future harmonization of agricultural policies (Canada 2003, 40).

Another example where potential deepening would have positive benefits for FDI is the never-ending problem of antidumping and countervailing duties, which had recently become more serious as a result of the Byrd Amendment (Canada 2003, 43–44). This amendment, becoming U.S. law in October 2000, encouraged U.S. firms to file antidumping and countervailing duty complaints by making it possible for the firms to share in the collected duties. Canada and Mexico, along with several other countries, challenged the Byrd Amendment at the WTO. Both the 2002 interim and 2003 final WTO reports concluded that the amendment violated GATT principles. The U.S. government is expected to comply with this ruling. It may also be possible, within the context of the current Doha Round of trade negotiations, for the administrative trade policies of the three NAFTA countries to be brought closer together, for example, by treating NAFTA as a single entity with respect to research and development subsidies and developing a common methodology for measuring costs (Harris 2001, 25–26). A much more difficult proposal would be to scrap national trade remedy laws and replace them with a NAFTA-wide competition policy; as advocated by Graham and Warner (1994).

A second possibility would be the *harmonization of external tariffs* in the major FTAs, such as NAFTA (Wonnacott 1996), in effect, replacing complex rules of origin with a common external tariff. While some argue that this is likely to raise tariff rates to the "highest common denominator," in many sectors tariffs are close enough to zero such that harmonization would be feasible. In addition, given the unequal bargaining power among the three NAFTA members, the most likely political outcome is that tariffs would converge to the U.S. level, typically the lowest of the three rates. A second major gain from moving to a common external tariff would be the reduction of transaction costs in cross-border trade as rules of origin were eliminated and border processes expedited.

There are problems with the common external tariff policy option, however (Dobson 2002; Harris 2001; Weintraub 2003). For example, Dobson (2002, 21) notes that "Canadians would still have to face capricious U.S. trade-remedy laws authorizing the use of [countervailing duties] and [antidumping] penalties," national sovereignty in trade policy would be compromised, and the three countries would have to adopt common negotiating policies at the WTO. In addition, each country now has one or more RTAs with a non-NAFTA country and Mexico has several; this suggests that complex negotiations with outsider countries would be required to deepen NAFTA into a customs union. For example, Weintraub (2003, 2) argues that Mexico would have to terminate its FTA with the European Union in order to enter a North American customs union.

If moving to a customs union proves impossible, three simpler possibilities suggest themselves. First, all three countries now have an FTA with Chile. A short quadrilateral negotiation should be sufficient to bring Chile in as a full member of NAFTA, fulfilling its request for entry first submitted in 1994. Second, common external tariffs could be negotiated on a sectoral basis, following the example of computers in NAFTA. Dobson (2002) suggests that a NAFTA commission be set up that would regularly examine country tariffs by commodity and propose sectoral common external tariffs. Third, the member countries could liberalize rules of origin on a sector-by-sector basis. There is some precedent for this. In January 2003, at the request of industry associations, Canada and the United States liberalized rules of origin for seven products, including alcoholic beverages and petroleum/topped crude oil; Mexico was to follow later during 2003 (Canada, 2003: 39). This liberalization should encourage intra-NAFTA exports.

A third major initiative could be *ending the proliferation of bilateral RTAs*. For example, Canada, Mexico, and the United States now all have bilateral RTAs with Chile (the U.S. one must still be ratified). Harmonizing these three bilaterals would reduce administrative costs for firms; if it were done consistently, Chile could be brought in as a full member of NAFTA. A broader alternative would be to sweep many of the smaller RTAs into the FTAA commitments, removing many of the hub-and-spoke distortions that have crippled the potential economies of scale and scope gains from regional integration. The FTAA talks are apparently entering their "last stage" of negotiations and are on track for January 2005 (*International Trade Reporter* 2003), although Brazilian officials may attempt to slow the pace of negotiations (*International Trade Daily* 2003). At present, it looks as if the FTAA will coexist with other RTAs, with preexisting arrangements taking precedence except where all member countries agree to substitute the FTAA rules for the specific RTA's rules (Canada 2003, 50). This suggests that the FTAA will not end the proliferation of RTAs unless national governments push for harmonization under the FTAA umbrella.

In addition to trade policy changes, more attention should be paid to the *proliferation of bilateral FDI agreements*—particularly BITs and BTTs—within the Western Hemisphere. These also create hub-and-spoke arrangements that offer fewer benefits and higher costs than a comparable multilateral FDI accord. The failure of the Multilateral Agreement on Investment should not prevent the adoption of regional approaches to investment policy. Replacing the three bilateral tax treaties with one trilateral tax treaty with common withholding tax rates would be a relatively simple way to deepen NAFTA (Eden 1996b; Harris 2001). This is one more example where regionalism can precede multilateralism.

It is clear from the empirical work above that the formation of an RTA advantages certain countries over others in terms of attracting inward FDI flows. Not all countries benefit equally from regional integration in terms of FDI, and some may well lose. For countries that have suffered disinvestments and a declining share of intraregional FDI (e.g., Canada within NAFTA), a key policy issue is how to reverse the situation and attract inward FDI. Deepening regional integration may well worsen the situation, causing a vicious circle and disagglomerations as capital flows to areas with higher returns. This suggests that *domestic policy reforms must accompany the RTA process.*

Levy Yeyati, Stein, and Daude (2002a) discuss two polar strategies to attract FDI. The first strategy, "competition in incentives," entails the aggressive use of fiscal and financial incentives to attract foreign investors. Blomstrom and Kokko (2002) suggest that the use of investment incentives focusing exclusively on foreign firms, although motivated in some cases from a theoretical point of view, is generally not an efficient way to raise national welfare. The main reason is that the strongest theoretical motive for financial subsidies to inward FDI spillovers of foreign technology and skills to local industry is not an automatic consequence of foreign investment. The potential spillover benefits are realized only if local firms have the ability and motivation to invest in absorbing foreign technologies and skills. To motivate the subsidization of foreign investment, it is therefore necessary, at the same time, to also support learning and investment in local firms.

Incentives competition has been a real problem between Canada and the United States during the past 15 years, with state and local governments in both countries engaging in bidding wars to attract businesses. The Buy America initiative and small business set-aside provisions in U.S. government procurement contracts have also negatively affected export sales by Canadian and Mexican firms in the U.S. market (Canada 2003, 44–45). Regional integration in North America would benefit if these tax incentives and subsidies were either curtailed or applied uniformly to firms in all three countries. Carrying this one step further, with the removal of tariffs and the curtailment of nontariff barriers, corporate income taxes assume more importance in FDI location decisions. Deepening regional integration might also involve some harmonization of corporate income tax policies in North America (Eden 1996a; Harris 2001).

The second strategy, the "beauty contest," involves improving the quality of institutions, educating the labor force, and developing the country's infrastructure. The advantage of this strategy is beyond the effects on FDI; it can benefit society as a whole. In particular, domestic firms will clearly benefit from improvements in infrastructure, education, or the quality of the institutional environment. The results reported in Stein and Daude (2001) suggest that, beyond these general benefits, improving the quality of institutions can have a major impact on FDI inflows. In terms of institutional policy changes in Latin America, better governance would clearly have positive effects on FDI. Globerman and Shapiro (2002) show that good governance has positive impacts on both inward and outward FDI flows. More specifically, a reduction of public sector corruption in Latin America could lead to sharply increased inward FDI flows because corruption acts as a tax on firms, encouraging less stable bank borrowing at the expense of FDI (Wei 2001).

In North America, a focus on improving and coordinating infrastructures, particularly in transportation and telecommunications across the three NAFTA countries, would reduce transaction costs within the region, facilitating both trade and FDI (Canada 2003; Harris 2001). The call to improve cross-border transportation within North America is an old argument, and the common example was Mexican trucking—but no longer. Since September 11, 2001, it has become abundantly clear that borders open for "goods" (trade, FDI) are also open for "bads" (illegal immigration, drugs, terrorists). As a result, national security demands now conflict with just-in-time delivery systems predicated on rapid border crossings. The Smart Border action plan is a necessary first step in rebuilding borders that are "open for business but closed to terrorists" (Canada 2003, 37).

CONCLUSIONS

Pendulums swing in both directions. Regional trade agreements were highly popular in the 1960s and the 1990s but fell out of favor in the 1970s and 1980s. In this chapter, we have examined the economic relationships between the new regionalism and foreign direct investment in the Americas. We reviewed the literature on differences between the old and new regionalisms, linked this work to the literature on FDI and locational responses by multinationals to regional integration, and compared it with the recent empirical research findings on the Americas. We concluded by examining several policy options for deepening the relationship between FDI and regional integration in the Americas.

Given the macroeconomic recession that now plagues the Americas, the focus on terrorism and national security after September 11, 2001, rising budgetary and balance of payments deficits, and the public's resentment of multinational corporations and globalization, policymakers must be sensitive to the conditions that could set the pendulum swinging again. Could it be possible that the United States, having finally opened the door with fast track to new regional agreements after years of sitting on the sidelines while other countries filled their "dance cards" with RTAs, could be met by Latin American countries closing the door due to macroeconomic and political crises at home? The key test of the new regionalism in the Americas will be the Free Trade Area of the Americas, which is due for implementation in 2005.

Notes

1. ECLAC (1994) first used the term "open regionalism" to describe the difference between old and new regionalisms in Latin America. We are indebted to Enrique Dussel Peters for this point.

2. We coded the United States–Chile provisions based on the draft text, released on April 2, 2003, and posted at www.mac.doc.gov/chileFTA/FTAtext.html.

3. Most economists would argue that the elimination of antidumping and countervailing duties within a regional agreement is an improvement, leading to deeper regional integration. In this case, Mercosur is an improvement over NAFTA; customs unions typically eliminate these policies on internal trade, whereas FTAs continue to use them to protect domestic producers. In fact, one of the principal (and unmet) goals of the Canadian negotiators in the Canada–United States and NAFTA agreements was the removal of U.S. antidumping and countervailing duties against Canadian exports.

4. For example, Mexico responded to the peso crisis in 1995 by raising more than 500 tariffs against nonmember countries while leaving those against its NAFTA partners unchanged.

5. This is the investment equivalent of trade creation; similarly, investment diversion is the equivalent of trade diversion.

6. Information on each country's practices can be found, using the search engine for "international investment position," at http://dsbb.imf.org/Applications/web/keyconceptfiscalsec/.

7. UNCTAD's FDI data is accessible at http://r0.unctad.org/en/subsites/dite/fdistats_files/fdistats.htm; while ECLAC's statistics can be found at www.eclac.cl/estadisticas/default.asp?idioma=IN.

8. See, e.g., Landefeld and Lawson (1991), Statistics Canada (2002, chap. 16, "Direct Investment Position") and Gray and Rugman (1994).

9. Blomstrom, Kokko, and Globerman (1998) argue that total FDI flows into Mexico should have been overstated prior to 1995 because they were based on notifications, not actual investments; although it is less clear that the over-

statement was biased in favor or against intraregional FDI flows. Their data indicate that U.S. FDI flows into Mexico were relatively little changed (in absolute value) in the immediate post-NAFTA period compared with the pre-NAFTA period.

10. See Deardorff (1998) for a history and analysis of gravity models in international trade.

11. Globerman and Shapiro (2001) caution that year-to-year changes in FDI values may be heavily influenced by a small number of very large mergers and acquisition (M&A) activities. The examples provided by Globerman and Shapiro are two specific acquisitions in 2000 that accounted for virtually all of the inward FDI to Canada through the M&A channel: Vivendi's acquisition of Seagrams and Alcatel's purchase of Newbridge.

12. Regional integration in automobiles had an interesting policy spillover. As a result of Japan taking Canada to the WTO, Canada was forced in 2002 to end the 1965 Canada–U.S. Auto Pact and replace it with a uniform Canadian tariff on motor vehicle imports from non-NAFTA countries, ending the differentiation between the Big Three and Asian assemblers (Eden and Molot 2002).

References

ADB (Asian Development Bank). 2002. *Asian Development Outlook*. New York: Oxford University Press.

Aizenman, J., and N. Marion. 2001. The Merits of Horizontal versus Vertical FDI in the Presence of Uncertainty. Paper presented at the 4th International Economics Conference at University of California, Santa Cruz.

Andresen, M.A., and A.S. Pereira. 2002. Structural Change and Foreign Direct Investment. University of British Columbia, Department of Economics Working Paper.

Baldwin, R., and C. Wyplosz. 2003. *The Economics of European Integration;* http://heiwww.unige.ch/~baldwin/papers/BW/bw.htm.

Bertrand, O., and N. Madariaga. 2002. *U.S. Greenfield Investments and M&A Location: Impact of American Continental Integration and Insider vs. Outsider Position.* Working Paper. Paris: TEAM, Université Paris I Sorbonne et CNRS.

Bhagwati, J., D. Greenaway, and A. Panagariya. 1998. Trading Preferentially: Theory and Policy. *Economic Journal* 108: 1128–48.

Bhagwati, J., and A. Panagariya. 1996. *The Economics of Preferential Trade Agreements.* Washington, D.C.: AEI Press.

Blomstrom, M., and A. Kokko. 1997. *Regional Integration and Foreign Direct Investment*. NBER Working Paper 172. Cambridge, Mass.: National Bureau of Economic Research.

———. 2002. The Economics of Foreign Direct Investment Incentives. Paper presented at the Foreign Direct Investment in the Real and Financial Sector of Industrial Countries conference organized by the Deutsche Bundesbank, Frankfurt, May 3–4.

Blomstrom, M., A. Kokko, and S. Globerman. 1998. *Regional Economic Integration and Foreign Direct Investment: The North American Experience*. NBER Working Paper 269. Cambridge, Mass.: National Bureau of Economic Research.

Bloningen, B.A. 1999. *In Search of Substituting between Foreign Production and Exports*. NBER Working Paper 7154. Cambridge, Mass.: National Bureau of Economic Research.

Buckley, P.J. 2002. Is the International Business Research Agenda Running out of Steam? *Journal of International Business Studies* 33, no. 2: 365–73.

Buckley, P.J., and M.C. Casson. 1998. Models of the Multinational Enterprise. *Journal of International Business Studies* 29, no. 1: 21–44.

Buckley, P.J., J. Clegg, N. Forsans, and K.T. Reilly. 2003. Evolution of FDI in the United States in the Context of Trade Liberalization and Regionalization. *Journal of Business Research* 56, no. 10.

Canada, Government of. 2003. *Opening Doors to the World: Canada's International Market Access Priorities—2003*. Department of Foreign Affairs and International Trade. Ottawa: Government of Canada.

Deardorff, A.V. 1998. Determinants of Bilateral Trade: Does Gravity Work in a Neoclassical World? In *The Regionalization of the World Economy*, ed. J.A. Frankel. Chicago: University of Chicago Press.

Devlin, R., and A. Estevadeordal. 2001. *What's New in the New Regionalism in the Americas?* Institute for the Integration of Latin America and the Caribbean (INTAL); Integration, Trade, and Hemispheric Issues Division (ITD); Statistics and Quantitative Analysis Unit (STA) Working Paper 6. Buenos Aires: INTAL, ITD, and STA.

Dobson, W. 2002. *Shaping the Future of the North American Economic Space: A Framework for Action*. Commentary 162. Toronto: C.D. Howe Institute.

Dunning, J.H. 1993. *Multinational Enterprises and the Global Economy*. Reading, Mass.: Addison-Wesley.

———, ed. 2002. *Regions, Globalization, and the Knowledge-Based Economy*. Oxford: Oxford University Press.

Eaton, B., L. G.R. Curtis, and A.E. Safarian. 1994a. The Theory of Multinational Plant Location: Agglomerations and Disagglomerations. In *Multinationals in North America*, ed. L. Eden. Industry Canada Research Series 3. Calgary: University of Calgary Press.

———. 1994b. The Theory of Multinational Plant Location in a Regional Trading Area. In *Multinationals in North America*, ed. L. Eden. Industry Canada Research Series 3. Calgary: University of Calgary Press.

ECLAC (Economic Commission for Latin America and the Caribbean). 1994. *El regionalismo abierto en América Latina y el Caribe. La integración económica al servico de la transformación productiva a con equidad.* LC/G.1801(SES.25/4). Washington, D.C.: ECLAC.

———. 2002. *Foreign Investment in Latin America and the Caribbean.* Santiago: ECLAC.

———. 2003. Foreign Direct Investment Flows into Latin America and the Caribbean Plunged by One-Third in 2002. ECLAC Press Release, Santiago, April 8.

Eden, L. 1994. Who Does What after NAFTA? In *Multinationals in North America*, ed. L. Eden. Industry Canada Research Series 3. Calgary: University of Calgary Press.

———. 1996a. Deep Integration: Tax Harmonization and Investment Policies in North America. In *Investment Rules for the Global Economy: Enhancing Access to Markets*, ed. Pierre Sauvé and Daniel Schwanen. Policy Study 28. Toronto: C.D. Howe Institute.

———. 1996b. The Emerging North American Investment Regime. *Transnational Corporations* 5, no. 3: 61–98.

———. 2002. Regional Integration and Foreign Direct Investment: Theory and Lessons from NAFTA. In *The Challenge of International Business Research*, ed. M. Kotabe, P. Aulakh, and A. Phatak. Cheltenham, UK: Edward Elgar Publishing.

Eden, L., and M.A. Molot. 1992. The View from the Spokes: Canada and Mexico Face the U.S. In *In North America Without Borders? Integrating Canada, the United States, and Mexico*, ed. S. Randall, H. Konrad, and S. Silverman. Calgary: University of Calgary Press.

———. 1993. Insiders and Outsiders: Defining "Who Is Us?" in the North American Auto Industry. *Transnational Corporations* 2, no. 3: 31–64.

———. 1996. Made in America? The U.S. Auto Industry, 1955–95. *International Executive* 38, no. 4: 501–41.

———. 2002. Insiders, Outsiders and Host Country Bargains. *Journal of International Management* 8, no. 4: 359–433.

Eden, L., and A. Monteils. 2000. Regional Integration: NAFTA and the Reconfiguration of North American Industry. In *Regions, Globalization and the Knowledge-Based Economy*, ed. J.H. Dunning. Oxford: Oxford University Press.

Ethier, W. 2001. The New Regionalism in the Americas: A theoretical Framework. *North American Journal of Economics and Finance* 12: 159–72.

Evans, T. 2002. *Foreign Direct Investment Monitor*. Ottawa: Export Development Corporation.

Feinberg, S.E., M.P. Keane, and M. Bognanno. 1998. Trade Liberalization and "Delocalization": New Evidence from Firm-Level Panel Data. *Canadian Journal of Economics* 31, no. 4: 749–77.

Fontagne, L. 1999. *Foreign Direct Investment and International Trade: Complements or Substitute?* OECD Directorate for Science, Technology and Industry 3. Paris: Organization for Economic Cooperation and Development.

Frankel, J.A., and A. Rose. 2000. *Estimating the Effect of Currency Unions on Trade and Output*. NBER Working Paper 7857. Cambridge, Mass.: National Bureau of Economic Research.

Globerman, S. 2002. Trade, FDI, and Regional Economic Integration: Cases of North America and Europe. Paper presented at the Enhancing Investment Cooperation in Northeast Asia conference, Honolulu, August 7–9.

Globerman, S., and D.M. Shapiro. 2001. Assessing Recent Patterns of Foreign Direct Investment in Canada and the United States. Working Paper, Western Washington University, Bellingam.

———. 2002. Global Foreign Direct Investment Flows: The Role of Governance Infrastructure. *World Development* 30, no. 11: 1899–1919.

Graham, E.M. 1999. Foreign Direct Investment Outflows and Manufacturing Trade. In *Japanese Multinationals in Asia*, ed. D.J. Encarnation. Oxford: Oxford University Press.

Graham, E.M., and E. Wada. 2000. Domestic Reform, Trade and Investment Liberalisation, Financial Crisis, and Foreign Direct Investment into Mexico. *The World Economy* 23, no. 6: 777–97.

Graham, E.M. and M. Warner. 1994. Multinationals and Competition Policy in North America. In *Multinationals in North America*, ed. L. Eden. Industry Canada Research Series 3. Calgary: University of Calgary Press.

Gray, S.J., and A.M. Rugman. 1994. Does the United States Have a Deficit with Japan in Foreign Direct Investment? *Transnational Corporations* 3, no. 2: 127–37.

Hanson, G.H., R.J.J. Mataloni, and M.J. Slaughter. 2001. *Expansion Strategies of U.S. Multinational Firms*. NBER Working Paper W8433. Cambridge, Mass.: National Bureau of Economic Research.

Harrigan, J. 2001. *Specialization and the Volume of Trade: Do the Data Obey the Laws?* Federal Reserve Bank of New York 140. New York: Federal Reserve Bank.

Harris, R. 2001. *North American Economic Integration: Issues and Research Agenda.* Discussion Paper 10. Ottawa: Industry Canada.

Hejazi, W., and A.E. Safarian. 1999. Trade, Foreign Direct Investment, and R&D Spillovers. *Journal of International Business Studies* 30, no. 3: 491–511.

———. 2001. The Complementary between U.S. Foreign Direct Investment Stock and Trade. *Atlantic Economic Journal* 29, no. 4: 420–37.

Helpman, E. 1984. A Simple Theory of Trade with Multinational Corporations. *Journal of Political Economy* 92: 451–71.

Helpman, E., and P. Krugman. 1985. *Market Structure and International Trade.* Cambridge, Mass.: MIT Press.

Hunter, L., J.R. Markusen, and T.F. Rutherford. 1995a. North American Free Trade and the Production of Finished Automobiles. In *Modeling North American Economic Integration*, ed. T. Kehoe and P. Kehoe. Boston: Kluwer.

———. 1995b. Trade Liberalization in a Multinational-Dominated Industry. *Journal of International Economics* 38: 95–118.

IDB (Inter-American Development Bank). 2002. *Beyond Borders: The New Regionalism in Latin America.* Washington, D.C.: IDB.

Iglesias, E. 2002. Global Positioning of the European Union and MERCOSUR: Towards a New Model of Inter-regional Cooperation. Paper presented at the Annual Lecture at the Chaire Mercosur of the Institut d'Etudes Politiques de Paris, Paris, April 4.

International Trade Daily. 2003. Brazil Seeks to Slow Down Tempo of FTAA Talks, Foreign Minister Says. April 25. http://web.bna.com.

International Trade Reporter. 2003. FTAA Talks Enter "Last Stage," Trade Officials Say after Meetings. April 16. http://web.bna.com.

Krueger, A.O. 2000. NAFTA's Effects: A Preliminary Assessment. *The World Economy* 23: 761–75.

Landefeld, J.S., and A.M. Lawson. 1991. Valuation of the U.S. Net International Investment Position. *Survey of Current Business*, May: 40–49.

Levy Yeyati, E.L. 2001. On the Impact of a Common Currency on Bilateral Trade. *Economic Letters* 79, no. 1: 125–29.

Levy Yeyati, E.L., E. Stein, and C. Daude. 2002a. The FTAA and the Location of FDI. Paper presented at the Inter-American Development Bank–Harvard University Conference on the Free Trade Area of the Americas in Punta del Este, December 7.

————. 2002b. Regional Integration and the Location of FDI. Unpublished manuscript, Inter-America Development Bank, Washington, D.C.

Lipsey, R.G. 1960. The Theory of Customs Unions: A General Survey. *Economic Journal* 70, no. 279: 496–513.

Love, J.H., and F. Lage-Hidalgo. 1999. Is There Competition for U.S. Direct Investment? A Perspective on NAFTA. *The World Economy* 22: 207–21.

MacDermott, R. 2002. NAFTA and Foreign Direct Investment. Working Paper, Rutgers University, New Brunswick, N.J.

Makhija, M., and S.D. Williamson. 2000. The Globalization of U.S. Industries. In *Globalizing America*, ed. T.L. Brewer, and G. Boyd. London: Edward Elgar.

Markusen, J. 1994. Multinationals, Multi-Plant Economies, and the Gains from Trade. *Journal of International Economics* 16: 205–26.

Markusen, J., and K. Maskus. 1999. *Discriminating among Alternative Theories of the Multinational Enterprise*. NBER Working Paper 7164. Cambridge, Mass.: National Bureau of Economic Research.

Markusen, J., and A. Venables. 1998. Multinational Firms and the New Trade Theory. *Journal of International Economics* 46: 183–203.

Mauro, F.D. 2000. *The Impact of Economic Integration on FDI and Exports: A Gravity Approach*. Working Document 156. Brussels: Center for European Policy Studies.

McMorriston, S. 2000. Recent Development on the Links between Foreign Direct Investment and Trade. Unpublished manuscript, University of Exeter, Exeter, UK.

Molot, M.A., ed. 1993. *Driving Continentally: National Policies and the North American Auto Industry*. Ottawa: Carleton University Press.

Monge-Naranjo, A. 2002. The Impact of NAFTA on Foreign Direct Investment Flows in Mexico and the Excluded Countries. Working Paper, Northwestern University, Evanston, Ill.

Moreno, A. 2002. Mexican Public Opinion toward NAFTA and FTAA. In *NAFTA in the New Millennium*, ed. E.J. Chambers and P.H. Smith. San Diego: University of California, and Edmonton: University of Alberta Press.

Morton, P. 2003. U.S. Hammers Canadian Wheat with New Duty. *National Post*, May 3.

Narula, R. 2003. Multinational Firms, Regional Integration and Globalising Markets: Implications for Developing Countries. In *Trade and Regional Integration in the Development Agenda*, ed. R. Devlin and A. Estevadeordal. Washington, D.C.: Brookings Institution Press and Inter-American Development Bank.

Nevitte, N., L. Anderson, and R. Brym. 2002. Canadian Attitudes toward Continentalism. In *NAFTA in the New Millennium*, ed. E.J. Chambers and P.H. Smith. San Diego: University of California, and Edmonton: University of Alberta Press.

OAS (Organization for American States). 1996. *Trade and Integration Arrangements in the Americas: An Analytical Compendium.* www.sice.oas.org/cp061096/english/section1.asp.

Rosenberg, T. 2003. Why Mexico's Small Corn Farmers Go Hungry. *New York Times,* March 3.

Rugman, A. M. 1990. *Multinationals and Canada-United States Free Trade.* Columbia: University of South Carolina Press.

————, ed. 1994. *Foreign Direct Investment and NAFTA.* Columbia: University of South Carolina Press.

Rugman, A.M. 2001. *The End of Globalization.* New York: AMACOM/McGraw Hill.

Rugman, A.M., and C. Brain. 2003. Intra-Regional Trade and Foreign Direct Investment in North America. Paper presented at the Canada–United States Business Conference, Indiana University, Bloomington, April 11–12.

Rugman, A.M., and M. Gestrin. 1993a. The Investment Provisions of NAFTA. In *Assessing NAFTA: A Trinational Analysis*, ed. S. Globerman and M. Walker. Vancouver: Fraser Institute.

————. 1993b. The Strategic Response of Multinational Enterprises to NAFTA. *Columbia Journal of World Business* 28: 318–29.

Safarian, A.E., and W. Hejazi. 2001. Canada and Foreign Direct Investment: A Study of Determinants. Unpublished manuscript, University of Toronto, Toronto.

Statistics Canada. 2002. *Canada's Balance of International Payments and International Investment Position.* Catalogue 67-506-XIE. Ottawa: Statistics Canada.

Stein, E., and C. Daude. 2001. Institutions, Integration, and the Location of Foreign Direct Investment. Unpublished manuscript, Research Department, Inter-American Development Bank, Washington, D.C.

Swimmer, D. 2000. Investment Framework Policies and Canada's Declining Share of Inward Foreign Direct Investment. Unpublished manuscript, Industry Canada, Ottawa.

Taylor, L. 2003. Squealing on NAFTA: Mexican Farmers Angry over Trade Pact. *Newsday,* January 26.

UNCTAD (UN Conference on Trade and Development). 1998. *World Investment Report 1998: Trends and Determinants.* Geneva: UNCTAD.

———. 2001. *World Investment Report 2001: Promoting Linkages*. Geneva: UNCTAD.

———. 2002. *World Investment Report 2002: Transnational Corporations and Export Competitiveness*. Geneva: UNCTAD.

Vernon, R. 1994. Multinationals and Governments: Key Actors in NAFTA. In *Multinationals in North America*, ed. L. Eden. Industry Canada Research Series 3. Calgary: University of Calgary Press.

Waldkirch, A. 2001. The "New Regionalism" and Foreign Direct Investment: The Case of Mexico. Working paper, Oregon State University, Eugene.

Warf, P., and S. Kull. 2002. Tepid Traders: U.S. Public Attitudes on NAFTA and Free Trade Expansion. In *NAFTA in the New Millennium*, ed. E.J. Chambers and P.H. Smith. San Diego: University of California, and Edmonton: University of Alberta Press.

Wei, S. 2001. *Corruption and Globalization*. Policy Brief. Washington, D.C.: Brookings Institution Press.

Weintraub, S. 1993. The North American Free Trade Agreement as Negotiated: A U.S. Perspective. In *New Dimensions in Regional Integration*, ed. J.D. Melo and W. Michael. Cambridge: Cambridge University Press.

———. 2003. *Strains in the Canada–U.S. Relationship*. Issues in International Political Economy 40. Washington, D.C.: CSIS.

Weintraub, S., and C. Sands. 1998. *The North American Auto Industry under NAFTA*. Washington, D.C.: CSIS.

Wonnacott, R. 1996. Trade and Investment in a Hub-and-Spoke versus a Free Trade Area. *The World Economy* 19: 237–52.

WTO (World Trade Organization). 2002. Regional Trade Integration under Transformation. Paper presented at the Seminar on Regionalism and the WTO, Regional Trade Agreements Section, Trade Policies Review Division, WTO Secretariat, Geneva.

CHAPTER THREE

PROSPECTS FOR NORTH AMERICAN MONETARY COOPERATION IN THE NEXT DECADE

Rogelio Ramírez de la O

Monetary issues were among of the first ones in economics to pose practical problems for classical theoretical economists, drawing them into controversies over policy. Unlike other branches of economics, monetary theory and monetary policy have a straight connection to the real world; this makes them natural domains of economists and practitioners.

The link between international trade and monetary issues explains many attempts to explore further developments of the North American Free Trade Agreement (NAFTA) through monetary cooperation. Economic forces drive trade, but economies are also driven by monetary factors. Henry Thornton, in his *Enquiry into the Nature and Effects of the Paper Credit of Great Britain*, published in 1802 (Thornton 1939), was the first to see the effect that domestic monetary policy has on inflation and the real exchange rate. His work preceded Ricardo's *The High Price of Bullion, a Proof of the Depreciation of Bank Notes*, published in 1810 (Ricardo 1966), which addressed the fall in the domestic value of paper money as a result of monetary growth. In the debates on currency instability and the suspension of cash payments by the Bank of England in 1797, economists and practitioners split into two camps. The bullionists (Thornton, Ricardo, Malthus, et al.) argued that excessive issues of paper currency caused the price of bullion to rise. The anti-bullionists, grouped at the Bank of England, argued that the fall in value of the currency was caused by wars disrupting export trade. According to them, any central bank could not issue notes in excess of needs, because borrowers would not borrow more than they could use profitably.

I thank CSIS's Sidney Weintraub for critical comments that helped improve this chapter, and I thank Frederick Dudet for providing me with a myriad of statistical data.

These two camps with radically differing views over the causality between monetary policy and inflation broadly remain the same today. A group known as "monetarists" and some central banks claim that monetary expansion should be kept in check, with its growth close to that in output as an essential condition for price stability. Another group argues that money can only be issued in the quantities demanded by the public to facilitate transactions and clear markets.[1]

It is thus logical that before countries can achieve advanced forms of monetary cooperation, they should first be in agreement on how inflation is caused and what should be the role of policy. Once this is acknowledged, different degrees of cooperation are possible, from informal consultations only, involving no need for common views or objectives, to a currency union involving the need for them. In general, the more similar the economic structures of countries, the greater the scope for monetary cooperation.

THE BACKGROUND AND PAST TEN YEARS OF NAFTA

In the decades before NAFTA, Mexico often grew at high rates, even when the U.S. economy was slowing or in recession. The driver of growth was domestic demand and only marginally exports, which reached 15.3 percent of gross domestic product (GDP) in 1985. After Mexico liberalized trade and exports boomed, their share of GDP rose to 28.9 percent in 2002.

In the earlier period, because Mexico's economy depended mainly on domestic demand, business investment often followed the signals set by the government, which in various instances in the 1970s tried to expand public investment and engaged in development projects without regard for macroeconomic stability. As the private sector followed such signals, Mexico kept growing and absorbing imports, even as export growth fell. This led in the 1970s, in the early 1980s, and again in 1994 to macroeconomic crises whose common characteristic was a huge current account deficit, an overvalued peso, and foreign indebtedness.

International trade of Mexico was in any event highly concentrated with the United States long before NAFTA. Most foreign firms investing in Mexico were from the United States; at first, they were mainly interested in selling in the domestic market, and by the late 1980s they were equally interested in manufacturing for export. The first export-oriented foreign plants in the late 1970s and early 1980s were in automobiles and electronics, using American materials and Mexican labor and selling their products in the United States. The share of the United States in Mexico's exports rose from 80 percent in the early 1990s to 85 percent in 2002, despite the fact that Mexico signed many trade agreements with other countries after it had signed NAFTA with the United States and Canada.

Mexico's macroeconomic policy, and monetary policy in particular, suffered in the same period a transformation as significant as that of its trade policy; to focus on fiscal deficit reduction and low inflation. For that reason, an orthodox macroeconomic policy is often associated with NAFTA, which is not entirely correct. Although in the early 1990s Mexico had made great progress eliminating fiscal deficits and reducing inflation from 159 percent in 1987 to 7 percent in 1993, its economy was still far from converging naturally with the economies of the United States and Canada. During the same period, the peso had become over-valued, partly as a result of the tools employed by the government in reducing inflation, mainly by keeping the nominal exchange rate within preannounced ranges against the U.S. dollar. This was despite the fact that prices of domestic factors and nontradable goods had risen much more than the nominal rate and hence more than the prices of imports for a number of years. The strong currency hurt profits of Mexican exporters and, consequently, their investments and employment. As impressive as the reduction of inflation appeared to be, it was largely artificial, for it relied on an overvalued currency. When the peso succumbed to speculation and to an unsustainable current account deficit of 6.8 percent of GDP, inflation jumped again to reach 52.0 percent in 1995.

This devaluation caused debate and a radical shift in views over the role of monetary policy and the exchange rate regime. In this debate, Mexico and its two North American partners took part, because the latter had contributed fresh injections of emergency finance and the U.S. Treasury kept supervision over Mexico's adjustment program. The devaluation also hurt many companies indebted in dollars and especially commercial banks, but it was welcomed by exporters and foreign investors interested in investing in manufacturing industry. Exports jumped from $61 billion in 1994 to $161 billion in 2002; gross fixed investment jumped 13.6 percent a year in the four years after the devaluation, while manufacturing output grew 7.8 percent a year.

Foreign investors also acquired many private businesses that had gone bankrupt or had fallen into serious financial difficulties, investments that brought the Mexican and the North American economies much closer. These included two of the largest North American banks

(Nova Scotia and Citigroup) acquiring control of two Mexican major banks and another (Bank of America) acquiring a minority position in a third. The road to increasing financial and monetary cooperation was open.

Cooperation had in fact existed before, but it was significantly reaffirmed in 1995, when the U.S. government led a massive financial rescue of Mexico for more than $50 billion, which included $20 billion of its own Treasury funds. Discussions at the International Monetary Fund and between governments and academics of the three countries drew a key lesson: Reducing inflation should only be attempted with hard, constant work to raise productivity and reduce fiscal deficits, and certainly not by fixing the nominal exchange rate to the dollar.[2] This experience only reaffirmed the faith of the authorities in the United States and Canada in floating exchange rates, which Mexico eventually acquired; flexible exchange rates gained further credibility after they performed well during the Asian crisis of 1997 and later on during the crisis of Russia and Brazil.

NAFTA as a trade and investment agreement did not address monetary issues, but it certainly set the ground for future economic integration and cooperation because it induced a rapid expansion of trade and cross-border investment. The experience of Mexico after NAFTA is that most investment was focused, at least until 2000, on manufacturing for export, while imports and financial transactions were also growing. Both Canada and Mexico have their trade highly concentrated with the United States, but in the case of Mexico, such trade became the main vehicle for growth in subsequent years, as the record of manufacturing output, exports, and employment shows. Although Canada and the United States experienced significant increases in external transactions, the two countries already had a bilateral free trade agreement in place since 1989 and their economies were much more integrated with each other. NAFTA's effects were undoubtedly greater on Mexico than on either of its two partners.

Greater economic integration, largely stemming from NAFTA and trade, has made the Mexican business cycle follow ever more closely the U.S. cycle. Domestic demand responded within a relatively short time in 2001 to the reduction in exports to the United States. Though this makes Mexico dependent on U.S. activity, it has given it an automatic stabilization mechanism that slows exports and investment when U.S. growth slows down. As long as Mexican macroeconomic policy does not try to change this natural link, Mexico will not run too high current account deficits, as was a frequent problem in past decades.

Mexican policymakers accept that the economy had to slow down after the U.S. economy did and will recover when the U.S. economy picks up. Given the fact that growth in the United States provides a sustainable ground of growth for Mexico, foreign investors are more certain today than they were in past decades over the direction of Mexico's economy. This was an important factor for rating agencies to grant "investment grade" to Mexican sovereign debt, which led to lower costs of foreign debt service and peso interest rates.

We must be cautious, however, not to take this coupling of business cycles in Mexico and the United States as permanent. This is still a relatively new feature of Mexican macroeconomics, and for the same reason it needs time to be reaffirmed and recognized by investors in the whole economy and not only in the export sector. It also needs to pass various tests, for example, whether macroeconomic policy will maintain its emphasis on stabilization if the U.S. recovery takes longer than is expected.

Given the background of increased trade and investment as well as a more integrated business cycle in North America, much can be gained from closer integration, but this does not mean, as some have suggested, that the course for action must include greater monetary integration or in particular a common currency.[3] For that reason, and taking into account the experience that Mexico has with exchange rate regimes, changing the present floating exchange rate regime will have profound implications for output and employment. That is, any change of regime carries risks that at this stage seem unnecessary, because Mexico is still enjoying the benefits of trade-based growth, whereas consolidating profound structural changes will take time.

The experience of Mexico after trying to follow the dollar in the early 1990s was in many ways just as ill advised as the experience of the United Kingdom with the European Exchange Rate Mechanism. In both cases monetary policy, being focused on the exchange rate and not on the domestic price level, caused high unemployment, loss of competitiveness, and eventually capital outflows. The present skepticism in the United Kingdom about joining the euro area, and the self-imposition of five macroeconomic tests before deciding that joining the euro area is a sound policy, are based on this experience. Mexico should heed these lessons, which advise it to moderate its claim on convergence with the

U.S. economy, as it announced it would do since 2000, which has encouraged markets to expect nominally stable exchange rates but not necessarily ones based on economic fundamentals.

THE NEXT TEN YEARS OF NAFTA

At the end of 2000, hearing the call of the Bank of Mexico to achieve convergence with U.S. inflation, influential voices suggested that formalizing monetary integration could lock in low inflation and the exchange rates. This could be done through "dollarization," which would enhance business confidence and bring about a sharp reduction in interest rates. Similar suggestions were to fix the exchange rate of the peso to the dollar as an intermediate step, whether or not this would ultimately lead to dollarization. And others suggested a common currency for the NAFTA region, along the lines of the European Union (Grubel 1999). President Vicente Fox, encouraged by his foreign minister, Jorge Castañeda, voiced the idea of enhancing NAFTA with a currency union and infrastructure development funding during his first trip to Canada and the United States in August 2000 (Ramírez de la O 2002).

What these proposals have in common is the notion that NAFTA's success in increasing trade and investment is a good platform for deepening economic and financial integration in North America. This is correct, but most researchers seem confused about the forces that cause trade to increase, which leads them to assign excessive importance to the monetary regime. As I mentioned above, the literature shows that greater trade, and eventually the greater economic integration arising from it, does not require fixed exchange rates between countries, let alone a currency union. For example, the United Kingdom and other members of the European Union, such as Denmark and Sweden, have chosen for now not to be members of its currency union, without fearing that they are losing trade opportunities.

Because NAFTA is not even a customs union, let alone a common market, such proposals on monetary integration are premature, to say the least. But discussing them in the light of the future of monetary cooperation is appropriate. The first thing to bear in mind is that the three countries have floating exchange rate regimes and their monetary authorities attend to domestic economic conditions to control inflation and, in the case of the United States, to support economic growth as well. None of the three countries manages monetary policy by following an international benchmark. Having started a float in 1995, in the midst of a financial crisis and after years of pursuing a peg to the dollar, the Bank of Mexico has gradually accepted that a floating rate is the appropriate regime.

Avenues for Monetary Cooperation

Monetary cooperation between NAFTA members can be enhanced under various monetary regimes. One is a floating rate, whereas others may involve fixed or managed exchange rates. Any country can adopt a fixed rate objective, unilaterally or in coordination with the other countries.

Floating Exchange Rate Regime. Having experienced major currency crises while pursuing fixed exchange rates and pegs to the dollar for the past 30 years, Mexico took a more pragmatic view in late 1994, allowing the peso to float. Since then, its experience with stabilization during the period 1995–96, and later in coping with the effects of the Asian crisis in 1997 and the Russian crisis in 1998, suggests that the floating regime is entirely appropriate.

In 1998, the peso depreciated 20 percent, and one of the effects was an inflation rate higher than the objective of the Bank of Mexico. This experience illustrated that while floating provides a flexible nominal exchange rate to absorb the effects of external disturbances, it also may mean some disruption of short-term inflation targets. In the end, however, inflation in Mexico regained its downward trend, and in 2001 was 4.4 percent, in line with the Bank of Mexico's objective. The record is that a floating rate contributes to sustained economic growth by reducing the negative effect of a slowdown in export markets.

Partly because of this success, in 2000 the Bank of Mexico felt confident enough to announce its objective for achieving "convergence" with the rate of inflation in the United States, which it set at 3 percent for 2003. This was probably a mistake, partly because it was unnecessary for the fulfillment of the bank's objective of continuing to reduce inflation. That is, convergence entails much more than meeting a target for inflation, because it involves matching inflationary conditions of another country and another currency over which the national authority has neither control nor influence. If the rate of increase in domestic prices is not converging with that in the United States, the monetary authority will be compelled to tighten its policy. While the economy is growing and inflation is rising, this is the appropriate response for any central bank, but during periods of economic weakness, a tighter policy will cause other problems. For example, output and employment would fall even more if interest rates rise. Another problem is that if the United States is easing its monetary policy, tightening in Mexico causes interest rates to offer unusually high premiums to portfolio investors, which brings about speculation and makes the peso appreciate. These problems often make a floating exchange rate inconsistent with explicit pledges on convergence with lower inflation in another country.

Targeting Nominal Exchange Rates. Monetary policy may involve nominal targets for the exchange rate in addition to inflation targets or targets for the growth of monetary aggregates. Canada and especially Mexico have had much experience with nominal targets for exchange rates. Such experience justifies the great skepticism in Canada and the United States about nominal targets, because they are known to cause unnecessary pressure on monetary policy and may provoke large and potentially disruptive short-term capital flows. This is contrary to the need of these countries to have all monetary instruments available, especially at times of market volatility.

If Mexico and Canada were to participate in a scheme to target nominal rates, whether unilaterally or with U.S. support, they would have to conduct their monetary policy not necessarily with an objective for inflation but with an objective for the exchange rate to the dollar. If the exchange rate weakened, the central bank would have to increase interest rates; at a time when the economy is weak, employment and output would suffer more than is necessary and the flexibility for the authority would be considerably diminished.

Although it can be admitted that a nominal target for the exchange rate will probably render greater financial stability in the short term, it also requires the economy to adjust to external disturbances by allowing output and employment to fluctuate more than they would under a floating regime. Consequently, the country would have to accept potentially higher unemployment, at least during certain periods.

With a nominal target, domestic monetary policy in effect becomes determined by the policy of the reference country, as if the country were to outsource the services of monetary policy to the U.S. Federal Reserve. When the United States tightens up and interest rates rise because of domestic inflation, Mexico will have to tighten and tolerate higher interest, independent of the Mexican inflation rate. Such a system was successfully followed in Mexico between 1954 and 1976, but its success owes much to the fact that it was part of a relatively stable world order under

Bretton Woods, whereby countries maintained exchange rate controls. Mexico also had import controls, which gave it additional flexibility to control the expansion of its trade deficit as the U.S. economy fluctuated.

At present, no import controls are possible, and by the same token any system of fixed rates in the world is out of the question. Among other reasons, this is because of the unstable nature of global capital markets, major differences in business cycles among large countries, and very dynamic international competition. Although it may be possible for a small country to have a fixed rate with the agreement of a larger country, such cases are rare today, for they require that the latter give its full support to maintaining the exchange rate.

Dollarization.   In theory at least, with or without Canada, Mexico could adopt the dollar as its currency, with or without agreement of support from the United States. In case of agreement, it would be backed by the U.S. authorities, which would ensure that Mexico has enough foreign exchange to finance external or internal deficits. Without backing from the United States, Mexico would have to generate enough exports and attract foreign investment or slow down its rate of economic growth in order to limit import growth to what can be financed.

As for the United States, if it were supporting dollarization in Mexico, it could not possibly grant unlimited finance to Mexico. Thus, dollarization requires that the economy of Mexico becomes efficient and competitive enough to ensure that its external accounts are in equilibrium over the long run. This means that the rate of growth of productivity must be at least as high in Mexico as in the United States. In practice this would be difficult for Mexico, because its economic structure is sharply different from that of the United States and its possibilities to lift productivity growth are much more limited. This is because Mexico is still a traditional economy in the sectors of agriculture and small industry and services, despite the major modernization that has taken place in the past 10 years. Mexico also has a lesser capacity to integrate all its activities to the latest developments in telecommunications, capital markets, and services, among others. It suffers from much greater government regulation than the United States, and labor skills and education standards are much lower. Such conditions certainly imply that there are opportunities for raising productivity, as Mexico makes progress in all of those areas, but such a task will take many years and in any event should not be timed with monetary targets, given the great scope for failure or delays.

If the United States backs dollarization in Mexico, the risk is that it may have to provide large flows of finance for as long as Mexico takes to complete the daunting task of modernizing its economy and developing its untapped resources to match the productivity outlook of the U.S. economy. Such a possibility sounds too utopian to be a good guide for policymakers. If, on the contrary, the United States does not back dollarization, Mexico's economy will be forced to grow at low rates when export growth slows and access to international credit is restrained. In that case, monetary policy would have to keep high interest rates if investors perceived the risk of high trade deficits or insufficient finance. One of the original purposes of dollarization—low interest rates—would then be defeated. Of course, dollarization would also preclude any large fiscal deficit, for this would have to be financed with dollars borrowed abroad. Either of these two possibilities—infinite foreign finance, or a restrained rate of growth of the economy to guarantee external equilibrium—is unrealistic for a country as large as Mexico, with high growth potential and a large population.

Other problems of dollarization are institutional in nature. One is that if the United States backs dollarization in Mexico, the mandate and scope of the U.S. Federal Reserve would have to change to accept a wider responsibility to provide emergency finance to Mexico and to be the lender of last resort to the Mexican banking system. The fact that as recently as 1998 Mexican banks were bailed out by the government for $100 billion resulting from imprudent lending and a financial crisis suggests that this is a risk that U.S. financial institutions will not easily assume.

Another institutional hurdle is related to the often-cited question of seigniorage, which applies to Mexico because it can issue its own money for transactions for $30 billion to $40 billion (which is the present amount of notes and coins held by the public), for which it pays no interest. The measurement of such an interest, equivalent to seigniorage, would no longer accrue to Mexico, which is a strong disincentive of dollarization. But a counterpoint is that the authorities would benefit from lower interest rates on the public debt, such that loss of seigniorage might be offset by lower debt service. Whether this compensation will hold over time is subject to the discussion above on perceived risk or insufficient liquidity causing interest rates to rise. In the final analysis, however, there is little doubt that the authorities would lose at least their sovereign capacity to decide whether to increase the money supply or not.

In light of these limitations, dollarization does not have much to recommend it for Mexico. The essential objection is that its expected benefits may be obtained by consistently disciplined macroeconomic rules without any need to lose sovereignty or the capacity to use fiscal and monetary policy in its national interest. Such macroeconomic rules imply, under any conditions, certain constraints as a matter of good policy; for example, inflation has to be kept under control and fiscal deficits should not be high.

Transitional Regimes.   It is possible that a floating exchange rate would, over time and under natural conditions, evolve into a fixed rate and perhaps a monetary union—but only if we can imagine that North Americans see such a union as in their interest, admittedly a situation very difficult to visualize presently. A fixed rate is possible if adopted unilaterally by Mexico. As the proponents of fixed rates argue, once such a system proves its usefulness in helping authorities to control inflation and reduce the cost of debt service, the case for dollarization would have been made in practice and its implications would become acceptable to the Mexican and U.S. authorities. In this role, the fixed rate would be a transitional regime for as long as convergence of the two economies takes place and for as long as the two countries take to realize the benefits of such a regime.

This reasoning is fine and can be enhanced by a further description of ideal conditions. It has, however, a fundamental problem, as do all ideal scenarios, which is discounting the future prematurely when so many structural changes essential to its success are, at best, uncertain. Furthermore, assigning such a precisely transitory role to a fixed exchange rate regime can be dangerously misleading to both policymakers and markets, when the transition to such ideal conditions is long.

A fixed exchange rate policy that is regarded as a transition toward greater monetary integration is a bad idea. This is because policymakers would probably try to accelerate the transition to the formal new regime, pretending that conditions are ripe before they actually are in order to obtain the political credit for the new regime. During such a transition, markets would cause capital flows and speculation as firms and banks increase their liabilities in the hard currency and their assets in the national currency, because the latter will yield higher interest.

This is in fact one of the mistakes made by the Bank of Mexico when it embarked on convergence in 2000. This was done without being precise as to what role convergence had for the fulfillment of the bank's mandate and whether it was a transitory step. With hindsight, we can see that the pledge to converge added nothing to the bank's capacity to reduce inflation, while it created problems with speculation and appreciation of the peso.

Still, in the realm of scenarios, a successful monetary policy focused on inflation under a floating exchange rate might conquer convergence with the United States and Canada in three to five years. The converging of inflation rates, however, would only be a first step toward macroeconomic convergence. Because Mexico must modernize and deregulate to make its markets consistent with U.S. and Canadian markets—in energy, agriculture, infrastructure, education, the labor market, and the tax and the legal systems, to name a few areas—this task would take a long time, between 10 and 15 years. A fixed exchange rate would not be feasible until then. The longer the political debate over how Mexico restructures these sectors of the economy, the longer it will take to achieve convergence.

This time frame makes the entire issue of fixed exchange rates and dollarization highly speculative and not useful as a guide for medium-term policy. Whether Mexico in the end decides to make the dollar its currency will largely depend on the success of the floating exchange rate regime to deliver low inflation and stability. Judging by experience since 1995, and especially that of Canada, it is most likely that a floating rate may be the regime in Mexico for many years to come.

Monetary cooperation within North America will still have great scope under floating rates, through enhanced consultations between central banks, banking supervision, and capital market development oriented toward improving standards in Mexico, leading to greater efficiency of financial services and greater competition. This cooperation is likely to evolve in the desirable direction and will not necessarily have to be part of NAFTA negotiations.

Hurdles for Convergence. Convergence is a step in the evolution of a monetary system gradually integrating itself with a larger one, like Canada's and Mexico's to the dollar, and it is therefore convenient to examine some of the hurdles it faces in light of Mexico's experience. Convergence is easier said than done, as the Bank of Mexico discovered after 2000. In 2001, the bank issued increasingly frequent warnings that insufficient tax collection and a lack of reform threatened convergence in electricity, labor, and other areas of the economy. The bank implicitly acknowledged that it had adopted a target that was out of its mandate, for it depended on the macroeconomy operating in a synchronized fashion in areas over which it had no control.

Given the failure to meet its inflation target in 2002, the Bank of Mexico now makes no mention of convergence, but it will probably revisit it in the future. What has been significant since 2001 is that the 4.5 percent inflation target in 2002 was not met and that of 3.0 percent for 2003 was unlikely as of this writing, despite recession forcing many prices downward and a tight monetary policy applied consistently.

By announcing so emphatically its objective to converge, the Bank of Mexico took away flexibility for its policy. Because the economy has been in recession, tightening monetary conditions made it even weaker, which contributed to deterioration in credit quality and a reluctance of banks to lend. At the same time, the peso appreciated, as interest rates remained high in Mexico while in the United States they were moving downward. Foreign capital flew into pesos to capture higher yields, while large companies borrowed dollars to create long asset positions in pesos, guessing rightly that a large depreciation was unlikely, for it contradicted the bank's plan to converge. In the end, by 2003, the peso had to depreciate sharply, threatening the official inflation target. At the time of writing, the bank and the Treasury Ministry agreed on a mechanism to increase the supply of dollars to the market from the revenues of Petróleos Mexicanos (Pemex). The peso stands to weaken when oil prices fall, now that such a direct link has been established between oil revenues and the exchange rate.

During the same period, while the Bank of Mexico was trying to reach convergence, making matters ironic, U.S. inflation fell below 3 percent, which was the benchmark that Mexico's monetary authority had established to achieve convergence. This episode illustrates that monetary objectives set with a view to get closer to U.S. macroeconomic indicators imply a myriad of practical difficulties for policy.[4] Clearly, the Central Bank can guarantee a realistic target for inflation, but the bank must be flexible about it during times of volatility and uncertainty. It cannot pledge to match the monetary conditions of another country.

To be effective, convergence must be natural and not forced, attending to the great differences between Mexico and the other North American countries.[5] Mexico would not converge correctly if it meets ambitious inflation targets at the cost of a high appreciation of the real exchange rate. This is what happened from 2000 to 2002, which explains the large recent peso depreciation and the change in policy to allocate

Table 3.1. Economic Performance of North America, 2000–2002

	United States		
Performance Indicator	2000	2001	2002
Real GDP (percent change from previous period)	3.8	0.3	2.4
Net export contribution to GDP growth (percentage points)	–0.9	–0.2	–0.8
Unemployment rate (percentage of labor force, official reports)	4.0	4.8	5.8
Real exports of goods and services (percent change from previous period)	9.7	–5.4	–1.6
Effective exchange rate (index 1995 = 100)	127.5	134.3	134.8
Ratio of exports to GDP	0.12	0.12	0.11
Compensation per employee in the business sector (percent change from previous period)	6.5	2.5	2.5
Nominal short-term interest rate (percent)	6.5	3.7	1.8
Real short-term interest rate (percent)	2.8	2.0	0.6
Comparative unit labor cost (index 1993 = 100)	85.68	86.75	85.39
Relative unit labor cost (index 1995 = 100)	118.4	122.9	120.5
Inflation rate (percent at year end)	3.39	1.55	2.38

Source: Data from Organization for Economic Cooperation and Development.

Pemex's dollar revenues to the foreign exchange market. Ideally, artificially low inflation, relative price distortions, and a change of signals regarding direct or indirect forms of intervention in the foreign exchange market should be avoided.

A floating exchange rate is the only feasible regime for now, and it will likely be a long time before any other can be successfully attempted. Mixing this regime with any hidden or explicit attempt to drive the exchange rate toward a certain level is an aberration of free floating, and for that reason the authorities should only intervene with foreign exchange sparingly.

Table 3.1. *(continued)*

	Mexico			Canada	
2000	2001	2002	2000	2001	2002
6.6	–0.3	0.9	5.3	1.9	3.3
–1.9	–0.7	–0.1	0.2	0.6	–0.3
2.2	2.5	2.8	6.8	7.2	7.6
16.4	–3.6	1.4	8.8	–3.1	–0.1
72.1	74.1	71.8	98.0	95.1	93.6
0.25	0.23	0.24	0.40	0.38	0.39
11.5	9.3	5.2	4.8	2.2	2.7
16.2	12.2	7.6	5.8	4.0	2.6
8.1	9.1	4.0	2.4	3.2	1.3
70.14	80.18	76.84	85.07	86.06	87.20
122.0	129.5	131.4	101.4	101.8	102.4
8.96	4.40	5.70	3.23	0.70	3.88

EVIDENCE OF MACROECONOMIC PERFORMANCE

Economic performance speaks volumes about the working of monetary policy in NAFTA. The experience of the past three years shows that Canada and the United States are close to a de facto real and monetary integration, whereas Mexico is a long way off. The past three years include a period of high growth in the region followed by severe economic adjustment. Monetary policy in the United States and Canada has been naturally focused on reducing output losses from recession, while in Mexico it has remained focused on reducing inflation. For this reason,

Figure 3.1. Inflation in North America, 1997–2002 (annual percentage rates of growth)

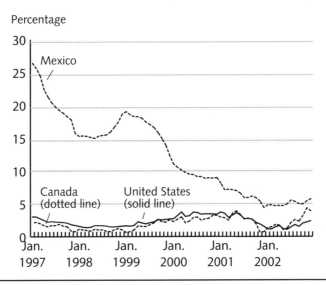

Sources: Banco de Mexico and Organization for Economic Cooperation and Development.

Note: Series are nonseasonally.

short-term market interest rates in Canada and in the United States fell much in line between 2000 and 2002, by –3.2 and –4.7 percentage points, to 2.6 percent and 1.8 percent respectively, as is shown in table 3.1.

In Mexico real rates fell more, by 8.6 points, but they maintained absolute levels much higher than in the rest of North America, at 7.6 percent on average in 2002. This high level of interest caused speculative inflows, to which I referred above, explaining the steady appreciation of the peso through 2002. Table 3.1 shows that the effective exchange rate was weakening for Canada as recession hit, but instead kept appreciating in Mexico, only to start weakening late in 2002, when output had already stabilized at a low level. The real exchange rate of the peso measured against the dollar appreciated by 14.1 percentage points in the two years through the end of 2001. The problem confronting the Bank of Mexico when it wanted to maintain a stable peso was that cumulative inflation for the past few years was much higher than in Canada or the United States, as figure 3.1 shows.

The dispersion of inflation across time was also much greater in Mexico than in the United States, which suggests that relative prices are

Figure 3.2. Dispersion of Inflation Rates, 1997–2002 (percent)

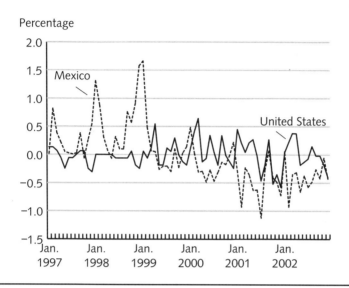

Percentage

Sources: Banco de México and Bureau of Economic Analysis.

Note: Dispersion is measured by subtracting average inflation for the period from inflation in each month.

changing much more than in the United States and Canada. At times of currency appreciation, such changes mean that profits in manufacturing and in exports, in particular, fall relative to profits and prices in the domestic economy. If continued for a period of time, this leads to lower investment in these sectors. The fact that many maquiladoras have closed down and other manufacturing firms have moved from Mexico to other Latin American and Asian countries suggests that currency appreciation may have gone too far in hurting long-term investment. Eventually, when the currency depreciates, relative prices will move in the reverse direction, all of which is disruptive to long-term investment. The dispersion of inflation rates is shown in figure 3.2.

Although inflation picked up in 2002 in the whole North American region, its increase in Mexico was from a relatively high level. Therefore, it affected comparative unit labor costs significantly and resulted in higher rates of increase in compensation per employee and in unit labor costs, as was shown in figure 3.1.

The Bank of Mexico maintained a policy of tight monetary policy throughout the period 2000–2. Figure 3.3 shows that real interest rates

Figure 3.3. Real Interest Rates, 1998–2002 (annualized monthly rates of short-term commercial paper)

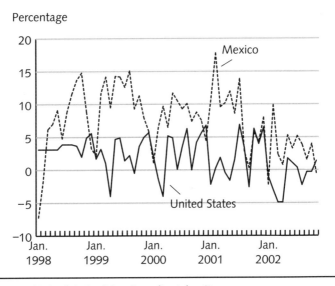

Source: Instituto Nacional de Estadística, Geografía e Informática.

Note: Commercial 28-day paper rates.

remained much higher than in the United States through 2000, continuing through the spring of 2003.

The reason for high interest in Mexico is that it has taken it much longer to bring its rate of inflation to levels as low as those recorded in the rest of North America. As late as 1998, Mexico had 18.6 percent inflation, which only fell to approach the level of U.S. rates in 2001, in the midst of recession and temporarily.

CONCLUSIONS

NAFTA, during its first decade, created solid ground for greater economic integration in North America by increasing trade and investment and boosting new business opportunities. Greater integration is likely now in a variety of areas, including monetary and financial cooperation. How this integration materializes will depend on the circumstances affecting each sector and on the global economic and political environment.

There are good prospects for continuing with monetary integration, which has started to occur de facto as Mexico continues to reduce inflation and interest rates, as foreign investment increases, and now (unlike in the early 1990s) that the country has a large foreign participation in banking. But any explicit attempt to integrate Mexican monetary conditions with those of the United States, to be effective, must not be at the expense of output and employment, which typically occur when the authorities try to accelerate the process of integration by tightening monetary policy. Inasmuch as this integration is natural and the gradual result of the modernization of economic structures and institutions, it will be sustainable. Mexico has much to gain from orderly integration with the rest of North America, but also much to lose from forced integration.

There are risks for Mexico in trying to converge with the low rate of inflation in the United States, when the monetary policy required to reach this end is inconsistent with economic growth, as was demonstrated by the ambitious objective announced in 2000 of reaching progressively lower inflation rates down to 3 percent in 2003. Included among these risks is the resistance of the authorities to allow the peso to float when it faces downward pressure from markets, when they attempt to contain public price increases below what would be economically reasonable, or when they try to dissuade private firms from adjusting their prices upward. These risks have also materialized during the past three years.

During the transition from high to low inflation, Mexico's floating exchange rate helps the economy to adapt with minimum losses in output and employment to changed external circumstances and lower oil prices. This is the record of the floating exchange rate that Mexico adopted in 1995, which for that reason is likely to continue, because more adjustment is likely in the future. In particular, the NAFTA-induced manufacturing boom seen in Mexico since the early 1990s has led to higher foreign direct investment and growth in employment. But such gains should not be taken for granted; preserving them is as important as instituting monetary conditions of greater stability. In particular, an appreciating peso in the midst of global excess capacity in manufacturing and increasing international competition makes no sense.

For the next 10 years, Mexico is likely to maintain sound macroeconomic policies, which by themselves work in favor of convergence, whether or not this is an explicit objective. Nevertheless, it will not be wise to make it an explicit objective until other things that are necessary for the full convergence of economic conditions fall into place. These are deregulation and reforms in energy, in the legal system, in tax collection, and in the labor market, to name a few. Transforming Mexico in these areas and others is a prerequisite for a process of effective monetary integration. The tasks are so daunting that they may take 15 years. Consequently, a floating rate and inflation targets, as in Canada, are the most appropriate regime for Mexico if it wants to reduce the risk of currency crises. In that framework, monetary cooperation with the United States and Canada is likely to become closer through consultations among central banks, improved standards for Mexican banking, better supervision of financial and capital markets, and replacement of old regulations by new ones.

Notes

1. The Bank of Mexico (1999) is somewhere between these two schools. Since 1993, it has held a monetary base target, but such a target has become less meaningful to the public and the markets. The bank pledges, at the same time, to supply all demand for money, but at a higher interest rate if inflation is heading to a level higher than the target. By using an instrument called the "short," which applies to balances of commercial banks at the Bank of Mexico, it tightens and expands liquidity and thus induces the movement in interest rates.

2. Mexico could have heeded the lesson of the pound sterling devaluation of September 1992. This had been foreseen by some (Walters 1990), on the basis that successful monetary policy cannot be applied at the same time that policy is trying to maintain a certain nominal exchange rate, in this case with the deutsche mark. Such a policy ended in tears as the pound was ejected from the European Exchange Rate Mechanism, prompting the devaluation of the lire, the Swedish krona, and the peseta in the same year.

3. Trade does not necessarily rise significantly because of a common currency, according to Walters (1995), Feldstein (1992), and Persson (2001), though there are counterpoints to this view by Rose (2001). Bachette and van Wincoop (2000) use a stochastic general equilibrium model based on microeconomic foundations, with which they conclude that a fixed exchange rate does not lead necessarily to increased trade.

4. Jerry Jordan (1996), the president of the Federal Reserve Bank of Cleveland, put this problem in clear terms: "For better of for worse, people have always liked to organize things. . . . As we ponder the question of monetary union, we should keep in mind the essential elements of survival of any arrangement in a dynamic global environment."

5. Jürgen Stark (1998), deputy governor of the Deutsche Bundesbank, warns against seeking international cooperation through attempts "to force exchange

rates into a more or less narrow regime . . . not desirable or feasible . . . when fundamental differences in the participating economies are too great . . . and the internally conducted policies are not directed at the same ends."

References

Bachette, Philippe, and Eric van Wincoop. 2000. Does Exchange Rate Stability Increase Trade and Welfare? *American Economic Review* 90, no. 5: 1093–1109.

Bank of Mexico. 1999. *Informe anual 1998.* Mexico City: Bank of Mexico.

Feldstein, Martin. 1992. Europe's Monetary Union. *Economist,* June 13.

Grubel, Herbert G. 1999. *The Case for the Amero: The Economics and Politics of a North American Monetary Union.* Critical Issues Bulletin. Vancouver: Fraser Institute.

Jordan, Jerry L. 1996. Economic Forces versus Monetary Institutions. In *Money and Markets in the Americas,* ed. J. A. Dorn. Vancouver: Fraser Institute.

Persson, Torsten. 2001. Currency Unions and Trade: How Large Is the Treatment Effect? *Economic Policy* 33 (October): 433–48.

Ramírez de la O, Rogelio. 2002. *Nafta and the Prospects for North American Integration.* C. D. Howe Border Paper 172. Toronto: C. D. Howe Institute.

Ricardo, David. 1966. The High Price of Bullion. In *The Works of David Ricardo,* vol. 3, ed. Piero Sraffa. Cambridge: Cambridge University Press,

Rose, Andrew. 2001. Currency Unions and Trade: The Effect Is Large. *Economic Policy* 33 (October): 449–61.

Stark, Jurgen. 1998. The Worldwide Currency Situation and International Monetary Cooperation. Speech given at a meeting of the European League for Economic Cooperation, Kronberg, December 4. (Printed by Deutsche Bundesbank, Frankfurt.)

Thornton, Henry. 1939. *Enquiry into the Nature and Effects of the Paper Credit of Great Britain,* ed. F. A. von Hayek. London: London School of Economics and Political Science.

Walters, Alan. 1990. *Sterling in Danger.* London: Fontana.

———. 1995. Do Common Markets Require Common Currencies? In *Money and Markets in the Americas,* ed. J. A. Dorn. Vancouver: Fraser Institute.

PART TWO

LABOR AND THE ENVIRONMENT

CHAPTER FOUR

MIXING ENVIRONMENT AND TRADE POLICIES UNDER NAFTA

Jan Gilbreath and Janine Ferretti

Living in Mexico City in the late 1980s was a rough experience for anyone with a chronic lung condition. Rapid growth in the near absence of air quality regulation had created an air pollution problem of such magnitude that a series of government-designated "air emergencies" forced industries to periodically shut down operations and the city's citizens to flee southward to the relative safety of Cuernavaca, free from the dark haze that hovered over the Valley of Mexico.

The implementation of the North American Free Trade Agreement (NAFTA) and its environmental side accord, the North American Agreement on Environmental Cooperation (NAAEC), did not clear up Mexico City's air pollution, any more than it resolved long-standing water or air management problems in the U.S.–Mexican border region or forced changes in industrial behavior in Canada, the United States, or Mexico. What NAFTA did do, however, was to elevate the issue of natural resource use and environmental protection to a continental level. By raising the stakes—or forcing the issue into the trade arena—the Mexican government was held accountable both to its own citizens and its trading partners for a level of environmental performance that was

At the time of this writing, Jan Gilbreath was a senior associate of the Center for Strategic and International Studies. She currently serves as an international policy specialist for the U.S. Environmental Protection Agency. The views she expresses in this chapter do not reflect the views of the U.S. Environmental Protection Agency. Janine Ferretti is chief of the environment division of the Inter-American Development Bank. The views she expresses in this chapter do not represent the views of the Inter-American Development Bank.

routine in the United States or Canada but unthinkable in the Mexican political landscape of the 1980s.

Paradoxically, the Mexican government's new accountability stems in large measure from the growing strength of nongovernmental organizations (NGOs), which opposed the signing of NAFTA but nevertheless gained considerable influence from its implementation. Coalitions of NGOs formed in each of the NAFTA countries and across North American boundaries to address a broad range of environmental issues. For these organizations, the NAFTA environmental agreement established a new high-water mark for public participation, which was ultimately translated into stronger participation in other international forums.

In Mexico, the results of the new accountability have been significant. Mexico City has implemented air quality standards that are becoming more similar to those of the United States. Any sudden worsening of the city's air quality is scrutinized not just by a select number of high-profile intellectuals and artists, as was the case in the 1980s, but also by a broad variety of trained professionals and community activists who have banded together by the thousands into nongovernmental groups and are strengthened by local, national, and international linkages. At the same time, the proliferation of international environmental agreements in which the Mexican government participates with Canada and the United States gives Mexico's federal government—or local or state governments—new avenues of technical cooperation that can be tapped for solving environmental problems. Also, Mexico's recent membership in the Organization for Economic Cooperation and Development provides it with access to technical analysis and cooperation on environmental management instruments and regulations.

The Mexican government has been energized by its deeper level of interaction with Canadian and U.S. environmental agencies. The government has tentatively begun to extend its own developing view of environmental protection to Central American neighbors and to become increasingly active in international environmental efforts. Victor Lichtinger, Mexico's environmental minister, regularly participates in and hosts international meetings on sustainable development. During the 1990s, Mexico signed at least 32 international environmental agreements, in addition to the many binational environmental agreements signed with the United States (Gilbreath 2003).

The United States and Canada also benefited from linking NAFTA to environmental protection. As the host country for the North American Commission for Environmental Cooperation (CEC), the trilateral institution established by NAFTA's environmental side agreement, Canada has taken a leading role in forging similar environmental arrangements with other Latin American countries. The United States has benefited by deepening an already existing relationship with Mexico on transboundary issues, and by broadening the scope and number of its cooperative environmental arrangements with Mexico. For example, since 1992, the year NAFTA was signed, the Mexican and U.S. governments have implemented a binational environmental management plan that broadens in scope each time it is periodically renewed, and the funding commitment to that plan has increased over time.

Partly as a result of NAFTA, environmental concerns are increasingly established in trade relations throughout the hemisphere. U.S. trade policy now embraces environmental reviews of proposed trade agreements, and negotiations for a Free Trade Area of the Americas, a Central American free trade agreement (FTA), and a U.S.–Chilean FTA all contained environmental negotiations. Although not directly linked to NAFTA implementation, environmental ministers of the Americas periodically meet to discuss common challenges in the management of natural resources, reflecting a shift in environmental consciousness throughout the hemisphere. Additionally, when the hemisphere's trade ministers convene a Summit of the Americas, they are briefed by the region's environmental ministers and often include in their summit declarations a set of environmental priorities.

ENVIRONMENTAL POLICY CONVERGENCE

In North America as a whole, a semblance of a common environmental policy has begun to emerge, particularly on the reduction, elimination, or use of certain toxic chemicals and on biodiversity. The transformation is most evident in Mexico, where 10 years of NAFTA implementation have generated some visible changes in domestic environmental policy. In the United States and Canada, the changes have been less profound because of well-established environmental programs and a long history of environmental cooperation in areas such as transboundary waters, acid rain control, and wildlife management.

In devising a NAFTA environmental performance "score card," one must link the purposes of its environmental institutions to outcomes.

Although never officially stated, NAFTA's environmental institutions were designed for three primary purposes: preventing environmental disputes from becoming trade disputes; providing institutional frameworks in which environmental issues of mutual concern could be addressed; and raising Mexico's level of environmental capacity in dealing with natural resource and environmental protection issues.

The institutions have never been tested as a medium for avoiding trade disputes.[1] The dispute mechanism established under the NAAEC is for the limited purpose of ensuring that governments enforce their own domestic environmental laws and is not designed for the issue that most often preoccupies the environmental community: investor–state disputes.[2] The institutions' second purpose—providing forums for addressing issues of mutual concern—has been amply served. And the third purpose—raising Mexico's environmental capacity to a level shared by Canada and the United States—is enhanced somewhat by both the Border Environment Cooperation Commission and the trilateral NAAEC.

NAFTA's environmental institutions and related cooperative efforts have had a more limited impact on the economic integration occurring in other parts of the Americas. While environmental issues are now routinely negotiated in trade agreements to which the United States and Canada are a party, they rarely are included when Latin American countries negotiate trade agreements among themselves. The Mexican government has shown no enthusiasm for a NAFTA-style environmental accord for other trade agreements. In fact, Mexico has negotiated trade agreements with 12 countries or groups of countries since 1992—the year when NAFTA was signed. Not a single one of those agreements had a parallel environmental agreement (see Organization of American States 2003).

The Canadian and U.S. insistence on inclusion of strong environmental components to NAFTA reflect higher levels of demand for environmental protection within those societies. Yet, despite that higher societal demand for environmental protection, none of the trade agreements that the United States has negotiated since NAFTA have contained as comprehensive an environmental agenda, such extensive mandates, or the elaborate environmental institutional arrangements put in place by NAFTA's environmental side agreement.

NAFTA SUCCESS: ENVIRONMENTAL TEST OF THE NEW MEXICAN DEMOCRACY

Some media and academic writing during the past decade has chronicled both the opening of Mexico's economy and the simultaneous shift to effective suffrage and more open government. The consensus has been that the two types of openings—political and economic—must operate in tandem for both to be successful. The NAFTA experience shows that the integration of trade and environmental policies operates under the same principle. The transparency that is needed in government to optimize economic policies is the same transparency needed to optimize environmental policies. Transparency, in turn, empowers the public by holding government accountable for its actions.

The emerging role of NGOs during NAFTA negotiations and implementation set a precedent not only for Canadian and U.S. groups but also most importantly for Mexican groups, whose political influence at the domestic level had been more limited before trade negotiations began. Since NAFTA implementation, Mexican environmental groups have been more involved in both domestic and trilateral decisionmaking on trade and economic policy issues—issues that would have been beyond the scope of most Mexican environmentalists before 1990. However, the scope of Mexican NGO participation in domestic trade policies is not as broad as it is in the United States or Canada. For example, Canadian and U.S. environmental organizations are represented on federal trade policy advisory committees that serve trade negotiators.

New Institutions Empower Mexican NGOs

NAFTA provided two institutions in which public participation tends to push the three parties into greater transparency and accountability for environmental actions. The institution that affects citizens in all three countries is the CEC, which was established under the NAAEC.[3] The other institution, the Border Environment Cooperation Commission (BECC), affects only the U.S. and Mexican publics.

The NAAEC reinforced public participation and principles of transparency and the right of public access to information about government operations by setting out obligations for all three signatories in these areas. These obligations helped to provide the conditions for Mexican NGOs to change their relationships to their federal government. The agreement emphasized transparency and public participation by providing opportunities for NGOs to comment on a broad range of proposed laws, regulations, procedures, and administrative rulings in each country. It promoted public access to information by setting out detailed procedures that the public could use to air complaints about a government's failure to enforce its own environmental laws and by instituting cooperative efforts with Mexico to develop a broad-based emissions inventory that would be available to the Mexican public.

The agreement also contained other, indirect pressures on the three federal governments to expand the scope of the environmental information made publicly available. For example, article 10 of the NAAEC encouraged the CEC Council, which consists of the environmental ministers from each country, to promote the exchange of information on criteria and methodologies used in establishing domestic environmental standards, to promote public awareness of environmental issues, and to establish a process for developing recommendations on greater compatibility of environmental technical regulations, standards, and conformity assessment procedures.[4] Article 13 makes provision for most CEC reports to be issued to the public in draft form so that individual citizens or NGOs may comment on them. Other parts of the agreement emphasized that council reports should be made public and that council proceedings must be transparent.

The CEC's broad-based mandate generally tended to reinforce the importance of public participation in the governance structures of the three NAFTA parties. In Mexico, the mandate also had the effect of raising public expectations about the environmental performance of its government and the role that environmental groups would play as government watchdogs. These expectations were fueled in part by the establishment of new national and trilateral committees designed to promote the concerns of civil society in the operations of the CEC Council and its secretariat. The NAAEC, for example, created a Joint Public Advisory Committee to assist the CEC Council. This committee consists of five environmental specialists from each country charged with promoting the interests of civil society to the CEC Council. It holds public meetings and has initiated public hearings in all three countries on a wide range of issues.

At the national level, the NAAEC encouraged each government to develop new mechanisms of including the public in environmental decisionmaking by establishing national advisory committees that consist of members of civil society who provide advice on a broad variety of issues to each environmental minister. The U.S. committee has been quite active; the Mexican committee less so.

Reinforcing the Environmental Resolve of Governments

One of the principal aims of the NAAEC was to ensure that each NAFTA country effectively enforces its domestic environmental legislation, to lessen the chances that lax enforcement would provide a cost advantage over industries from the two other parties. Part 5 of the NAAEC, which addresses environmental dispute resolution, provides all three parties the option to initiate consultations over environmental disputes. If consultations were to fail, an arbitration panel could be convened, and ultimately trade sanctions could be imposed on the party that loses the dispute. However, this dispute-resolution mechanism has never been used.

What has been frequently used are the complaint processes provided under articles 14 and 15 of the agreement. Under these articles, anyone living in any of the three member countries may bring a complaint to the CEC about the enforcement of environmental legislation on the books of any of the NAFTA parties. This citizen submission process also is designed to empower citizens to play an active role in monitoring government enforcement of environmental laws, thus vesting NGOs with new roles in both domestic and international governance.

The complaint process has had an impact, particularly in Mexico and Canada, on each party's environmental policy by providing new channels for NGOs to increase pressure on federal governments to consistently enforce laws and to make environmental planning and review processes more transparent and open to public participation. In Canada and Mexico, however, access to the judicial system to encourage governments to enforce environmental laws continues to be more limited to than in the United States. For Canada, the citizen complaint process on enforcement was introduced at the same time that spending on environmental protection, including monitoring and inspection, began falling.

The CEC's complaint process does not operate in a policy vacuum. At the same time that the three North American governments are held more accountable by the CEC's citizen complaint process, they also are held accountable for consistent application of its laws, provision of information, and transparency of operations through other NAFTA provisions.

Dealing with Complaints

A quick review of the volume and type of complaints that have been filed with the CEC from citizens in all three countries reveals something of the environmental issues that preoccupy the public. From 1995, when the CEC's secretariat first began accepting complaints, until February 1, 2003, a total of 36 complaints of failure to enforce environmental laws have merited at least a staff review at the CEC secretariat level. Eight complaints merited the most serious investigation and documentation, called a "factual record." This includes factual records prepared by the secretariat and those under study by its council. By the spring of 2003, three had been developed in response to complaints against Mexico, four in response to complaints against Canada, and one against the United States.[5] Of all complaints reviewed at the secretariat level, eight were filed against the United States; 11 against Canada; and 17 against Mexico.

Canada has been forced to review enforcement of environmental laws governing livestock processing, mining, logging, and the protection of fish and fish habitat caused by hydroelectric dams. The United States has responded to allegations of failure to enforce wildlife protection laws, failure to enforce a United States–Canada treaty limiting airborne pollution over the Great Lakes, failure to protect the spotted owl, and failure to prohibit leaks from underground storage tanks.

The adverse publicity that the Mexican government endured after a handful of high-profile complaints filed by NGOs under articles 14 and 15 helped to initiate changes in the government's regulation and review processes. The public pressure also forced the Mexican government to open its planning and enforcement processes to public participation, and to publish statistics on enforcement actions, fines, and the number and types of environmental reviews and permits it grants.

Failure to enforce regulations stemming from environmental impact assessments has been the most common complaint against Mexico. Much of Mexico's land use regulation occurs by forcing developers and industry to comply with a set of environmental impact conditions that are set in order to get project authorization.

The handling of complaints filed against the government for failing to assess the environmental impacts of development projects has become a litmus test within Mexican society about the resolve of the administration of President Vicente Fox to make Mexican government decisionmaking more transparent, more open to public participation, and to make government information more readily available to the public. The fact that Mexican NGOs air their grievances against the government in an international forum like the CEC reinforced arguments for public access, transparency, and accountability in the Mexican debate on democratic change. The challenge to domestic policy within the international community focuses both domestic and international scrutiny of government promises to change, and it focuses them on specific issues that have broader implications.

One of the most crucial challenges to the Mexican government on environment and economic development policy centered on a complaint filed by Mexican environmental groups in 1996, well before President Fox took office in December 2000. The Fox Administration's response to this challenge proved important both in signaling a changing attitude toward environmental protection and in mobilizing civil society opposition to certain long-standing development policies in Mexico. In the case filed against the Mexican government at the CEC, three Mexican groups—Comité para la Protección de los Recursos Naturales, AC, Grupo de los Cien Internacional, AC, and Centro Mexicano de Derecho Ambiental, AC—complained that the Mexican government failed to effectively enforce environmental laws during the impact assessment for construction of a new terminal for cruise ships off the island of Cozumel in the state of Quintana Roo (North American Commission for Environmental Cooperation 1996). The opening of once pristine beaches along the Yucatán and the Quintana Roo coastline to new cruise ship ports and resorts had been an issue of concern in Mexico for a decade before the complaint was filed.

The complaint, against a single proposal for a new port at Cozumel, helped Mexican environmentalists gain domestic and international exposure for their more general concerns about development throughout this region. Although the environmentalists were not successful in stopping development, their complaint had other, more far-reaching effects. Protests erupted sporadically over the next six years, spurred by local environmentalists who argued that frequent dockings by big ships threatened the coral that lines the coast from Cancún down to Honduras, the world's second-largest barrier reef.

As a result of the publicity, in April 2001, Victor Lichtinger, Mexico's environmental minister, withdrew a permit for a 1,400-room hotel development at Xcacel, a beach 67 miles south of Cancún. That was one of the first such actions based on environmental considerations in Mexico's history. Lichtinger's decision took into account the fact that Xcacel is one of the world's last sanctuaries for several endangered species of sea turtles.

Mexican environmentalists have identified other significant impacts on Mexican environmental policy from the Cozumel case. Gustavo Alanís, executive director of the Centro Mexicano de Derecho Ambiental, has documented the following effects (Alanís Ortega 2002):

- Former president Zedillo's declaration of Cozumel's coral reefs as a natural protected area. The federal government agreed to develop an ecological zone and management plan, and established a trust fund to manage the protected areas.

- A 1996 reform of Mexico's environmental law. The new law strengthens regulations on environmental impact assessments.

- Increased environmental awareness, within the Mexican state of Quintana Roo, throughout Mexico, and in international forums.

THE MODERNIZATION OF MEXICO'S ENVIRONMENTAL PROGRAMS

Mexico enacted its first comprehensive environmental law in 1988, shortly before the push began for a North American trade agreement. The promulgation of this law was not related to economic integration with the rest of North America but instead reflected rising domestic demand to clean up the air pollution that was threatening to limit future development of Mexico City, as well as the growing internationalization of environmental concerns. The NAFTA debate that focused on Mexico's environmental performance reinforced the domestic and international pressures for change, and it caused that change to accelerate.

U.S., Canadian, and Mexican environmental groups forced the issue of Mexico's environmental performance into the trade debate, partly out of a sense of fear that Mexico's lax environmental laws and poor enforcement record would create a haven for polluting firms, and partly from a sense of concern that transboundary pollution and resource depletion would increase with rapid economic development associated with trade.

The linkages that the debate fostered between Mexican environmentalists and their U.S. and Canadian counterparts helped the Mexican groups gain financial and political independence from their government. New avenues of financing for NGOs opened up within United States–based nonprofit foundations. With increased independence, Mexican environmentalists were able to more effectively push their own environmental agenda, which focused primarily on the government's poor protection of Mexico's natural resources.

The combined pressure of domestic environmental groups and international pressures to modernize environmental programs or risk rejection of a much-coveted FTA with the United States and Canada prompted the Mexican federal government to compress what might have been several decades of environmental program reform into a few short years. These actions were not completely driven by NAFTA, but Mexico's environmental program today bears little resemblance to the program that existed in 1988, when the nation's first comprehensive environmental law was enacted. Highlights of changes include:[6]

- In 1991, the Mexican federal government held what may have been its first public hearings to seek opinions on environmental planning. These hearings, held jointly with the U.S. Environmental Protection Agency, sought comment on a joint U.S.–Mexican border environmental management plan.

- Before 1992, Mexico had no federal governmental unit dedicated specifically to enforcement of environmental regulations. That year, President Carlos Salinas de Gortari established the Federal Office of Environmental Attorney General.

- Before 1988, enforcement of Mexico's existing environmental laws was virtually non-existent. From the time President Salinas took office in December 1988 up to September 1992, shortly before NAFTA's signing, the federal government (1) suspended the operating licenses of 1,926 facilities for noncompliance with environmental regulations; (2) permanently closed more than 100 facilities in the Mexico City area at a cost of $500 million in federal revenue; (3) forced 2,112 industries to install pollution control equipment; and (4) inspected more than 7,668 industrial sites (Secretaría de Desarrollo Urbano y Ecología 1992).

- In 1994, President Salinas elevated environmental protection to a cabinet-level position within the Mexican government.

- Mexico strengthened its omnibus environmental law in 1996 and adopted some economic measures to achieve the government's environmental management objectives.

- In 1996, as part of a general strengthening of environmental law, Mexico expanded the types of activities for which environmental impact assessments are required. Environmental impact assessments are now used in with regional land use plans to evaluate the environmental effects of projects and the adequacy of mitigation measures.

- From 2000 to the present, Mexican coalitions of environmentalists and political figures have launched a number of public awareness campaigns and protests aimed at (1) limiting tourist projects, (2) forcing the government to undertake more rigorous environmental assessments of these projects, and (3) preserving species and biodiversity.

- In 2001, the administration of President Vicente Fox established an office within the Mexican Environmental Secretariat (commonly known as Semarnat) to provide environmental information to the public.

- That same year, the Mexican government established the first publicly accessible emissions inventory for Mexico. The CEC's secretariat, over a six-year period, had been instrumental in providing the capacity-building support to Mexican government agencies needed to implement the registry.

- In 2002, President Fox gained congressional approval for Mexico's first comprehensive freedom of information law that broadly guarantees Mexicans the right to know what their government is doing. The law is forcing the release of many new types of information, including information compiled by Semarnat (United Mexican States 2002).

NAFTA ENVIRONMENTAL LINKAGES TO TRADE AGREEMENTS IN LATIN AMERICA

During the past 10 years, NAFTA's environmental side agreement has never been duplicated in any other U.S. trade agreement. However, it has served as a point of reference for negotiating the environmental provisions of other trade agreements. As one example, the U.S.–Central American free trade agreement negotiated in 2003 and early 2004 contains a provision under which citizens may generate submissions alleging that a trading partner has failed to effectively enforce its environmental laws. This provision is somewhat similar to the citizen submission procedures provided within the NAFTA side agreement.

Canadian Negotiations after NAFTA

After NAFTA's implementation, Canada was the first of the three countries to promote the incorporation of environmental issues in trade negotiations with other Latin American and Caribbean countries. In signing trade agreements with Chile and Costa Rica, the Canadian government negotiated environmental cooperation agreements. Although the Costa Rican environmental accord, signed in April 2001, imposed no substantial obligations, the Chilean agreement, signed in February 1997, was closely modeled on the NAFTA environmental agreement.[7]

Canadian and Chilean negotiators modeled their environmental agreement on the provisions of the NAAEC with the belief that Chile might someday become a NAFTA member. In fact, article 48 of the agreement states, "The Parties shall work toward the early accession of Chile to the North American Agreement on Environmental Cooperation."

In the Canadian–Chilean environmental agreement, the two trading partners incorporated the concept of imposing monetary penalties against a party that persistently failed to enforce its own environmental laws. Although the Chilean government in the environmental accord with Canada agreed to monetary assessments in cases where environmental disputes could not be otherwise resolved, the proposed method of assessing such penalties was changed. NAFTA's environmental side accord had called not only for monetary penalties of up to $20 million in the first year of implementation but also made a provision for trade sanctions. After the first year of implementation, a penalty for failure to enforce domestic environmental laws could, in theory, be assessed up to 0.007 percent of total trade in goods between the parties.[8] The Canadian–Chilean environmental agreement called for maximum penalties of up to $10 million.[9] Such penalties, if assessed and collected, would be used to improve or enhance the environment or environmental law enforcement of the country complained against.

The Canadian and Chilean governments decided to reduce costs of implementing the environmental accord by avoiding the expense of establishing a separate secretariat. Instead, the two countries established offices within their individual governments to carry out provisions of the accord.

As in the NAFTA environmental agreement, Canada's agreements with Chile and Costa Rica encouraged the filing of citizen complaints against governments for failure to effectively enforce environmental laws, and both agreements made provision for government transparency and publication of environmental information.

The Costa Rican–Canadian environmental agreement, however, was a greatly scaled down version of the NAAEC. It called for each party to effectively enforce its own environmental laws, but the formal procedures by which complaints could be filed and reviewed were missing. Instead, the agreement stipulated that citizens or NGOs in each country could submit written "questions" to either the Canadian or Costa Rican government about the government's ability to effectively enforce its environmental laws.[10] Responses to these questions are required in writing, but responses to several similar questions can be combined into a single response.

Also missing from the Costa Rican–Canadian environmental agreement was the threat of penalties or trade sanctions for a party's failure to enforce its own environmental laws. The areas of potential environmental cooperation were not as broad as in the NAAEC, no formal mechanism was suggested for joint projects, and no joint secretariat or even national offices were established to carry out the provisions of this agreement. In essence, the Costa Rican–Canadian agreement was simply a framework from which future cooperative efforts could grow.

Although the Costa Rican environmental accord with Canada is substantially weaker than the Chilean one, the Canadian government's persistence in negotiating these accords helped set the stage for future environmental negotiations for a Free Trade Area of the Americas (FTAA). These accords also served as additional political pressure on U.S. trade negotiators as they undertook trade negotiations for an FTA with Chile.

U.S. Negotiations after NAFTA

The United States, like Canada, has incorporated some of the environmental lessons learned under NAFTA implementation into other FTAs on a smaller scale. When Chile and the United States conducted an FTA in 2003, the two countries included an environmental chapter within the text of the agreement itself, detailed specific areas for future cooperative efforts on environmental protection, and agreed to negotiate a separate environmental accord. Both governments committed themselves to enforce their domestic environmental laws, and the agreement contained an enforcement mechanism under which monetary assessments could be made. Either the United States or Chile can raise issues about any other provision in the environmental chapter to the political level by requesting a meeting of the Environmental Affairs Council established under the FTA.

The Environment Affairs Council in the Chilean FTA will meet annually to discuss the implementation of the chapter. The council is required to seek public input in designing agendas for its meetings and to hold public sessions at each meeting.

Environmentalists immediately complained after the U.S.–Chilean agreement was signed on June 6, 2003, that its environmental provisions were too weak to serve as a model for either a Central American FTA or an FTAA. Mark Van Putten, president of the National Wildlife Federation, said in a press release issued at the time of the signing that the U.S.–Chilean FTA had failed to do the following (National Wildlife Federation 2003):

- Include a citizen submission process that allows citizens of both Chile and the United States to allege a failure to effectively enforce environmental laws. Such a 'sunshine' mechanism allowing for the production of a limited factual record (and no penalties) is in place in the NAFTA and Canada-Chile environmental side agreements.

- Preclude foreign investor suit provisions that can be used to undermine U.S. and Chilean environmental laws.

- Establish an independent environmental cooperation institution.

- Be accompanied by specific resource and financial commitments to implement the environmental cooperation goals of the agreement.

NEW ENVIRONMENTAL CHALLENGES FOR NORTH AMERICA

Despite the relative success of NAFTA's environmental institutions in fostering cooperation, all three NAFTA partners continue to face natural resource depletion and environmental protection issues that have the potential to limit future benefits of the region's deepening economic integration. These issues arise in large measure because NAFTA has been successful in stimulating economic growth and dropping barriers to foreign direct investment throughout the region. Most of these challenges require substantial effort and policy reform at the national level.

The CEC's ability to effectively address citizen complaints of a government's failure to enforce environmental laws also is coming under intense scrutiny. Since 2000, the CEC's Council, which consists of the environmental ministers of each NAFTA party, has shown increasing reluctance to develop the intense reviews and public documentation of these complaints, which are known as factual records. Often, the council has rejected the recommendations of its own secretariat that such review and documentation be compiled. As a result, environmental groups increasingly voice their concerns that the ability of the citizen submission mechanism to help improve the effectiveness of environmental enforcement at the national level has diminished.

In May 2000, for example, the CEC's Council rejected a recommendation to develop a factual record about the Quebec government's enforcement of environmental laws for large-scale hog farming. In 2001, the council restricted the scope of four other factual records so much that the petitioners saw little relevance to pursuing their complaints.[11] In 2002, the council rejected a secretariat recommendation to develop a factual record of a complaint filed against the Mexican government for failure to enforce hazardous waste law. In April 2003, the council decided that its secretariat should compile additional information before determining that a factual record was warranted for a complaint about logging operations in Ontario.

Investor–State Disputes under NAFTA

One goal of an FTA is to speed the settlement of cross-border commercial disputes. To accomplish this goal, NAFTA negotiators gave individual investors—corporations—new powers to dispute local, state, or national laws affecting their investments. A number of investor–state disputes filed under NAFTA during the past five years focused on the effect of environmental laws on foreign investment. Some of these disputes center on state or local environmental measures that reflect different goals from national regulations. On at least two occasions, aspects of these investor complaints also surfaced as citizen complaints filed with the CEC.[12] In both cases, the complaints lodged at the CEC did not completely proceed through the CEC process because both were the subject of investor litigation under NAFTA.

As a result of the NAFTA experience, new questions have arisen about the role that investors should have as regional or national law is shaped, and these concerns have spilled into negotiations for an FTAA. Some experts, including lawyers who otherwise support the dispute settlement procedures, worry that the court proceedings, held before special NAFTA tribunals instead of traditional national courts, are too secretive. Activists, especially environmentalists, have said NAFTA's investment dispute provisions give only companies and investors the legal power to take their complaints into court. Other groups, including labor unions and environmentalists, cannot do that. The clause does not require the tribunals to hear the opinions of those outsiders.

Under NAFTA's chapter 11, foreign investors have the right to bring their cases to the International Center for Settlement of Investment Disputes (ICSID), which is housed in the World Bank. Most of the investor disputes filed with the ICSID against Mexico—whether through NAFTA or other investor-related agreements—have focused on Mexico's application of hazardous waste law. Since 1997, a total of five investor complaints concerning Mexico's application of hazardous waste laws have been filed with the ICSID (see World Bank Group and ICSID 2003).

Whether or not these disputes as a whole threaten to weaken Mexican environmental waste law or simply pinpoint existing weaknesses in the application of that law is not clear. Mexico traditionally has had little capacity to process hazardous wastes, and the federal government, until the NAFTA era, did not focus much attention on establishing environmental policy in this area.

As hazardous wastes have grown over the decades with increasing industrialization, the Mexican government has struggled to address the issue. The World Bank estimated that 5.29 million tons of hazardous waste were generated in 1992, of which 3 million tons were abandoned (World Bank 1992). Meanwhile, the number of Mexican facilities that can handle waste disposal has declined over the years (Gilbreath 2003). In 2001, only one hazardous waste disposal facility was in operation—near Monterrey in northern Mexico—and that facility held an estimated 550,000 tons of waste.

NAFTA guarantees that each signatory may set its own environmental standards, and critics of the investor dispute settlement procedures believe that commitment has been undermined by several high-profile investor disputes. These include the following:

- U.S. hazardous-waste company S. D. Myers sued Canada for $20 million over a law banning transport of polychlorinated biphenyls to the United States and between Canadian provinces.

- Ethyl Corporation sued Canada for $20 million over a law banning the chemical MMT, a gasoline additive.

- The Canadian firm, Methanex, which produces ingredients for the gasoline additive methyl tertiary butyl ether, sued the United States for $1 billion because of California's ban on the chemical.

- Metalclad Corporation of Newport Beach, California, sued Mexico in 1996 after a local government outlawed a facility that it had constructed in the state of San Luis Potosí.

- Waste Management, Incorporated, has twice filed NAFTA investor challenges against Mexico over provision of waste management services under a concession granted by the city of Acapulco in the state of Guerrero (American Society of International Law 2002).

Methanex Case. The Methanex case is one that has drawn significant attention to California's environmental standards, which are generally higher than elsewhere in the United States. The CEC refused to allow the Methanex complaint to proceed because of pending NAFTA chapter 11 litigation in the ICSID over the same issue.

Methanex Corporation, a Canadian company, makes the gasoline additive methyl tertiary butyl ether (MTBE), which was banned by California governor Gray Davis after a study found a possible carcinogen in 10,000 groundwater sites in the state. Governor Davis issued his order in 1999 and said all MTBE should be removed from gasoline sold in the state by December 31, 2002 (Dhooge 2001). As a result of the governor's action, Methanex claimed $970 million in damages. MTBE had been used in U.S. gasoline since the 1970s, first as a source of octane when lead was phased out of gasoline and then as an oxygenate to meet the requirements of the Clean Air Act Amendments of 1990 for cleaner-burning fuel. In 1999, MTBE was used in 70 percent of the gasoline sold within the state of California. Governor Davis acknowledged that MTBE had been beneficial in achieving clean air standards, but he said that this benefit was overshadowed by a significant risk to groundwater and drinking water that occurs when MTBE leaks from underground fuel storage tanks.

Metalclad Case. In 1996, the Metalclad Corporation of Newport Beach, California, complained that Mexican officials had blocked the opening of a hazardous waste landfill that Metalclad had built in the central state of San Luis Potosí (DePalma 2001). Metalclad said it had obtained all the necessary federal permits, and it had invested more than $20 million in the project before the state governor designated the site an ecological preserve, preventing the landfill from opening.

Metalclad argued that the government's actions were tantamount to expropriation. A NAFTA tribunal that heard the case agreed. Mexico appealed, and the case was heard in a court in Canada, considered neutral in the dispute (DePalma 2001). The Canadian judge upheld the ruling, and said Metalclad was owed $15.6 million in compensation.

U.S.–Mexican Transboundary Resource Depletion

As NAFTA has spurred economic growth in the U.S.–Mexican border region, transboundary political tensions over water allocation and management also have grown. Both sides of the border are running out of water both for agricultural and municipal use, and the scarcity is creating a series of unresolved disputes between agricultural and municipal users. NAFTA's implementation and its resulting impact on growth in border region aggravated the demand for water for both uses but did not cause it. Even so, failure to address the water management issue over the next decade will have an adverse impact on the ability of the United States and Mexico to continue their process of economic integration or to sustain regional economic growth.

The problem is more acute on the Mexican side of the border because existing supplies are threatened by municipal contamination. Mexico's National Water Commission reported in 2001 that Mexico's northern border towns and cities, strapped for funds, could adequately treat less than 35 percent of the sewage generated daily (Thompson 2001). One area of growing concern was Ciudad Juárez, across the Rio Grande from El Paso, Texas. As of 2001, this city of 1.3 million residents was growing by about 50,000 people a year, but the underground aquifer that supplies the city and El Paso was declining by about 5 feet per year. City officials estimated that the aquifer would contain no usable water in 20 years (Thompson 2001).

Water is running short on the U.S. side of the border as well. Failure to conserve water and failure to regulate underground water pumping are two of the issues that threaten to limit economic development in the southwestern United States. U.S. per capita use of water declined from 1,900 gallons of water per person per day in 1980 to 1,500 gallons per day in 1995, but by global standards, the United States is one of the world's most gluttonous water users (Jehl 2002).

The depletion of the nation's giant Ogallala aquifer, which supplies eight states, including Texas, has slowed but continues. In the United States, part of the water problem stems from the antiquated Texas water law. Texas's lax law governing underground aquifers allows private property owners virtually unrestricted water use, which allows consumption to increase faster than in other states. By 2050, Texas water planners predict the state's population will reach 40 million people, up from about 21 million in 2000, and they expect municipal water use to rise by nearly 67 percent. By the same year, the Texas Water Development Board has warned that Texas's supply of water, from existing sources, will be 19 percent less than in 2002 (Jehl 2002).

In addition to the pressures to conserve underground water sources, California officials are in the middle of a confrontation with six other states—Arizona, Colorado, New Mexico, Nevada, Utah, and Wyoming—over allocation of water from the Colorado River. This is the same river from which the United States must supply water to Mexico under a 1944 water treaty. Tensions over U.S. state allocations from the Colorado River rose so high in early 2003 that for the first time since it was given authority four decades ago, the U.S. Department of the Interior prohibited California from taking more than its allotted share from the river (Murphy 2003).

NAFTA established two institutions capable of dealing with a limited number of these water issues—the Border Environment Cooperation Commission and the North American Development Bank (NAD Bank). The BECC is charged with certifying environmental infrastructure projects for NAD Bank funding. In that capacity, it helps local communities to plan and implement water supply use, wastewater treatment, and other environmental infrastructure projects. Although an important function, the institution's impact on broader water management issues is small.

Both the U.S. and Mexican governments aim to use the NAD Bank to fund a wide variety of water projects and air pollution control projects, but until recently the bank has contributed only a small amount of funding for infrastructure projects. The two governments clearly intend to rely on NAD Bank funding to implement their binational environmental management plan, however. Much of their joint border environmental management plan, currently called Border 2012, relies on NAD Bank funding for water improvement projects that will reduce municipal contamination and extend municipal supplies.

The NAD Bank cannot fully address the water management issue on either side of the border. In 1999, the NAD Bank estimated that $2.1 billion was needed over a 10-year period in environmental infrastructure funding for the border region. The bank, which is jointly financed by the Mexican and U.S. governments, provided only $35 million in loans for 12 projects between September 1995, when the BECC first certified a project for funding, and September 30, 2002 (North American Development Bank 2003). Of these 12 loans, three loans totaling $11.3 million were granted in 2002 by the NAD Bank's new low-interest rate lending facility (BECC and NAD Bank 2002). The NAD Bank has issued substantially more environmental infrastructure funding through its grant programs. As of September 30, 2002, the NAD Bank had awarded $422 million in grants for these infrastructure projects.

Mexico's Domestic Natural Resource Challenges

Mexico's environmental policy gains in recent years have been impressive, but the rate of environmental degradation continues to pose significant risks to its economic growth. The deforestation, soil erosion, and water supply and contamination challenges that Mexico currently faces will limit the nation's ability to fully realize its economic potential under the trade accord unless many costly actions are taken now. In a 2002 interview, Victor Lichtinger, Mexico's environmental minister, said that Mexico must have at least 20 years of strong environmental policies to recover from decades of abuse that ravaged the country's forests and polluted its air and water (Reuters 2002).

A few months after he became president, Vicente Fox declared water a "national security issue" (Weiner 2001). He said that Mexico in 2001 had 60 percent less water per capita than it had 50 years before, and he added that one out of eight Mexicans had no easy access to drinking water at all. His government reported that greater Mexico City, home to nearly 20 million people, was draining its immense underground aquifer by as much as 11 feet a year. With the aquifer close to being depleted, the city was pumping water from as much as 125 miles away, and half of that trickled away in leaks and cracks (Weiner 2001).

In addition, Lichtinger declared that 73 percent of Mexico's surface and underground water supplies were contaminated and a danger to public health (Weiner 2001). He said that most of the surface water—93 percent—was contaminated. The National Water Commission reported that some states, such as Chiapas, did not have a single functioning wastewater treatment plant.

What Mexico needs most is the funding to address its water and deforestation problems. As one example, Mexico's National Water Commission estimated in 2001 that Mexico must spend $30 billion over a 10-year period to stop water contamination and to treat enough water to keep up with human demand (Weiner 2001).

This is a formidable challenge. Multilateral lending institutions can provide some, but not all, of this funding. Fiscal reform in Mexico is urgently needed in order to establish a user-fee base for environmental protection programs and the elimination of water subsidies that distort water consumption patterns. As one example of this need, Lichtinger has pointed to the fact that agribusinesses, mining firms, and cattle ranchers across Mexico get their water free, even though these industries consume at least 70 percent of the nation's water.

Mexico also faces a serious challenge in reversing deforestation and related soil erosion that is having an adverse impact on agricultural fertility. Mexico's annual rate of deforestation has long been one of the fastest in Latin America, but over the past several years, it has increased substantially. A 2001 Mexican multiagency study of satellite images from 1993 through 2000 suggested that Mexico is losing forest cover almost twice as fast as previously estimated, making it the country with the second-highest deforestation rate in the world after Brazil (*Orlando Sentinel* 2001). In announcing the results of the satellite survey in 2001, Lichtinger said that before 1993, the annual loss of forest was about 600,000 hectares per year. But after 1993, that rate rose to 1.1 million hectares per year (Efe News Services 2001). If this rate of deforestation continued unchecked, he said, Mexico would lose all its forests in 127 years.

United States–Canada Growth in Pollution and Resource Deterioration

In U.S.–Canada relations, successful economic integration and economic growth in both countries since the inception of the Canada–U.S. Free Trade Agreement in 1989 are generating new environmental challenges in the energy and logging sectors, and in an overall rise in land-based toxic chemical releases. The CEC monitors some of these trends, accepts citizen complaints about each government's resolve to enforce its own environmental laws, and urges all three of the NAFTA countries to consider the environmental consequences of increasing electricity-generating capacity over the next several years.[13]

The growth in timber cutting during the past decade in both the United States and Canada has drawn the ire of many environmental groups in both countries, who have filed complaints with the CEC alleging that both governments are failing to protect wildlife as the logging sector booms. High-profile complaints have been filed against logging operations in British Columbia and Ontario, and one against the U.S. government for broad-scale failure to protect migratory birds during logging operations.[14] In the most recent complaint, against Ontario, the CEC asked the Canadian federal government to defend itself against allegations that it allows 85,000 nests containing eggs and baby birds to be destroyed every year. A coalition of environmental groups claimed the federal government does not enforce the Migratory Birds Convention Act against Ontario forestry companies that destroy nests by clear cutting. But forestry companies say that while some nests are destroyed when trees are cut down, the companies follow regulations that protect the overall migratory bird habitat (Jaimet 2002).

Rising energy demand in all three NAFTA countries is creating trilateral tensions over pollution from new electricity-generating facilities. The CEC addressed this issue in a 2002 report on electricity generation in North America, warning that the continent's air quality will worsen with the addition of 2,000 new power plants over a five-year period beginning in 2002 (Leatherdale 2002). The growth of the energy sector is a reflection not only of growth-led demand in all three countries but also of the recent deregulation of electricity in 16 U.S. states and the Canadian provinces of Alberta and Ontario. In all, the CEC report predicted that electricity demand will grow during the next decade by 66 percent in Mexico, 21 percent in the United States, and 14 percent in Canada.

ENVIRONMENTAL IMPLICATIONS
OF DEEPER AND BROADER INTEGRATION

Economic integration in North America as well as the Western Hemisphere will continue to include negotiations aimed at deepening levels of environmental cooperation. These negotiations are not likely to result from fears that pollution havens will be established in countries with few environmental controls over industries, as was the case in the public debate leading to the establishment of NAFTA's environmental institutions. The negotiations instead are likely to focus on technical transfers, technical assistance, and funding for programs to protect natural resources in countries that lack the capacity to fully integrate environmental and economic policies.

The likelihood of negotiations for technical assistance increase when emerging or middle-income economies identify the benefits that can accrue from such assistance. The Mexican government, for example, has expressed a desire to extend the mandate of one of its environmental institutions—the NAD Bank—to a geographic region that encompasses all of Mexico. The bank funds environmental infrastructure projects—water supply, wastewater treatment, solid waste disposal, and other forms of infrastructure that reduce pollution.

Mexico has two interests in financing urban infrastructure that also reduce pollution. First, a large component of Mexico's economic growth during NAFTA's implementation has been the increased level of foreign direct investment it can attract from the United States. Foreign corporations cannot start up new operations without adequate environmental infrastructure, and the strains on urban infrastructure represent one reason that U.S. assembly plant operations in northern Mexico increasingly look elsewhere in Mexico to establish facilities.

Second, Mexican federal and state governments increasingly link the protection and conservation of water supplies to continued economic growth. That linkage is particularly clear in northern Mexico, where water shortages have forced the government of Monterrey, Nuevo León, to turn away companies that want to establish water-intensive operations. The linkage also is clear in the agricultural sector in northern Mexico. The cost of producing agricultural products for export in Mexico's northern-state "breadbasket" is increasing in part because irrigation systems need to be modernized and water use must be reduced.

The Mexican government has not only emphasized its need for environmental infrastructure funding and technical assistance but is also using this same concept as it attempts a greater level of economic integration with Central America. In June 2001, President Fox announced a new development program for southern Mexico and Central America, called the Plan Puebla-Panama (*New York Times* 2001). Funding sources for the program have not been identified, but it was President Fox's intention to promote tourism, trade, education, environmental protection, and disaster relief planning over a 20-year period for a nine-state region of Mexico and seven countries of Central America. President Fox's plan also envisioned a series of infrastructure linkages, including roads, power lines, telephone lines, and natural gas grids in this region, and ultimately linking the region to the rest of North America.

Environmentalists' demands for the U.S.–Chilean FTA demonstrate that many of the principles incorporated into the NAAEC remain strong priorities. In a November 2002 letter written to U.S. trade representative Robert Zoellick, four United States–based environmental groups asked for the following provisions:[15]

- an independent citizen petition mechanism aimed at focusing attention on a government's failure to enforce its own environmental law;

- a commitment from each country to effectively enforce its environmental laws;

- a commitment on the part of each country not to weaken its environmental standards;

- a commitment to strengthen environmental standards, enforce environmental laws, and strengthen the capacity to prevent and mitigate trade-related environmental effects; and

- a joint environmental council.

To enhance the benefits of free trade and make trade negotiations operate as efficiently as possible, the Office of the U.S. Trade Representative has established a unit aimed at enhancing the trade capacity of U.S. trading partners. Although environmental issues are not specifically addressed within this unit, the creation of such an office points to the growing recognition that a government's performance across many functions has a direct bearing not only on its capacity to trade but also on its ability to sustain the benefits of trade. In this sense, a government's environmental capacity—the ability to preserve and protect its resource base—is directly tied to the economic growth and prosperity that it hopes to enjoy from expanding trade relations.

Notes

1. Very little of Article 10:6, which lays out the mandate of the CEC in resolving or preventing trade disputes, has been used, except for 10:6(d). Article 10:6(d) calls on the CEC to monitor the effects of NAFTA on the environment. Article 10:6 instructs the CEC Council to cooperate with the NAFTA Free Trade Commission to achieve NAFTA's environmental goals and objectives.

2. Chapter 11 of NAFTA allows firms to initiate and pursue dispute settlement if they feel that a foreign country through environmental or other regulations has infringed their rights.

3. See *North American Agreement on Environmental Cooperation between the Government of Canada, the Government of the United Mexican States and the Government of the United States of America* (1992).

4. *North American Agreement on Environmental Cooperation*, article 10, "Council Functions" (1992).

5. The Secretariat has drafted three factual records in response to complaints against Canada, and these are under study by the CEC Council. The three are "Oldman River II," submitted April 17, 2003, "BC Logging," submitted April 15, 2003, and "BC Mining," submitted March 28, 2003 (respectively, North American Commission for Environmental Cooperation 2003e, 2003b, 2003c). A fourth factual record concerning Canada, "BC Hydro, SEM-97-001," was released in 2000 (North American Commission for Environmental Cooperation 2000). In addition to the two factual records released in response to complaints against Mexico, a third draft factual record is under council review. It is "Aquanova," submitted to the council on March 7, 2003 (North American Commission for Environmental Cooperation 2003a). Another factual record released April 24 responded to allegations that the United States did not effectively enforce the Migratory Bird Treaty Act when logging killed great blue herons and destroyed osprey nests in 1995 and 1996. Information on factual records is available at www.cec.org/citizen/.

6. These highlights are drawn from Gilbreath (2003).

7. See *Agreement on Environmental Cooperation between the Government of Canada and the Government of the Republic of Costa Rica* (2001) and *Agreement on Environmental Cooperation between the Government of Canada and the Government of the Republic of Chile* (1997).

8. *North American Agreement on Environmental Cooperation between the Government of Canada, the Government of the United Mexican States and the Government of the United States of America* (1992), annex 34, "Monetary Enforcement Assessments."

9. *Agreement on Environmental Cooperation between the Government of Canada and the Government of the Republic of Chile* (1997), annex 33, "Monetary Enforcement Assessments."

10. *Agreement on Environmental Cooperation between the Government of Canada and the Government of the Republic of Costa Rica* (2001), article 9, "Accountability for Effective Enforcement."

11. On November 16, 2001, the council instructed its secretariat to prepare factual records for five submissions. In four of those cases, the council limited the scope of the factual records, declining to approve broader reviews for complaints titled "Oldman River II (SEM-97-006)," "Aquanova (SEM-98-006)," "Migratory Birds (SEM-99-002)," "BC Mining (SEM-98-004)," and "BC Logging (SEM-00-004)" (respectively, North American Commission for Environmental Cooperation 2003e, 2003a, 2003d, 2003c, 2003b).

12. See North American Commission for Environmental Cooperation (2002c). Also see North American Commission for Environmental Cooperation (1999), "Methanex"; the June 30, 2000, update on this file states, "The Secretariat determined to proceed no further because the matter is the subject of a pending judicial or administrative proceeding."

13. For information on the air emission impacts of increased electricity production in the NAFTA region, see North American Commission for Environmental Cooperation (2002a). For information on toxic chemical releases in Canada and the United States, see North American Commission for Environmental Cooperation (2002d). For information on the most recent complaint by environmentalists against the U.S. government for failure to enforce migratory bird protection laws, see North American Commission for Environmental Cooperation (1999). For information on the most recent complaints by environmentalists against the Canadian government for failure to enforce wildlife laws in the logging sector, see North American Commission for Environmental Cooperation (2003b, 2002b).

14. For information on the most recent complaint by environmentalists against the U.S. government for failure to enforce migratory bird protection laws, see North American Commission for Environmental Cooperation (1999). For information on the most recent complaints by environmentalists against the Canadian government for failure to enforce wildlife laws in the logging sector, see North American Commission for Environmental Cooperation (2003b, 2002b).

15. Natural Resources Defense Council, Friends of the Earth, Defenders of Wildlife, and Center for International Environmental Law (2002).

References

Published and Photocopied Materials

Alanís Ortega, Gustavo. 2002. Public Participation within NAFTA's Environmental Agreement: The Mexican Experience. In *Linking Trade, Environment, and Social Cohesion: NAFTA Experiences and Global Challenges*, ed. John Kirton and Virginia Maclaren. Burlington, Vt.: Ashgate.

American Society of International Law. 2002. International Center for Settlement of Investment Disputes: *Waste Management, Inc. vs. United Mexican States. International Legal Materials*, 41 I.L.M. 1315. November.

BECC and NAD Bank (Border Environment Cooperation Commission and North American Development Bank). 2002. *Joint Status Report*, September 30; www.nadb.org/Reports/Joint_Report/english/status_eng.pdf.

DePalma, Anthony. 2001. Nafta Dispute Is in Court Once Again. *New York Times*, October 19, 1.

Dhooge, Lucien F. 2001. The Revenge of the Trail Smelter: Environmental Regulation as Expropriation Pursuant to the North American Free Trade Agreement; California MTBE Ban. *American Business Law Journal* 38, no. 3: 475.

Efe News Services, Spanish Newswire. 2001. Mexico-Ambiente: Advierten que sector forestal mexicano "ha tocado fondo." December 5.

Gilbreath, Jan. 2003. *Environment and Development in Mexico: Recommendations for Reconciliation, 2003*. Washington, D.C.: CSIS.

Jaimet, Kate. 2002. Loggers Insist They Obey Rules on Bird Habitat: NAFTA Panel Wants Canada to Answer Charge That 85,000 Nests Are Destroyed Every Year. *Ottawa Citizen*, February 27, 5A.

Jehl, Douglas. 2002. Saving Water, U.S. Farmers Are Worried They'll Parch. *New York Times*, August 28, 1.

Leatherdale, Linda. 2002. Greed Bad for Health; Electricity Deregulation Means More High-Polluting Coal Power Plants. *Toronto Sun*, June 19, 52.

Murphy, Dean E. 2003. In a First, U.S. Puts Limits on California's Thirst. *New York Times*, January 5, 1.

National Wildlife Federation. 2003. United States–Chile Free Trade Agreement Is Inadequate Model to Address Environmental Concerns. Press release, June 6. Available at www.insidetrade.com.

Natural Resources Defense Council, Friends of the Earth, Defenders of Wildlife, and Center for International Environmental Law. 2002. Letter to Ambassador Robert Zoellick: Environmental Provisions of the U.S.–Chile Free Trade Agreement. November 5, Washington, D.C. (photocopied).

New York Times. 2001. Central America Joins Mexican Regional Plan. June 16, 5.

North American Commission for Environmental Cooperation. 1996. Cozumel. Citizen Submissions on Enforcement Matters Database, submission SEM-96-001, January 17; www.ced.org/citizen/submissions/details/index.cfm?varlan= english&ID=32.

————. 1999. Methanex. Citizen Submission on Enforcement Matters Database, submission SEM-99-001, October 18.

————. 2000. BC Hydro. Citizen Submissions on Enforcement Matters Database, submission SEM-97-001, March 28.

————. 2002a. *Environmental Challenges and Opportunities of the Evolving North American Electricity Market, Secretariat Report to Council under Article 13 of the North American Agreement on Environmental Cooperation* (June). Available at www.cec.org/files/PDF//CEC_Art13electricity_Eng.pdf.

————. 2002b. Ontario Logging. Citizen Submissions on Enforcement Matters Database, submission SEM-02-001, February 6; www.cec.org/citizen/index. cfm?varlan=english.

————. 2002c. Submission Regarding Mexican Landfill Denied Factual Record. Press release, December 16, Montreal; www.cec.org/news/details/index. cfm?varlan=english&ID=2513.

————. 2002d. *Taking Stock 1999: North American Pollutant Releases and Transfers* (May); www.ce.org/files/PDF/POLLUTANTS/TSSummary99_EN.pdf.

————. 2003a. Aquanova. Citizen Submissions on Enforcement Matters Database, submission SEM-98-006, March 7.

————. 2003b. BC Logging. Citizen Submissions on Enforcement Matters Database, submission SEM-00-004, April 15; www.cec.org/citizen/submissions/details/index.cfm?varlan=english&ID=64.

————. 2003c. BC Mining. Citizen Submissions on Enforcement Matters Database, submission SEM-98-004, March 28.

————. 2003d. Migratory Birds. Citizen Submissions on Enforcement Matters Database, submission SEM-99-002, November 19; www.cec.org/citizen/submissions/details/index.cfm?varlan=english&ID=64.

————. 2003e. Oldman River II. Citizen Submissions on Enforcement Matters Database, submission SEM-97-006, April 17.

North American Development Bank. 2003. Infrastructure Project Database. Available at www.nadbank.org/english/projects/Infrastructure/infra_proj_frame. htm.

Organization of American States. 2003. Foreign Trade Information System database. Available at www.sice.oas.org/Trade/mex_e.ASP.

Orlando Sentinel. 2001. Mexico Losing Forests Fast. December 4, A-11.

Reuters. 2002. Mexico Sees 20-Year Effort to Clean Up Environment. *San Diego Union Tribune*, January 17, A-21.

Secretaría de Desarrollo Urbano y Ecología. 1992. Mexico: Environmental Issues. Fact sheets, Embassy of Mexico, Washington, D.C., September, 3–4.

Thompson, Ginger. 2001. Chasing Mexico's Dream into Squalor. *New York Times*, February 11, 1.

Weiner, Tim. 2001. Mexico Grows Parched, with Pollution and Politics. *New York Times*, April 14, 3.

World Bank. 1992. Staff Appraisal Report: Mexico Environmental Project. Washington, D.C., World Bank (photocopied).

World Bank Group and ICSID (International Center for the Settlement of Investment Disputes). 2003. ICSID Cases; www.worldbank.org/icsid/cases/cases.htm.

Legal Instruments

Agreement on Environmental Cooperation between the Government of Canada and the Government of the Republic of Chile. 1997. Signed February 6. Washington, D.C.: Organization of American States; www.sice.oas.org/TRADEE.ASP#canchi.

Agreement on Environmental Cooperation between the Government of Canada and the Government of the Republic of Costa Rica. 2001. Signed April 23. Washington, D.C.: Organization of American States; at www.sice.oas.org/Trade/cancr/English/enve.asp.

Environmental Cooperation Agreement between the United States of America and Mexico. 1983. Signed at La Paz, August 14. Web-based version of the document, Treaties and Other International Acts Series 10827, U.S. Mexico Border Program, U.S. Environmental Protection Agency; http://yosemite.epa.gov/oia/MexUSA.nsf/df4e4d197bb5eba886256bde006202d8/208f81d47fde81b9882566b10061cbc2?OpenDocument.

North American Agreement on Environmental Cooperation between the Government of Canada, the Government of the United Mexican States, and the Government of the United States of America. 1992. Signed December 17. Washington, D.C.: Organization of American States; www.sice.oas.org/trade/nafta/env-9141.asp.

United Mexican States. 2002. Ley federal de transparencia y acceso a la información pública gubernamental. *Diario oficial de la nación*, June 7, 3.

CHAPTER FIVE

LABOR REGULATIONS AND TRADE UNION CONVERGENCE IN NORTH AMERICA

Graciela Bensusán

Ten years after initiating negotiations of the North American Agreement on Labor Cooperation (NAALC), this chapter examines the agreement's main results as well as its repercussions on the strategies of regional labor unions. NAALC is a supplemental agreement to the North American Free Trade Agreement (NAFTA), whose effects on labor were much more modest than had been anticipated in that the potential to improve opportunities available to workers in the region was less than expected. Although the results of NAFTA have been much more positive in other areas, such as the significant growth of Mexican exports, it is indispensable to reflect upon changes that could promote a fairer and more equal distribution of the costs and benefits of integration, both in the formal agreement as well as in the policies, organizations, and labor institutions of each country. In this sense, the balance of achievements and limitations of NAALC have particular relevance as an international labor regulation arrangement parallel to NAFTA intended to translate the economic opportunities generated by the latter to an improvement in labor standards as well as living and working conditions for the participating countries.[1]

Although this objective was not met, among NAALC's main achievements was the creation of a basis for cooperation among governments for the resolution of labor problems, and the (admittedly unintentional) promotion of greater cooperation among trade unions and social organizations that fought for improved labor conditions—and has had a significant impact on the evolution of these organizations. In this respect, leaving aside some of the discrepancies that arose during the NAFTA negotiations, there exists today a relative convergence of labor standards in North America as a result of the changes experienced by labor organizations in the three member countries, many of which had their origin in the overall restructuring process of which the labor agreement formed a part. These changes have increased the possibilities for cooperation among labor organizations, and they should translate into a greater capacity of such organizations to shape the continent's integration process within the framework of the Free Trade Area of the Americas (FTAA).

To support and develop this argument, this chapter first examines employment, productivity, and salary trends in North America. Then the chapter analyzes the advantages and limitations of NAALC, bearing in mind both its objectives and the results achieved. Finally, the chapter discusses the principal changes experienced by the labor union movement, the strategies it has used, and the convergence of its positions and proposals in the face of advancing integration in the region.

THE IMPACT OF NAALC

It is difficult to establish which of the transformations in the labor realm have been a direct result of NAFTA, which have resulted from the broad economic restructuring that has taken place in the three countries over the past two or three decades, and which, if any, are simply a result of the economic cycle.[2] This chapter analyzes some of the tendencies more directly linked to NAFTA without establishing causal relationships between the above phenomena. Another factor to be taken into account is the fact that the opportunities generated by NAFTA coincided with the onset of severe financial crisis in Mexico in December 1994, a crisis from which Mexico was rescued thanks to the support of the United States in exceptional circumstances. Similarly, many of the advances (e.g., the increase in employment in the maquiladora industry) were hindered by the impact of the economic recession in the United States that began in 2000. Under these conditions, NAFTA has been credited with fostering economic dynamism, increasing trade, and maximizing productive advantages, although these effects are primarily concentrated in export companies and have generally not extended to the rest of the Mexican productive system, thus contributing to the country's vulnerability vis-à-vis fluctuations in the U.S. economy.[3]

As for the impact of exports in job creation, it should be noted that exporting companies generated only 25 percent of jobs created in Mexico between 1994 and 2001, representing 9.58 percent of national employment in 2001, suggesting that NAFTA by itself may not be able to solve our sluggish growth in this area, given the urgency of restructuring Mexico's internal market (INEGI 2002a, 2002b). In some industrial sectors, NAFTA's impact was considerable, whether as a result of plant transfers or the closure of uncompetitive plants. For example, between 1988 and 2001, employment in the transportation sector grew by an average of 2.35 percent annually in Canada, whereas it fell by 0.75 percent in the United States and grew by 9 percent in Mexico, the main beneficiaries being automobile-part assembly plants.[4] In the electronics sector, there was an annual average increase of 4.72 percent in Canada and 8.7 percent in Mexico (98 percent of jobs were created by the maquiladora industry), while the sector was stable in the United States. Finally, in the apparel sector, employment declined by 4.3 percent annually in the United States, while the rate was stable in Canada and grew by 10.5 percent in Mexico (ILO 2001). Also, in these sectors, particularly automotive and apparel, the greatest proportion of U.S. workers are registered with the NAFTA Transitional Adjustment Assistance Program, which is intended to provide training and to reinsert workers displaced by trade and industrial relocation (Campbell et al. 1999).

Employment in the manufacturing sector as a proportion of the employed population diminished between 1988 and 2001 both in the United States (1.71 percent) and in Canada (0.65 percent), which may have been due to the global tendency toward using third parties in manufacturing as well as to commercial policies and the impact of regional integration. In contrast, Mexico's manufacturing sector employment increased by 31.8 percent. It is worth noting that a significant change has taken place in the composition of manufacturing employment in Mexico, in that the maquiladora industry grew by 84.5 percent in the period whereas employment in the manufacturing industry declined by 3.5 percent.[5]

However, the gains in manufacturing employment diminished with the onset of the U.S. recession of 2000, as evidenced by the loss of more than 25,000 jobs in the manufacturing sector between January 2001 and October 2002, and a total of 212,448 jobs (16.2 percent) lost in the maquiladora industry. In addition to these losses, it is important to acknowledge that the quality of the employment generated in this industry is low; even though salaries in this sector have increased at a greater rate than those in the manufacturing industry since 1997, in

2001 salaries in the maquiladora industry were 60 percent of those being paid in the manufacturing sector (IMSS 2002; INEGI 2002a,
2002b). Whereas in Canada and the United States, average salaries in
manufacturing were stable in the second half of the 1990s, Mexico witnessed a drop of 5 percent in that period (1994–2001).

Consequently, the gap that existed when NAFTA came into effect has
widened instead of narrowed; seven years after the implementation of
NAFTA, Mexican manufacturing salaries went from $2.10 an hour ver-
sus $11.7 an hour in the United States to $1.90 an hour versus $13.80 an
hour in the United States, a trend that was mirrored in relation to Canadian salaries (INEGI 2000a, 2000b). At the same time, labor power
productivity in Mexican manufacturing grew by 34.1 percent, more
than in the other two countries (although obviously starting from lower levels). All this translated into a greater reduction of unit costs of
labor power in Mexico—31 percent between 1993 and 2001—but in
Canada and the United States this share was less than 15 percent (INEGI
2000a, 2000b, 2002a, 2002b).

These statistics may be explained by the limited capacity of Mexican
trade unions to translate productivity growth into proportional salary
improvements, which was partly due to institutional restrictions that
prevented the revitalization of trade unions, as has been demonstrated
in comparative studies of the maquiladora industry and in the majority of complaints presented within the NAALC framework (Bensusán
and Reygadas 2000); the latter will be dealt with in the next section.
What is important to underscore is that although U.S. and Canadian
trade unions saw greater productivity increases than salary increases in
the manufacturing industry, profitable business opportunities to attain higher earnings from productivity growth are much greater in
Mexico.[6]

Although the deterioration of real salaries of lower-income workers
in the United States seemed to confirm the fear that this was the result of
trade with a less-developed country with lower salaries (Lee 1999), the
fact is that this tendency predated NAFTA and tended to reverse itself in
the second half of the 1990s, even though the losses experienced by lower-income groups between 1987 and 1996 have not been totally recovered (Mishel and Bernstein 1994).

RESULTS OF NAALC

The experience of NAALC offers proof of the few opportunities and numerous limitations of the agreement in its current state to achieve the objectives and challenges associated with the expansion and strengthening of labor unions within the NAFTA framework. These limitations are partly the result of an insufficient presence of trade union organizations from Canada, Mexico, and the United States in the NAALC negotiations as well as the difficult balance that must be achieved in this area in order to gain the approval of the U.S. Congress. U.S. legislators considered the demands of NAFTA opponents (including the AFL-CIO, nongovernmental organizations, and Democratic legislators) and the resistance of the U.S. Chamber of Commerce and Republican legislators, along with the Mexican government, its trade union allies, and businesspeople, to the inclusion of anything that would condition free trade (Bensusán 1994). In the United States, President Bill Clinton calmed fears that marked labor asymmetries—mainly low salaries in Mexico—would negatively affect the U.S. workforce.

Having been resisted by the governments of the other two countries, which sought to avoid any external interference in this matter of Mexican labor standards constituting a threat to U.S. jobs, the prospects for the creative use of a labor agreement to influence the course of employer–employee relations in North America became all the more somber with the victory of a Republican presidential candidate in 2000. Even so, the near simultaneous alternation in the Mexican presidency weakened the resistance to pursue a deeper integration in several areas, including the free circulation of workers and compensatory funds for the weaker economies. A conservative administration linked to a business viewpoint stymied the possibility of improving the opportunities for independent trade unionism in Mexico. This group took advantage of loopholes in NAALC to frustrate the most frequent violations of workers' rights that impeded trade union renewal. As experience has demonstrated, at the end of almost a decade of failed efforts, NAALC practically fell into disuse.

NAALC's Accomplishments

NAALC boasts accomplishments in three main areas: (1) the high degree of institutionalization of labor agreements between countries with marked economic, political, and labor asymmetries; this is considered "the first non-unilateral form of a social clause" which links free trade and compliance with national legislation; (2) the creation of institutions and procedures for monitoring, cooperation, and conflict resolution; and (3) the effective participation of labor unions and social organizations in these procedures through the submission of claims related to the violation of labor rights (Dombois 2002, 5). Other accomplishments include the scope of the 11 labor standards recognized in the agreement, the opportunities to identify basic points in compliance with national legislation, and the absence of requirements for groups to present violation claims (Verge 2002).

NAALC's Limitations

The meager results of NAALC can be explained by problems in the agreement's design and implementation that have been manifest throughout its existence. Eight among them are particularly worth noting.

First, there is no intent to harmonize workers' rights, which allows each country to maintain its respective comparative advantages. In the face of arguments against the agreement, ranging from the strictly commercial nature of NAFTA to the defense of national sovereignty, NAALC aimed exclusively at strengthening national labor regulations.[7]

Second, under the pretext of defending sovereignty, NAALC member countries reserve the right to establish and amend their own labor standards without being required to create independent agencies or organizations with true supranational powers to supervise national authorities in the enforcement of these laws and regulations.[8] Consequently, it is incumbent on the national authorities—many times those responsible for the violations—to guarantee in each country the existence and effectiveness of "high labor standards consistent with high quality and productivity,"[9] which for various reasons are not fully guaranteed internally in either Mexico or in the United States.[10]

Third, even though NAALC's objectives are broad and are centered on promoting cooperation, the exchange of information, and compliance with labor regulations in each country, there were no effective mechanisms established to promote cooperative solutions to conflicts of interest among labor organizations and employers of the region (Bensusán 2000).

Fourth, in addition to NAALC's restricted potential to punish labor violations, the agreement is further constrained by weaknesses in the patterns and strategies of interaction between governmental and nongovernmental actors. This is compounded by restrictions on the powers of the trinational secretariat, contradictory objectives, mutual mistrust, obstructionism on the part of the governments, and expectations by social organizations and labor unions weakly tied to the objectives of the NAALC (Dombois 2002).

Fifth, restrictions on protecting the 11 NAALC principles limit the application of sanctions to only three cases (child labor, minimum salaries, and safety and hygiene standards in the workplace) and leave collective labor rights—those violated with the greatest frequency—unprotected. Furthermore, there is no mechanism to form expert committees or arbitration panels in the latter cases.

Sixth, the slowness of the arbitration process allows violations to remain unpunished.[11] According to one estimate, a complaint can take 6 to 8 weeks to be accepted and another 26 weeks for its first review. Afterward, ministerial consultations, when recommended, can take more than 30 weeks; in one case they took an entire nine months (Daamgaard 1999).

Seventh, there was a lack of adequate incentives—such as material compensation or the possibility to adopt common solutions from which all may benefit—to encourage government cooperation with NAALC objectives and generate significant changes in its policies and practices. In all fairness, however, NAALC was conceived with an inclination toward monitoring compliance with a series of labor standards and not toward creating a broader agenda or coordinated labor policies to the benefit of the three countries.

Eighth, an equally adverse factor is the procedural disparity in each National Administrative Office (NAO) to study claims or communications presented by the public. Whereas in the United States and Canada a meticulous examination of the situation under examination is made, in Mexico the review process is much more general (Bensusán 1994; Dombois 2002; Verge 2002).

Outcomes of the Claim Process

With regard to NAALC's most contentious dimension—the resolution of controversies (complaints, ministerial consultations, expert committees, arbitration panels, and sanctions)—NAOs have received a total of 25 complaints, most of which dealt with violations of the right of association in the Mexican assembly industry.[12] The evolution in the number of complaints (4 in 1994, 1 in 1995, 2 in 1996, 3 in 1997, 10 in

1998, 2 in 1999, 1 in 2000, 2 in 2001, and none in 2002) demonstrates the loss of interest by trade union organizations in Mexico and United States in testing the effectiveness of this instrument, mostly due to disenchantment with the unsatisfactory results obtained in the early cases, although occasionally a case attracted media interest and international public attention.[13] Indeed, one case was ultimately withdrawn by the denouncing organization, United Electrical (UE), of the United States to protest the inefficiency of NAALC procedures (Damgaard 1999).

Nevertheless, the number of organizations supporting these complaints gradually increased. There was also an increase in the level of detail with which these organizations described alleged violations, and the content of claims filed expanded to include other NAALC principles, such as the violation of safety and hygiene standards, prevention of risks and professional diseases, discrimination in the workplace, and protection of migrant workers. All of this was the result of apprenticeship among organizations in the three countries, which constitutes a necessary step to raising the profile of the regulatory organization.[14]

In 1998, NAALC became more dynamic because of the intensification of transborder labor union cooperation, and this translated into a significant increase in the number of complaints filed. Although accusations of labor violations in the United States were rather important insofar as they demonstrated that such irregularities were not limited to Mexico,[15] there was not a single case in which expert committees undertook evaluations, nor was there much prospect for imposing sanctions for violations of labor standards. Besides, repeat violations and inconsistency in the recommendations did little to address the question of reparations for damages caused to workers. In addition, the lack of interest on the part of the new U.S. administration in clarifying the issue of workers rights ended up reducing the credibility of NAALC, even though Mexican organizations continued to see the possibility of using the agreement to draw attention to irregularities in the regulatory process (Dombois 2002).

The distribution of the total number of complaints by country from 1994 to 2001 supports the initial assumption that Mexico is the country with the greatest challenges in complying with labor laws (16 complaints), followed by the United States (7 complaints) and Canada (2 complaints). It should be clarified, however, that the low number of complaints in Canada may not be the exclusive result of greater compliance with labor legislation but instead due to the fact that this instrument has been ratified by only four provinces, given the provincial jurisdiction of labor legislation in Canada.[16]

To date, none of the cases has gone beyond the first procedural review (ministerial consultations) of the complaint,[17] nor has a single case created sufficient pressure to generate voluntary revision of national labor legislation.[18] This demonstrates that the instrument is virtually useless in solving conflicts of interests between companies and workers in the region. This can be explained by the fact that the governments of the three countries are more interested in avoiding repercussions from labor-violation-related decisions from affecting their mutual relationships. NAALC is still received very differently in each of the countries, as evidenced during the Clinton administration, which was more interested in the contentious dimension of this instrument than its value.[19]

Among the meager short-term positive results of NAALC, the following deserve mention:

- a commitment on the part of Mexican labor authorities to implement a public registry of collective contracts and the adoption of practices ensuring the secrecy of the vote to determine labor union preferences (although they have yet to comply);

- the imposition of a fine by Mexican authorities against a company (Hang Young) the day after submission of a claim alleging violations to safety and hygiene standards (in addition to others relating to union elections and the existence of a "protection contract");

- the requirement for pregnancy tests in Mexican maquiladoras has been reduced if not eliminated entirely;

- the elaboration of a manual on labor legislation in the three languages; and

- the reduction in the practice of denouncing a worker's migratory status by work inspectors in the United States (Verge 2002, 122).

Experience shows that in addition to the aforementioned results, a practice has been created to build transnational solidarity networks to better understand and monitor the consequences of NAFTA, the underlying integration model, and the corresponding systems of labor relations, especially in their more problematic aspects. The ability to disseminate information to the general public regarding legislation and practices in each country has been enhanced; previously, claims were filed only by victims and their local legal counsels (Herzenberg 1998; Compa 1998; Damgaard 1999; Robinson 1999; Dombois 2002). In addition, the three countries have pooled their organizational skills and competencies despite strong competitive pressures, laying the groundwork for lasting alliances between trade unions and NGOs to deal with transnational corporations and governments of the region in the area of labor standards (Compa 1998; Haathaway 2002b).

Another consideration is the disproportionate importance assigned to NAALC by trade unions in each of the three countries. For example, it is evident that American trade unions and organizations constituting the "new unionism" in Mexico, Sindicatos de Telefonistas de la República Mexicana (STRM) and the Frente Auténtico del Trabajo (FAT), among others, have been the most active, even though today the former union is more disillusioned than the latter regarding the usefulness of NAALC. This is due to discrepancies in the expenses and time invested in the dispute-resolution process and the meager results achieved to date. In addition, the fact that the only participation formally recognized by NAALC is the presentation of claims (other forms of cooperation are largely ignored) erodes NAALC's legitimacy and may ultimately lead to its complete ineffectiveness (Dombois 2002).

It must also be considered that the application of NAALC not only favored new forms of reconciliation but also altered traditional alliances between Mexican and U.S. trade unions. For example, the relationship between the AFL-CIO and the Confederación de Trabajadores de México (CTM) today is of a much lower profile, due in part to the denunciations implicating affiliated trade unions. From the outset, both CTM and other organizations linked to the Congreso de Trabajo (LC) opposed the adoption of regional labor regulations with supranational powers, sanctioning capacity, and the intention to harmonize national laws. These groups were affected by the cohesiveness provided by the U.S. organization to independent trade unionism. Even after the political transition in Mexico in December 2000, the members of the LC continued to show little interest in the progress of the agreement. In the case of CTM, a single case, supported by the Mexican government, was filed for violations committed in the United States against the labor conditions, discrimination, and risks faced by migrant workers. This situation represents a significant difference with other cases of claims in the United States and Canada, where conflicting interests tend to origi-

Table 5.1. Main Characteristics of the 25 Claims Filed under the North American Agreement on Labor Cooperation, 1994–2002

Characteristic	Country of Violations		
	Mexico	United States	Canada
Total denunciations[a]	16 cases	7 cases	2 cases
Main reason	Right of association violations	Violations of rights of migrant workers	Right of association violations
Petitioners from more than one country	11 cases	4 cases	2 cases

Source: Author's data.

[a] Some of the denunciations were about the same case.

nate within the same labor union movement, instead of within or to the benefit of the employer, as was the case Mexico (table 5.1).

Cooperative Activities

Cooperative activities have been centered primarily on comparative research and seminars on a range of topics, including labor markets, labor legislation, the relationship between income and productivity, and difficulties in trade union organization.[20] These exchanges brought to light circumstances that were previously unfamiliar to the public with regard to labor legislation in the other member countries, such as the precarious existence of collective rights in the country with the largest economy in the world.[21] Without denying the importance of the results achieved (as was the case with the investigation into business closures linked to the exercise of the free right of association or the inquiry into the main indicators used to evaluate the labor market; CCL 1997), to date there has been little progress toward correcting or rectifying such deficiencies, nor has there been progress in the adoption of policies and regional mechanisms to discourage or sanction labor violations, improve the opportunities for trade union formation, reduce salary asymmetries, or jointly solve fundamental problems such as those of Mexican migrant workers in the United States.

As occurred with NAALC's dispute-resolution dimension, cooperative activities were intense in the first year (more than 15 activities were performed) and have declined in subsequent years. It has been estimated that almost half of the cooperative activities (about 50 total) dealt with the themes of health and social security (Verge 2002).

Proposals for Change

The negative appraisal of NAALC's results has given rise to numerous reform proposals from trade unions and social organizations. These proposals were intended to strengthen the instrument by recognizing collective rights, adopting more efficient procedures, and increasing the participation of society in the dispute-resolution process.[22] Five years after its creation, NAALC underwent consultations designed to assess the opinion of labor unions and organizations of the effectiveness of the instrument. Indeed, one of the conclusions of a meeting between the labor ministers of the three countries was the partial recognition of the instrument's limitations in this area, pointing out the need to "strengthen the cooperation mechanisms established by the Agreement itself" without taking into account the weaknesses of the dispute-resolution mechanisms. Whereas Mexico took this opportunity to state its intention to foster cooperation in matters related to migrant labor, the United States expressed concern about whether or not integration would benefit all citizens equally.[23]

Meanwhile, groups such as FAT and Red Mexicana de Accion Frente al Comercio (RMALC) that had questioned this model of integration and underlined the limitations of NAALC from the beginning reaffirmed their objections and requested a revision of the agreement. Their major proposals included the following:

- harmonize labor laws in North America and guarantee their effective compliance, taking into account the more important International Labor Organization (ILO) conventions and beginning with their ratification by the three countries;

- allow for surveillance of compliance with labor legislation and establish specific sanctions for offending companies, considering the violations a form of unfair competition and disrupting commercial flows of companies that engage in this type of behavior;

- incorporate the 11 labor principles as a substantive part of NAALC in the chapter on dispute resolution and sanctions;

- include NAALC within NAFTA; and
- guarantee social participation in NAALC.[24]

From the perspective of the unions making these proposals, the possibility to advance workers' rights depends on the strengthening of trade unionism in the region, which in the Mexican case presupposes the democratization of the Mexican trade union movement. This objective depends, in turn, on the reform of labor legislation to eliminate corporate loopholes to achieve a labor justice system independent of the executive branch, and to facilitate international membership in Mexican labor organizations. Similarly, it is noted that the transnational space created by NAALC must be taken advantage of to present joint denunciations and to propose changes to the agreement, as well as to strengthen alliances in the fight for the democratization and expansion of the trade union movement, to develop exchanges at the sector level, and to design common strategies.

Coinciding with the FAT approach, in a document presented to the president of AFL-CIO in 1998, the Federación de Sindicatos de Empresas de Bienes y Servicios (FESEBS) advised that procedures established in NAALC were not consistent with its broad objectives and proposed the renegotiation of the agreement with the input of representatives of workers from the three countries. International oversight of labor regulations would be fundamental. The negligent conduct of Mexican authorities would constitute the main concern of labor organizations.

Finally, it is important to point out that workers from the three countries should lobby for freedom of transit for migrant workers in the region through the signing of a collective agreement designed in consultation with labor representatives from the three countries. To achieve the effective renegotiation of the agreement, the formation of a representative commission been proposed.[25] With the exception of the Mexican Electricians Union, organizations associated with FESEBS and organizations that took part in the creation of the National Workers Union in 1998 (to which FAT also belongs) have recently prioritized the question of how to reform Mexican labor legislation without abandoning their interest in strengthening NAALC.

In Canada, the Canadian Labor Congress (CLC) and the Canadian Action Network have concerned themselves primarily with questioning the negotiation of NAFTA and with pursuing the inclusion of a social clause in the General Agreement on Tariffs and Trade. In paying greater attention to the limitations of NAALC, these groups seek to strengthen the conventions of the ILO. In turn, the francophone centers (Quebec Workers Federation, the National Trade Union Confederation, the Quebec Education Central, and the Quebec Coalition) shifted from an initially favorable position on NAFTA to questioning the sufficiencies of NAALC, ultimately opposing both instruments.

When the Quebec Network was subsequently created with the Continental Integration (1994), its actions were oriented toward achieving the inclusion of social and labor regulations in NAFTA and the extension of these principles to other countries engaging in FTAA talks. A statement from this network in 1995 at the International Conference about Social Dimensions contained 10 points to be considered at any negotiation for continental integration. One of those points referred to the inclusion of a charter on labor rights and norms based on ILO conventions. The intention was to make NAALC more comprehensive as well as to establish a mechanism to monitor and impose sanctions in cases where violations were not properly addressed. Similarly, it proposed incorporating clauses to protect the rights and of migrant workers and to support Mexico in reducing its debt. It must be pointed out that the aim of this proposal was also to achieve the broad societal participation (including the popular sector, women, trade unions, and business organizations) in negotiating any hemispheric agreement (Robinson 1999, 152, 153).

In this vein, Canada's anglophone trade unions aimed to promote the integration of a social dimension in trade agreements to a continental level. It was considered that compliance with NAALC ought to be required from any new NAFTA signatory, and that it would be replaced in the future by compulsory social clauses designed to prevent the downward harmonization of labor standards in the region. One model to consider was the European Union's model, which required broad participation of social actors. Although this model has been presented several times, a concerted effort has not yet been made to take advantage of NAALC in its present form. The CLC maintains a neutral position on the question of the agreement's ratification, probably due to the lack of enforcement of workers' rights. Nonetheless, this group sends representatives to participate in various forums organized in the United States and Mexico in order to maintain its relationships with labor unions in both countries with which it actively participates in building the social dimension of continental integration (Robinson, 1999, 157).

REPERCUSSIONS FOR LABOR UNIONS

Throughout the 1990s, the position of North America's trade unions toward the adoption of trade agreements experienced significant changes in the direction of increased convergence. North American trade unions tempered the protectionist views opposed to commercial liberalization and regional integration, and they channeled their energies into a search for viable alternatives. Another factor that contributed to greater convergence were the simultaneous changes within the U.S. trade union movement and within important sectors of the Mexican trade union movement. The conservative business strategies of trade unionism and state corporatism were abandoned and replaced by the socially dominated trade union movement in Canada, which was centered on the rejection of neoliberal policies, the inclusion of broad sectors of society, and the mobilization and creation of broad social networks (Bensusán 2002).

With the exception of Mexican trade unions, which were traditionally loyal to the government (which demonstrates scarce interest in coordinating social efforts to influence the direction of regional and continental integration), there has been a relative recuperation of activism in trade unions and a greater orientation of unionism toward social organizations through joint participation in diverse forums and protests against the globalization process. From Seattle (November 1999) to Porto Alegre (2001, 2002, and 2003), protests have been gaining momentum both in terms of participation and effectiveness, having benefited from some material resources from U.S. and Canadian unions and from other social organizations from these countries.[26]

Trade Unions in the United States

Following the AFL-CIO's failure to block Congress's authorization to the president for fast-track negotiating of NAFTA in 1991, an opportunity opened up with the triumph of the liberal candidate Bill Clinton in the 1992 presidential elections. There was no longer an outright rejection of the commercial instrument but rather a request that the new president not submit the agreement to Congress for approval without mechanisms to avoid a decline in regional development supported by low salaries. Trade unions that had argued against the agreement on the grounds that it would lead to job loss due to the relocation of companies to low-wage countries, or competition from products originating in

those countries, found that their open protectionism had not produced positive results (Botto 2000, 6).

U.S. trade unionism at the time had been weakened by a decade of
Republican governments practicing labor policies that neglected workers' collective rights and the antiunion strategy of companies and corporations. The fight against the NAFTA integration model was
undertaken by the Industrial Trade Unions Department of the AFL-
CIO, an important aspect of trade unionism that aims to revamp organizational strategies to regain strength in the new context of regional
integration and globalization (Robinson 2000b).

One of the most important resources of organized labor, along with
the increase of funds for organizing campaigns, was the construction of
networks with other social organizations opposed to the signing of the
agreement (environmentalist, human rights, and other groups). The
intention was to increase the capacity to apply pressure and to generate
an opinion in American society that was favorable to the demands represented by these groups. In this manner, the position of trade unions
was improved and the balance of power within the AFL-CIO was affected; the faction that opposed NAFTA within the AFL-CIO earned the
presidency of the organization in 1995 and proposed a significant ren-
ovation of its power resources (Robinson 2000b). As part of that strategy, American trade unions softened their traditional protectionist
tradition in opposition to NAFTA and sought better relationships with
Canadian and Mexican trade unions. This was done in an attempt to
jointly propel the revision of NAFTA and to replace it with a more efficient instrument in defense of workers' rights. Likewise, successful efforts achieved the unionization of migrant workers in the U.S. service
sector. In February 2000, the AFL-CIO took a step forward in this direction when it proposed a radical change to the migration policy of
the United States, calling for the government to declare an amnesty and
equal rights for those who work illegally in the United States (Hathaway 2000b, 20).

The greatest AFL-CIO contribution toward the reorientation of
trade policy in the United States has been the effort of several social organizations to change the course of the proposed FTAA. Following the
first Miami Summit in 1994, many social organizations demanded the
inclusion of the following provisions: strong labor regulations, mechanisms to prevent artificially depressing salaries; and an understanding
of the consequences of capital relocation. President Clinton's request to

Congress to negotiate fast-track negotiating authority for trade agreements was not even put to a vote in 1997, and it was not presented again
during his presidency. This was due to the importance of the AFL-CIO
in election years (1998) as well as to the rigidity of government resistance in Mexico to the renegotiation of NAALC, which would have expanded its scope and sanctioning power, interested as it was in
maintaining its comparative advantage in wages (Osorio 1998). Nevertheless, following the fateful events of September 11, 2001, President
Bush was finally able to get Congress to approve the fast-track negotiation of trade agreements. This has created new expectations among the
proponents of FTAA and has disillusioned its opponents.

Canadian Trade Unions

When NAFTA was negotiated, Canadian trade unionism was in a better position than both of its neighbors to the south because it had more
favorable legislation recognizing individual rights for workers and offering better guarantees to exercise collective rights, all of which contributed to greater unionization. Although the political situation at
the federal level was not any better than that of the American unions,
the New Democratic Party, a traditional ally of the CLC, regained provincial power, thus avoiding further weakening of Canadian trade
unions. Another favorable factor was the broad support of Canadian
society for the country's critical position against economic policies that
could negatively affect social well-being. Many maintained serious res-
ervations regarding the processes of commercial opening (Robinson
2000a).

   In addition, Canadian unions sought to create alliances with other
organizations opposed to NAFTA, coordinating their efforts through
the Canadian Action Network. For Canadian unions, the threat not
only came from Mexico but also from the United States, although in the
United States there were fewer protections for individual and collective
labor rights. Participation by Canadian unions in international forums allowed them to articulate a coordinated strategy in opposition
to trade opening. The exchange of information was constant, as was the
case with the Common Borders forum of 1989. This organization carried out studies on the possible impact of the trade agreement on the
Mexican economy and on relationships between Canadian and Mexican companies, primarily in the maquiladora industry. During the
NAFTA negotiations, Common Borders attained renewed importance,

helping to promote a more internationalist orientation on the agreement within Canadian unions and adopting a favorable position toward the search for alternatives to the neoliberal model (Robinson 2000a). However, the CLC did not wish to take part in the NAALC negotiations, which in turn impeded its ability to join forces with NGOs in the United States and Mexico that sought to improve the scope and efficiency of the labor agreement (Robinson 2000a).

Trade Unions in Mexico

Unlike Canada and the United States, Mexican trade unionism is linked to the government. LC and CTM, the organizations with the greatest membership, supported the government's discourse in favor of NAFTA.[27] The labor unions' primary concern was to avoid the parallel labor regulations sought by President Clinton and the AFL-CIO. This could endanger its economic privileges as well as its recruitment process. In this manner, although LC sent a representative to participate in the advisory committee of the Mexican government, it did not have any influence upon the final terms of NAFTA. It could, however, affect the scope of NAALC to its benefit. The Mexican government accepted this condition because it coincided with the interests of exporting firms in the country, which opposed the development of an independent trade union (Bensusán 1994).

Alternatively, another faction of Mexican unionism under FESEBS (created in 1992 to defend workers from the privatization process of state enterprises) maintained a pragmatic position, supporting NAFTA in exchange for the inclusion of guarantees of respect for labor rights and mechanisms to mitigate the agreement's negative effects on workers. This was done through albeit marginal participation in the networks forged by opponents to the trade agreement; such as FESEBS. Some of the members of FESEBS, including the Sindicatos de Telefonistas de la República Mexicana, established alliances with their employers to seek the conditions favorable to delaying the opening of telecommunications sector to international competition, a goal that was of mutual benefit (Sánchez 1998).

The group most opposed to the NAFTA negotiations was a minority faction of Mexican union organizations. This group, which was on the far left of the political spectrum, included the Frente Auténtico del Trabajo,[28] a small organization that was close in principle to the Canadian unionism, openly questioned the government's position on trade liberalization, and took part in intense activity to consolidate a broad social network opposed to the model of integration agreed upon by the governments. FAT pointed out that instead of solving them, NAFTA would accentuate the structural problems in the Mexican economy and its asymmetries vis-à-vis the other two countries. FAT did not oppose NAFTA openly but insisted on the need to seek alternatives, regulate the social aspects of integration, and strengthen bonds with trade unions in Canada and the United States.

The changes experienced by Mexican trade unions in 1997, when the National Union of Workers (UNT, after its name in Spanish) was formed in a merger of LC, FESEBS, and independent union members that characterized themselves as having greater autonomy and higher internal democracy levels, which translated into a greater convergence of their positions, greater international activism, and more favorable conditions for transnational cooperation. It must be pointed out that UNT's formation occurred in an environment of great economic instability, when the effects of the 1994 financial collapse were still being felt and after the death of Fidel Velázquez, CTM's legendary leader.

Since then, UNT has led an intense campaign to denounce the existing restrictions to expanding its membership both in terms of legislation and implementation. In addition to seeking reform of labor legislation in Mexico and active participation in the search for international solidarity to defend its trade union interests, UNT has taken advantage of NAALC's mechanisms; it recently allied itself with the peasant movement to bring about a revision of NAFTA in anticipation of the opening of the agricultural sector the following year (*Reforma*, January 14, 2003).

It is important to explain the importance of international alliances and regulatory instruments for independent unionism. Even since the signing of NAFTA and the political transition in Mexico, there have been substantial difficulties in putting an end to the corporatist trade union regime. This is due to the presence of strong institutional restrictions as well as an environment of state corporatism, against which both the new president, proceeding from the National Action Party, as well as the traditional trade union leadership, proceeding from the Institutional Revolutionary Party, continue to be aligned.

Continental Integration and Convergence

As a member of RMALC,[29] FAT has sought to demonstrate the limitations of NAFTA and subsequently those of NAALC. Despite its small size and the limited material and institutional resources at its disposal, FAT—thanks to its traditional autonomy and previous international experience—has become a force both inside and outside the country in the fight for an alternative model of global and regional integration. It is pertinent to add that FAT's presence in this fight reduced the scrutiny of the AFL-CIO and CLC.

Similarly, through RMALC, FAT took an active role in evaluating NAFTA's impacts and in the formation and development of the Continental Social Alliance, which aimed to prevent an FTAA constitution under a limited integration model and offered an instrument to propose alternatives.[30] The document prepared by this alliance was meant to promote debate and consensus as well as to educate the participants in the need to build viable alternatives to FTAA. Because it is a product of the collective efforts of hundreds of individuals and social organizations in the region, it is the most comprehensive such document available on the subject matter. The ability to pursue a continental integration model with greater scope and with increased concern for possible social impacts hinges on the ability and willingness to follow the patterns offered by the European Union.[31] Democracy and social participation in decisionmaking constitute one of its guiding principles, giving a special place to the most oppressed and vulnerable groups and leaving behind closed negotiations among government and corporate elites. Citizen participation is seen as a requirement to control transnational companies whose activities cannot be supervised exclusively by government action. Aside from reforming multilateral institutions—principally the United Nations—the importance of the nation-state is taken up again, as well as its responsibility to fulfill the social and economic requirements of its citizens.

In November 1999, just before the fifth trade ministerial meeting of FTAA negotiations, a union forum was held; it was called Los Trabajadores/as contra el Área de Libre Comercio de las Américas (Workers against FTAA). The Organización Regional Interamericana organized the forum, in which the most important unions of the region participated. This organization requested that all trade negotiations and regional integration processes include social, labor, and environmental dimensions. At this meeting, the AFL-CIO representative demanded that trade ministers acknowledge the presence of the labor forum as a permanent interlocutor in FTAA negotiations in recognition of the irreversible character of globalization. This position was backed by the president of the CLC, who underscored that union organizations must demand inclusion of basic rights for workers in commercial agreements.

In parallel with the union forum, other civil society organizations united under the Continental Social Alliance sought a forum to strengthen coordination mechanisms among organizations and social movements in the region with the intent of bringing greater stability, endurance, and influence to the organization in the continental integration process. Participating organizations were able—with the support of the government of Canada—to hold a meeting with trade ministers, during which they requested the creation of more efficient channels for citizens to take part in the integration process. Although only modest results were achieved, it was an unprecedented step in commercial negotiations to date (RMALC, *Revista alternativas*, no. 24, March–April 1999, 13, 14).

Transnational Union Cooperation

With the approval of NAFTA, the defense of labor rights in Mexico became a fundamental criterion in the defense of American and Canadian standards of living. The recognition by the AFL-CIO that problems of collective action were not unique to Mexico and the need to take advantage of the modest resources offered by NAALC compelled the AFL-CIO to collect more precise information of labor systems in the three countries. This contributed to greater convergence through the formation of diverse alliances that strengthened the capacity of its members to file complaints and stage protests. In this respect, cooperation in this area predated the signing of NAFTA. In 1987, the National Union of Farm Workers and the AFL-CIO's Organizing Committee of Farm Workers aligned to counteract pressures from American companies, which threatened the transfer of jobs to Mexico should unions continue to demand higher salaries.

This type of antiunion behavior expanded in the United States following the signing of NAFTA. Guarantees for capital mobility were increased, making corporate threats about business closures more plausible, as was demonstrated in a study commissioned by the NAALC Labor Cooperation Commission in 1997.[32] Another factor that helped increase cooperation was the fear that the NAFTA integration model would be extended to other countries, as had occurred in the case of the free trade agreement signed between Chile and Canada.

In 1998, an AFL-CIO delegation made its first visit to Mexico in 50 years. The new president, John Sweeney, led the delegation. Sweeney established agreements between the AFL-CIO and the newly created UNT to work together to revise NAALC and, in particular, to develop common strategies on the organizations' policies on migrant workers. The meeting prompted the establishment of an AFL-CIO Solidarity Center in Mexico. The organization follows the evolution of the Mexican labor and union situation and organizes joint activities with the different sectors of union organizations. One such activity supported the creation in 1998 of the Instituto de Estudios del Trabajo (Institute for Labor Studies) in Mexico, which is made up of academics and union members devoted to supporting Mexican unions with research projects in their interest.

It is pertinent to point out that the AFL-CIO's position on the existing disputes within trade unionism in Mexico was different from that held by Canadian union organizations. Although the AFL-CIO maintained its relationship with CTM, this connection cooled with the growing connection of that organization to UNT and its cooperation in violation denunciations regarding the right of association in Mexico under the NAALC framework.

Transnational cooperation not only affected labor unions but also had a "multidimensional" character that included environmental, human rights, and gender organizations (Treillet and de la Vega 2000, 192). The protests that have taken place throughout NAFTA's history have used different strategies, including coordinating simultaneous pressures on companies in the region (e.g., strikes in automotive companies and in other sectors),[33] taking advantage of NAALC mechanisms to demonstrate its limitations, the linkage between unionism and the reform of trade agreements and NAALC, and, more broadly, criticizing the path of the current globalization process.[34]

CONCLUSIONS

Experience indicates that labor asymmetries will persist and that neither NAFTA nor NAALC has fulfilled its objective of improving living and working conditions in the region. NAALC has not coerced the Mexican government to level the playing field among the different union options, though it does constitute a requirement for a true representative trade union movement and the need for more strict application of the present regulations. In this sense, Mexican opposition to the inclusion of a labor clause in NAFTA and other trade agreements and safeguards against the artificial lowering of salaries and the absence of true union formation is being exposed as a short-term and inadequate strategy. This is due to the fact that, while internal pressures for political democratization, increased transparency, and better compliance with existing regulations in the labor realm will continue, internationally Mexico will always be exposed to competition from countries such as China, where basic workers' rights remain unprotected and where no regulatory instruments have been put in place to allow workers to defend themselves.

It is also evident that the solutions to the structural problems afflicting the most fragile member economy will not come simply from an increase in exports in the absence of efforts to expand the domestic market as an engine for economic growth. This goal, essential for Mexico as well as for the other two countries, depends to a great extent on the possibility of increasing domestic consumption by establishing a close link between real salaries and productivity. This in turn would require strengthening workers' rights and unionism in countries or sectors where these mechanisms are most fragile or where they have deteriorated as a result of competitive pressures.

It is worth noting that although there is more evidence today than in the past of Mexico's problems in comparison with the other two countries, the precariousness of workers' rights in the United States deserves greater attention than it currently receives in trade negotiations. This is so because of the fact that if there are no convincing signals of any significant commitment to those rights in the country with the largest economy in the world, it will be very difficult to expect progress in other Latin American countries. The low profile of individual labor regulations in the United States and the difficulties in advancing collective negotiation do not make demands for greater compliance with workers' rights in less-developed countries particularly actionable or credible, whereby creating political conditions favorable to the reform of those regulations ought to be at the center of the U.S. agenda. Also, UNT has greater clarity with regard to the need to seek substantive reform of Mexican labor legislation as a requirement to achieve the improvement of labor rights and their effective compliance.

Trade unions have experienced important changes in the three countries. They have expanded their agendas and increased opportunities for cooperation. However, significant adjustments to national and regional institutional frameworks are required to further increase the effectiveness and facilitate greater participation of social actors in shaping the integration process. Expectations for a deeper integration depend to some extent on the ability of North American unions to recover lost ground in the context of greater competitive pressures, which would permit them to add their proposals to those of the governments and other interested parties in the area of deepening trade agreements.

The advances achieved in this direction should not be overlooked and, contrary to the many predictions of an impending state of crisis for the unions of the region, NAFTA's contribution to this process cannot be denied. However, there are also disheartening signs that continue to compromise these perceived accomplishments. The greatest danger comes from companies threatening workers who seek to unionize, collective contracting simulation practices in Mexico, and limitations on unionism in each country—all of which prevent many from taking advantage of the favorable conditions which, in the political and economic realm, would permit their strengthening.

Finally, it must be pointed out that all efforts oriented toward a broader integration occur in an adverse scenario marked by the slowness of U.S. economic recovery from the impact of September 11, 2001, and the beginning of war against Iraq. In a similar context, the political symmetry achieved with the alternation of the Mexican presidency in December 2000 and a turn in the country's foreign policy in favor of a new relationship with the United States centered on the adoption of an immigration agreement and a request for funds to support structural adjustment in the weakest economy. These efforts have not produced the desired results. For this reason, it is fundamental to underscore the importance of promoting greater participation by unions and social organizations interested in changing the course of integration in the three countries and in removing the obstacles that the governments have not been able or do not intend to overcome so that the benefits of integration can be extended to the most diverse sectors of society.

Notes

1. Preliminary and partial versions of this work are in Bensusán (2002a, 2002b).

2. The author thanks Jorge Horbarth, professor, Facultad Latinoamericana de Ciencias Sociales, Mexico City campus, for his cooperation in updating the information related to this section.

3. Dussel (2000); Tockman and Martínez (1997). Mexican exports increased by 160 percent between 1994 and 2001, while world exports reached 19 percent and the increase of foreign direct investment was 165 percent. Mexico became the second provider of goods and services to that country, and 67.6 percent of Mexican imports came from the United States and 88.6 percent of Mexican exports were shipped to the United States (U.S. Department of Commerce 2002). See chapter 1 of this book by Sidney Weintraub and the analysis by Borja (2001).

4. According to Carrillo's definition (1994, 31) by maquiladora industry manufacturing plants, devoted to the assembly or manufacture of components and/or raw material processing as intermediate or final products using to a great extent imported raw materials or components almost exclusively for export markets.

5. ILO (2001); INEGI (2001a, 2001b). Another important change is the relocation of assembly industries by moving or by installing them in nonborder states; whereas 90 percent of plants were located on the border in 1990, according to data from INEGI, this share was reduced to 77.4 percent by 2000.

6. The gap between salary increases and productivity in Canada translated itself into a salary loss of 10 percentage points during the 1980s and as much in the 1990s (equivalent to roughly half of that experienced by Mexico), which cannot have originated exclusively with the impact of commercial agreements, but rather on account of the greater pressure exerted in the 1980s upon salaries for greater international competition (Robinson 2000a, 2000b).

7. Concerning the main arguments stated in Mexico against the adoption of an agreement with greater scope and capacity to sanction violations to labor rights in the northern part of the continent, see Bensusán (1994).

8. The reluctance of governments to transfer regulating or punishing power to a supranational organization in the field of labor relations is due to the fact that it is a very sensitive theme because it expresses social power and political relationships, configuring an "area of protected sovereignty from outside interventions, which might question internal social commitments, liberate conflicts or change power relationships" (Dombois 2002, 24).

9. ACLAN (NAALC), *Diario Oficial de la Federation*, December 21, 1993.

10. In Mexico, the labor regulation model is statist and corporate, which, joined to the fragility of democracy, leaves a broad discretional margin to the executive to apply labor laws. On the contrary, the U.S. model is liberal and individualist, and this means a low protection profile of labor laws and a prominent role of employers to avoid collective negotiation from working conditions. Even if differences are substantial, the results are similar favoring employers: prevalence of unilateralism in determining these conditions (Bensusán 2000).

11. See an evaluation of the first three years applying LCANA in Verma et al. (1999).

12. Both in denunciations (also known as public communications) and the ministerial consultations refer to the 11 NAALC principles. In this respect, there is a possibility to verify the protection laws offered to each of them, the suitability of government or administrative measures to apply said laws, existence of administrative recourses, quasi-judicial or appropriately judicial as well as the procedural guarantees destined to its exercise and about access to public dissemination of pertinent legislation (articles 1 to 8 of NAALC).

13. Conflicts connected with the right of association in Mexican maquiladoras, protected by NAALC principle 1, gave rise to most of the denunciations. Linked to this principle, the Sony case—in which the workers wanted to form a trade union apart from the central trade union supported by the government and transnational companies—was presented in 1994. It gained great notoriety and gave rise to the adoption of a tripartite cooperation program for workers dismissed for labor union activities. Similarly, it gave rise to the start of a study of the role of labor courts in cases of firing for this reason, having recommended the beginning of ministerial consultations (in June 1995), which will be continued in public seminaries where national procedures were analyzed for recognition by labor unions. Independent experts made also a specific study about labor union registration procedure according to Mexican legislation. Other similar denunciation cases culminated in the signature of an interdepartmental agreement, promoted by NAO in the United States in May 2000, and that three years on continues unfulfilled, whereby the Mexican government should implement a collective contract registration system, promoting their knowledge (to put an end to "protection" simulation contracts that benefit employers by protecting them from a true unionization) and installing transparent and impartial secret voting procedures in inter–labor union disputes. See Verge (2002, 119).

14. A detailed account of all alliances forged among these organizations in the cases of General Electric, Honeywell, Echlin, Itapsa, Congeladora del Rio, and others can be found in Hathaway (2000b).

15. The Sprint case, tabled before the Mexican NAO resulting from a denunciation presented in 1995 for illegal firing of workers who tried to form a labor union, gave rise to a study by Cornell University, in keeping with instructions from the departments of labor of the three countries, in order to know the effects of sudden closure of companies, especially about the right of association. The study demonstrated that Sprint's behavior in the company known as "Family Connection", in closing down its installations during a labor union organization campaign, was a well-used practice and that NAFTA had created an appropriate climate for such practices. See a synthesis of the result of the study in Verma et al. (1999, 131 ff.).

16. A detailed analysis of these rules, contained in annex 46 of NAALC, can be seen in Robinson (1999, 131 ff.).

17. In 12 of the 25 cases presented, some ministerial consultations were recommended.

18. It has been pointed out, however, that on one occasion, the threat from several Canadian organizations to denounce the Alberta government's inaction to privatize surveillance and application of labor laws in that province stopped the measure Robinson (1999, 112). Likewise, a change in practices has been observed in Mexican maquiladoras, by having stopped requiring a nonpregnancy condition as a contracting requirement.

19. Dombois (2002). In this respect, it has been held that intergovernmental relationships move in this area between conflict and "low intensity" or "halfway" cooperation, with a high dosage of mutual suspicion, refraining from going beyond bilateral consultations and action programs limited to realizing seminars and informative meetings, all of which contrasts with aspirations of NGOs and trade unions presenting the complaints.

20. In connection with this last point, the study relating to threats of business closures as a maneuver to avoid trade unionism, where the increase of this practice was documented in the United States following NAFTA coming into effect (CCL 1997). Another contribution was the comparative summary about the manner in which national legislation regulates the 11 NAALC principles (Verge 2002).

21. An excellent report from Human Rights Watch (2000) documents the reprisals thousands of workers are subjected to for their wish to join or form a trade union in the United States, establishing that both in law and in practice there is an "impunity culture," which, paradoxically, that country has failed in assuming its responsibility to protect workers rights when it demands it from other countries as a condition to enter into bilateral agreements. The examination of cases under study permits to conclude that U.S. laws and practices allow an "irregular advantage" to employers, calling for more effective laws to ensure that all workers in the United States have freedom of association.

22. A summary of the main proposals for change put forth by FAT and RMALC can be found in Luján (1999).

23. In connection with the ministerial meeting, see RMALC (1998).

24. These mechanisms would be the plural and demographic participation of social organizations in the Commission for Labor Cooperation; creation of National Labor Commissions with trade union participation to ensure compliance with labor standards; creation of a Regional Labor Commission formed by the government and social organizations for the elaboration and implementation of salary recuperation programs and for training of NAFTA displaced workers, and expansion of functions and the role of the Advisory and Evaluation Committees provided for in NAFTA for them to play a real function in sup-

port and compliance and surveillance of labor norms in the region (Luján 1999, 176).

25. Document presented by FESEBS to AFL-CIO in Mexico, January 23, 1998.

26. The Porto Alegre World Social Forum (Foro Social Mundial de Porto Alegre) had the greatest calling capacity, when more than 100,000 activists from more than 120 countries met. During its last meeting, held in January 2003, there were representatives of most Latin American trade unions and two presidents (*La jornada*, January, 23, 2003).

27. Whereas CTM had 476,751 members in 2000 in 353 organizations belonging to federal jurisdiction, UNT counted a total of 326,367 members in 25 organizations, and this gives an idea of the greater size and importance of the latter (Bensusán 2000; Bensusán and Alcalde 2000a, 2000b).

28. FAT was founded in 1960 resulting from the international solidarity of several farming and cooperative European and Latin American organizations near the Catholic church; it is made up by farming and cooperative organizations. Since the 1970s, it has broken its links to the church, although FAT's relationship with European and Canadian organizations (mainly from Quebec) was strengthened. At the present time, it has close to 30,000 members, of which only a third are salaried workers. The history and development of this organization are given in Hathaway (2000a, 2000b).

29. RMALC was formed April 11, 1991, as a coordinating venue for organizations and persons interested in influencing economic cooperation and integration processes. The incorporation of an environment and social agenda within NAFTA and the adoption of compensation funds are RMALC's basic claims (RMALC 1996, 1–15; RMALC 1997, 189–98).

30. At the second summit of hemispheric presidents and chiefs of government held in Santiago in April 1998, an action plan was approved that included precise goals and mechanisms to progress in the continental trade opening, and a social agenda that included a commitment to protect the rights of migratory workers and to promote forming civil society organizations as well as dialogues and alliances among governments and civil society (RMALC, *Revista alternativas*, September–October 1998, 29). The Summit of Peoples of the Americas was held in parallel, in which RMALC took part. See, in this connection, *Revista alternativas*, published by RMALC, especially its issue number 24, March–April 1999.

31. An initial version of a document entitled "Alternative for the Americas" was prepared during the Summit for the Peoples of the Americas, in Santiago, April 1998. More than 30 people from eight countries cooperated in writing the first draft, which was presented at the Forum on Socioeconomic Alternatives for the Americas of the Summit of Peoples and at other similar gatherings, leading to a second draft of the document (RMALC, *Revista alternativas*, September–October 1998).

32. The 1991 agreement between United Electrical and FAT, which gave rise to numerous meetings and joint organizational activities, like that held in 1992 in the telecommunications sector among STRM, CWA, and the Communications Electrical Workers of Canada, which also constituted important antecedents for transnational cooperation (Treillet and de la Vega 2000, 195).

33. The 1996 strike by the UAW against the General Motors plant in Dayton, Ohio, paralyzed 26 plants and 180,000 workers in the three countries. Another strike against General Motors in Michigan not only paralyzed the plant where the strike occurred but also six more U.S. assembly plants, along with 30,000 workers in Mexico and 15,000 in Canada (Cook 1998).

34. Cook (1998, 196). The UE–FAT alliance, having combined these strategies for a decade, achieved positive results by permitting the latter to establish links with several unions in the United States and Canada, which enabled it to increase its understanding of the labor Mexican situation and to lay the basis for the political fights taking place in the three countries (Hathaway 2000b, 7). One of the alliances was between a Mexican labor organization—UNT—and the Coalition Pro Justice in the Maquiladora (an NGO particularly active in the border area) to strengthen trade union action in this important economic activity, where more than 1 million Mexican workers are employed, and where low-salaried jobs prevail, with strong labor insecurity and extended forms of unionism simulation.

References

Bensusán, Graciela. 1994. Entre candados y dientes: La agenda laboral del TLCAN. *Revista perfiles latinoamericanos* 4 (Facultad Latinoamericana de Ciencias Sociales, Mexico City).

———. 1999. Integración regional y cambio institucional: La reforma laboral en América del Norte. In *Estándares laborales después del TLCAN*, ed. G. Bensusán. Mexico City: Plaza y Valdés.

———. 2000. *El modelo mexicano de regulación laboral*. Mexico City: Plaza y Valdés.

Bensusán, Graciela, and Arturo Alcalde. 2000a. Estructura sindical y agremiación. In *Trabajo y trabajadores en el México contemporáneo*, ed. Graciela Bensusán and Teresa Rendón. Mexico City: Porrúa.

———. 2000b. El marco jurídico del trabajo. In *Trabajo y trabajadores en el México contemporáneo*, ed. Graciela Bensusán and Teresa Rendón. Mexico City: Porrúa.

Bensusán, Graciela, and Bodil Damgaard. 1999. Estándares laborales y distribución del ingreso en su relación con el comercio. *Revista integración y comercio* 4 (INTAL/BID, Buenos Aires).

Bensusán, Graciela, and Luis Reygadas. 2000. Relaciones laborales en Chihuahua: Un caso de abatimiento artificial de los salarios. *Revista mexicana de sociología* 62, no. 2: 29–57.

Bensusán, Graciela, and Landy Sánchez. 2002a. Efectos Laborales del TLCAN. In NAFTA in The New Millennium, ed. Edward Chambers and Peter Smith. San Diego: USMEX Press.

———. 2002b. Estrategias sindicales en América del Norte. Paper presented at a seminar of the Programa Interinstitucional de Estudios de la Región de América del Norte, COLMEX.

———. 2002c. La experiencia del ACLAN: Posiciones de los sindicatos, ponencia presentada al 4° Congreso Regional de las Américas. Paper presented at the 39th annual meeting of the Asociación Internacional de Relaciones de Trabajo and Asociación Canadiense de Relaciones Industriales, Toronto, June 25–28.

———. 2003. La dimensión laboral de los procesos de integración el TLCAN– MERCOSUR. In *Políticas públicas de trabalho e renda na América Latina e no Caribe*, ed. Aytor Fausto, Marcela Pronko, and Silvia C. Yannoulas. Brasília: Abaré and Facultad Latinoamericana de Ciencias Sociales.

Borja, Arturo, ed. 2001. *Para evaluar al TLCAN*. Mexico City: Porrúa.

Botto, Mercedes. 2000. Civil Society Participation in Regional Integration Processes. Unpublished manuscript, Facultad Latinoamericana de Ciencias Sociales, Buenos Aires.

Campell, Bruce, et al. 1999. *Labour Market Effects under CUFTA/NAFTA*. Employment and Training Paper 29. Geneva: International Labor Organization. Available at www.ilo-org.

Carrillo, Jorge. 1994. *Dos décadan de sindicalismo en la industria maaquiladora de exportación: Examen de las ciudades di Tijuana, Juárez y Matamoros*. Mexico City: Porrúa.

CCL (Comisión para la Cooperacíon Laboral). 1997. *Cierre de emprasas y derechos laborales*. Washington, D.C.: CCL.

Compa, Lance. 1998. El acuerdo laboral paralelo del TLCAN: Un recuento de tres años. In *Estándares laborales después del TLCAN*, ed. Bensusán Graciela. Mexico City: Plaza y Valdés.

Cook, María. 1998. Estrategias sindicales en la industria automotriz. EEUU, Informe final de investigación, proyecto CONACYT-PRIAN. Unpublished manuscript, Estrategias Sindicales en el TLCAN, Mexico City.

Damgaard, Bodil. 1999. Cooperación laboral transnacional en América del Norte a finales de los noventa. *El cotidiano* 94.

De La Garza, Enrique. 2000. *El sindicalismo mexicano ante la transición política*. Mexico City: Trabajo y Democracia Hoy, Cenpros.

Dininio, Phyllis. 1992. North American Free Trade Agreement: Free for Whom? Boston: Harvard Business School Press.

Dombois, Rainer. 2002. ¿En el camino hacia relaciones laborales internacionales? El caso del ACLAN y los problemas de la regulación laboral internacional. *Revista latinoamericana de estudios del trabajo*, 44.

Dussel, Enrique. 2000. *Polarizing Mexico: The Impact of Liberalization Strategy.* Boulder, Colo.: Lynne Rienner.

Hathaway, Dale. 2000a. Allies across the Border: Mexico's Authentic Labour Front and the Global Solidarity. Cambridge: South End Press.

————. 2000b. Transnational Support of Labour Organizing in México: Comparative Cases. Paper prepared for Latin American Studies Association meeting, Miami.

Herzenberg, Stephen. 1998. El ACLAN y el desarrollo de una alternativa al neoliberalismo. In *Estándares laborales después del TLCAN*, ed. G. Bensusán. Mexico City: Plaza y Valdés.

Human Rights Watch. 2000. Unfair Advantage. New York: Human Rights Watch.

ILO (International Labor Organization). 2001. *Yearbook of Labor Statistics 2001.* Geneva: ILO.

INEGI (Instituto Nacional de Estadística, Geografía e Informática). 2000a. *Encuesta industrial mensual.* Mexico City: INEGI.

————. 2000b. *Estadística de la industria maquiladora de exportación.* Mexico City: INEGI.

————. 2001a. *Encuesta industrial mensual.* Mexico City: INEGI.

————. 2001b. *Estadística de la industria maquiladora de exportación.* Mexico City: INEGI.

————. 2002a. *Encuesta industrial mensual.* Mexico City: INEGI.

————. 2002b. *Estadística de la industria maquiladora de exportación.* Mexico City: INEGI.

Lee, Thea. 1999. Los sindicatos frente al TLCAN. In *Estándares laborales después del TLCAN*, ed. G. Bensusán. Mexico City: Plaza y Valdés.

Luján, Bertha. 1999. Los sindicatos frente al TLCAN. In *Estándares laborales después del TLCAN*, ed. G. Bensusán. Mexico City: Plaza y Valdés.

Mayer, Frederick. 2001. Juego de dos niveles: Las negociaciones del TLCAN. In *Para evaluar al TLCAN*, ed. Arturo Borja. Mexico City: Porrúa.

Mishel, Lawrence, and Jared Bernstein. 1994. *Is the Technology Black Box Empty? An Empirical Examination of the Impact of Technology on Wage Inequality and Employment Structures.* Washington, D.C.: Economic Policy Institute.

Osorio, Víctor. 1998. *Agenda social y libre comercio en las Américas.* Mexico City: Red Mexicana de Accion Frente al Comercio.

Ramírez, Juan Carlos. 2001. Los efectos del TLCAN sobre el comercio y la industria de México. In *Para evaluar al TLCAN*, ed. Arturo Borja. Mexico City: Porrúa.

RMALC (Red Mexicana de Accion Frente al Comercio). 1996. *Cinco años de lucha.* Mexico City: RMALC.

———. 1997. Espejismo y realidad: El TLCAN cinco años después. Mexico City: RMALC.

Rendón, Teresa, and Carlos Salas. 2000. La evolución del empleo. In *Trabajo y trabajadores en el México contemporáneo*, ed. Graciela Bensusán and Teresa Rendón. Mexico City: Porrúa.

Robinson, Ian, 1999. El ACLAN y el Movimiento Sindical Canadiense. In *Estándares laborales después del TLCAN*, ed. G. Bensusán. Mexico City: Plaza y Valdés.

———. 2000a. National Level Analysis, Canada. Informe final de investigación del proyecto estrategias sindicales frente al TLCAN. Unpublished manuscript, CONACYT-PRIAN, Mexico City.

———. 2000b. National Level Analysis: United States of America. Informe final de investigación del proyecto estrategias sindicales frente al TLCAN. Unpublished manuscript, CONACYT-PRIAN, Mexico City.

Sánchez, Landy. 1998. *Entre la apertura comercial y la transición política: La estrategia del Sindicato de Telefonistas de la República Mexicana.* Mexico City: Tesis de Maestría en Ciencias Sociales, Facultad Latinoamericana de Ciencias Sociales.

Silverstein, Jeff. 1993. *A Nation Undecided: Canada Thinks Twice about NAFTA,* U.S. Latin Trade. Mexico City: No publisher.

Tockman, Víctor, and Daniel Martínez. 1997. Costo laboral en el sector manufacturero de América Latina. In Costos laborales y competitividad en América Latina, ed. Edward Amadeo et al. Lima: Organización Internacional del Trabajo.

Treillet Stéphanie, and Xavier de la Vega. 2000. Vers des stratégies syndicales transnationales. In *Le syndicalisme dans la mondialisation*, ed. Annie Fouquet et al. Paris: Editions de l'Atelier and Editions Ouvrièr.

U.S. Department of Commerce. 2002. *Second Government Report 2002.* Washington, D.C.: U.S. Government Printing Office.

Verge, Peter. 2002. *Presentación analítica del ACLAN.* In Dimensión social de la globalización y de los procesos de integración, ed. Juan Somavía et al. Lima: Organización Internacional del Trabajo.

Verma, Anil, et al. 1999. Haciedo el libre comercio más justo: La evolución en la
proteción del los direchos laborales. In *Estándares laborales después del TLCAN*,
ed. G. Bensusán. Mexico City: Plaza y Valdés.

PART THREE

GOVERNMENTAL AND PRIVATE LINKS

THE FUNCTIONING OF NAFTA AND ITS IMPACT ON MEXICAN–U.S. RELATIONS

Rafael Fernández de Castro

January 1, 2004, marked the tenth anniversary of the North American Free Trade Agreement (NAFTA). Several events were held to commemorate what has been, without doubt, a major milestone in the bilateral relationship between Mexico and the United States. During the past 10 years, a great deal of information has been generated and ample time has passed to assess NAFTA's impact, and, not surprisingly, several studies dealing with various aspects of the agreement have appeared.

The studies on NAFTA can be grouped into three basic types depending on their focus. The first and most abundant type analyzes NAFTA's direct impact on the Mexican and American economies. These studies cover such issues as the increase in trade between the two nations; how the composition of this trade has changed over time; and the agreement's impact on the various sectors of the economy and on employment figures.[1] The second type of study deals with the indirect impact of free trade, especially in noneconomic fields such as the environment, culture, and even the political system. These works analyze the unintended consequences of free trade that range from the way in which income distribution has been affected to the differences in regional development that have emerged since NAFTA was signed. These studies also analyze the effect of free trade on the transition to democracy in Mexico.[2] One could also include within this second group some studies that criticize NAFTA, albeit with varying degrees of analytical rigor, and that tend to focus on its noneconomic effects. These criticisms include claims of the loss of sovereignty and the erosion of the capacity of nation-states to confront the negative effects of free trade and globalization that have resulted from the agreement.

The third type of study, by far the least abundant of the three, focuses on issues that generally have not been frequently analyzed, including such topics as NAFTA's operating procedures; how the institutional arrangements envisioned by the agreement have evolved over time; and what effect the negotiation and implementation of NAFTA has had on Mexican policy toward the United States and on the bilateral relationship as a whole.[3]

This chapter focuses on this last point and attempts to answer two related questions. First, how well have the institutions created to manage and monitor NAFTA worked over the past 10 years? And second, how has NAFTA affected Mexican policy toward Washington and the bilateral relationship as a whole? This second question has to do with the spillover effects of free trade into other areas of bilateral relations and, in particular, with the way in which the two governments interact and deal with the various topics that make up the rich and complex bilateral agenda.

To answer these two questions, this chapter is organized in three basic sections. The first section contains an assessment of NAFTA's institutional framework that analyzes the original intentions behind these arrangements and how they have evolved over the past 10 years. The second section looks at how Mexican policy toward the United States has changed as a result of NAFTA and, in particular, highlights the efforts made by the Mexican government to institutionalize the bilateral relationship through the creation of formal structures, working groups, commissions, mechanisms, and institutional agreements so as to better manage what became an increasingly complex relationship. The third section outlines a series of recommendations for the improvement of bilateral relations in the context of the security concerns that have emerged since the terrorist attacks of September 11, 2001.

OPERATION AND EVOLUTION OF NAFTA'S INSTITUTIONAL FRAMEWORK DURING THE PAST TEN YEARS

Cooperation between countries requires an institutional structure, which is usually based on existing governmental organizations but often rests on institutions set up for a specific purpose. NAFTA operates through a combination—a skeletal structure established especially for NAFTA but placing most reliance on three-country intergovernmental decisions. NAFTA does not have the elaborate, and often supranational, decision-making process that exists in the European Union.

Original Intentions

The philosophy behind free trade in North America was, from the beginning, different from the one that gave birth to the European Union. In sharp contrast to the Old World, where economic integration was, in many ways, a stepping-stone to political integration, in North America all that was desired was economic integration, and one governed by market forces. As a result, from the start of the negotiations in 1991, two fundamental decisions were made that would have a profound effect on NAFTA's institutional framework: The agreement would only be a free trade agreement; and government involvement would be kept to a minimum. The institutional model that emerged was thus the antithesis of the European one. There was no customs union, and no complex supranational institutions were created.

Sidney Weintraub, one of the intellectual fathers of free trade in North America, has argued that behind the conscious decision to keep to a minimum the institutional framework surrounding NAFTA was an "abhorrence of creating new institutions" shared by both the U.S. executive branch and Congress.[4] This initial American preference found an echo in the Canadian and Mexican governments. Indeed, one could claim that all three countries shared two concerns regarding NAFTA's future institutional framework—to minimize the impact on national sovereignty and the cost of running the agreement—which severely restricted the options analyzed during the negotiations.

Given the basic asymmetry between the United States, on the one hand, and Mexico and Canada on the other,[5] it is important to single out Washington's attitude with respect to NAFTA's institutional framework. Paradoxically, the sovereignty issue, that is, the capacity of every country to decide key issues for itself, although a concern shared by all three governments, was more important to the Americans even though their country was by far the most powerful. The basic question that seemed to be in every American negotiators' mind when discussing issues ranging from the possible mechanisms for the resolution of disputes to the creation of a commercial secretariat was "Why should we compromise our decisionmaking capacity given the relative weakness of Mexico and Canada?"

This somewhat narrow-minded attitude of the United States is clearly reflected in chapter 19 of NAFTA, which deals with the resolution of disputes and is one of the most important chapters as far as NAFTA's institutional framework is concerned. The Americans decided that in the event of having to interpret the various clauses relating to unfair competition—antidumping and countervailing duties—each country should apply its own laws. In other words, there was no attempt to develop common legislation, North American norms and regulations, and a standard operating procedure with regards to disputes, but rather each country was left on its own to do as it thought fit.

This idea that each country should follow its own norms and regulations was, in general terms, the formula adopted with regard to all agreements and institutions of NAFTA. For example, the spirit behind the parallel labor and environmental agreements is precisely that each country should apply its own laws. As a result, these agreements are no more than a simple mechanism that allows others to make sure that each country properly applies the relevant national legislation. In short, from the beginning the attitude of all three countries was to design a minimal institutional framework so that only those institutions that were strictly necessary would be set up.

In order to assess how the institutions created by NAFTA have worked and evolved during these first ten years, it is worth bearing in mind the neoliberal institutionalist tenets of how states relate to each other. Institutionalists claim that there can only be cooperation among states if and only if they have shared interests and the outcome of such cooperation is more beneficial than that of unilateral action. In this way, coordination or cooperation between states is a rational strategy adopted by particular states to achieve their goals.[6]

According to Robert Keohane, one of the main theorists of interdependence, an offshoot of neoliberal institutionalism, international organizations and institutions are no more than a series of permanent and interconnected rules that restrict and mold the conduct of actors within the international system. As far as the economist Douglas North is concerned, institutions are any and all forms of restrictions developed by humans as they interact (North 1993). One of the basic premises behind this perspective is that there are degrees of institutionalization of interstate relations. The greater the level of institutionalization, the more likely the behavior of the respective states is to reflect the established norms. Given this premise, an international convention represents the lowest form of institutionalization, because it consists solely of implicit rules. International regimes represent an intermediate level, because as they consist of negotiated rules between states that regulate the activities of international actors in given areas or topics. It is at this level that NAFTA operates. Finally, the most advanced level of institutionalization, according to Keohane, is to be found where an international institution operates through a bureaucracy with specific rules and tasks assigned to particular individuals or groups within the organization (Keohane 1983, 4–5). Clearly, the three countries involved in the NAFTA negotiations never considered this higher level of institutionalization.

According to Keohane's classification, NAFTA is a type of trilateral commercial regime. The three countries involved decided to structure their commercial activities in accordance with the text of an agreement. In contrast to the parallel labor and environmental agreements that have secretariats, NAFTA's free trade commission does not have a secretariat or any formal trilateral bureaucratic organization. In 1997 it was decided that the commercial secretariat should not be opened in Mexico City, though it should be noted that the creation of such a secretariat did not form part of the agreement. Rather, it was an informal "gentleman's agreement" among the three countries to balance the distribution of the new institutions created by NAFTA: The United States would house the secretariat for the North American Agreement for Labor Cooperation, the secretariat for the Environmental Agreement would be based in Canada, and Mexico would provide a home for the commercial secretariat. However, during the first two years of NAFTA's operation, the commercial authorities of the United States did not have the necessary resources to open an office in Mexico City. By the time that the U.S. Congress had authorized the required funds, the Mexican government had decided not to create the secretariat in question because, they argued, it did not have clear objectives and specific tasks, while the mere keeping of all the documents relating to the agreement did not justify a new trilateral bureaucratic organization.[7]

In a recent study of the effects of international institutions and regimes on environmental cooperation among states, Hass, Keohane, and Levy (1994, 12–17) provide a list of three criteria that can be used to judge how well NAFTA has worked as an international regime and whether it truly has had a positive impact on the conduct of the three countries involved. The three criteria are

- an increase in the interest shown by governments in the relevant issues;
- a decrease of transaction costs and levels of uncertainty for key players; and

■ an improvement in the government's capacity to make decisions.

Government Interest

The negotiation of NAFTA obviously raised the level of interest in free trade shown by all three governments. As far as the Mexicans were concerned, it became the main foreign policy objective during the administration of Carlos Salinas de Gortari (1988–94). For the U.S. administration of George H.W. Bush (1989–92), the agreement also became a key foreign policy initiative. Thus, Robert Zoellick, the then undersecretary for economic affairs at the State Department, has claimed that the reunification of Germany, NAFTA, and the Uruguay Round became the three core components of U.S. foreign policy during the Bush presidency. And because NAFTA was not sent to Congress during the Bush administration but was pushed through under President Bill Clinton, both Mexico and the ratification of NAFTA became top priorities for the Clinton administration from the beginning. Indeed, this continued interest in Mexico during Clinton's first term, as well as the familiarity and trust among government officials from both countries that was built up during this time, are key factors that help explain why Clinton, notwithstanding significant opposition from Congress, took a historic step and put together a financial rescue package of an unprecedented magnitude to help Mexico through its severe economic crisis at the beginning of 1995 (Lustig 1998).

When Vicente Fox (December 2000) and George W. Bush (January 2001) both took office simultaneously (as happens every 12 years), the relationship between Mexico and the United States again reached a high point. One should here recognize that Fox's ambitious proposal of working toward a North American Economic Community that would further integrate the three countries had NAFTA as its backdrop. The apparent novelty of the proposal consisted in a "deepening" of free trade in North America and an improvement in the terms of integration, adding a labor component to the agreement, and making the United States (and, to a lesser extent, Canada) partly responsible for the development of Mexico's more backward regions where most of the migrants to the North came from.

However, the terrorist attacks of September 11 abruptly put an end to this "special relationship" between Fox and Bush. The highly propitious international environment at the end of the 1990s took a sudden turn at the beginning of the present millennium and the United States

under Bush entered a kind of neo–Cold War, though this time confronting an enemy—Islamic terrorists—that was far more elusive than
the Soviet Union. As a result of this changed environment, disenchantment on both sides soon set in: Fox believed that the White House had
not kept its word as far as working toward an migration agreement;
and Bush was never able to understand Mexico's unwillingness to support the position of the United States in the UN Security Council with
regard to Iraq (Fernández de Castro 2002, 111–129; Fernández de Castro and Rozental, forthcoming).

What is relevant in all this for the present analysis is that it is clear
that NAFTA does not have an internal or intrinsic capacity to keep the
three governments working toward a deepening of free trade in the region, especially when facing a highly adverse international environment such as the one that emerged after the September 11 attacks.
NAFTA's lack of institutional autonomy is clearly evident and sorely
missed at a time when the Mexican, U.S., and Canadian heads of government appear to have banished the creation of a North American
Economic Community from their list of priorities.

Transaction Costs and Uncertainty

To understand the way NAFTA has reduced transaction costs and the
level of uncertainty for key players—exporters and importers and the
commercial authorities of both the United States and Mexico—requires
bearing in mind the difficulties that the bilateral commercial relationship faced five years before negotiations for a free trade agreement. In
1985, Mexico had the dubious honor of being the country with the
highest number of proceedings in the United States initiated against it
for unfair trade practices. From 1980 to 1986, Mexico accumulated 27
petitions of countervailing duties and antidumping. With NAFTA,
notwithstanding the fact that trade between the two countries has
greatly increased, the number of such proceedings has significantly decreased. Thus, in a study of the use of trade remedies, Beatriz Leyceguí
and Mario Ruiz Cornejo show that even though Mexico was the United
States' second most important commercial partner in 1997, it occupied
the eighth place in a list of countries that had *peticiones* from the United
States (Leycegui and Ruiz Cornejo 2002, table 1).

Until the unilateral adoption of lower trade barriers by the Mexican
government in 1985–86, its commercial relationship with the United
States, its main trading partner, was anarchic and confrontational.

Since 1950, when the 1943 Economic Complementarity Agreement expired, the Mexican and American governments did not have a single instrument that governed the commerce between these two countries, except for the textile agreement of 1975. Moreover, given that Mexico was not then a member of the General Agreement on Trade and Tariffs (GATT), it is understandable that trade between these two nations was chaotic. And, not surprisingly, this state of affairs led to constant problems and confrontations. As a result, the increase in Mexican exports to the United States that resulted from the economic crisis of the early 1980s helped by a highly favorable exchange rate, encountered both greater protectionism disguised as accusations of unfair practices, or new forms of protectionism such as the Voluntary Export Restriction Agreements imposed on Mexican steel in 1985 and 1989.

In sharp contrast to this situation, NAFTA established a detailed regulatory scheme that defined the obligations assumed by each country in close to 300 articles distributed in 22 chapters and several appendixes. In other words, NAFTA contains a highly detailed legal framework that seeks to eliminate the discretionary power of the executors of the agreement, establishing the procedures that should be followed to avoid confrontations. In this way, NAFTA has effectively diminished the level of uncertainty and considerably reduced transaction costs. With few exceptions, the countries involved know how to behave and can predict how their counterparts will conduct themselves.

Admittedly, NAFTA did not create a central body responsible for the operation of the agreement. A Free Trade Commission exists, which supposedly is the highest authority, but is nothing more than the meeting of all three secretaries of commerce, who must get together for a regular session at least once every year. Nevertheless, to further develop and fine-tune certain topics covered by the agreement and establish permanent channels of communication, NAFTA created committees and working groups for practically all its chapters.[8]

Moreover, during the first years of its operation, four further working groups were created: government purchases, antidumping and countervailing duties, investment and services, and emergency actions. Even though the responsibilities and purpose of each committee and working group varies depending on the area with which it deals, practically all of them directly supervise a specific aspect of NAFTA. At the same time, they have also functioned as consultation forums, so that they have helped prevent or tackle problems as soon as these emerged.

Table 6.1. Meetings of the NAFTA Antidumping and Countervailing Duties Working Group

Mexico	United States and Canada
February 16, 1995	May 17, 1995 (Washington)
November 7, 1995	September 6, 1995 (Ottawa)
November 30, 1995	September 21-22, 1995 (Washington)

Source: Leycegui and Fernández de Castro (2000).

An example of one such group responsible for updating and developing the agreement was the Antidumping and Countervailing Duties Group, which got together three times but was dissolved upon reaching an impasse in 1995 (see tables 6.1 and 6.2).

These committees and working groups have operated as effective channels of communication at a technical level enabling the authorities to periodically update the agreement. Thus, the Working Group on Rules of Origin allowed for the modification of various appendixes (e.g., 401 and 403), while the Committee on Measures Relating to Normalization solved some of the problems surrounding labeling and certification of tires in each country, for which a specific agreement was created known as the Tire Agreement. However, one should recognize that the various committees and working groups are restricted to technical revisions of the agreement, so that when the three countries involved face a particularly complex and/or politicized problem these institutions created by NAFTA are clearly not enough.

Government Capacity

In matters relating to trade, NAFTA has, without doubt, improved the technical and decisionmaking capacity of all three North American countries. This change is particularly evident in Mexico. Given that the country was practically closed up to the mid-1980s, free trade led to significant changes in the government structure, as well as in the technical capacity of its officials. The Ministry of Commerce and Industrial Promotion (Sistema de Información Empresarial Mexicano, SECOFI), today renamed the Ministry of the Economy, underwent an important transformation as a result of NAFTA. When the negotiations began,

Table 6.2. Proceedings Related to NAFTA Antidumping and Countervailing Duties In the United States, 1987–97

Rank	Country	Number of Initiatives	Percentage of Initiatives	Number of Final Measures	Percentage of Measures	Success Ratio
1	Japan	60	10	39	14	0.7
2	China	55	9	32	11	0.6
3	South Korea	40	7	22	8	0.6
4	Taiwan	35	6	17	6	0.5
5	Canada	33	6	9	3	0.3
6	Brazil	30	5	12	4	0.4
7	Italy	29	5	19	7	0.7
8	Mexico	20	3	8	3	0.4
	Others	296	49	125	44	—
	Total	598	100	283	100	0.5

Source: Leycegui and Fernández de Castro (2000).

SECOFI had only one small department in charge of international commercial negotiations. This department was significantly expanded during the negotiations and by the time of their conclusion its structure and that of SECOFI as a whole clearly reflected the new importance that international trade had for Mexico. Two new undersecretaries that dealt with international trade were created: International Commercial Negotiations and Promotion of Industry and Trade.[9] Moreover, as a result of the agreement, several new specialized departments were created, such as the Department of Unfair Competition, that provided the bureaucratic and technical capacity that Mexican authorities needed to be able to abide by the terms of the agreement. The Mexican government also significantly increased its presence in Washington. During the negotiations, SECOFI's Washington office grew considerably, and by the end of the negotiations it had almost as many people as the Mexican embassy itself.

Though the Mexican government underwent the most significant structural changes as a result of NAFTA, one can also identify such changes in all three bureaucracies. Thus, for example, in the United States, the Department of Commerce as well as the Office of the U.S. Trade Representative (USTR) opened new North American departments that dealt with Mexico and Canada, and both increased the number of people working in this area.

However, 10 years after the implementation of NAFTA, it is clear that this initial drive to improve bureaucratic capacity so as to facilitate the operation of the agreement has waned. And indeed, in some areas, there has been a movement in the opposite direction. Thus, for example, Mexico's commercial representation in Washington has been reduced in size and the number of people directly involved with NAFTA within the USTR's office has also declined. Of the eight original officials responsible for commerce with Mexico and Canada within the USTR's office, only two are left and these two, moreover, do not work full time on Mexican issues.[10]

In sum, of the three items previously enumerated—an increase in the government's interest in issues relating to trade, a reduction in transaction costs and uncertainty for all parties involved, and an improvement in the decisionmaking capacity of the three governments—it would seem that although NAFTA had a positive impact during the first years of its implementation, during the past two or three years and in particular since September 11, the initial momentum has been lost. There is far less interest shown by all three governments in NAFTA, as can be seen by the fact that fewer resources have been assigned for its operation. If this tendency is not reversed, the three countries involved could face serious problems in the next few years. In fact, this institutional erosion is already of great relevance because 2003 was the year in which much of the agricultural sector, traditionally one of the most protected sectors, was being opened.

Finally, during NAFTA's first years, the interest that it sparked, together with the strengthening of existing trade-related bureaucratic structures in all three governments, allowed for the relatively smooth operation of the agreement despite the nonexistence of a central governing body with its own bureaucracy. However, now that the initial enthusiasm has faded, the lack of a solid and autonomous institutional framework is clearly a serious obstacle to the further development and improvement of the original agreement and the inclusion of new areas such as labor.

NAFTA'S IMPACT ON MEXICAN FOREIGN POLICY TOWARD THE UNITED STATES AND ON BILATERAL RELATIONS

It has been said, and with reason, that since Mexico's independence in 1810 there have been two negotiations with the United States that have been defining. The first, the Guadalupe-Hidalgo agreement of 1848, was an outcome of Mexico's defeat in the Mexican–American War and led to the loss of half of its territory to the United States. The second is, of course, NAFTA, which seeks to take advantage of Mexico's proximity to the biggest market in the world and thus promote the economic integration of North America.

Given its great scope and scale, NAFTA had, both during the negotiation phase and throughout its implementation, significant repercussions in the way in which Mexico interacts with its northern neighbor. There have been two main diplomatic spillover effects of NAFTA.[11] The first has to do with changes in Mexico's relationship with Washington, including new ways in which the Mexican government sought to operate and promote its interests in the United States. The second relates to the manner in which the bilateral relationship itself was managed, and in particular, the attempt made by the two governments to replicate the order imposed on trade in other spheres, that is, the attempt made at further institutionalizing intergovernmental relationships.

PLAYING THE WASHINGTON GAME

During the Cold War, Mexican foreign policy toward the United States was passive and cautious. The spirit behind this strategy adopted by Mexican diplomats can be summarized as follows: "Mexico does not intervene in the internal affairs of the United States in the hope that the United States will not intervene in the internal affairs of Mexico." Jorge Espinosa de los Reyes, Mexican ambassador to the United States during the Miguel de la Madrid administration (1982–88), is in many ways a typical example of the traditional Mexican diplomat. He rarely ventured near the Capitol, and when he did go there it was usually for social reasons, such as the Cinco de Mayo celebrations. Ambassador Espinosa only once lobbied Congress, and that was in 1988 in relation to the Senate's vote to decertify Mexico in its fight against drugs. Espinosa met with Jim Wright (Democrat-Texas), the then the speaker of the House of Representatives, who responded to the Mexican ambassador's request by announcing that the measure to decertify Mexico would not be passed by Congress.

In sharp contrast to this passive and cautious foreign policy, the Salinas administration adopted a far more proactive strategy. The first objective that Salinas set himself was to persuade a reluctant USTR to negotiate a free trade agreement with Mexico. The USTR, Carla Hills, who initially favored the negotiation of the GATT's Uruguay Round, eventually capitulated to the persuasive arguments put forward by Mexican technocrats.[12] However, after a highly auspicious start, American environmentalists and trade unions lobbied Congress to stop the U.S. president from using the fast-track procedure for the agreement. In the face of this opposition, the Salinas administration decided to play by the local rules and hired professionals to lobby on its behalf. Furthermore, the Mexican government decided to underpin this strategy by strengthening Mexico's diplomatic presence in Washington, as well as in most other major cities and regions where a significant Mexican population was to be found.

Thus, during his first visit to Washington as president, Salinas inaugurated the new offices of the Mexican embassy, now housed in a modern building on Pennsylvania Avenue, three blocks from the White House. The move from 16th Street in a largely Hispanic neighborhood to a new prime location symbolized Mexico's enhanced presence in the United States. The NAFTA negotiations as well as its implementation made necessary a significant increase of Mexican personnel in Washington. Both the Ministry of Foreign Affairs as well as other Mexican ministries, in particular SECOFI, significantly increased the number of government officials working in Washington. Furthermore, during the 1990s, the number of ministries with offices in Washington increased from four to nine. As a result, the role of the Mexican ambassador to the United States, traditionally a political appointee,[13] became that of coordinating the efforts of the various Mexican government agencies to influence policy in Washington.

To be able to directly influence legislators and other key players such as leaders of Hispanic origin on their home ground, the Mexican Ministry of Foreign Affairs strengthened its network of consulates and assigned them specific political tasks. Their activities now went beyond protection to include duties that traditionally corresponded to the embassy in Washington. The consuls were to act as "regional ambassadors," promoting Mexico's image and lobbying local political leaders.

All consulates general opened a press and public relations office as well as a cultural institute. The strengthening of Mexico's consular network in order to promote NAFTA partly explains why the Mexican government today has the biggest such network in the United States, with 45 consulates, 12 of which are consulates general.

This increased presence in the United States went along with a new diplomatic attitude that dropped the previous reticence to intervene in the internal politics of that country. Mexico developed a highly proactive diplomacy, which sought to promote its interests at the very center of power. And because the law in the United States allows for the hiring of lobbyists by foreign governments to promote their interests, the Salinas administration, through SECOFI, hired a large team of professionals to assist in the smooth progress of the NAFTA negotiations and ensure its safe passage through Congress (Velasco Márquez 1996). After the successful conclusion of the negotiations, Mexico again turned to professional lobbyists, law firms, and political managers to help it promote its interests with regard to other important bilateral issues: legal issues, drug trafficking, and migration. In the spring of 1998, as the Mexican government faced what seemed like an inevitable decertification, Ambassador Reyes Heroles hired three firms to prevent this from happening—and was successful.[14]

More recently, during President Fox's first year in office, Jorge Castañeda, then minister of foreign affairs, decided to hire a large team of lobbyists and communication specialists to help his ministry promote a migration agreement. However, once it became clear at the beginning of 2002 that any such agreement was unlikely to become a reality, these contracts were not renewed. It is worth noting in passing that Mexican government officials were not the only ones who decided to play the Washington game and intervene in local politics. The opposition also decided to play this game. Thus, during the NAFTA negotiations, Castañeda, along with several other Mexican opposition leaders, flew to Washington to participate in a congressional hearing on the agreement and opposed it.

ATTEMPTS TO INSTITUTIONALIZE INTERGOVERNMENTAL RELATIONS

The Mexican political system, although on paper a democratic presidential system, is very different from the U.S. one. While in the United

States the system of checks and balances operates effectively and the decisionmaking process is decentralized, in Mexico, until very recently, the executive branch was all-powerful, and in particular had complete control of foreign policy. These differences, along with the fact that Americans are far less interested in Mexico than the Mexicans are interested in the United States, has resulted in a problematic and often querulous relationship.

Historically, there have been three major strategies through which both governments have sought to improve their relationship: the appointment of a special "Mexico coordinator" in Washington, through a "broker" and an institutional strategy that has sought to formalize certain aspects of the relationship. The first strategy—the appointment of a special coordinator—was tried during the administration of Jimmy Carter (1977–80). The National Security Council and the State Department, as a result of a perceived lack of coordination between the various government agencies that dealt with Mexico, appointed a coordinator with the rank of ambassador within the State Department who would oversee and coordinate all dealings with Mexico. The results of this effort were not particularly satisfactory, and the experiment ended when Ronald Reagan took office.

The second strategy—the use of a "broker"—has been tried at different times under different administrations and involves the identification by the Mexican government of someone within the U.S. administration that is willing and able to act as "broker" on its behalf. The idea is for this person to guide Mexicans through the bureaucratic maze that is Washington and to help them overcome obstacles and problems that often require the intervention of the Oval Office. Two clear examples of such a "broker" are the role played by Robert Zoellick in the administration of George H.W. Bush and that played by Thomas McLarty in the administration of Bill Clinton. Zoellick, as undersecretary of state for economic affairs and probably the most influential official at the State Department after the secretary, James Baker III, helped to unravel important problems, such as the tuna embargo and the kidnapping of a Mexican citizen by the Drug Enforcement Agency. During the Clinton administration, the president's chief of staff and later a special assistant for Latin America, and a confidant, Thomas McLarty, assumed the role of broker on Mexico's behalf and was instrumental in ensuring the financial rescue package in the spring of 1995.

Table 6.3. Mexico's NAFTA-Related Presidential Meetings, 1988–2000

President	Number of Meetings
Carlos Salinas de Gortari	13 (1 as president-elect)
Ernesto Zedillo Ponce de León	9 (1 as president-elect)
Vicente Fox Quesada	1 (as president-elect)[a]

Source: Leycegui and Fernández de Castro (2000).
[a] Up to August 2000.

The third strategy that has been adopted to manage the highly complex and asymmetric bilateral relationship—the institutionalization of the intergovernmental relationship—emerged along with NAFTA. The order imposed by the various agreements that were reached in commercial maters—five bilateral agreements were negotiated between 1985 and 1989, and then NAFTA in 1994—significantly reduced the level of conflict and led to a smooth administration of bilateral economic issues. Indeed, NAFTA, as was noted above, is a trilateral commercial regime that fulfills the three basic requirements any such regime should seek to satisfy: It establishes clear rules that translate into specific patterns of behavior; it reduces transaction costs by clearly stating what can and cannot be done; and it facilitates the transfer of information and reduces uncertainty for key players.

The order imposed on trade between the two countries, one of the most important aspects of the bilateral relationship, had a demonstration effect or, as the literature on European integration would phrase it, important spillover effects into other areas of the relationship, where a similar process of institutionalization was attempted. This effort at institutionalizing existing relations was particularly noticeable in the consultation mechanisms, and not only were existing ones strengthened, but new ones were created dealing with specific issues such as drug trafficking. Also, bilateral regimes were created for different areas, such as the environment, labor, and migration.[15]

During the Salinas administration (1988–94) in particular, the existing bilateral consultation mechanisms were strengthened: presidential meetings, the Binational Commission, the conference of governors from border states and interparliamentary meetings. Presidential talks

Table 6.4. NAFTA Working Groups

Rules of Origin

Customs Problems

Agricultural Subsidies and Market Norms

Competency Issues

Temporal Entry of Technical Personnel and Businessmen

Emergency Measures

Government Procurement

Services and Investments

---

became more frequent. Salinas met Bush and Clinton 11 times, that is, almost twice a year (see table 6.3). However, the mechanism that underwent the greatest transformation was the Binational Commission. This mechanism was created in 1981, under Presidents de la Madrid and Reagan, as an attempt to better coordinate relations between the two countries. The commission, which meets once a year, invariably involves three ministries: foreign affairs as coordinators, and the finance and commerce ministries. For the Seventh Binational Commission in August 1989, during the first year of the Salinas and Bush presidencies, 10 cabinet members were present from each country, a clear demonstration that both governments were willing to dedicate a whole working day to improve the bilateral relationship. By 1995, with the further institutionalization of the commission, several working groups were created that dealt with the main bilateral issues (see table 6.4).

The Binational Commission became very effective at coordinating the various government agencies involved in the bilateral relationship. Above all, this mechanism became a useful tool for the Mexican Ministry of Foreign Affairs and the State Department, which preside over the commission. However, by the end of the 1990s, at least for some of those involved, such as the commerce and justice ministries, the commission became redundant as it merely went over issues already discussed in other forums or in the various meetings of counterparts throughout the year. As a result, since the end of the 1990s, the commission has been in crisis. The level of participation by high-ranking officials has gone down dramatically, the number of working groups has also decreased, and, all too often, the agreements reached have been merely cosmetic. A thorough revision of the mechanism is therefore needed if it is to survive as a useful instrument to manage the bilateral relationship.

As for drug trafficking, probably the most conflictual aspect of the bilateral relationship, both governments established in 1996 a High-Level Contact Group of ministerial rank to ensure coordination at the highest level. During its first years of operation, the group met twice a year. In May 1997, the GCAN Insurance Company published a report describing the problems faced by both countries in this area, titled "Assessment of the Bilateral Drug Trafficking Challenge for Mexico and the United States," which led, a few months later, to the "Joint Statement by Mexico and the United States against Drug Trafficking."

Vicente Fox's migration agreement represented an opportunity for constructing a bilateral regime for this issue similar to that provided by NAFTA for trade. Mexico's insistence that such an agreement should be broad enough to included some regularization, a host program for workers, co-responsibility for the development of the areas where most of the migrants came from, and a shared administration of the border zone, is evidence of the desire to replicate for migration the sort of order imposed on commercial issues by NAFTA (Mexico–United States Working Group on Migration 2001).

CRISIS AND RECOMMENDATIONS

The September 11, 2001, terrorist attacks complicated an already difficult situation as far as the bilateral relationship was concerned. Exactly four days after the climatic state visit by Fox to Washington from September 5 to 7, which marked the highest point of the Fox–Bush honeymoon, the terrorists struck. Once the dust settled, it became clear that the various efforts made to institutionalize the bilateral relationship through regimes, working groups, and the strengthening of the consultation mechanisms were in trouble. Mexican foreign policy toward Washington had as its key component a broad migration agreement, but the strategy adopted went against the accumulated wisdom of how the decisionmaking process worked in the U.S. capital. Mexico's efforts during the first nine months of the Bush administration focused entirely on the president himself. When President Bush adjusted his priorities as a result of the terrorist attacks, Mexico in general and the migration agreement in particular found themselves without an advocate.

What has and has not worked in the management of the bilateral relationship since the implementation of NAFTA? A strong diplomatic presence in the United States through the embassy in Washington and the network of consulates is still essential. The same can be said of playing by the local rules in Washington and hiring professional lobbyists. Mexico now has experience in this game and can play it reasonably well. A pragmatic attitude still prevails, as does a technical approach to problem solving by "specialists" which, however, remains above (or below) politics, failing to involve the major political players and shunning the media. It is probable that the foreign minister and Mexican ambassador in turn may give a particular flavor to this strong diplomatic presence and activism in the United States. Thus, Fox's first minister of foreign affairs, Jorge Castañeda, was very assertive, while the present minister, Luis Ernesto Derbez, has been more discreet. Nevertheless, the need for activism at the very center of the decisionmaking process in Washington and the United States remains clear.

The trust that was built up over time through the various negotiations, and increased contact that resulted from NAFTA, remain an important resource for the management of the bilateral relationship. For example, with the simultaneous change in administrations in Mexico and the United States in December 2000 and January 2001, respectively, many of the government officials at the second and third levels did not change (especially in the United States, where there is a professional civil service), and this continuity no doubt facilitated the learning process of the new people in charge.

Independent of the priority now given to the fight against terrorism, the two governments have been unable to conquer the astonishingly dynamic nature of their relationship. The rapid economic integration that NAFTA stimulated has increased the number of actors involved in bilateral affairs as well as the intensity of their participation. Thus, governments at both the state and local levels have become increasingly involved, and the relationship between the two countries has become increasingly decentralized. Also, demographic changes along with migration have significantly altered the context in which the bilateral relationship unfolds. The exponential growth during the past 10 years in the number of Americans of Mexican origin as well as of Mexicans living in the United States has surpassed all estimates. The big surprise of the census carried out in 2000 by the American government was precisely the increase of the Hispanic population. Approximately 60 per cent of this population is of Mexican descent. The very fact that there are 24 million people of Mexican origin living in the United States, 10 million of whom were born in Mexico, and that their number is likely to increase further, provides a special context for the management of the bilateral relationship. For example, the electoral authorities now face a new phenomenon: the transnationalization of politics. As a result, some groups have pressed for the creation of electoral districts for Mexican voters in the United States given the large number of Mexicans in that country. Also, several governors and even President Bush use their close relationship with President Fox when campaigning in regions where there is a significant number of Mexican Americans.

The dynamic nature of the bilateral relationship over the last decades—the decentralization of bilateral affairs and the surprising growth of the Hispanic population in the United States—makes necessary an adjustment of both federal governments' strategies, so as to be able to deal with the new circumstances. However, rather than strengthening the existing mechanisms and institutions, including those of NAFTA, both countries do not seem to be particularly interested and have let their guard down. The reasons for this attitude on the Mexican side are many and include a lack of leadership and the quick internal political payoff that resorting to crude and simplistic criticisms of the United States represents. Having initially been very pro-American, over the past two years the Mexican government has increasingly adopted a nationalist discourse with a clear anti-American tendency. Undoubtedly, this is in part a reaction to the aggressive unilateralism of Washington since George W. Bush took office. At the same time, one must understand that no mechanisms or institutions exist that could enable anyone to manage the bilateral relationship in an autonomous manner and permit constant adjustment in the face of an ever-changing reality.

Today, after 10 years of NAFTA's operation, the international environment clearly is not a favorable one for undertaking significant transformations in bilateral affairs. The "new international order" that George H.W. Bush announced at the end of the Cold War has clearly been left behind, and the peaceful and quiet times that led to the election of George W. Bush visibly ended on September 11. Furthermore, the economies of the United States and Mexico are going through difficult times. As a result, it is important that both countries set a critical path that will enable them to manage a bilateral relationship that has become increasingly complex.

NAFTA First

The operation of NAFTA has led to serious problems that need to be overcome. Some of the issues involved here, such as transport, sugar, and artificial sweeteners, continue to contaminate the general atmosphere in which free trade between the two countries unfolds. It is not a question of the intrinsic importance of these sectors but rather the negative image that these unsolved issues project with regard to NAFTA as a whole—namely, its inability to solve basic problems. It is this inability that has led some critics to suggest that redress be sought in a different forum or, indeed, that the agreement should be abandoned altogether. To confront this problem, it is essential that the NAFTA chapters that deal with the resolution of controversies—chapters 19 and 20—be revised and updated. Moreover, NAFTA's highest authority— the Binational Commission—needs to look at the institutional framework of the agreement and, if necessary, set up specialized working groups to solve problems that have arisen. Thus, the tenth anniversary is not so much a time to celebrate but to meditate. It is an opportunity to thoroughly analyze what has and has not worked in what, undoubtedly, has been a key instrument enabling the Mexican and the U.S. economies to be more competitive in an increasingly globalized world.

The Border Zone

Even before September 11, 2001, the management of the border between Mexico and the United States and the lack of infrastructure in this area had become an impediment to the further expansion of free trade. The very idea of a border needs to be analyzed and rethought, especially because it is essential that this area be managed jointly; yet the dominant strategy seems to be that of unilateralism. The threat of terrorism has injected new resources into the border area and has made increased security a top priority. Nevertheless, the commercial authorities from both countries, along with the private sector engaged in trade, must emphasize the importance of efficiency. Now is the time to lobby and lobby hard.

Migration and Oil

Paradoxically, the two issues deliberately left out of the original NAFTA negotiations need to be revived. President Fox's initiative to negotiate a broad migration agreement received the support of all political sectors in Mexico. It is essential that the Mexican government take advantage of this rare internal consensus to push for an incremental solution to the main migration problems that should include, at the very least, some sort of regularization of undocumented workers and increased border security to prevent the numerous deaths that result from attempted crossings every year. As for oil, it is a very sensitive issue for Mexico, because most Mexicans feel very strongly about the national ownership of oil.

Nevertheless, it should be possible for two neighboring countries with a 10-year-old free trade agreement to have such an incipient dialogue concerning a vital subject for both their economies. If Mexico has more oil than it needs and the United States has a supply deficit, some sort of agreement should be possible. Castañeda, Mexico's former foreign minister, is today promoting the view that the only way to get Americans interested in a migration agreement is by also talking about the possibility of opening up the energy sector in Mexico.

Privileged Relations with the Mexican Community

In an effort designed to coincide with Salinas's visit to the United States in 1989 and a few months before announcing the start of the NAFTA negotiations, the Mexican government launched the Program for Mexican Communities Abroad. This program has today evolved into the Institute of Mexicans Abroad (known as IME by its Spanish initials), which was created in 2002. The IME has an advisory board of 120 leaders, including both Mexican Americans and Mexicans, from every sector of society. This institute is an attempt at organizing the Mexican diaspora in the United States at a national level, so that it may become a genuine and privileged mediator between Washington and Mexico City. The Mexican community in the United States will continue to grow at a high rate as a result of both the birthrate and migration. This growing community requires special attention from the Mexican government as an organized diaspora could greatly help the lobbying process.

The Binational Commission and Innovative Mechanisms for New Players

Given the increasing complexity of the bilateral relationship, the Binational Commission should not be forgotten, especially because this mechanism has, in the past, proven to be useful in coordinating the various government agencies involved in this relationship. Undoubtedly, the mechanism needs to be updated. One possibility is that a fixed annual date be chosen for the meeting, so that the various ministries involved can avoid scheduling bilateral meetings near that date. One could also imagine certain working groups, such as the one dealing with migration and consular matters, becoming more independent of the commission. Finally, the federal governments of both Mexico and the United States should play a more active role in the annual conference of border governors. Nonborder states such as Illinois and Zacatecas should probably be included in this annual gathering, given that they have a significant stake in the bilateral relationship.

Notes

1. See Leycegui and Fernández de Castro 2000; Weintraub 1997; Leycegui, Robson and Stein 1997; Fernández de Castro, Verea Campos and Weintraub 1993; Lipsey, Schwanen, and Wonnacott 1994; Hufbauer and Schott 1992, 1993; Garber 1993; Lustig, Bosworth, and Lawrence 1992; and Orme 1996.

2. Rubio 1999; Mayer 1998; Mac Ari and Saunders 1997; Cardero 1996; Anderson 1993; Grinspun and Cameron 1993; Robert 1992.

3. McKinney 2001; Von Furstenberg 2001; Boyd 2001; various documents from the page of the NAFTA Secretariat, www.nafta-sec-alena.org/spanish/index.htm.

4. Weintraub (1994, 28), quoted in Leycegui and Fernández de Castro (2000, 480).

5. This asymmetry relates not only to the greater size of the American economy and the greater power that Washington wields in the international arena, but also to Mexico's and Canada's dependence on the United States. Thus, whereas for Mexico and Canada their trade with the United States represents approximately 85 percent of their total international trade, for the United States, the sum total of its trade with these two countries represents approximately 31 percent of its total international trade.

6. Neoliberal institutionalism derives from complex interdependence paradigm. In 1977, Robert Keohane and Joseph Nye, in their book *Power and Interde-*

pendence (Keohane and Nye 1977), presented a strong criticism of the realist perspective, the then dominant perspective within the discipline. This latter approach does not acknowledge the possibility of cooperation, because it conceptualizes all states as maximizers of power in an anarchic international society. For Keohane and Nye, international institutions are the most highly developed instruments that account for cooperation between states. See Keohane 1983.

7. Interview with a high-ranking SECOFI official, who asked to remain anonymous.

8. The 2000–1 appendix contains a list of these committees and groups. The meetings that took place between 1994 and 1998 are described in Leycegui and Fernández de Castro (2000, table 3).

9. With the appointment of Luis Ernesto Derbez as minister of foreign affairs in February 2003, the possibility of transferring the area responsible for commercial negotiations from the Ministry for the Economy to Foreign Affairs is being considered.

10. Interviews with Javier Mancera, head of the Commercial Department in the Mexican Embassy in Washington, and with the trade representative of the United States, Washington, February 2002.

11. The concept of "spillover" comes from functionalist theory, which claims that the process of integration involves spillover effects, so that the benefits in a specific area where integration has taken place leads to attempts a integration in other areas so as to obtain similar benefits. This process can take place in two different ways: as a result of the activities of "technicians" and bureaucrats who exchange information or as a result of an increased functional dependency.

12. With Salinas, a new elite came to power, which displaced the postrevolutionary leadership, composed mainly of lawyers and professional politicians that worked their way through the Institutional Revolutionary Party or government hierarchy. The new elite that came to power in 1988 was made up mainly of economists or professionals with graduate degrees from the most prestigious universities in the United States. They had no prejudice against the United States, knew the country well, and understood how it worked.

13. Since 1970, there has been 1 career ambassador in Washington and 8 political appointments. In general terms, out of the 103 Mexican ambassadors around the world, 53 are political appointees.

14. At the end of the day, there was no real opposition from Congress, and Mexico obtained the certification without much trouble (Estévez 2001).

15. Chapter 5 in this volume by Graciala Bensusán analyzes the efforts at institutionalization in the labor and environmental areas.

References

Anderson, Terry L., ed. 1993. *NAFTA and the Environment.* San Francisco: Pacific Research Institute for Public Policy.

Boyd, Dan S. 2001. Strategies for Enforcing Cross-Border Judgments. Paper presented at the Texas–Mexico Bar Association Eight Annual Conference, El Paso, September 27–29.

Cardero, María Elena, ed. 1996. *¿Qué ganamos y qué perdimos con el TLC?* Mexico City: Siglo XXI Editores.

Estévez, Dolia. 2001. Los medios en la relación bilateral México–Estados Unidos. In *México en el mundo: Los desafíos para México en 2001,* ed. Rafael Fernández de Castro. Mexico City: Instituto Tecnológico Autónomo de México.

Fernández de Castro, Rafael. 2002. La migración sobre la mesa de negociación. In *Cambio y continuidad en la política exterior de México (México en el Mundo 2002).* Mexico City: Ariel.

Fernández de Castro, Rafael, Mónica Verea Campos, and Sidney Weintraub, eds. 1993. *Sectorial Labor Effects of North American Free Trade.* Austin: University of Texas Press; Mexico City: Universidad Nacional Autónoma de México and Instituto Tecnológico Autónomo de México.

Fernández de Castro, Rafael, and Andrés Rozental. Forthcoming. El amor, la decepción y cómo aprovechar la realidad: La relación México-Estados Unidos 2000–2003. In *En la frontera del imperio (México en el Mundo 2003).* Mexico City: Ariel.

Garber, Peter M., ed. 1993. *The Mexico–U.S. Free Trade Agreement.* Cambridge, Mass.: MIT Press.

Grinspun, Ricardo, and Maxwell A. Cameron. 1993. *The Political Economy of North American Free Trade.* New York: St. Martin's Press.

Haas, Peter M., Robert O. Keohane, and Marc A. Levy, eds. 1994. *Institutions for the Earth: Sources of Effective International Environmental Protection.* Cambridge, Mass.: MIT Press.

Hufbauer, Gary Clyde, and Jeffrey J. Schott. 1992. *North American Free Trade: Issues and Recommendations.* Washington, D.C.: Institute for International Economics.

————. 1993. *NAFTA: An Assesment.* Washington, D.C.: Institute for International Economics.

Keohane, Robert. 1989. *International Institutions and State Power: Essays in International Relations Theory.* Boulder, Colo.: Westview Press.

Keohane, Robert, and Joseph Nye. 1977. *Power and Interdependence: World Politics in Transition.* Boston: Little, Brown.

Leycegui, Beatriz, and Rafael Fernández de Castro, eds. 2000. *TLCAN, ¿Socios naturales? Cinco años del Tratado de Libre Comercio de América del Norte.* Mexico City: Instituto Tecnológico Autónomo de México and Porrúa.

Leycegui, Beatriz, and Mario Ruiz Cornejo. 2002. Restoring Competition or Granting Protectionism? Trading Remedies to Remedy Trade: The NAFTA Experience. Available at www.farmfoundation.org/flags/leycegui.pdf.

Leycegui, Beatriz, and Rafael Fernández de Castro, eds. 2000. *¿Socios naturales? Cinco años del Tratado de Libre Comercio de América del Norte.* Mexico City: Instituto Tecnológico Autónomo de México and Porrúa.

Leycegui, Beatriz, William B. P. Robson, and S. Dhalia Stein, eds. 1997. *Comercio a Golpes, las prácticas desleales del comercio internacional bajo el TLCAN.* Mexico City: Instituto Tecnológico Autónomo de México and Porrúa.

Lipsey, Richard, Daniel Schwanen, and Ronald J. Wonnacott. 1994. *The NAFTA: What's In, What's Out, What's Next.* Toronto: C. D. Howe Institute.

Lustig, Nora. 1998. Los Estados Unidos al rescate de México en crisis: ¿Repetición de la historia? In *Nueva agenda bilateral en la relación México–Estados Unidos,* ed. Mónica Verea Campos, Rafael Fernández de Castro, and Sidney Weintraub. Mexico City: Instituto Tecnológico Autónomo de México, Centro de Investigaciones sobre América del Norte, and Fondo de Cultura Económica.

Lustig, Nora, Barry P. Bosworth, and Robert Z. Lawrence, eds. 1992. *North American Free Trade, Assessing the Impact.* Washington, D.C.: Brookings Institution Press.

Macari, Emir José, and F. Michael Saunders, eds. 1997. *Environmental Quality, Innovative Technologies, and Sustainable Economic Development: A Nafta Perspective.* Portland: Book News, Inc.

Mayer, Frederick W. 1998. *Interpreting NAFTA: The Science and Art of Political Analysis.* New York: Columbia University Press.

McKinney, Joseph A. 2001. *Created from NAFTA: The Structure, Function, and Significance of the Treaty's Related Institutions.* Armonk, N.Y.: M. E. Sharpe.

Mexico–United States Working Group on Migration. 2001. *Mexico–United States Migration: A Shared Responsibility.* Mexico City: Instituto Tecnológico Autónomo de México and Carnegie Endowment for International Peace,.

North, Douglas C. 1993. Toward a Theory of Institutional Change. In *Political Economy: Institution, Competition, and Representation,* ed. William A. Barnett, Norman Schofield, and Melvin Hinich. New York: Cambridge University Press.

Orme, William A., Jr. 1996. *Understanding NAFTA: Mexico, Free Trade, and the New North America.* Austin: University of Texas Press.

Robert, Maryse. 1992. *Negotiating NAFTA: Explaining the Outcome in Culture, Textiles, Autos, and Pharmaceuticals.* Toronto: University of Toronto Press.

Rubio, Luis. 1999. *Tres Ensayos, Privatización, Fobaproa y TLC.* Mexico City: Ediciones Cal y Arena.

Velasco Márquez, Jesús. 1966. Visión panorámica de la historia de los Estados Unidos. In *¿Qué son los Estados Unidos?* ed. Claudia Franco Hijuelos and Rafael Fernández de Castro. Mexico City: McGraw-Hill.

Von Furstenberg, George M., ed. 2001. *Regulation and Supervision of Financial Institutions in the NAFTA Countries and Beyond.* Dordrecht, Netherlands: Kluwer Academic Publishers.

Weintraub, Sidney. 1994. *NAFTA: What Comes Next?* Westport, Conn.: Praeger/ CSIS.

———. 1997. *NAFTA at Three: A Progress Report.* Washington, D.C.: CSIS.

CHAPTER SEVEN

CIVIL SOCIETY ORGANIZATIONS, FREEDOM OF INFORMATION, AND TRANSPARENCY IN MEXICO'S AGENDA IN THE CONTEXT OF NAFTA

A NORMATIVE APPROACH

Ernesto Villanueva

Civil society, as a separate notion from the general society of human-kind, is a concept that continues to evolve in Mexico, even at the beginning of the twenty-first century. However, there is no unequivocal definition of what civil society is, and consequently no definition of a civil society or nongovernmental organization (Olvera 1999, 16–17). Although this chapter takes a normative rather than a sociological approach, it is nonetheless important to have at least a notion of what may be understood by "civil society." To begin with, as scholars concur (Cohen and Arato 2001, 43–44), civil society is constituted by associations or movements that do not belong to the political society, that are voluntary, and that have as a purpose promoting the effective exercise of rights of the first, second, and third generations, from the classification of human rights in three groups based on the time of their establishment in the development of overall human society.[1]

As Diamond maintains, "Civil society is an intermediate entity between the private sphere and the state. It excludes, therefore, individual and family life, inter-group activity (i.e., recreation, entertainment or spirituality), private business enterprises, and political efforts to control the state. Actors in civil society require the protection of an institutionalized legal system in order to preserve their autonomy and freedom of action. In this manner, civil society not only restricts the power of the state, but it can also legitimate State authority when it is based on the rule of law" (Diamond 1997). This chapter discusses the emergence of nongovernmental organizations (NGOs), which constitute a fundamental sector (although not unique to civil society organizations)[2] in the period prior to the signing of the North American Free

Trade Agreement (NAFTA) between the United States and Canada, as well as the evolution of this sector in the 10 years since NAFTA.

The normative approach of this work is intended to tackle the topic by giving priority to two angles. The first relates to the legal basis upon which Mexico's NGOs operate in general, and the second and more important concerns the relationship between performance of the NGOs and the transformation of the more authoritative means of expression contained in the Mexican legal framework, which have been gradually ceding to a legal and political regime that advocates the construction of a social and democratic state based on the rule of law. How the agenda of Mexico's problems has been formed, and what impact the NGOs have had on that logic, and why, is the primary purpose of this chapter: to better understand the advances and challenges for citizen participation in building a democracy.

This theme gives rise to more questions than answers for several reasons. Among them are a lack of clarity regarding the profile NGOs should project, the absence of reliable information and transparency about activities performed by the organizations, and the lack of clear rules about the criteria for and follow-up on the delivery of public resources to this sector, all endemic problems that continue unattended. On the contrary, these concerns are an important part of the very agenda of civil society organizations: to understand their role in the long road toward democracy in Mexico.

THE SOCIAL IMPACT OF NGOs
DURING THE PERIOD BEFORE NAFTA

It is important to start by assuming that Mexico is a country in the process of building a democratic state. There are more than 200 federal laws that stipulate inconsistent compliance with NGO-related legislation depending on the degree of activism and the availability of information about the existence, benefits, and possible damage caused by NGOs to individuals, social sectors, or general society. In this context, it is not surprising that the political Constitution of the United States of Mexico—in addition, of course, to consecrating in article 9 the fundamental freedom of union and free association, as is the case in practically all modern constitutions of the world—stipulates in its article 3 a model of social democracy as part of the nation-building project that must guide the actions of the Mexican state (cf. García Ramírez 1994).

This constitutional article has certain social transcendence in citizen organizations to the extent that it establishes the basis upon which the Constitution defines the concept of democracy through education as an instrument for the socialization of knowledge and the capacity to form opinions. The above-mentioned article 3 suggests, for example, how democracy should be considered "not only as a legal structure and a political regime, but as a living system based on the constant social, economic and cultural improvement of the people." Thus from a legal standpoint, article 9 of the Constitution empowers people to organize themselves naturally, that is, without being subject to any type of direction or objective. On the contrary, article 3 of the Constitution establishes an end goal that goes beyond electoral democracy and rests instead on social participation. In both cases, we are dealing with the constitutional basics that have historically fulfilled more of a commemorative mission than an effective guarantee of the functions of NGOs in Mexico.

Civil society organizations surfaced, in their early stage, as a sum of various independent efforts, most of which previously had little impact on public decisionmaking for several reasons, among which three deserve mention. First, the Institutional Revolutionary Party (Partido Revolucionario Institucional, PRI), which ruled Mexico for 70 years, had the political sensitivity to include within its traditional structure of sectors (workers, *campesinos*, and the popular sector) the diverse expressions of organized citizen groups. In the period from the 1930s to the early 1980s, several social organizations were able to find participatory spaces within the PRI at a time when this party solely dominated all participatory spaces and access to public power at all levels under a so-called corporatist model. The PRI's popular sector created an organization known as the National Confederation of Popular Organizations to maintain that power, which for many years served as a primary meeting space and vehicle of social participation for political purposes.

A second factor was the absence of public resources of all kinds devoted to emerging NGOs as opposed to discretionary contributions to organizations connected to the PRI or the work of the postrevolutionary political regime. Likewise (until just a few years ago), under the biased interpretation of articles 9 and 33 of the federal constitution, the federal government took on a public and active policy to prevent the financing of social organizations by international organizations and foundations. Article 9 establishes that "only citizens of the republic may do so [organize] to take part in the political affairs of the country." In the same vein, the last paragraph of article 33 stipulates that "foreigners may not intervene in the country's political affairs" under any circumstances. The country's "political affairs" were understood for many years to be any and all activities that had the capacity to alter the status quo. Nor was private initiative during that time a source of support for NGOs devoted to objectives outside of the limited national priorities that were seen as having the potential to cause even a slight disturbance to the Mexican political regime. The sum total of all these factors was dissuasion from involvement in social organizations with broad independent space from the PRI or to make systematic or constructive criticism of the status quo and its corresponding *establishment*.

The third factor was the role played by the overwhelming majority of the media with strong linkages to federal, state, or municipal governments. Today it is a common affirmation that the media are an important part of society's right to know. Furthermore, the media play a fundamental role in the formation of public opinion. The notion of public opinion does not enjoy a definition of universal validity. For some it is a question of "opinions of national interest freely and publicly expressed by people not belonging to the government, but demanding the right for their opinions to influence or determine actions, personnel, or government structure" (Speir 1950). For others, it is the "aggregate of individual opinions collected by opinion analysts" (Beniger 1977). In this scholar's judgment, public opinion may be understood conditionally as the predominant opinion concerning the more diverse topics of collective interest. The questions then are: What are the sources of public opinion? How is public opinion formed? It is understood in the current analysis as where the media intervene as a nondefining but definitive factor. It is important to remember that most of the information of public interest received by citizens—information to which they are entitled as a result of the right to know in its broadest sense—comes from the media and not from direct sources.

The problem becomes more complicated to the extent that the media are not objective as a messenger between information sources and the public but, on the contrary, are an instrument of alliance with the authorities that may actually obstruct the public's right to be informed. First of all, it is necessary to consider the theory of the "agenda-setting function." Maxwell McCombs (McCombs and Pla 2003, 83–106), on the basis of a series of opinion polls, documented that the media transferred to the citizenry its own agenda concerning the country's most important problems. In Mexico, the national agenda was not created by the media but rather by various government authorities to which the majority of media organs were loyal. This was compounded by the fact that the regime provided subsidies in the annual budget of expenditures for the dissemination of major news. In this manner, limited only by their own imagination, high-level public administration officials have traditionally taken advantage of the broad discretionary powers the law gave them to finance political careers, presidential projects, and a veritable universe of means of communication, which lack a social base in the majority of cases and is solvent because of the subsidies provided by the federal, state, and municipal governments.

The culture of patrimonial exercise of power is by nature antidemocratic. This begs the question: How can the right to information be honored when political propaganda is published disguised as factual information, thus deceiving readers? How can the citizenry fully enjoy freedom of information in Mexico when the majority of the media lack economic independence, that is, the ability to survive through private advertising? How can the political and editorial information be distinguished from advertising when more than 50 percent of the economic resources a newspaper receives come from a single donor: the government? The media's lack of economic independence is accompanied by a lack of informational and editorial autonomy, which has traditionally cast doubt on the exercise of the right to information.

There is a principle with an empirical base that establishes that what is not acknowledged by the media does not exist. NGOs lacked the possibility for this type of coverage and were relegated in most cases to residual spaces. This treatment given to NGOs forced them to seek marginal broadcasting channels to communicate their viewpoints. To mitigate this situation, an NGO called Centro Nacional de Comunicación Social was created in 1964 to provide a voice for NGOs, and it served as practically the sole vehicle to open media spaces for NGOs.

During the second half of the 1980s, the possibilities for the emergence of NGOs grew as a result of an increase in tolerance by the Mexican political regime for the incipient but gradual increase of people in charge of democratizing the political participation formulas in the PRI. At that time, some internal cracks began to appear because the PRI was no longer uniquely positioned to initiate political change "from within," an expression that was coined subsequently by many activists and politicians to justify their militancy in the party.

Two main factors precipitated NGOs to increase in number and become less marginalized, in some cases abandoning their radical political instincts to undertake more proactive measures with a modern discourse that had a greater appeal to political actors within the PRI and other political parties. The first factor was the devastating earthquake of 1985 that partially destroyed Mexico City. As a result of this event, the federal government was temporarily paralyzed, and the emergent network of NGOs instinctively filled the vacuum. The earthquake affected several offices of the Procuraduría General de Justicia of the Federal District (the Attorney General's Office of the Federal District). Rescue efforts at the offices uncovered several illegally buried cadavers with visible torture marks to the extent that many assumed that what was being uncovered were the bodies of the "politically disappeared," whose existence the government had categorically and vehemently denied. Faced with such evidence, the government was at a loss to explain the facts to the satisfaction of public opinion, which prompted the relatives of those disappeared and other sectors of society to seek coverage in the foreign press.

This constituted the most opportune moment for some NGOs to emerge with greater visibility to protect human rights in the broadest sense. Thus, between 1983 and 1988, 53 civil society organizations dealing with human rights and its electoral objectives emerged (Aguayo and Parra 1997, 23). One of the most significant was the Mexican Academy of Human Rights, established in 1984 and devoted initially to work in the areas of research, education, analysis, documentation, training promotion, and dissemination and broadcasting of information about human rights.

The second factor had its roots in the first great fracture of the PRI, which took place in 1988 with the exit of Cuauhtémoc Cárdenas and several high-ranking military officials to form the National Democratic Front (which had the possibility to include several left-wing opposition parties and social groups) to nominate Cárdenas as a presidential candidate under growing support from diverse social sectors. This chain of events for the first time created the possibility that a candidate from a political party other then the PRI might gain the presidency of the republic. But it was not to be. Instead, it incentivized social participation networks outside the government and the ruling party. The fall of the Berlin Wall and the demise of "real socialism" was a complementary external factor that permitted other sectors to devise mechanisms for citizen participation from *within* society.

Thus, two years after the polemic presidential elections of 1988, about which there have always existed doubts that the calculated votes were an accurate reflection of the popular will at voting time (cf. Olvera 1999, 11), in August 1990 the Convergencia de Organizaciones Cívicas para la Democracia was formed by 76 civil society organizations. In 1991, a similar umbrella organization was born, which was called the National Network of Civil Organizations for Human Rights: Full Rights for All. It was during this time that great efforts were made to provide a common thread to the diverse work being done in defense of civil rights. Those efforts generated inconsistent results concerning the reform of the legal framework because only a normative reform could guarantee a total change in the treatment of these rights.

It is important to point out that this initial stage was characterized by the creation of the first NGOs with a certain degree of social importance. These organizations, however, acted without limitations between activities suitable for modern social organizations and the search for political power in concert with the parties, as demonstrated by the active sympathies for the National Democratic Front and its organizational sequels as an expression of disillusionment with the influence and electoral omnipresence of the PRI.

THE EVOLUTION OF NGOs DURING THE FIRST TEN YEARS OF NAFTA

The approval of NAFTA by the legislatures of Canada, the United States, and Mexico in 1993 did not have a discernible impact on the strengthening of existing NGOs and the creation of new ones in Mexico. But in an implicit manner, NAFTA—which brought together many NGOs in opposition to the agreement under the logic that the asymmetry of the three countries would be damaging to Mexico—created the environment for NGOs to develop under better conditions than those prevailing in previous years for three basic reasons.

First, the approval of NAFTA was based on the principles of transparency and access to information, which served as an antecedent for future legislation on the issue of transparency, and the subject matter has become a part of the agenda of civil society organizations in terms of their financing. The government criteria used to decide the basis on which to assign public resources to NGOs (especially NGOs that previously accepted money from the government), and the social value of the right to know—which, in Mexico, despite being generically guaranteed under article 6 of the Constitution, was never applied directly, and even less so in secondary legislation. What is worse, a culture of secrecy was maintained not only among public officials and entities under obligation to inform but also among people who had an unwritten understanding that the principal holders of power (government officials) were the natural constituents of the media and that the "real" constituents (the people) were only their agents.

Second, the ability to consult and compare with other models, such as those of Canada and United States, was a valuable tool in the formulation of practices and models that had never been considered (and much less put into practice) in Mexico, especially concerning public information, transparency, and accountability. The perception of the Canadian and U.S. media about Mexico has been gradually but consistently transformed as a result NAFTA. If, in days gone by, editorials in Canada and the United States covered only issues related to drug trafficking, insecurity, and illegal immigration to the U.S. and, to a lesser extent, to Canada, other aspects of the Mexican reality appeared in the newspapers of Mexico's new commercial partners following the approval of NAFTA. The spectrum of media coverage was expanded to cover developments and issues that were previously untreated in Canadian and U.S. newspapers, such as education in marginal areas of Mexico, efforts toward democratization, human rights, defense of the right to vote, and environmental protection.

A third, closely related factor helps to explain not only that more NGOs have been formed during the last 10 years than ever before but also the fact that these organizations have persevered. The closed system of the Mexican political regime needed to open up its doors and permit exchanges among different groups in Canada, the United States, and Mexico in order to sell a self-reforming democratic image, as a political strategy to quiet the foreign voices that advocated the approval of NAFTA only on the condition that the agreement incorporated safeguards designed to encourage an effective democratic transition in Mexico.

In this context, it can be said that between 1993 and 2003, the increase of NGOs in Mexico has been remarkable. Suffice it to say that according to some sources, 51 percent of the NGOs in Mexico have emerged in the past 10 years, with a more recent trend toward environmentally related NGOs.[3] If human rights and the electoral struggle had become the basic axis upon which the work of NGOs evolved during the 1980s, in the following 10 years the topics of interest and concern of such organizations also recorded a change and a significant thematic diversification. In addition to what has been stated above, what prompted Mexican NGOs to experience such explosive growth?[4] This seems to be the fundamental question. It can be argued that Mexico's NGOs were able to reach that status as a result of the ease with which they interacted with NGOs from Canada and the United States, interactions from which they learned the know-how to collect funds, professionalize their activities, and gain a clearer understanding of the role of NGOs in a democratic society.

As a result of this increasing interaction, money began to flow from abroad to finance projects in the most diverse sectors of social activity. A share of those projects was oriented toward strengthening the rule of law and the defense of civil rights in Mexico. However, these very resources generated an unfortunate residual effect: Some of the new NGOs became a modus vivendi for certain activists because they perceived an incipient business opportunity. In addition, during this period a broader resource base became available to provide public subsidies for NGOs, although this also gave rise to corrupt practices, whether through ignorance or collusion with public servants. For example, the same project was often presented to several different public entities for funding, and in many cases different public departments financed the same project more than once. This period was also characterized by a lack of follow-up on the projects that were funded.

It became clear that the absence of transparency and information about the rules of the game had a negative effect on the process of organizing citizen participation in Mexico. At the same time, the Mexican media were experimenting with various reform ideas to ensure their survival during this period in the market. Public resources had become scarce for the media, particularly the printed media, and the first controls were placed on the discretionary powers of public servants to assign public resources freely for official publicity.[5] This circumstance caused the media to turn back to society as the base from which to recover the credibility it had lost after so many years of interacting only with public powers. This phenomenon implied that NGO activities had a greater niche in an ever-increasing number of media outlets, something previously unheard of.

THE IMPACT OF NGOs ON MEXICO'S
DEMOCRATIC REFORM PROCESS

Although NGOs have been able to maintain their presence in society over time, only in exceptional cases have they been able to create broad media visibility to participate actively in national agenda setting. As a result, of the 5,000, 7,000, or 10,000 NGOs existing in the country (depending on who one consults), fewer than 1 percent (of the smallest figure) have been able to transcend the collective anonymity. They have become thematic points of reference, social actors influencing the formation of public policies, observers of civil rights, human rights activists, or the champions of new laws promoting Mexico's democratic development. In other cases, training, meetings and thematic workshops have been sufficient to survive almost unnoticed in the organized world of civil society. This work is not intended to study the NGOs that make up part of an organizational paradigm. Nor is there a dominant typology to measure which of these NGOs is in accordance with international democratic standards, although some empirical evidence suggests what should *not* be done based on the Mexican experience of recent years.

One example of a successful NGO with a strong impact on public opinion and the public sector is the Alianza Cívica (Civic Alliance), which was formed in April 1994 within the context of growing expectations that a presidential candidate from a party other than the PRI could win the election. Civic Alliance was formed as an umbrella organization uniting several state organizations, professional experts, activists, and academics, all of which shared the goal of pursuing free and fair elections. Civic Alliance had an impact on the 1994 elections, participated successfully in several local elections, and, on account of its credibility and stature, was consulted in the organization of electoral processes in various social sectors.

In 1997, however, when the opposition party obtained an absolute majority in the Chamber of Deputies for the first time,[6] Civic Alliance was forced to recast and diversify its objectives in light of the fact that electoral oversight no longer had the same importance in the national agenda. It is important to remember that opposition parties had successfully passed legal reforms that granted a new profile to the Federal Electoral Institute (the authority responsible for organizing and supervising the legality of federal elections) by assigning citizen counselors unaffiliated with any political party with the sole responsibility for the decisions of that body. This was incorporated into the Federal Code of Institutions and Electoral Procedures of 1996. Civic Alliance revised its priorities, giving emphasis to the themes of accountability and transparency, and adopted several programs designed to popularize the theme in Mexican society, with inconsistent results among sectors of Mexican society.

One positive precedent for which Civic Alliance should take credit is for having questioned the president of the republic about his own salary in an effort to legally exercise the right to information, as stipulated in the last paragraph of article 6 of the constitution. This effort had more of a testimonial effect than concrete results because of the timing and circumstance in which this particular exercise of the right to access public information was carried out.

The 2000 presidential elections created, for the third time in Mexico's modern history, possibilities that the PRI, having held the presidency for more than 70 years, would lose the election. Many NGOs considered it a legitimate strategy to support, either explicitly or implicitly, the campaigns of opposition candidates, especially the candidate of the National Action Party (PAN), Vicente Fox, with whom some agreements had already been brokered should he be victorious in the elections of July 6, 2000. This inquiry became the subject of a broader debate: Should NGOs take part in political campaigns in support of certain policies and demands, or should they remain uncommitted to any political party, demanding the same from all candidates? This was the great question mark that some time later would be answered to the effect that NGOs should serve as a counterweight to public and private powers.

Reality trumped theory, and the aspiration for public power caused the presidents of various NGOs to accept public appointments in the government of President Vicente Fox. The inclusion of former activists on the public payroll was viewed with surprise and concern by several sectors (Petras 2000). This raised more questions about the work of NGOs following the alternation in political power in Mexico—a transition that did not necessarily extend to all of the structures upon which the Mexican authoritarian regime had been built. One concern was expressed by several groups: Should political parties act as legitimate institutions to attain and exercise public power, or should there be a mixed system in which NGOs may also be vehicles to obtain public power? How can NGOs profess a discourse based on society's oversight of public power while at the same time seeking to exercise power not through the long line of aspirants to political power and party militancy, but by means of a fast-track route based on a nonpolitical discourse? This identity crisis among NGOs prompted several former activists to offer a range of explanations as to how the organizations had gone from guarding the chickens to eating them: (1) what better than an individual who has been involved from the early stages of a policy or law to be paid with public funds in order to guarantee the enactment of that policy or law? No personal interest is involved, only Mexican society's right to employ the specialized knowledge of an individual to enact policy; (2) the problem with the creation of the new NGO regime is that a new profile is required and is necessary to demonstrate absolute independence. One who has taken part in that process knows its spirit better than anyone; he or she knows its strengths and its likely weaknesses such that his or her presence becomes something like a bond of democratic authenticity and a show of respect for the autonomy of the emerging institution; and (3) what better for one to participate in the process than for his internal capacity to propel the freedom and independence of the civic organization to which he or she belongs? One may not be interested in a public appointment, but the country and the social movement morally compels him or her to work from within the government to initiate the reform process from a position from which it is uniquely possible to change attitudes.

The 2000 presidential elections sent many of the major NGOs into a state of crisis following the decision of many of their main executives to move into public service, presumably in order for everything to continue as normal. In effect, no one in Mexico could prove that these former activists had undertaken a reform of the Mexican legal framework in favor of the consolidation of the rule of law, or that their presence in the government constituted a historical watershed that fell into the periods before and after their entry into government service. In this new framework, a group of academics, activists, journalists, and media proprietors recognized the need to create a social movement to initiate comprehensive structural and legal reform—in other words, to create a legal framework that would accommodate change far beyond the change based on fragile personal voluntarism.

The right of access to public information was a point of convergence among sectors that had historically been incongruous, which in the best of cases were actually pursuing similar goals. The reduction of tensions and mistrust and, alternatively, the formation of an "esprit de corps" around a shared concern, enabled the collaborative work of NGOs to become a constructive reality. The founding of the so-called Oaxaca Group constitutes a historical precedent in the organization of the citizenry in alliance with the media,[7] which gave a stronger voice to the ideas and proposals for legal reform in matters of transparency, access to public information, and accountability.

In the Oaxaca Group, priority was given to reaching consensus on fundamental matters, leaving aside those issues where no agreement was reached, or those issues deemed best dealt with at a later date. An effective division of labor was established whereby everyone had a task to fulfill based on his or her comparative advantages and particular area of knowledge and personal and institutional ability. For the first time in history, a social movement made common cause with the media to give voice to and position the topic on the national agenda as a sine qua non requirement for the emergence of a democratic state under the rule of law. The media, academics, and participating activists did not set their own agenda. Instead, they forged consensus agreements for the good of Mexico.

Also for the first time—and this is a significant precedent—a step was taken from preoccupation to occupation, from criticism to proposal. Unlike the federal government, which has mechanisms to develop legal initiatives and projects, the Oaxaca Group operated without a public budget but instead with a shared commitment to serving the nation. The management and strategy displayed by the Oaxaca Group positioned it to achieve the approval of a Federal Transparency and Access to Government Information Law despite government resistance (the government favored a more superficial law). If Civic Alliance introduced the debate about accountability and the right to know in the 1990s, the Oaxaca Group offered Mexico a federal law in this matter.[8]

As a follow-up effort, in August of 2002 many of the actors of the Oaxaca Group formed a new NGO called Freedom of Information–Mexico AC (Libertad de Información–México AC, or LIMAC), which became the institutionalized arm of the Oaxaca Group devoted to continuing to monitor these issues in the federal realm, promoting access to information legislation throughout the states of the republic, and educating people about the purpose and means of exercising the law allowing access to public information.

It was necessary for these new organizations to experiment with unfamiliar organizational structures, partly due to the fact that the public realm in Mexico suffers from serious credibility problems. Few believe in political institutions, and social participation can offer no guarantees of credibility, on account of what has been stated above. The increasing erosion of traditional institutions is, in a broad sense, a premise that can be demonstrated. This context, however, has given rise to experimental forms of circumstantial behavior. Civil society, as an organization, must fulfill three basic requirements: representativeness, legitimacy, and results.

These elements condition a social movement's ability to have an impact on the structure of public life. Knowledge must be put to use for the benefit of all citizens. The only way to achieve this is to envision and put into practice new forms of societal participation. The principal concern in the creation of this new NGO was to keep the advocates of the movement from ending up holding public office, as had occurred previously in the Mexican experience. For this reason, and because the group's membership included the most recognized journalists and the more influential companies of the national press, LIMAC took measures to prevent the possibility that political careers might be created for personal benefit under the discourse of civil society participation by taking advantage of the good faith of the media.

For this reason, LIMAC became the first NGO in the history of Mexico to establish the following principles in its statutes:

1. Upon becoming a member, an individual must renounce the right to occupy any public office in matters related to the association's social objectives. Public estrangement, to be enforced by the organization's management council, was established as an effective sanction against any person intending to use the association for his own purposes under the banner that his actions are motivated by a profound sense of sacrifice and love for Mexico. Similarly, the association is banned from nominating any candidate for public office. This is a matter of utmost importance insofar as it empowered the management council to launch a media campaign to compel any government employer to think twice before contracting an NGO executive on account of the political cost that would imply, together with loss of prestige of said executive for trying to use the NGO as a stepping-stone to launch his political career.

2. The association shall not be a source of private wealth for anyone. All members shall participate as honorary, unsalaried members.

3. The organization is philanthropic in nature, politically neutral, secular, and all its services will be provided free of charge.

In just over a year, owing to the high standards of its membership, LIMAC has successfully worked to create 10 freedom-of-information laws in different states. Six of these have been developed directly by the LIMAC legal team, which has also signed cooperation agreements with the National Association of State Congresses to promote the topic of transparency, access to information, and accountability with 27 local congresses. Even so, NGOs' integration in Mexican society has still not evolved toward new horizontal and transparent forms that the outcome of the 2000 elections might have produced in these organizations.

NGOs IN MEXICO: PERSPECTIVES AND CHALLENGES FOR THE NEXT TEN YEARS

Henceforth, and particularly in the next 10 years, different challenges and perspectives must be considered if NGOs are not to revert to the marginal space and alternative forums they once occupied. Four main factors will foster development of a new profile for NGOs in Mexico.

First, it must borne in mind that a clear separation must be maintained between an NGO's function and objectives, particularly those NGOs involved in political, social, and economic matters, and the aims of political parties (including the political groups envisaged in the electoral law that are *not* parties and, consequently, cannot put forward candidates directly for public office, but which can associate with political parties to support legally registered candidates), which have a legal obligation in Mexico to seek, obtain, and exercise public office in order to develop an electoral program. NGOs must serve as a counterweight to the exercise of public power in order to promote new laws, reforms, or additions to existing laws to foster a legal system consistent with the image of a democratic state under the rule of law, to supervise compliance with the law, and above all to socialize knowledge and develop an informed citizenry. NGOs fill a fundamental rather than accessory role in the construction of the broad concept of citizenship by empowering people to exert their rights and fulfill legal obligations in a society seeking democracy.

Following the 2000 presidential elections, the separation of the mission of NGOs and the quest for public appointments and power brought about the emergence of a bureaucratic political class that generally earned higher incomes than those they had previously received as civil society activists, although at a high social cost. On one hand, civil society organizations that had been constituted in previous decades generally became weaker; many NGOs created during the 1980s and 1990s now lack convening power and are relatively powerless to set their own agendas to affect the country's democratic life. Some of these organizations have in fact disappeared, and many lack their own Web sites. On the other hand, it has not been empirically demonstrated that this new bureaucratic-political class has made the change to better serve the country or that its presence in the public sector has led to better government.

Second, as a consequence of the foregoing, it is incumbent upon NGOs to undertake an institutional commitment to democracy and accountability as mechanisms to restore social credibility and to ensure their survival as a sector of organized civil society. Rhetorical statements are not enough; it is necessary to develop a normative system with incentives, sanctions, and prohibitions. Therefore, regulatory provisions must be included in NGO statutes regarding prohibitions or mechanisms to prevent NGO executives from getting involved in conflicts of interest by seeking or accepting public positions related to social purposes.[9]

There must also be clauses reflecting in an unambiguous manner the organizations' commitment to transparency in the management of internal resources and their accountability for those resources not only before partners or members but also before society at large. This will allow them to demonstrate that their protests and social activities have long-term viability in Mexico's transition to democracy.

Cooperative relationships among Mexican NGOs will not only strengthen their relationships with NGO counterparts in Canada and the United States but will also create stronger bonds within the national NGO community. In the same way, through internal reform, social organizations will be able to leverage additional funds from foundations and organizations in Canada and the United States interested in Mexico's transition.

Third, two main factors have conditioned the lack of reliable data on the number of Mexican NGOs in existence: (1) the fact that many NGOs exist de facto; they are not legally registered as civil associations under the terms of the civil code and are therefore subject to paying taxes and presenting authorization as donors; in other words, entities without a profit motive whose donors may exempt part of the tax due when making the respective donation; and (2) the (declining) lack of clarity in public property registries where all civil associations must be registered and formalized before a notary public is an indispensable requirement to issue fiscal identity cards to exempt such organizations from paying a portion of their taxes. The Federal Transparency and Access to Public Information Law, as well as similar laws at the state level, should be utilized to clearly identify how many NGOs exist in the country and their areas of interest. The trend in the next few years will be to professionalize the activities of these social organizations in order to provide greater impetus to the work performed by this sector.

Fourth, it is important to develop clear and systemic rules for NGOs, particularly with respect to the delivery of public resources and the forms of social participation in public decisionmaking. With this in mind, some NGOs undertook a project called the Ley de fomento a las actividades de desarrollo social realizadas por organizaciones sociales (Law to promote social development activities carried out by social organizations). This initiative was adopted by several members of Congress and approved by the Chamber of Deputies, although it has not passed in the Senate. This underscores the lack of negotiating capacity of most NGOs. Many NGOs are unfamiliar with professional lobbying processes and lack experience working with the media on common objectives. As a result, this legal initiative was never considered a priority on the national agenda. It ought to be said that the initiative in question is in reality much like a brochure of good intentions. It lacks a legal foundation to the extent that it does not guarantee the enforcement of its aims; in its generality, the initiative lacks sanctions against improper behavior and leaves all procedural enforcement to the executive branch.

It is therefore incumbent on Mexico to enact a new law in this matter, one with an improved legal framework, guaranteeing freedom of action on the one hand and clear participatory rules in its public management on the other, leaving the smallest possible margin of discretion to regulatory officials. In this manner, NGOs in Mexico will have meaning and value outside of politics and the exercise of public power, thus lessening the temptation of executives of such organizations to utilize the organization as a means for personal gain. This is the internal challenge facing NGOs in Mexico and is also the point of departure for these organizations to improve their contribution to the process of democratization of relationships between leaders and the citizenry.

Notes

1. The three generations of human rights refer to the following: first generation: civil and political rights; second generation: economic, social, and cultural rights; and third generation: solidarity rights.

2. Excluded from this analysis are other civil society organizations, such as popular, professional, and socially charitable movements that do not fit within the strict scope of the nongovernmental organizations, which are only mentioned in an accessory manner.

3. According to data from the Directorio de Organizaciones de la Sociedad Civil del Instituto Nacional de Desarrollo Social, where most of the NGOs are registered—although not all that exist in Mexico, bearing in mind that there is no reliable record and figures—these vary according to sources checked. It can be said also that only those organizations having a legal status are counted here, leaving unaccounted those which are de facto operators.

4. As far as the government is concerned, the number of NGOs is approximately 7,000; other believe the figures are double that. It is important to reiterate, however, that in Mexico no one can affirm the precise number of existing organizations

5. On November 22, 1992, the Secretaría de Gobernación, Secretaría de Hacienda y Crédito Público, and the Secretaría de la Contraloría issued "Guidelines for the Application of Federal Resources Destined to Advertising and Broadcasting." That is considered as a starting point to regulate public resources destined to the media.

6. This is of great importance, if we take into account that although the federal legislative power in Mexico is constituted by two chambers, of deputies and of senators, and that the former has the exclusive faculty to approve the Budget of Expenditures of the Federation, signifying how public monies are to be to spent among federal dependencies and organizations and with the economic participation of states and municipalities.

7. The Oaxaca Group is so called because it was in the city of Oaxaca where its members first met, and the first that was so identified at a meeting with the author of this essay was journalist Ginger Thompson of the *New York Times*.

8. Following approval of the law, tension developed among some members of the Oaxaca Group. Some, not too many, thought that there should be members of the group in the independent regulatory body as provided in the Federal Transparency and Access to Government Information Law as part of a membership ensuring a good performance. Others, the majority, insisted that the group' s

objective was not to exercise power but to create legal norms to promote the democratic system, that it was not convenient to repeat the experience of the year 2000 with the NGOs while holding the perception that the law had been enacted to occupy public office. This last position triumphed, but the original group disappeared as a result of those perception and criteria differences.

9. This does not refer to other legal formulas of the social organizations, because those that differ from civil associations have been fundamentally devoted to giving legal life to philanthropic and social assistance organizations whose operating features are not the concern of this chapter.

References

Aguayo, Sergio, and Luz Paula Parra. 1997. *Las organizaciones no gubernamentales de derechos humanos en México: Entre la democracia participativa y la electoral.* Mexico City: Academia Mexicana de Derechos Humanos.

Beniger, James. 1977. Toward an Old New Paradigm: The Half-Century Flirtation with Mass Society. *Public Opinion Quarterly* 51: 46–66.

Cohen, L. Jean, and Andrew Arato. 2001. *Sociedad civil y teoría política.* Mexico City: Fondo de Cultura Económica.

Dabas, Elina, and Dense Najmanovich, eds. 1995. *Redes: El lenguaje de los vínculos—Hacia la reconstrucción y el fortalecimiento de la sociedad civil.* Mexico City: Paidós.

Diamond, Larry. 1997. Reprensar la sociedad civil. *Metapolítica*, no. 2 (April–June): 186–94.

García Ramírez, Sergio. 1994. Citizen Participation: An Essay in Constitutional Systematization (in Spanish). In *Participación ciudadana y control social*, ed. María Elenam Vázquez Nava. Mexico City: Porrúa.

McCombs, Maxwell, and Issa Luna Pla, eds. 2003. *Agenda-setting de los medios de comunicación.* Mexico City: Universidad Iberoamericana–Universidad de Occidente.

Olvera, Alberto J., ed. 1999. *La sociedad civil: De la teoría a la realidad.* Mexico City: Colegio de México.

Petras, James. 2000. Las dos caras de las ONG's. *La Jornada*, August 8.

Speir, Hans. 1950. Historical Development of Public Opinion. *American Journal of Sociology* 55, no. 4: 376–88.

Vázquez Nava, María Elenam, ed. 1994. *Participación ciudadana y control social.* Mexico City: Porrúa.

PART FOUR

SECURITY

CHAPTER EIGHT

MEXICAN POLICY AGAINST DRUGS: FROM DETERRING TO EMBRACING THE UNITED STATES

María Celia Toro

Even before thinking about NAFTA, Mexican president Carlos Salinas de Gortari (1988–94) seemed determined to put an end to the increasing deterioration of U.S.–Mexican relations that began in the early 1980s. The Mexican debt crisis played an important role in changing U.S. perceptions about Mexican stability and capacity to develop. A drastic increase in the smuggling of cocaine also contributed to raising doubts about the firmness of U.S.–Mexican traditional security relations. As the 1980s unfolded, drug trafficking soon became the most immediate security concern and the most important source of bilateral conflict.

In December 1988, President Salinas announced to a group of U.S. legislators that he would "make life miserable" for drug traffickers (Rohter 1988). The message was intended for U.S. ears in an effort to soften U.S. aggressive unilateralism, which the murder of Drug Enforcement Administration (DEA) agent Enrique Camarena in February 1985 in Mexico had unleashed. The U.S. search for leverage to change Mexican drug policy, while not new, took many forms and was strongly exerted as of that year. To modify the contentious dynamic of U.S.–Mexican relations and to confront the immense domestic challenge that drug trafficking had come to represent by the mid-1980s, Salinas came up with an unprecedented promise to work more closely with the United States and to bolster Mexican programs against drug smuggling.

Salinas was building, to be sure, on President Miguel de la Madrid's decision to raise antidrug policy to the top of Mexico's internal and foreign policy priorities. The torture and murder of Camarena is frequently referred to as a major turning point in the U.S.–Mexican history of

I thank Gabriela Pérez for her proficient work as a research assistant.

fighting drug smuggling because it triggered sustained and open U.S. pressure on a reluctant Mexican government that, according to the United States, was not ready to collaborate in the "war against drugs," a U.S. foreign policy priority in the Western Hemisphere. Less attention is given, however, to the tremendous impact of the Camarena affair in Mexico. As a result of the scandal, an astonished Mexican public learned about the presence and work of DEA agents in Mexico.[1] It also became clear to the Mexican government and society that drug-related corruption and violence had to be addressed.

Until the early 1980s, Mexicans had little reason to worry about the abuse of drugs in the United States; the long-existing concern in Mexico with the illegal production of marijuana and opium poppies had been taken care of. The decision—which went largely unnoticed in the United States—to send 25,000 soldiers to conduct a national eradication program in 1983 was the last in a series of efforts to curb the illegal cultivation of drugs by Mexican peasants, a program that remains in place.[2] The massive transportation of cocaine through Mexican territory that began in those years as a result of more stringent U.S. interdiction efforts was not, however, then perceived as a major threat. Mexico was unable to foresee the consequences that U.S. interdiction programs in Florida, launched in the early 1980s with the purpose of elevating the risks and costs for cocaine traffickers at selected U.S. ports of entry, would have on the Mexican drug market. The dramatic increase in the U.S. import price of cocaine, of which drug smugglers were the main beneficiaries, allowed Colombian traffickers to change their contraband routes, to avoid detection, from Caribbean waters to Mexican soil.[3] Neither was the Mexican government able to fully grasp the major change in U.S. policy introduced in those years by the Ronald Reagan administration's war on drugs, which included a more forceful and daring internationalization of the U.S. police and judiciary that threatened Mexico's exclusive jurisdiction over law enforcement.

Thus, Mexico had to confront the twin security threats that massive narcotics trafficking and the U.S. policy against drugs came to represent by the mid-1980s. Acknowledging the magnitude of these political challenges, in 1987 President de la Madrid declared drug trafficking a "threat to national security," a "state affair" that required preventing traffickers and foreign police from challenging internal and sovereign authority. This novel definition of what was all too frequently considered a "U.S. problem" in Mexico was also a first step, probably unacknowledged, in the direction of fully engaging and participating in the U.S. drug war.

Two policy strategies were adopted to advance Mexican interests in deterring both traffickers and U.S. cops: restructuring ineffective law enforcement programs and negotiating the scope and limits of bilateral cooperation, in particular, the presence and activities of U.S. security agents in Mexico.

Accurately assessing the limited capacity of eradication and inter-diction programs to reduce drug smuggling (and their unintended consequences on the organization of the international drug market), U.S. analysts were convinced that the immobilization of drug-trafficking organizations was the best approach. Dismantling the most powerful criminal organizations, however, required, in their view, sophisticated intelligence, a properly working judiciary, and high-security prisons— all of which were lacking in Mexico. It also required, Americans argued, the introduction of more intrusive police techniques like wire-tapping, witness protection programs, infiltration of criminal organizations, and undercover operations, some of which were part of the Mexican police repertoire but were basically illegal until the second half of the 1990s. This diagnosis, which depicted drug trafficking as organized crime, was adopted by Mexican officials. Toward the end of the 1980s, the Mexican government began working along these lines.

The Mexican government could rely only on a police force that, at best, could incarcerate people by the thousands and detain the more dangerous criminals (usually with the assistance of the military) to de-liver them to the judiciary, which was also ill prepared to handle con-victions of such resourceful delinquents. Increased corruption, the abuse of authority, and violence were the most conspicuous and perni-cious results of the new antidrug strategy. Launching a major offensive against the largest criminal organizations thus amounted to a severe weakening of the Mexican criminal justice system, the consequences of which are still being suffered by Mexicans today.

THE SALINAS YEARS

President Salinas forcefully reiterated that drug trafficking represented a threat to national security because of its capacity to affect Mexican poli-tics and society. His drug policy maintained an internal and a foreign policy orientation. Externally, the Mexican president tried to prevent

U.S. policing and evidence gathering without Mexican consent and to assuage U.S. anger against ineffective drug programs, which was expressed—and profusely covered by journalists in both countries—every year during congressional debates leading to the "certification" of countries that were "fully cooperating" with the United States in countering the illegal drug trade.

Salinas hurriedly tried to restructure both U.S.–Mexican relations regarding drugs and Mexican antinarcotics programs. The latter required the creation of an intelligence office, a special antinarcotics police force, and special training for agents at the Federal Prosecutors Office (Ministerio Público Federal, MP).

The most important intelligence agency since 1947, the Dirección Federal de Seguridad (DFS), had been disbanded in 1985. It had become involved in drug trafficking over the previous decade. Bringing together the remnants of the DFS and the General Directorate of Political and Social Investigation, President de la Madrid had previously begun creating "an early version of a national security apparatus," the General Directorate of Investigation and National Security (Secretaría de Gobernación, DISEN; Doyle 1994, 84; see also Aguayo 1996). Salinas immediately abolished the DISEN and, in December 1988, created the Centro de Investigación y Seguridad Nacional (CISEN) and placed it in charge of organizing and operating the country's security information and investigative system. Aguayo claims that CISEN "represented the Mexican government's first serious attempt to create a genuine intelligence service," and a clear commitment to professionalism (Bailey and Aguayo 1996, 149). Unfortunately, this effort would not last long. In 1992, President Salinas removed the first director of CISEN and tasked him to take charge of antidrug policy.[4]

A new, highly visible post, the assistant attorney general for the investigation and combat of drug trafficking, was created during Salinas's first year in office, and the budget for the office of the attorney general was doubled. By the end of the de la Madrid administration, this office was already spending more than half of its budget on antidrug law enforcement.

Between 1,200 and 1,500 new agents were hired and trained in antinarcotics operations during the Salinas administration, and 344 agents from the federal public prosecutor's office were trained as specialists in narcotics (U.S. Department of State 1992, 4). Reliance on the Mexican military as the main eradication force increased; by 2000, soldiers were destroying an annual average of more than 30,000 hectares of marijuana and opium poppies, approximately 70 percent of national eradication programs.[5]

The Federal Judicial Police (FJP) and the new assistant attorney general for narcotics (called the "iron prosecutor," *el procurador de hierro*) were granted considerable power and leeway when it came to enforcing antidrug laws. They managed, indeed, to make life miserable for drug dealers—but not only for them. In frequently circumventing the Ministerio Público (in charge of conducting investigations and authorizing police activities), security agents adopted unacceptable and illegal police practices. Many honest public prosecutors (*agentes del* MP) left; others stayed to become victims, bystanders, or beneficiaries of irregular practices. The police went literally out of control.

The assistant attorney general for the investigation and combat of drug trafficking was dismissed in 1990 as a result of strong public pressure and outcry against human rights violations by police agents enforcing antidrug laws. The head of the National Commission for Human Rights was named the new Mexican attorney general. That same year, Salinas created the National Drug Control Center (CENDRO) to work as an intelligence agency that would provide the FJP with information.

Major efforts were made to prevent corruption and abuse of authority: 270 Procuraduría General de la República (PGR) officials and FJP agents were referred for prosecution on those kinds of charges in 1992 (U.S. Department of State 1992, 4). Penal codes and articles of the Mexican constitution were amended in 1993 to legalize new police practices, classify a set of criminal activities as organized crime, introduce stiffer penalties, enhance respect for human rights, establish new guidelines for criminal investigations and public prosecutors, and so on.[6]

Many legal and organizational changes were made in hasty response to public scandals resulting from extraordinarily violent acts by drug traffickers and from knowledge about practitioners of high-level corruption. In response to the murder of Cardinal Juan Jesús Posadas Ocampo in 1993, mistakenly shot, according to the attorney general, by drug traffickers,[7] Salinas created the National Institute for the Control of Drugs (INCD), which was responsible for conducting antidrug policy and took over many of the functions of the assistant attorney general for narcotics. In 1997, only four years after its creation, the INCD was dissolved in the midst of a political scandal involving its head, a high-ranking member of the Mexican military.

Interdiction efforts were basically bilateral. Following U.S. advice, both Mexican borders were patrolled via radar, after the acquisition of an expensive radar system. A new interdiction unit at the FJP was created, with U.S. support, to intercept the aerial cocaine traffic massively crossing the U.S.–Mexican border. The Northern Border Response Force (Operación Halcón) was a bilateral team consisting of 1,800 members of the FJP, which through the use of UH-1H helicopters leased from the U.S. and relying on intelligence provided by the DEA and the U.S. military, was able to seize close to 50 tons of cocaine in 1990, an all-time high in the history of Mexican interdiction programs. Fewer than 17 tons were seized in 1988, and only 460 kilograms were confiscated in 1984.[8]

U.S. radar planes entering Mexican airspace in pursuit of aircraft believed to be carrying drugs was also allowed, but the flights were suspended in response to public protest. Both hot pursuit and the creation of joint task forces had been considered to be unacceptable U.S. proposals by President de la Madrid, Salinas's predecessor.

It was believed, at the same time, that bilateral treaties establishing the terms of bilateral police and judicial assistance would bind U.S. authorities. For example, with the purpose of deterring aggressive DEA tactics—specifically the irregular surrender of fugitives and evidence-gathering activities in Mexico to prosecute Mexican criminals in U.S. courts—the Mexican attorney general urged the signing in 1987 of a Mutual Legal Assistance Treaty, in force as of May 1991, and proposed the modification of the 1978 U.S.–Mexican extradition treaty.[9]

Similar concerns and goals animated Salinas's proposal to sign, in 1989, the bilateral Agreement on Cooperation in Combating Narcotics Trafficking and Drug Dependency, which stressed that the parties to the agreement would act "in accordance with the principles of self-determination, non-intervention in internal affairs, legal equality, and respect for the territorial integrity of States."[10]

In 1990, the kidnapping of Alvarez Machain, who was illegally taken to the United States to stand trial, was perhaps the most important source of public contention between Mexico and the United States in those years. The 1992 U.S. Supreme Court decision in *United States v. Alvarez Machain*, upholding the kidnapping of foreign nationals by U.S. police, was much debated and criticized in Mexico. The decision reminded Mexican officials that incidents like this were not only the result of U.S. "policemen working on their own" but were rather part of a more permissive political and legal context in the United States.[11] The participation of Mexican police in this and other kidnappings, and their being paid or otherwise cajoled by DEA agents, led the Mexican government to introduce new legislation in an effort to have effective jurisdiction over both national and foreign police in Mexico. As he forcefully protested unacceptable police practices by "foreign agents" (and threatened to suspend all collaboration with the United States), Salinas sent Congress a new law that made transnational kidnapping "a crime against the homeland." Mexican citizens who participated in the abduction of persons for the purpose of delivering them to foreign authorities would be severely punished; foreigners would be subjected to "immediate expulsion."

In July 1992, during the meeting between Salinas and U.S. president George H.W. Bush in San Diego, Salinas publicly rejected as invalid the U.S. Supreme Court decision regarding abductions abroad and made reference to the rules that would guide the presence and operations of foreign agents in Mexican territory. According to the Decree on Rules for the Temporary Stay of Foreign Agencies Representatives, issued that same month, those agents would serve as liaisons only for the purpose of sharing information; information gathered in Mexico had to be immediately shared with the assigned Mexican counterpart; foreign agents were compelled to observe Mexican law; and they had to be properly accredited and registered and were not to be immune from Mexican penal codes.

In terms of U.S.–Mexican relations, Salinas tried what at the end would prove impossible: to deter the extraterritorial assertion of U.S. drug laws while depending on the United States for the effectiveness of Mexican programs. His successors would face the same dilemma.

Internally, Salinas's policy succeeded in modifying the Mexican drug-trafficking scene: Major traffickers were incarcerated; bilateral interdiction programs at the Mexican Northern border forced drug smuggling from the air to the ground, and toward the Pacific Coast; and more forceful antidrug law enforcement unleashed an unprecedented violent response by traffickers and propelled drug-related corruption to higher political levels, beyond police units, reaching the military and the judiciary.

The killing of Cardinal Posadas in 1993, as well as the assassinations of the secretary general of the Institutional Revolutionary Party (Partido Revolucionario Institucional, PRI), Francisco Ruiz Massieu, and of the PRI's presidential candidate Luis Donaldo Colosio in 1994 (many speculated that the three murders could have been drug related) left president Ernesto Zedillo (1994–2000) with a complicated implementation-of-justice crisis that had to be addressed immediately.

THE ZEDILLO ADMINISTRATION

Maintaining a similar discourse at home and abroad, Zedillo introduced far-reaching changes in U.S.–Mexican antidrug law enforcement relations and embarked on yet another major restructuring of Mexican programs to counter drug trafficking and, a most significant addition, non-drug-related criminal activities. That previous programs had been unable to destroy the drug-trafficking organizations was acknowledged by President Zedillo in 1996, when he declared that *narcotráfico* "had become the biggest threat to Mexican national security" (quoted in Turbiville 2002, 263). Actions taken to safeguard and strengthen Mexican institutions, a reiterated priority in Zedillo's antidrug policy, followed previous patterns: disbanding and reorganizing police agencies; massive dismissal of police officials; programs to professionalize security agencies and the judiciary; higher penalties; new police techniques, and so forth.

But Zedillo also followed the much-debated path of "militarizing" police and intelligence agencies to not only confront drug trafficking but also deal with what had become a national public safety crisis. Between 1991 and 1997, crime grew at a higher rate than did the population in Mexico, with delinquency rates growing significantly in the 1995–97 period. Though crime figures vary considerably in Mexico and analysts debate their validity, most researchers maintain that the delinquency crisis was particularly acute in Mexico City, where the number of crimes for every 100,000 inhabitants jumped from 1,918 to 3,081 between 1994 and 1997, and the average number of daily crimes reported increased by 64 percent in those same years (Alvarado and Davis 2001, 121, 127). Close to 1.5 million crimes, according to the Mexican Interior Ministry, were reported in 1997, which may have represented half the number of crimes that actually occurred considering the percentage of crimes that went unreported.[12] Moreover, delinquency became more violent and better organized. Truly dramatic was the inability of the authorities to enforce the law. Of the 1.49 million criminal complaints filed in 1998, only 249,000 cases were decided; of the 149,000 arrest warrants issued that year, only 85,000 were carried out (Bailey and Chabat 2002, 11).

In trying to quickly set up a properly working front against increasing violence and crime in Mexico City and the rest of the country, the Zedillo administration replaced thousands of civilian police with soldiers technically on leave and drastically enlarged police personnel and budgets. Financial resources for the new National Public Security System multiplied fortyfold in three years, between 1996 and 1998.[13] National policing was reorganized by separating preventive from investigative agencies. A new national police force, the Federal Preventive Police (Policía Federal Preventiva, PFP) was created in 1999, a decision considered by police specialists "the most important police-related initiative" of the Zedillo administration. By mid-2000, it had more than 11,000 agents, of which 5,000 came from the military, 1,000 came from CISEN, and 4,000 from the Federal Highway Police.[14] Between September 2001 and June 2002, the PFP hired 1,700 new agents (Sierra Guzmán 2003, 4).

To more effectively confront drug trafficking, the Zedillo administration opted for U.S. support and allowed for increased U.S. participation in the implementation of Mexican antidrug programs. An old expedient, the creation of elite police units, was restored. U.S. police and intelligence agencies, in particular the DEA and the Federal Bureau of Investigation (FBI), were active in the design and training of these special units. Support by the U.S. Department of Defense also grew, as will be noted below. The increased participation of U.S. security agencies and of the Mexican military in antidrug law enforcement was a matter of policy and an operational necessity.

The decision to get tough with crime required, again, the modification of penal codes and of the Constitution. The Mexican Supreme Court determined in March 1996 that the armed forces were allowed to support civilians in law enforcement efforts, at the request of civilian authorities. A landmark in Mexican history against crime was the passing of the Ley Federal Contra la Delicuencia Organizada (LFCDO) in 1996. Believed to be a much-needed reform to disrupt the drug cartels, the law largely expands police and judicial powers. It allows for the building of conspiracy cases and the creation of special crime units and special prosecutors; it introduces exceptional prosecutorial measures and legalizes practices like home detention, undercover operations, witness protection, and the reduction of sentences to cooperative criminals. This law has been criticized by Mexican criminal lawyers and academics as a dangerous tool that will inevitably lead to the abuse of human and civil rights.

The LFCDO mandated the creation of a crime unit for the investigation and prosecution of organized crime. A small but powerful Special Organized Crime Unit (Unidad Especializada Contra la Delincuencia Organizada, UEDO) accordingly was created. It is, legally, the only elite unit authorized to use the expanded police powers mentioned above.

In response to the arrest in early 1997 of the INCD commissioner, who was accused of protecting drug traffickers (Gutiérrez Rebollo had been in this office fewer than three months), the INCD was reorganized to become, in April 1997, the Office of the Special Prosecutor for Crimes against Health (Fiscalía Especial para Atención a los Delitos contra la Salud, FEADS). A member of the armed forces was appointed head—that is, special prosecutor—of FEADS.[15]

Both FEADS and UEDO have worked closely with U.S. agencies (DEA and FBI) and with officials at the U.S. Department of Justice. The Northern Border Response Force continued, though with major changes in its personnel. A Special Anti-Money-Laundering Unit (Unidad Especializada contra el Lavado de Dinero, UECLD) was also created in 1998. Because it lacked the required expertise, one researcher claims, the UECLD and the Ministry of the Treasury depend largely on the Financial Crimes Enforcement Network at the U.S. Department of the Treasury (Arzt 2002, 147).

Since 1996, the U.S. State Department has redirected part of its annual financial support to the PGR, to include the Mexican military. The main recipients of that aid during the past few years have been specialized antidrug agencies and units fighting organized crime, most notably FEADS, UEDO, the air services division, CENDRO, and the Agencia Federal de Investigación (AFI), all of which function as part of the Office of the Attorney General (Sierra Guzmán 2003, 10). Also, since the mid-1990s, the U.S. government has offered assistance in monitoring and hiring new security personnel, in particular those involved in high-level investigations and prosecutions. Applicants to UECLD, to UEDO, and to FEADS are scrutinized and tested, with DEA and FBI support, before they can join the organizations (Arzt 2002, 146–47).

Practically all drug law enforcement operations (eradication, interdiction, seizure of assets, intelligence, immobilization) have been handed over to military officers. This policy has been pushed even further by the Vicente Fox administration, which transferred investigation and arrest of traffickers to the military after dissolving the FJP in October 2001. The FJP was restructured at the beginning of 2002 to become the AFI, with new personnel, including members of the military, trained by the FBI.

A parallel strategy was to create bilateral forums that would allow U.S. and Mexican officials to explain their concerns and their programs, reach further agreements and, it was hoped, prevent U.S. security agents from engaging in unacceptable breaches of Mexican sovereignty. On the basis of this logic, the attorneys general of the two countries created, in February 1995, the Plenary Group on Law Enforcement, which would meet four to five times a year (Domínguez and Fernández de Castro 2001, 45). In March 1996, in an effort to influence U.S. perceptions and evaluations of Mexican antidrug programs, which many U.S. officials and congressmen regarded poorly, the Mexican government proposed the creation of a High-Level Contact Group for Drug Control (HLCGDC), which would meet twice a year.

Then, in May 1997, Zedillo and Clinton announced in Mexico City the United States–Mexico Alliance Against Drugs. Both countries committed themselves to forging an alliance against a "threat to the national security of both nations" and agreed on the principles that would guide bilateral cooperation. The HLCGDC organized a binational study group that issued the United States–Mexico Bilateral Drug Threat Assessment in an effort to agree on the most important threats (production, distribution, trafficking, and consumption of illegal drugs, as well as money laundering, diversion of chemical precursors, and arms smuggling) and the best means of coping with them. In February 1998, the high-level contact group issued the U.S–Mexico Bi-National Drug Strategy. "Both countries recognize"—according to the text of this document—"that bilateral cooperation, to be effective, can only be developed through adherence to the principles of sovereign equality and the integrity of national territory, as well as nonintervention in the internal affairs of other States."

"The HLCGDC"—according to Domínguez and Fernández de Castro (2001)—"was the first entity created at the highest level of both governments to coordinate and manage bilateral security relations from the policy to the operational level." It marked the beginning of a "bandwagoning alliance" that came to fully accept U.S. influence and operational activities in Mexico.[16] Consequently, Mexico agreed, among other things, to coordinate maritime operations with the U.S. Coast Guard, to allow surveillance operations by U.S. ships and aircraft in

Mexican waters and airspace, to accept military support and training, and to admit 12 additional U.S. law enforcement agents, 6 from the DEA and 6 from the FBI.[17] The two governments also agreed to create "Bilateral Border Task Forces to facilitate the actions of the two governments, each operating within its respective jurisdiction . . . to dismantle major drug trafficking organizations in both countries" (U.S. Office of National Drug Control Policy 1998).

According to participating Mexican officials, however, the cooperation/institutionalization strategy tried to achieve the same officially stated goals through different means. The strategy of striking a new deal with the United States by means of "institutionalizing the relationship" had the purpose of building trust through continuous communication. Mexican officials believed that a more open dialogue and explicitly agreed-upon bilateral programs would improve political relations and avoid unwelcome "surprises." There was also the hope, probably inspired by the NAFTA experience, that by creating bilateral collaboration mechanisms, the Mexican government would also have an opportunity to persuade the United States to cooperate on other drug-related and security matters, such as the use of drugs and arms smuggling (Ruiz-Cabañas 1998). The strategy was not fully successful, however.

In May 1998, the Mexican government learned about Operation Casablanca, a major anti-money-laundering investigation that had begun in November 1995 and had been conducted by the U.S. Customs Service. The targets were Mexican banks on the United States–Mexico border that were being used by drug traffickers to launder money. The operation involved more than 200 undercover agents and resulted in more than 150 arrests (about $100 million in drug-related profits were confiscated). The United States indicted, at the end, 22 bank employees from 12 Mexican banks (Hoffer 2000, 297).

Mexican officials were deeply disappointed. Just as the operation was widely praised in the United States, a Mexican deputy of the National Action Party (PAN) declared that the Casablanca indictments were "proof of a unilateral, deceitful, and disloyal relationship." President Zedillo formally protested and declared that Operation Casablanca violated Mexican law and U.S.–Mexican cooperation agreements. According to Hoffer, the Mexican government also denied a U.S. request for extradition of five individuals connected to the operation. At the end, the attorneys general of the two countries "pledged to keep each other fully informed about sensitive law enforcement activities" (Hoffer 2000, 303).

Mexican diplomats also had a keen interest in establishing a common evaluation mechanism to assess the effectiveness of antidrug programs, one that would eliminate the United States annual evaluation/certification. With a similar purpose, the Mexican government invested energies and resources to establish a Multilateral Evaluation Mechanism within the Organization of American States (OAS). Pressures from various Latin American countries within the OAS framework eventually led to the temporary suspension of the infamous certification process in 2001.

The policy of "certifying" or "decertifying" governments, according to their willingness to participate in the U.S. war on drugs, was another means by which the U.S. government tried to shape antidrug policy in other countries. As mandated by the Anti-Drug Abuse Act of 1986, which amended, among others, the Foreign Assistance Act, the U.S. executive branch was required to present to Congress an annual evaluation of more than 30 countries to establish whether they were "fully cooperating" with the United States in counternarcotics programs. Noncertification of a country could lead to the cancellation of U.S. economic and military aid, trade preferences, and support in multilateral lending institutions. The statute and its implementation for more than a decade gave the U.S. Congress an unprecedented vocal role in U.S.– Mexican relations, because members of the House of Representatives and of the Senate could ask for the decertification of a country like Mexico without major risks and at little cost. Though representatives and senators could reject the recommendation of the executive branch to extend certification to a country, the president could prevail if he considered that "vital national interests of the United States" were at stake.[18]

It was common in the late 1980s and during the second half of the 1990s for U.S. legislators to call for a decertification of Mexico, a political exercise that led to an annual round of criticisms and often to "supercilious pronouncements about Mexico's abundant imperfections" (Smith 1999, 208). Still, most accounts of the politics of certification suggest that approval of Mexico's performance was often pressed hard by the White House and the State Department for reasons that had little to do with a positive assessment of Mexican policy against drugs, such as the need to obtain support for NAFTA (before and after its ratification), or for the financial rescue package offered to Mexico at the beginning of 1995. U.S. advocates of taking the war on drugs more seriously lamented that U.S interests in NAFTA could hinder, one year after another, the decertification of the Mexican government.

For the Mexican government and public, the scrutiny represented a humiliating and unacceptable practice that invariably prompted nationalist responses from the Mexican executive branch, Congress, and media.[19] This U.S. instrument of foreign policy also accounted for the annual visit to Washington, before the congressional debates, of a multitude of Mexican officials who, aided by the Mexican embassy and by lobbyists hired by the Mexican government, tried to prevent a good number of members of Congress—each advancing their own, usually domestic interests—from rejecting the executive's certification. The creation of bilateral mechanisms to discuss and evaluate antidrug programs was yet another Mexican attempt to persuade the U.S. Congress and encourage the executive's support.

It is difficult to determine the precise influence on Mexican drug policy of this long-maintained threat of decertification. Many analysts in Mexico have claimed that for every annual certification, a long list of concessions was in order. The U.S. government certainly believed that it was an effective negotiating tool (e.g., see Storrs 1998). By the end of the 1990s, however, the practice of certifying countries had also become a political liability for the United States.

Two additional changes in Mexican policy have been identified as constituting important departures from traditional stances and practices: Mexican extradition policy, and the relationship between the Mexican and the U.S. military. Let us look briefly at each.

Extradition

As of the mid-1990s, the Mexican government decided to adopt extradition as an important tool in fighting organized crime. In 1996, "President Zedillo broke precedent by deciding to extradite two Mexican nationals" (U.S. Office of National Drug Control Policy 1997, vol. 1, sec. 5., p. 3, "Extradition"). For a long time, Mexico refused, as a matter of policy, to extradite Mexican nationals, an increasingly unbearable practice for U.S. officials during the 1990s. The Mexican law is contradictory.[20] The Penal Code grants the right to all Mexicans to be judged in Mexico and by Mexican judges; the Law of International Extradition as well as the U.S.–Mexican Extradition Treaty establish that Mexicans will not be extradited to foreign nations, unless the executive considers that "exceptional circumstances" warrant their extradition. To the extent that those exceptional circumstances are not defined, extradition of Mexican citizens remains a discretionary, usually presidential, decision. A defendant may challenge a judge's decision in favor of extradition by petitioning for an *amparo* (writ of habeas corpus).

Arturo Everardo Páez, a member of the Tijuana cartel, sought protection from extradition through an *amparo* on the grounds that as a Mexican he could not be extradited to the United States. The Second Circuit Collegiate Tribunal overturned this *amparo*, stating that the U.S.–Mexican Extradition Treaty authorized the Mexican government to extradite nationals under exceptional circumstances. A contradiction in sentences arose as the result of a previous decision by the First Circuit judges, based on the letter of the Mexican Penal Code, to uphold the *amparo* provision of another noted trafficker, Oscar Malherbe de León. The Mexican Supreme Court was called upon to resolve the contradiction of rulings. On January 18, 2001, in a 10 to 1 vote, "the Mexican Supreme Court handed out a historic ruling" in favor of a resolution that held that the Mexican executive had the legal right to extradite nationals. "The decision"—argues Pérez García—"ended a century-long tradition of protecting Mexicans from being tried outside their homeland" (Pérez García 2000, 1). Páez, charged with smuggling cocaine and laundering money, was extradited to the United States on May 4, 2001, after more than four years of fighting his extradition.[21]

Notwithstanding the importance of this Supreme Court ruling, it came after five years of Mexican decisions facilitating extradition procedures. As of 1996, the Zedillo government began to extradite Mexican citizens in an attempt to compensate for the failure of the Mexican criminal justice system to convict and incarcerate drug traffickers. According to the assistant attorney general for international affairs, "extradition was the best instrument for curbing impunity."[22]

The Mexican government realized the benefits of relying on the U.S. criminal justice system in 1996, when president Zedillo decided to expel Juan García Abrego, the reputed leader of the "Gulf cartel." García Abrego, whose extradition had been requested by the U.S. government, was deported to the United States immediately after his arrest. To hand him over to the neighboring country without initiating extradition proceedings, Mexican officials argued that he was an American citizen (he had double nationality) and declared him persona non grata.

This bold decision was taken out of fear that García Abrego's trial could become a political liability, resulting in extraordinary violence against police, judges, and witnesses, or in the dismissal of charges based on the intimidation or corruption of judicial authorities.

Thus would begin Mexico's new extradition policy. Tens of fugitives, both Mexican and U.S. citizens, have been extradited to the United States since then. A similar number have been extradited from the United States to Mexico. To avoid long legal procedures or to circumvent Mexican law prohibiting the extradition of defendants who may face death penalty or lifelong sentences,[23] the two governments are relying on the Fugitive Identification and Alert Program to deport fugitives on the grounds that they have violated immigration laws (U.S. Office of National Drug Control Policy 1997, 1).

A "temporary extradition" agreement that allows for individuals to be tried in both countries prior to the completion of their sentences in either country has also been approved. (This was a ratification of the protocol signed in November 1997 to amend the existing extradition treaty.) Under this provision, criminals tried and convicted in one country can be sent to the other country to stand trial before serving their sentence. After completing their sentence in the first country, they can serve prison time in the second country.

Mexico's turnaround regarding the extradition of nationals was based on extensive joint investigative and information-gathering operations. What is striking in these new extradition relations, "one of the areas of the bilateral partnership which has seen the most progress in the shortest period of time," is the fact that all major Mexican traffickers have been targeted for extradition to the United States (U.S. Office of National Drug Control Policy 1997, 7). Actually, as of the mid-1990s, most criminal investigations of well-known traffickers have been jointly conducted to ensure successful prosecution by Mexican tribunals, or, more likely, in the U.S. courts, for incarceration in the country where tried.

The Military

The "special strategic relationship" that Mexico and the United States maintained between 1941 and 1989 began changing, according to Latell, under the Salinas administration toward a "new, more open, and formal array of security collaboration and agreements" (Latell 2002, 285). The quiet and reluctant security collaboration characteristic of the Cold War years was effective and advanced the interests of both countries. Mexico was able to maintain its nationalist foreign policy and to avoid U.S. overt or covert intervention in Mexican domestic politics. The United States could be assured of Mexican cooperation when in need (i.e., important East–West issues) and could count on a stable, communist-free neighbor. "Relations between the Mexican and U.S. military establishments"—continues Latell—"do appear to have reflected to a considerable degree the parameters of the special strategic relationship" (2002, 291).

Relations between the Mexican and the U.S. armed forces began changing in the 1990s, mostly as a result of Mexico's decision to drastically accelerate the militarization of all the agencies in charge of enforcing antidrug laws. The decision to expand the role of the armed forces in interdiction and programs to immobilize drug-trafficking organizations is largely explained by the repeated failures to professionalize the police and the pressing need to address the conspicuous resilience of drug-trafficking organizations. However, this decision was also congruent with U.S. insistence on the need to use military personnel to bolster interdiction capabilities in the United States and other countries. The increasing militarization of the U.S. Southwestern border was meant to achieve the first goal; as for the second, "the United States launched its most ambitious program ever to arm and train foreign military forces for the war [on drugs]" (Doyle 1993, 86).

The increase in the participation of the Mexican military in antidrug law enforcement, other than the long-standing participation of the army in eradication programs, formally began during the Salinas administration with the creation of "a staff section for special operations that concentrated on developing antinarcotics activities" (Doyle 1993, 84). The United States and Mexico agreed then on the need to create an intelligence unit within the Mexican military that would not have to rely on information provided by the police. Salinas also allowed for an expanded participation of the armed forces in interdiction efforts by setting up military checkpoints along roads.

But appointing military personnel, on leave from the armed services, to head and staff all the agencies involved in antidrug law enforcement (as well as other police forces) began with the Zedillo administration and has continued under Fox. The INCD has been headed, since its creation, by military officers (retired or active). Under Fox, the number of soldiers within the Policía Federal Preventiva has increased, and 1,600 members of navy battalions were incorporated into it. President Fox appointed General Rafael Macedo de la Concha as attorney general, "marking the first time a military officer was chosen to direct the PGR." Consequently, many top level positions within the PGR are in charge of military officers. A military general has also been called to direct CENDRO. In late 2002, 107 members of the military were assigned to FEADS (Sierra Guzmán 2003, 4, 5).

Today, Mexican army personnel are directly in charge of dismantling the largest drug-trafficking organizations, mostly through special forces battalions trained by the U.S. military.[24] Among many other drug traffickers, soldiers arrested, in March 2002, the highest-ranking leader of the Tijuana cartel, Benjamín Arellano Félix, and 2,000 individuals believed to be part of the organization. The arrest was considered by the State Department spokesperson as "the most significant arrest ever of a wanted drug trafficker in Mexico" (Sierra Guzmán 2003, 2).

Even more striking is the fact that the military has investigated and arrested police agents of the special prosecutor for drug trafficking, FEADS. In January 2003, the army closed FEADS offices across the country to investigate drug-related corruption among its members.

Assistance offered by the U.S. Defense Department increased considerably as of 1996, a year after the visit to Mexico of the U.S. secretary of defense, William J. Perry. He was the first U.S. secretary of defense ever to visit Mexico, and he did so at the request of his counterpart, General Enrique Cervantes. The presence of Secretary Perry in Mexico is considered the beginning of formal military cooperation between the two countries. This cooperation would be oriented, according to Perry, "to develop new security relations" in various domains, and to "cooperate in helping Mexico improve its capabilities to defend its sovereign air and sea space" (U.S. Department of Defense 1995). A bilateral working group scheduled to meet every six months was established as a result of that visit. Perry also announced that the budget for education and training of Mexican officers would double.

Thus, the U.S. Department of Defense began supporting and training Mexican military elite units. It has paid in particular for the training of the Air-Mobile Special Forces Groups. Most aid has been channeled into the acquisition of equipment and the training of personnel both in U.S. military colleges and in Mexico. During the past six years, more than 1,000 Mexican officers have been trained in interdiction and reconnaissance techniques, searching vehicles, preserving evidence, helicopter transportation, equipment maintenance, and so forth.

Outstanding over the past two years has been the training of officials from the Mexican navy and air force. Mexican participation rose in the International Military Education and Training (IMET) programs, in which Mexico had participated for many years but on a small scale. Mexico became the number one recipient of IMET assistance from 1996 to 1999, and it was expected to be the top recipient in 2003 (Sierra Guzmán 2003, 11).

Financially, the most important assistance was granted in 1997 for the provision of 73 UH-1H helicopters to the Mexican military. This technical support offered by the U.S. military, however, did not end well. The Mexican military had finally decided it had to participate in the new policy of collaborating more actively with the United States. Consequently, the Mexican secretary of defense decided to take, on lease, the 73 helicopters that the U.S. government offered to help improve Mexican eradication programs. The UH-1H helicopters were surplus from the Vietnam war and needed maintenance and repair. Though technically on lease, these aircraft would have been eventually donated to Mexico. The Mexican army "remained suspicious, nonetheless, that the United States would take the equipment back and, therefore, invested little in the maintenance and operation of these helicopters" (Domínguez and Fernández de Castro 2001, 47). The Mexican secretary of defense decided, at the end, that it was better to buy new aircraft and returned the helicopters to the United States in late 1999, a year and a half after having received them.

The Mexican decision, however, was also influenced by U.S. insistence that the helicopters could only be used for counternarcotics operations, and nothing else. What for the U.S. government may have been routine (specifying the use of the military equipment transferred to other countries), for the Mexican army was a confirmation of its traditional fears, namely, that with aid comes oversight. The U.S. government was ready to repair 20 of the helicopters, but the Mexican government announced that it did not want them back. "The U.S. Department of Defense was furious, believing that this was an example of bad faith and breaking a commitment" (Domínguez and Fernández de Castro 2001, 47).

Although the recent rapprochement between the armed forces of the two nations may be interpreted in the years to come as the beginning of a new, post–Cold War strategic relationship, it has so far taken on great importance because of the increasing penetration of civilian law enforcement and intelligence units by members of the army. By and large, the Mexican military has maintained its independence and is by far the most autonomous agency participating in antidrug law enforcement.

CONCLUSIONS

The two-pronged Mexican policy against drugs has slowly but surely become one-sided, focusing on the formidable domestic criminal justice problem that has been, to an important extent, the result of wrongly conceived and poorly implemented antidrug programs. Maintaining the autonomy of antidrug law enforcement has become, conceptually, a second-order concern and, in practice, an impossibility.

Mexican policy changed during the 1990s to an extent that was difficult to predict at the beginning of the decade. The Mexican government considered that its traditional strategy of bolstering domestic programs and negotiating bilateral agreements with the United States was not rendering the desired results. The new strategy of trying to bind the United States by intensifying bilateral cooperation and creating bilateral mechanisms to build trust and agree on the rules to guide U.S. and Mexican policies has also been unable to advance Mexican interests.

Striking a "new deal" with the United States entailed internalizing U.S. drug policy and increased the costs of disagreeing with a partner that was providing fundamental support to Mexican programs. In comparison with the 1980s, bypassing the limits bilaterally agreed upon, once and again during the 1990s, became less risky for the United States. The institutionalization strategy has lost momentum (e.g., the HLCGDC is no longer in place); the United States is less interested today in maintaining it.

Embracing its neighbor allowed the Mexican government to get "off the hook" at critical junctures and facilitated the launching of antidrug programs that otherwise would have taken decades to implement. The United States can count today on a more willing partner. But aligning with the United States has not resulted in more effective antidrug law enforcement in Mexico (or in the United States). Mexico continues to be the main source of illegal drugs entering the U.S. market every year. Drug-related corruption has destroyed, quickly or slowly, all police agencies in charge of fighting drug trafficking. Violence has reached unsustainable levels and affects Mexican society in practically every state.

Current antidrug policies will not allow Mexico to domesticate its illegal drug market, regardless of how much help is provided. Nor will they significantly influence the use of drugs in the United States or in Mexico. More important, Mexico will have a hard time rebuilding its criminal justice system while implementing a strategy of immobilizing major drug-trafficking organizations.

NAFTA has been considered the triggering mechanism of the new U.S.–Mexican understanding in the realm of drugs. The trade agreement, according to this view, had a "spillover effect" that initiated a learning process whereby greater trust and shared commitments "permitted the design and implementation of subsequent agreements. . . . The scope of agreements widened beyond trade matters to encompass other issue areas" (Domínguez and Fernández de Castro 2001, 2, 3).

NAFTA did, in fact, influence many decision on both sides of the border, as it became a paramount interest for the two countries. Avoiding conflict with the United States and establishing a reputation as a reliable partner were certainly part of the Mexican realignment strategy. Salinas's decision to initiate a far-reaching rapprochement with the United States, of which NAFTA would become the centerpiece, provided a favorable context to begin Mexican accommodation to U.S. preferences. It also made the realignment politically more palatable in Mexico.

NAFTA created many expectations in Mexico and the United States; among others, that formalizing agreements and finally coming to terms with the realities of two highly intertwined economies and societies would launch both countries into a new era of international cooperation that best reflected the major changes in the international system and held the promise of protecting Mexico from U.S. unilateralism.

But focusing on Mexican incentives to get closer to the United States necessarily means pushing to the side the many heavy-handed strategies that the United States deployed for more than a decade to effectively export its antidrug policy. It also disregards the drastic change in the international distribution of power that so much favored the United States after the end of the Cold War. The strategy of setting up a common front against drug trafficking in the 1990s is better explained by a U.S. policy that clearly showed, as of the mid-1980s, a determination to participate more actively and directly in Latin American antidrug strategies (Toro 1999; Doyle 1993, 84). It is also accounted for by the extent to which fighting the "second generation" of drug traffickers by means of more stringent enforcement was dependent on U.S. intelligence, U.S. technical support, and (at times) on the U.S. judiciary. Put differently, Mexican policy against drugs would have changed in the same direction with or without NAFTA. A similar phenomenon, with national peculiarities, has been observed in many other Latin American countries during the past decade.

Notes

1. Enrique Camarena, who was engaged in undercover operations in Mexico, was kidnapped, tortured, and murdered by traffickers, who were operating with large-scale police protection. The traffickers involved in the murder are behind bars.

2. The number of hectares of marijuana and opium poppy plants eradicated by the Mexican army jumped from 910 in 1982 to 5,094 in 1983 in the case of marijuana, and from 625 to 5,240, in the case of opium poppies. See Toro (1995, tables 1.1 and 1.2).

3. It was believed that by the mid-1980s, approximately 30 percent of all cocaine entering the United States was crossing through Mexican territory.

4. By mid-1993, according to Aguayo, CISEN was "beset by disorganization, superficiality, and low morale"; some of its operational activities were illegal, among others political espionage (Bailey and Aguayo 1996, 151).

5. These data are from Mexico, *Informes presidenciales*, various years.

6. A thorough description of these changes and their rationale appears in Arzt (2002, 137–62).

7. This official verdict is still questioned today by members of the Catholic church.

8. All these figures can be found in Mexico, *Informes presidenciales*, various years.

9. The U.S. government sponsored, among others, the abduction of Verdugo-Urquídez in 1986. In *United States v. Verdugo Urquídez*, the U.S. Supreme Court refused to apply the Fourth Amendment to searches by U.S. law enforcement agents in foreign countries.

10. This agreement was signed in February 1989 and entered into force in July 1990. See SRE (1992, 54–55).

11. In fact, the "Anti-Drug Abuse Act of 1986" is a much-quoted piece of legislation because it introduced the famous "certification process." Far more consequential, however, was the outlawing of the manufacture and distribution of drugs outside the United States if they were intended for export to U.S. territory. The law thus provided the basis for U.S. federal grand jury indictments of foreigners, a quite common practice since then.

12. Report by the Secretario de Gobernación, *Public Security and the New Strategy Against Drug-Trafficking*, February 15, 1999, quoted in Bailey and

Godson (2000, 27). For a discussion of tendencies and statistics, see also Bailey and Chabat (2002, 9–13).

13. These figures are from the *Quinto informe de gobierno*, 1999, quoted in López Portillo Vargas (2002, 117).

14. The original team to direct the PFP was transferred from CISEN. See López Portillo Vargas (2002, 125, 126, 128).

15. The FEADS includes border task forces, the organized crime unit and the anti-money-laundering unit. For an analysis of the reorganization of PGR in those years, see Arzt (2000, 103–25).

16. Domínguez and Fernández de Castro (2001, 36, 46). The authors interpret Zedillo's attempt to forge a full-fledged security alliance with the United States as a change from a policy of abnegation to a bandwagoning strategy. Following Stephen Walt, they characterize this last strategy as one in which there is "unequal exchange; the vulnerable state makes asymmetrical concessions to the dominant power and accepts a subordinate role." For a similar interpretation, but for the Salinas period, see Aguilar (1992).

17. Domínguez and Fernández de Castro (2001, 46). See also "Balance de McCaffrey sobre México," *La jornada*, September 17, 1997.

18. Technically, a majority of votes in both chambers could lead to an overruling of a presidential decision—a highly unlikely event.

19. An account of the certification process from 1995 to 2000, as it affected Mexico, can be found in Chacón (2001).

20. The following paragraphs on extradition draw heavily on Pérez García 2000.

21. According to Pérez García, the day after the Supreme Court ruling, another famous trafficker, Joaquín "Chapo" Guzmán, escaped prison "fearing that he was next in line for extradition proceedings" (Pérez García 2000, 2).

22. *Reforma*, April 1, 2001. Quoted in Pérez García (2000, 19).

23. The Mexican government refused to extradite a member of the Amezcua organization, considered the largest metanphetamines smuggling group in Mexico, on these grounds.

24. A detailed account of these and other operations can be found in Sierra Guzmán (2003).

References

Alvarado, Arturo, and Diane Davis. 2001. Cambio político, inseguridad pública y deterioro del estado de derecho en México: Algunas hipótesis en torno del proceso actual. In *El desafío democrático de México: Seguridad y estado de derecho*, ed. Arturo Alvarado and Sigrid Arzt. Mexico City: El Colegio de México.

Aguayo, Sergio. 1996. Intelligence Services and the Transition to Democracy in Mexico. In *Strategy and Security in U.S.–Mexican Relations beyond the Cold War*, ed. John Bailey and Sergio Aguayo. San Diego: Center for U.S.–Mexican Studies at the University of California.

Aguilar, José Antonio. 1992. Realidades cambiantes: La reformulación de la política mexicana hacia Estados Unidos (1988–1990). Tesis de licenciatura, El Colegio de México.

Arzt, Sigrid. 2000. Scope and Limits of an Act of Good Faith: The PAN's Experience at the Head of the Office of the Attorney General of the Republic. In *Organized Crime and Democratic Governability: Mexico and the U.S.-Mexican Border-lands*, ed. John Bailey and Roy Godson. Pittsburgh: University of Pittsburgh Press.

———. 2002. Combatting Organized Crime in Mexico: Mission [Impossible]? In *Transnational Crime and Public Security: Challenges to Mexico and the United States*, ed. John Bailey and Jorge Chabat. San Diego: Center for U.S.–Mexican Studies at the University of California.

Bailey, John, and Sergio Aguayo, eds. 1996 *Strategy and Security in U.S.–Mexican Relations beyond the Cold War*. San Diego: Center for U.S.–Mexican Studies at the University of California.

Bailey, John, and Jorge Chabat, eds. 2002. Transnational Crime and Public Security: Trends and Issues. In *Transnational Crime and Public Security: Challenges to Mexico and the United States*, ed. John Bailey and Jorge Chabat. San Diego: Center for U.S.–Mexican Studies at the University of California.

Bailey, John, and Roy Godson. 2000. Introducción: El crimen organizado y la gobernabilidad democrática: México y Estados Unidos—las zonas fronterizas mexicanas. In *Crimen organizado y gobernabilidad democrática. México y la franja fronteriza*, ed. John Bailey and Roy Godson. Mexico City: Editorial Grijalbo.

Chacón, Susana. 2001. La toma de decisiones en política exterior: El caso de la certificación, 1995–2000. *Foro Internacional* 40, no. 4: 992–1044.

Domínguez, Jorge I., and Rafael Fernández de Castro. 2001. *The United States and Mexico: Between Partnership and Conflict*. New York: Routledge.

Doyle, Kate. 1993. The Militarization of the Drug War in Mexico. *Current History*, February.

Hoffer, Michael D. 2000. A Fistful of Dollars: "Operation Casablanca" and the Impact of Extraterritorial Enforcement of United States Money Laundering Law. *Georgia Journal of International and Comparative Law* 28, no. 2: 293–318.

Latell, Brian. 2002. U.S. Foreign Intelligence and Mexico: The Evolving Relationship. In *Transnational Crime and Public Security: Challenges to Mexico and the United States*, ed. John Bailey and Jorge Chabat. San Diego: Center for U.S.–Mexican Studies at the University of California.

Pérez García, Gabriela C. 2000. The Extradition of Mexican Nationals: New Challenges to an Old Practice. Unpublished manuscript, Yale University, New Haven, Conn.

López Portillo Vargas, Ernesto. 2002. The Police in Mexico: Political Functions and Needed Reforms. In *Transnational Crime and Public Security: Challenges to Mexico and the United States*, ed. John Bailey and Jorge Chabat. San Diego: Center for U.S.–Mexican Studies at the University of California.

Rohter, Larry. 1988. Mexican Leader Vows Action against Drugs. *New York Times*, December 12, A5.

Ruiz-Cabañas, Miguel. 1998. Intereses contradictorios y mecanismos de cooperación: El caso del narcotráfico en las relaciones mexicano-estadunidenses. In *México y Estados Unidos: Las rutas de la cooperación*, ed. Olga Pellicer and Rafael Fernández de Castro. Mexico City: Secretaría de Relaciones Exteriores and Instituto Tecnológico Autónomo de México.

Sierra Guzmán, Jorge Luis. 2003. Mexico's Military in the War on Drugs. *Drug War Monitor* (Washington Office on Latin America Briefing Series), April.

Smith, Peter H. 1999. Semiorganized International Crime: Drug Trafficking in Mexico. In *Transnational Crime in the Americas*, ed. Tom Farer. New York, Routledge.

SRE (Secretaría de Relaciones Exteriores). 1992. *Limits to National Jurisdiction: Documents and Judicial Resolutions on the Alvarez Machain Case*. Mexico City: SRE.

Storrs, Larry. 1998. *Mexican Drug Certification Issues: U.S. Congressional Action, 1986–1998*. Washington, D.C.: Congressional Research Service.

Toro, María Celia. 1995. *Mexico's War on Drugs: Causes and Consequences*. Boulder, Colo.: Lynne Rienner.

———. 1999. The Internationalization of Police: The DEA in Mexico. *Journal of American History* 86, no. 2: 623–40.

Turbiville, Graham H., Jr. 2002. Changing Security Challenges and Mexico–U.S. Military Interaction. In *Transnational Crime and Public Security: Challenges to Mexico and the United States*, ed. John Bailey and Jorge Chabat. San Diego: Center for U.S.–Mexican Studies at the University of California.

U.S. Department of Defense. 1995. New Generation of U.S.–Mexico Cooperation and Trust. Prepared remarks by Secretary of Defense William J. Perry at the Mexican Ministry of Defense, Mexico City, October 23. Available at www.defenselink.mil/speeches/1995/s19951023-perry.html.

U.S. Department of State. 1992. *International Narcotics Control Strategy Report 1992: Mexico*. Washington, D.C.: U.S. Government Printing Office.

U.S. Office of National Drug Control Policy. 1997. *Report to Congress: United States and Mexico Counterdrug Cooperation—Enhanced Multilateral Drug Control Cooperation, Enhanced Truck Inspections*. Available at www.white housedrugpolicy.gov/publications/enforce/rpttocong/usmexextra.html.

———. 1998. *U.S./Mexico Bi-National Drug Strategy*. Washington, D.C.: U.S. Government Printing Office.

CHAPTER NINE

SECURITY IMPERATIVES OF NORTH AMERICAN INTEGRATION

BACK TO A FUTURE OF HUB AND SPOKES

John Bailey

Security became the U.S. government's top priority following the terrorist attacks of September 11, 2001. The U.S. response was emphatic, as seen in the rapid passage of the USA Patriot Act, the creation of the Department of Homeland Security, and the proclamation of a new national security doctrine in which terrorism was identified as the principal threat and preemption was added to containment and deterrence as the central concepts. The U.S. government sought international support for its antiterrorist campaign, and the Canadian and Mexican governments, though with some delay and qualification, joined many others in pledging support. The response to the terrorist attacks presented an opportunity to revitalize and deepen the North American Free Trade Agreement (NAFTA). But this revitalization was missing at the crucial moment. This is interesting because wars and threats of war were arguably the primary engine that drove European integration from the outset.

TWO CLARIFICATIONS AND A PUZZLE

This chapter takes a largely U.S. perspective, and I begin with two clarifications. First, I use the term "security" in two basic ways. "National security" refers to the protection of the state and key state institutions, along with sovereignty, territorial integrity, and internal order from

The author thanks David King, Barbara Kotschwar, Martin Rudner, and David Shirk for providing helpful advice in the writing of this chapter. Martha Carro, Rachel Fedewa, and Arantxa Guillan helped with the research. The usual disclaimer of responsibility is hereby invoked.

threats from other nation-states or trans-state actors, including terrorists, organized crime, and so on. "Public security" refers to the protection of persons, their goods and assets, the rule of law, and democratic institutional development from threats posed by varieties of crime, violence, and corruption.

Security in both senses implies a special category of politics. "The special nature of security threats justifies the use of extraordinary measures to handle them. The invocation of security has been the key to legitimizing the use of force, but more generally it has opened the way for the state to mobilize, or to take special powers, to handle existential threats. Traditionally, by saying 'security,' a state representative declares an emergency condition, thus claiming a right to use whatever means are necessary to block a threatening development" (Buzan, Weaver, and de Wilde 1998, 21).

As a second clarification, we should recognize that regions and functions are defined and interact in a variety of ways. That is, both commercial and security regions include parallel and overlapping boundaries (e.g., NAFTA coexists with Mercosur and the Central American Common Market, and their members also belong to the World Trade Organization; the new U.S. Northern Command functions alongside the North American Aerospace Defense Command, or NORAD; and both Canada and the United States belong to the North Atlantic Treaty Organization, or NATO). There is no compelling reason that a security emergency for a given country should trigger reactions in a particular commercial agreement. Even so, if the agreement had vitality, one would expect at least symbolic responses. So our initial puzzle is: Why was a major trade agreement apparently irrelevant when its dominant partner was violently attacked?

Three preliminary hypotheses to address the puzzle include: the specialized role assigned to NAFTA, its lack of broad support and visibility, the lack of timely leadership, and the unpopularity of U.S. security policy in Canada and Mexico. First, NAFTA is seen as irrelevant to national security. Policymakers and the public apparently do not connect national security, perceived as armed forces and national defense, with NAFTA, which regulates trade, finance, and some additional areas.[1] Further, NAFTA lacks routine "summits" where matters such as security emergencies can be addressed, in contrast, for example, to the Group of Seven. The more significant North American policymaking venues are the hub-and-spokes binational commissions that bring the U.S.

government together separately with its Canadian and Mexican counterparts, or one-to-one summit meetings of the three countries' chief
executives. North American national security emergencies are dealt
with in other contexts, such as NATO, to which Mexico does not belong, or the 1947 Inter-American Treaty of Reciprocal Assistance
(TIAR, in its Spanish abbreviation, also known as the Rio Treaty), to
which Canada does not belong.

Second, NAFTA lacks broad-based support and visibility. It is not a
natural rallying point for the public in general in times of emergency.
News and commentary tend to focus—naturally—on NAFTA's problems, rather than its progress, emphasizing, for example, safety concerns about Mexican trucking, U.S. agricultural competition with
impoverished Mexican farmers, or disputes about Canadian softwood
exports.

Third, NAFTA went leaderless at the key moment. For NAFTA to
have figured in the response to the crisis, both Mexico's Vicente Fox and
Canada's Jean Chrétien would had to have taken coordinated and decisive action in the immediate aftermath of September 11. They did not,
for several reasons, and the moment passed.

SECURITY ISSUES FROM A U.S. PERSPECTIVE

If these hypotheses solve the puzzle, the fact remains that security has
become the top priority of NAFTA's dominant partner. Thus, both national and public security issues in a variety of forms will affect the
dominant partner's immediate neighbors. Some of these issues may
strengthen or weaken economic integration. If deepening is a result, it
may be formalized in ways that promote NAFTA's organizational development, or—more likely—it may lead to various special negotiations and organizational arrangements.[2] From the U.S. perspective,
there are six main national and public security issues.

The first such issue is safe borders. All three countries have assigned a
high priority to measures that facilitate the increased flows of legitimate commerce and travel while screening out the illicit flows. One
thinks immediately of the 7,500 miles of shared land borders among the
three countries, but the issue involves many thousands of miles of
coastlines and sea border zones as well (3.4 million square miles in the
U.S. case), and also air transport among the three countries and with
the rest of the world. If missile defense is considered, safe borders reach
the stratosphere. The issue might be broadened even further to include

Internet security and electronic commerce as well. Safe borders in the conventional sense of land, air, and maritime travel and shipping is the most immediately NAFTA-centric security issue.

The second issue is secure energy. The United States is a long-time, major importer of petroleum, and Canada and Mexico are among its top suppliers. Secure land access to petroleum is increasingly important to national security given the uncertainties of supply from elsewhere.

The third issue is migration control. Nearly a half-billion persons travel to the United States each year. In addition, an estimated 4 to 5 million Mexicans reside illegally in the United States. President Vicente Fox put regularization of their status at the top of the bilateral agenda prior to September 2001, and the George W. Bush administration had agreed to study the matter. After September 11, the U.S. priority became registration, that is, the location and identification of all persons residing in its territory. Even so, at some point, the regularization issue will reemerge. With respect to Canada, the issue concerns policies that regulate political refugees and asylum seekers. This issue typically is viewed in a public security lens.

The fourth issue is the water supply. Water scarcity has been a long-standing problem in the United States–Mexico border region and has become increasingly contentious in recent years. For its part, Canada has relatively abundant supplies but opposes large-scale exports of water. Both scarcity and abundance are sources of tension. At present, the issue is not typically viewed in terms of security, but in a 10-year horizon it likely will be.

The fifth issue is intelligence sharing and law enforcement cooperation. This is a vast and complex area that affects both public and national security, but potentially relevant aspects include, for example, monitoring the movements of persons and commerce, and cooperation against smuggling, money laundering, and counterfeiting of currency, documents, or products. Thus, cooperation against organized crime is the priority because of the potential ties between criminal and terrorist groups.

The sixth issue is defense and armed forces. As the traditional focus of national security, this would seem farthest from the commercial agreement, but some aspects of defense procurement and contracting might be affected, because these have been opened to companies in the partner members. At first glance, this is more significant to Canada, where the "interoperability" of defense forces and joint maneuvers with those of the United States is standing practice (Edgar 2002). Environmental issues might be involved in base agreements, joint operations, and the like.

THE ARGUMENT FOR A FUTURE OF HUB AND SPOKES

What is the likelihood that the increased U.S. emphasis on security will promote NAFTA deepening, as opposed to a series of ad hoc adjustments scattered among diverse bureaucratic and policy arrangements? The answer depends in good part on answers to two other questions: (1) Will the sense of a North American community increase to the point of supporting denser organizational arrangements? (2) Will future North American security cooperation be confined to a specialized bureaucratic and policy architecture or merged with more inclusive organizational arrangements?

The likely scenario, in my view, is that security will be largely confined to its own spheres, with some North American special arrangements but with greater emphasis on hemispheric and broader multilateral agreements. NAFTA was intentionally designed as a limited free trade agreement, and it will remain relatively "thin and narrow" in terms of organization and policy jurisdiction, with its future more closely tied to the evolution of hemispheric trade agreements, such as the Free Trade Agreement of the Americas. This is because (1) there is no apparent momentum to invigorate a North American vision generally, much less a vision that connects trade with security; (2) migration (including refugee and asylum issues), energy, and water are especially sensitive areas, whose negotiation may be easier outside the NAFTA framework (especially since reopening NAFTA under any circumstances is fraught with dangers); (3) U.S. security policy, with its unilateralist overtones, is unpopular with both its NAFTA partners; and (4) Mexico's withdrawal from the Rio Treaty and its announced intention to promote a new hemispheric defense treaty point away from a closer strategic security relationship with the United States and Canada and toward closer cooperation with other Latin American nations.

The area where security and commerce most directly intersect is the border. The new U.S. security bureaucracy and policy architecture, for example, the Department of Homeland Security and the reorganization of the Federal Bureau of Investigation and the Central Intelligence Agency, are taking shape to counter terrorist threats. One implication troubling to NAFTA is that the administration's strong security emphasis will reorient the incentive systems of key agencies—for example, Customs and Border Protection (the new name is itself telling), the Bureau of Citizenship and Immigration Services, the Animal and Plant Health Inspection Service, and the Transportation Security Administration—in ways that hamper rather than facilitate legitimate traffic across borders. Delays on either border are quite serious, but Canada's economy depends to an important extent on the exports of a key province, Ontario, many of whose firms could relocate to the United States if border delays create uncertainty.[3]

This said, it is easier to envision how the security imperative might promote deeper bilateral integration between the United States and Canada than between the United States and Mexico, for at least three reasons: (1) Beyond the shared language and culture, there is a longstanding history of closer cooperation between Canada and the United States with respect to defense, intelligence, and law enforcement; (2) the Canadian government and policy communities reacted promptly to the terrorist threat and are actively considering measures such as a customs union and joint customs inspections teams;[4] and (3) Canada's security bureaucracies that deal with intelligence, law enforcement, migration, customs administration, border control, financial regulation, and the like are professionalized and relatively effective.

Thus, barring another serious terrorist incident, the likely scenario is separate spheres of policymaking and organization with respect to commerce and security (with the "Smart Borders" exception) and the evolution of a hub-and-spokes security relationship between the United States and its neighbors.[5] National and public security cooperation with Canada will evolve more quickly and intensely than that with Mexico. In this sense, a longer historical pattern of hub and spokes will reassert itself, suggesting that the NAFTA innovation has had relatively limited effects in its first decade. None of this, however, forecloses the possibility that North American leaders in the future might restructure the new bureaucracies and policies along trilateral lines.

NORTH AMERICAN SECURITY COOPERATION FROM THE COLD WAR TO SEPTEMBER 11

Though sharing an anti-Soviet stance, Canada, Mexico, and the United States developed different security doctrines and practices over the course of the Cold War, through their negotiation of NAFTA in the early 1990s, and up to September 2001. National security with respect to the three member countries consisted of a core understanding that, in turn, supported two rather different hub-and-spokes arrangements. The core strategic understanding was that Canada and Mexico would actively support the United States in the event of a confrontation with the Soviet Union. Beyond this, national security cooperation diverged significantly. Canada and the United States for a variety of reasons— especially because of their close alliance in two world wars—developed a significantly closer defense relationship than did Mexico and the United States. Strategic cooperation and relations between the armed forces of Mexico and the United States remained rather distant and formal (Cope 1996).

With respect to public security, the three countries cooperated to implement land and maritime border controls, aviation regulation, intelligence sharing, and law enforcement cooperation. Here also, for much of the period from the late 1940s through the 1980s, the United States developed closer cooperation with Canada than with Mexico. Cooperation with Mexico at this "lower end" of security improved significantly in the latter 1980s, however, and improved even more so after NAFTA and after the election of Vicente Fox in 2000. These differences were not a significant factor in crafting NAFTA. Unlike the more inclusive and "thicker" organization that characterized European integration, NAFTA itself was explicitly limited to trade, finance, intellectual property, environmental, and labor issues, although its contribution to U.S. security was implicitly recognized.[6]

Threats of military action in North America have been irrelevant between Canada and the United States since the late 1800s and between Mexico and the United States since the 1930s, when Mexico's expropriation of U.S.-owned oil companies stoked nationalism in both countries. The United States, as the global superpower competitor with the Soviet Union, set the post–World War II security agenda for its North American neighbors. In this sense, the three countries formed a "security complex," defined as "*a set of states whose major security perceptions and concerns are so interlinked that their national security problems cannot reasonably be analyzed or resolved apart from one another*" (Buzan, Weaver, and de Wilde 1998, 12; emphasis in the original). Within this complex, the North American countries formed a "pluralistic security community in which states no longer expect or prepare to use force in their relations with each other" (Buzan, Weaver, and de Wilde 1998, 12).

FORMAL AGREEMENTS AND
INFORMAL UNDERSTANDINGS

At a formal level, the three countries entered a series of military allianc-es in World War II, and these alliances were subsequently adjusted to counter the Soviet Union. The alliances included formal treaties and specific understandings. At the bilateral level, Mexico and the United States formed a Joint Defense Commission in January 1942 and subse-quently both ratified the Rio Treaty of 1947. With Canada, the World War II alliance began with the Permanent Joint Board on Defense (1940), and the principal Cold War commitments included NATO (1949) and NORAD (1958). All three countries were founding mem-bers of the United Nations.[7]

But apart from formal arrangements, informal understandings an-chored the security community. In the United States–Canada case, the understanding became known as the Kingston Dispensation, which dates from August 1938, as Canada prepared for the conflict in Europe. "Each country understood that it had a 'neighbourly' obligation to the other, not only to refrain from any activities that might imperil the se-curity of the other, but also to demonstrate nearly as much solicitude for the other's physical security needs as for its own" (Fortmann and Haglund 2002, 18). These understandings were exchanged publicly.

The case of Mexico presents important contrasts. Declarations by Mexico to support continental defense were made openly in 1940. But assurances of support for and cooperation with the United States were conveyed privately in mid-1940 by President Lázaro Cárdenas through Mexico's ambassador to the White House. Mexico's concerns about the still-unsettled disputes over the 1938 petroleum expropriation, nation-alism in the 1940 presidential elections, and worries over civilian con-trol of the armed forces made open assurances more difficult (Paz 1997, 51, 66, 72, passim).

An informal assurance provided by the United States to Mexico was that, as long as its support was pledged on key strategic issues, Mexico was free to pursue an independent foreign policy. Further, the United States would not meddle openly and actively in internal Mexican af-fairs. This flexibility in turn provided the governments of the Institu-tional Revolutionary Party (Partido Revolucionario Institucional, PRI) with room to maneuver to employ foreign policy as an instrument of nationalism to bolster its legitimacy internally. Also, the United States granted Mexico something of an exemption from the more aggressive versions of its democracy and human rights policies (Bailey and Aguayo 1996; Mazza 2002).

Private assurances were reiterated by Mexico in the Cold War period, specifically in the Cuban missile crisis of October 1962. "Meeting with [assistant secretary of state for American republic affairs Edwin] Martin in March 1963, [President Adolfo Lopez Mateos] 'made it quite clear that Mexico would give its public support to any action against Cuba necessary to prevent a serious direct threat to the security of the United States or the hemisphere. . . . Lopez Mateos's successor, Gustavo Diaz Ordaz, is also known to have provided similar assurances'" (quoted in Latell 2002, 288).

Formal alliances and informal guarantees were of enormous significance to the United States, which—benefiting from peaceful neighbors and nonmilitarized borders—could project power much more effectively into Europe and Asia to pursue its anti-Soviet strategy. In the Western Hemisphere, U.S. strategy focused more on "strategic denial," or the resistance to Soviet influence in any form in Latin America and the Caribbean (Hartlyn, Schoultz, and Varas 1992, 4).

STRAINS AND TENSIONS IN THE AGREEMENTS

The notion of a pluralistic security community allows for considerable variation in policies and doctrines among the members; this indeed was and remains the North American case. Differences with Canada and/or Mexico, significant at times, emerged with respect to U.S. actions in specific cases (Guatemala, 1954; Cuba, 1959, 1962; Dominican Republic, 1964; Vietnam, 1964–73; Chile, 1973; El Salvador and Nicaragua, 1979–89; and Granada, 1983) and with respect to doctrines (for example, deterrence vs. arms control with respect to nuclear weapons). Canada and Mexico usually preferred to address conflicts through multilateral negotiation, preferably in accord with international law and within existing international organizations. The United States, while not rejecting international law or organizations (at least usually), typically chose bilateral diplomacy and was more willing to use coercion to pursue its interests. It is worth underlining the significance of Cuba, which was a constant irritant given U.S. belligerence toward the Castro regime in contrast with Canadian and Mexican policies of neutrality and accommodation. Even so, the formal alliances and basic understandings held up through several crises and shifts in strategic doctrines from the late 1940s to the end of the Cold War in 1989.

This said, the agreements held up arguably better with Canada than with Mexico. Major points of irritation with the Canadian government included its wavering on U.S. policies with respect to Cuba in 1962, its opposition to policy toward Vietnam (including the granting of asylum to U.S. citizens evading military conscription), its ambivalence about accepting an active role in nuclear deterrence, including its stance on an antiballistic missile defense, and its declining budgetary support for its armed forces. Prime Minister John Diefenbaker's reluctance to support the United States in the Cuban missile crisis led to an adverse reaction in Canadian public opinion and to tension in the bilateral relationship. "Perhaps this reaction encouraged John F. Kennedy's administration to help to topple the Canadian government, using the brusque brutality of a single press release in January 1963" (Granatstein 2002, 6).

The bilateral security relationship was tested as well during Pierre Elliott Trudeau's government (1968–79, 1980–84). Trudeau engineered a 50 percent cut in Canada's NATO contingent, abandoned the Canadian Forces' nuclear weapons, accelerated the process of military decline that had begun with Diefenbaker's government, and simultaneously moved to improve Canadian relations with the Soviet Union, China, and Cuba (Granatstein 2002, 6). Though open breaks were avoided, all of these policies directly opposed those of the United States and produced deep tensions.

With respect to Mexico, something close to a breaking point came in the period 1985–87, due to a convergence of problems. First, Mexico moved from symbolic and diplomatic opposition to U.S. policy in the case of the wars in Central America to a higher level of activism, for example, by joining Venezuela in the so-called San José Accord (1980) to provide subsidized petroleum to several Caribbean nations, including Nicaragua. Second, drug trafficking from and through Mexico became a serious irritant in the bilateral relationship in the mid 1980s. The murders of a U.S. Drug Enforcement Agency officer and his Mexican pilot in February 1985, followed by a perceived coverup by the Mexican government, provoked outrage in the U.S. government and public opinion. Third, for a variety of reasons, the Mexican government and PRI were perceived as more actively employing electoral fraud against a growing opposition, and the "democracy exemption" noted above came under active scrutiny. In the event, both presidents appeared to recognize the dangers of a breakdown in the understanding, and both moved to improve relations after 1987. New levels of co-operation were achieved as Mexico entered the General Agreement on Tariffs and Trade in 1986, and the Carlos Salinas de Gortari govern-ment (1988–94) actively promoted closer relations.

By way of overview, Canada and Mexico adopted contrasting strat-egies to cope with U.S. security initiatives. Canada adopted what King (2001, 2) has called a "defence against defense" strategy by which it might resist or object to U.S. initiatives, but ultimately it typically ac-cepted and participated in them with the logic that "being on the inside" gave them some influence on the exercise of U.S. power. Mexico, in con-trast, followed a strategy of employing sovereignty as an anti-U.S. sym-bol that was useful to generate broad public support for the hegemonic party. The implication was to emphasize its independent foreign policy and to reject *overt* security cooperation. This deeply ingrained habit relegated topics of military and intelligence cooperation to the catego-ry of "taboo" subjects for public debate.

NAFTA AND NEW LEVELS OF COOPERATION

NAFTA was negotiated in the period 1991–93 and implemented in Jan-uary 1994, in the period coinciding with the collapse of the Soviet Union and the end of the Cold War. In this context, the threat of war was insignificant. Even so, both national and public security played a role in persuading the U.S. Congress to support NAFTA. One of the central arguments, put almost in code, was NAFTA's role in helping to prevent a security problem by promoting rapid economic growth in the United States' southern neighbor (Benitez Manaut 2001). But this was a delicate argument to make, and NAFTA proponents accentuated the positive by connecting a robust Mexican economy with reducing illegal immigration and drug trafficking. Still, the multiplication of volumes of cross-border traffic implied substantial challenges to public security, especially with respect to law enforcement (e.g., antismug-gling) and safety (e.g., product inspection).

The period 1994–2002 saw marked improvements in U.S. public se-curity cooperation with Mexico and stability and continuity in close cooperation with Canada. The creation of a Mexico–U.S. High-Level Contact Group in 1996 helped to improve communications and coop-eration at the top levels of government, and contributed to more con-structive actions in law enforcement and border issues. During this time, and virtually unnoticed, the Mexican army grew from 110,000 in

1980 to 240,000 in 1998 and became more active in law enforcement, particularly against drug trafficking (Camp 1999, 131). Cordial relations with Canada masked the developing problem inherent in its declining budgetary support to its armed forces.

The terrorist attacks against the United States in September 2001 caused a distancing between the U.S. government and those of Mexico and Canada.[8] President Bush expected immediate and unconditional support for his antiterrorist policies. Even though the public declarations by Vicente Fox and Jean Chrétien were supportive, both governments gave delayed and qualified support to the U.S. response against al Qaeda and the Taliban in Afghanistan. Over time, as the U.S. government adopted a hard-line confrontational approach toward Iraq, support diminished further in the neighboring governments and in public opinion more broadly.

Two points should be stressed by way of summary. First, the North American nations make up a pluralistic security community in which military action is irrelevant to resolving differences, the three countries take into account each other's security interests in formulating their own security policies, and they pursue their own foreign and security policies within understood limits. Second, the United States developed closer security cooperation from the late 1930s to the present with Canada than with Mexico. Cooperation with Mexico improved significantly, however, in the late 1980s and even more so with the election of Vicente Fox in 2000.

THE REAFFIRMATION OF HUB AND SPOKES IN NORTH AMERICAN SECURITY

With the exception of the "Smart Borders" initiative, both public and national security cooperation in North America will likely be organized outside the NAFTA framework and will take the form of hub-and-spokes arrangements in which cooperation with Canada is more extensive and public than that with Mexico. An important reason for this is the absence of a strong North American vision advocated by energetic leadership and supported by public opinion. President Bush in mid-2004 was focused on antiterrorism. The newly elected Canadian prime minister, Paul Martin, made it a priority to improve bilateral relations with the United States. President Fox alone was attempting to reenergize ideas of "NAFTA-Plus," but has found little support thus far.[9]

Public opinion in Canada and Mexico opposes the preemptive and unilateralist themes U.S. security policy, and strongly opposed the United States–led war on Iraq. In this context, the priority becomes the protection of the present status of NAFTA, rather than an expansion of its roles. Viewed this way, the distance between commercial and security policies may be an advantage.

Energy and water are quite sensitive security issues that are easier to negotiate outside the NAFTA framework. Their solutions will likely promote deeper integration but through specialized bureaucracies. These are enormously complex issues that lie beyond my present scope. "Smart Borders" and migration, however, merit brief attention.

SMART BORDERS AND SECURITY

The terrorist attacks of September 11 prompted an immediate, temporary closure of U.S. borders with Canada and Mexico. Enormous flows of people and goods were halted, air traffic was grounded, and hundreds of international flights inbound to the United States were turned back or diverted to other countries. Subsequent delays at the border threw daily life for the millions of residents into turmoil. The growing number of companies whose production relied on just-in-time deliveries across border points suffered substantial losses. The three governments immediately recognized the need to quickly accelerate the border cooperation initiatives begun with NAFTA, or even before. Negotiations between the United States and Canada for a "Smart Border Accord" led to an agreement in December 2001, with the document formally signed on September 9, 2002. The United States and Mexico agreed on a "Smart Border: 22 Point Agreement" to begin working in February 2002, which was formally signed on March 22, 2002.[10] Both sets of agreements address secure flows of goods and people and secure infrastructure, and they contain several similar provisions. But the differences in purpose, substance, and effects suggest that the United States–Canada agreement goes further toward promoting integration in security and other policy areas.

With regard to the purpose of the border agreements, "NAFTA-Plus" proposals of various types had been aired in both Canada and Mexico before September 11.[11] With respect to security, the idea of a Canada–United States "security perimeter" had been debated since the negotiation of the Free Trade Agreement between the countries in the mid-1980s. Vicente Fox's proposals for a North American Community in early 2000 revived the security perimeter concept, to include Mexico as well. Ultimately, the concept of security perimeter was rejected by the Canadian parliament, which feared that it implied harmonizing laws and regulations and eliminating the border and also might hinder Canada's freedom to pursue a policy of "creative multilateralism" (Kitchen 2003, 3–4). Although Fox was more prepared than his predecessors to discuss security cooperation openly and spoke of a "shared strategic vision" with the United States, the concept of security perimeter gained little support in Mexico. The point of contrast in the purpose of the border agreements is that the Canadian and U.S. governments were prepared to use the crisis as a rationale to pursue rapid, wide-ranging cooperation across several policy areas. In contrast, the Mexican–U.S. agreement is about the immediate border region. This becomes clearer when we look at substance.

The U.S.–Canadian border agreement contains 30 points (in comparison with 22 in the U.S.–Mexican document) and pays more attention to law enforcement and intelligence cooperation. Further, the U.S.–Canadian agreement conveys more details about specific actions to be taken, whereas the U.S.–Mexican agreement contains fewer details, and the language is more general.

The U.S.–Canadian Smart Border agreement also appears to apply to a broader range of bilateral activities (with a greater impact on both defense and the interior) than the U.S.–Mexican agreement, which seems mainly focused on border-specific cooperation. The broader range of activities covered by the U.S.–Canadian agreement is partly facilitated by preexisting treaties and cooperative agreements between the United States and Canada, notably the North Atlantic organizations and agreements (NATO, NORAD) emerging from the Cold War. Meanwhile, the U.S.–Mexican agreement's border focus includes points covering cross-border collaboration, ports of entry, and funding projects at the border.[12]

Migration is treated in several points in both agreements, and I discuss some of these in the following section. The agreements are too complex and lengthy to cover in depth, but some examples from flows of goods, infrastructure, and law enforcement and intelligence cooperation illustrate the differences.

Both agreements promote the secure flow of goods (6 points in the U.S.–Canadian version and 5 in the U.S.–Mexican version). The U.S.–Canadian accord (point 15) discusses "approaches to move customs and immigration inspection activities away from the border to improve security and relieve congestion where possible." It also mentions an analysis of "the implementation of small and large shared facilities, located in one country of the other." Point 16 lists a dozen border corridors where shared facilities might be located. Point 18 describes a joint solution to targeting container inspections at seaports. In order that "containers can be examined where they first arrive, regardless of their ultimate destination in North America, Canadian and U.S. Customs agencies have created joint targeting teams at five marine ports." The U.S.–Mexican agreement (point 16) covers "Public/Private-Sector Cooperation," in order to "Expand partnerships with private sector trade groups and importers/exporters to increase security and compliance of commercial shipments, while expediting clearance processes." Point 18 on "Secure In-Transit Shipments" is to "Continue to develop a joint in-transit shipment tracking mechanism and implement the Container Security Initiative."

Both sets of agreements call for long-term planning to promote cooperation to protect critical infrastructure. The Canadian version (point 21) includes a "Joint Permanent Framework for Canadian–U.S. Cooperation on Critical Infrastructure Protection" and a "Binational Steering Committee," whereas the Mexican counterpart (point 1) is both vaguer and more border-centric: "Develop and implement a long-term strategic plan that ensures a coordinated physical and technological infrastructure that keeps pace with growing cross-border traffic."

Cooperation in law enforcement and intelligence sharing is also much more developed in the U.S.–Canadian accord. Points describe integrated border and marine enforcement teams in 14 geographic areas to deter border crossing by criminals or terrorists, a Canadian–U.S. Cross-Border Crime Forum, Integrated National Security Enforcement Teams by which Canada involves U.S. law enforcement and intelligence offers on a case-by-case basis, Canadian participation in the U.S. Foreign Terrorist Tracking Task Force in Washington, and cooperation between the Royal Canadian Mounted Police and the Federal Bureau of Investigation to exchange criminal records information, including fingerprints, using a standard communication interface. The agreement also calls for cooperation in freezing the assets of individuals and organizations designated as terrorist and joint counterterrorism training and exercises.

The U.S.–Mexican agreement calls for "safe border and deterrence of alien smuggling" to protect migrants while curbing migrant smuggling. A proposed liaison framework would improve cooperation between U.S. and Mexican federal agencies along the U.S.–Mexican border. Joint training in investigation and document analysis is proposed to detect document fraud and to break up alien smuggling rings. A point on "compatible databases" is to "develop systems for exchanging information and sharing intelligence."[13]

Finally, the broader effects of the border agreements differ with respect to promoting bilateral cooperation in a hub-and-spokes perspective. Kitchen (2003, 1) claims that the U.S.–Canadian agreement is "a major change in both concept and practice," that the "smart border model is being used as a blueprint in other issue areas, looking to capitalize on the combination of technical interoperability, policy co-operation, and bureaucratic co-operation it espouses." She argues that, while the border remains an important reality in U.S.–Canadian relations, the Smart Border Accord

> represents a new model of cooperation based on three pillars. First, policy co-operation concentrating on mutual recognition or on changing policies that have the same goals. Second, bureaucratic co-operation between governments that goes beyond agency-to-agency co-operation. Co-operation between policy makers in the White House and the Privy Council Office is key. Third, operationalization and implementation of plans across a specific issue area with defined goals and deadlines. This model allows for a series of technical initiatives to be linked together with a framework that allows for more progress than agency-to-agency cooperation would. (Kitchen 2003, 5)

The U.S.–Mexican agreement clearly advances bilateral cooperation in a number of ways, but it appears to have fewer systemic effects to promote bureaucratic and policy coordination.

MIGRATION AND SECURITY

International migration, both regulated and unregulated, affects both national and public security in complex ways, and I can treat only a few issues here. Currently, the main NAFTA provision is that of preferential visa treatment for business visitors, traders, investors, intracompany transferees, and so on. As Shirk (2003) points out, prior to September 11, undocumented migration was most usefully analyzed in an economic framework of supply and demand: The United States and Canada need cheap labor; Mexico needs employment. Push-and-pull factors, plus the workings of migrant networks and border controls, constitute the principal variables. The terrorist attacks, however, significantly altered this perspective. Economic forces remain important, but the security imperative takes precedence.

Terrorism and organized crime involve both domestic and transnational threats. An important dimension of the transnational threat concerns the stocks and flows of migrants. Taking a U.S. perspective, the Center for Immigration Studies, an anti-immigration think tank using U.S. government data, gives a sense of current stock: "The number of immigrants living in the United States has more than tripled [*sic*] since 1970, from 9.6 million to 28.4 million. As a percentage of the U.S. population, immigrants have more than doubled, from 4.7 percent in 1970 to 10.4 percent in 2000" (Camarota 2001, 1). A January 2003 report by the Immigration and Naturalization Service estimates that there are more than 7 million "unauthorized residents" present in the United States, with 4.8 million of these from Mexico (Shirk 2003, 7). As to flows, the U.S. government reports that more than 500 million persons are admitted into the United States annually, of whom 330 million are noncitizens. About 250,000 persons from Canada and 800,000 from Mexico legally enter the United States on a daily basis. The total number entering the United States illegally on an annual basis is about 175,000, and another estimated 125,000 enter legally but overstay their visas. In fiscal 2001, more than 1.2 million illegal aliens were apprehended and more than 700,000 were rejected at ports of entry (Ridge 2003, 1). The challenge is to identify the tiny fraction of these enormous numbers who present a credible threat. In this, the United States needs cooperation from the international community, and especially from its contiguous neighbors.

As with goods, the migration challenge to NAFTA is to promote the secure flow of legitimate persons while deterring those who are illegal or who present a threat. Though the vast majority of undocumented migrants present no threat in a direct sense, they may do so indirectly. Two points are usually raised here. First, the criminal groups that smuggle undocumented migrants can also smuggle terrorists and lethal products. Second, the industries that provide illegal documents and other services to undocumented residents can also service terrorists. This said, the fact remains that 16 of the 19 terrorists involved in the September 11 attacks entered the country legally (although three of these overstayed their visas). The implications are that the U.S. government needs effective border security, but much more it needs effective cooperation with foreign intelligence and law enforcement related to migration. In this sense, Canada and, to a lesser extent, Mexico have been quite forthcoming in a number of specific initiatives.

The Canada–U.S. Smart Border accord includes provisions to speed up legal transit and deter illegal or threatening transit. In the former category, the NEXUS system operates at four border crossings and was to be expanded to all other high-volume crossings by the end of 2003.[14] Efforts to screen out illegal or threatening migrants include several important provisions, beginning with the adoption of common standards for biometric identifiers and interoperable and compatible technology to read them. Also, Canada is issuing new permanent resident cards to all new immigrants and will issue these cards to existing permanent residents for the purposes of international travel.

Moreover, the two countries are developing an agreement to systematically exchange information on asylum seekers in order to identify potential security threats and to identify the so-called forum shoppers, who seek asylum in both systems. The agreement calls for close cooperation between their respective embassies overseas to share intelligence on high-risk individuals, and the two countries will consult about reviewing a third country for either requiring visas or granting exemption. Canada "preclears" in-transit passengers bound for the United States through its Vancouver airport, and preclearance is being expanded to other Canadian airports as well. The two countries share advanced air passenger information and personal name records on high-risk travelers, and they have agreed to a co-location of customs and immigration offers in joint passenger analysis units to identify potential risks. The two countries will deploy immigration officers abroad to deal with document fraud and cooperate with airlines and governments to deter the flow of illegal migrants to North America.

The United States–Mexico agreement also includes provisions to speed up legal border transit. It calls for expanding the use of the commuter lanes dedicated to the Secure Electronic Network for Traveler's Rapid Inspection to all high-volume ports along the border. Another provision specifically identifies transit by "NAFTA travelers," including special inspection lanes at high-volume airports. Whereas the agreement with Canada goes into detail about visa policy cooperation, the

agreement with Mexico merely instructs the parties to "continue frequent consultations on visa policies and visa screening. Share information from respective consular databases." It is clear on the screening of
third-country nationals, with this provision: "Enhance cooperative efforts to detect, screen, and take appropriate measures to deal with potentially dangerous third-country nationals, taking into consideration
the threats they may represent to security."

The border agreements deal mostly with flows of migrants, and the
question of stocks remains largely untreated. That is, what are the implications of the post–September 11 security environment for the foreign
born, including Canadians and Mexicans, residing in the United States,
especially for those residing illegally? In my judgment, we have a potentially dangerous combination of a U.S. federal government with quite
powerful tools and an ill-defined policy. Several of the tools are contained in the USA Patriot Act, and the policy is to detect and somehow
to neutralize (e.g., deport, imprison, monitor) individuals who are
considered security risks.[15] With the Canadian-origin community in
the United States, the issues concern profiling and civil rights. These are
significant with respect to the Mexican-origin community as well. But
this group differs in its sheer size: an estimated total of 21.6 million residents of Mexican origin, with 7.9 million of these born in Mexico, including 4.8 million undocumented.[16] The ways in which the powerful
tools are applied in policies affecting the NAFTA partners will affect the
broader commercial relationship in important respects. For example,
when the various databases in operation or under construction are interconnected and activated, what policies will guide their findings?
More specifically, as many thousands of undocumented residents are
identified, a large and pressing policy issue will be forced onto the agenda, not in the context of "NAFTA-Plus," as President Fox sought, but
rather in the context of U.S. security.[17]

CONCLUSIONS

To reiterate, the argument is that security has become the priority concern of the dominant NAFTA partner and that, while both Mexico and
Canada have responded positively to U.S. initiatives, Canada's responses are leading more quickly to security cooperation across a
broader front. This response was consistent with long-standing patterns of security cooperation that preceded NAFTA and reinforces incentives for a hub-and-spokes approach to North American security.

A related argument is that North American security cooperation will be organized outside NAFTA, which was intentionally kept "thin and narrow" with respect to bureaucracy and policy (although labor and environmental side agreements added some breadth). Here a historical analogy may be interesting. Recall that NAFTA came about in good part due to Canada's concerns about being left out of the free trade agreement being contemplated between the United States and Mexico. Might not something similar happen as Mexico contemplates closer security cooperation between the United States and Canada? Rather than hub and spokes, might not the Mexican government engage the Canadian in a joint approach toward the United States? As middle powers, they both have interests in multilateral, rules-based agreements and organizations (MacLean 2002).

My sense is that such an approach is unlikely. Mexico's public opinion and new democratic political system are not prepared to engage issues of security cooperation at a level that could support wide-ranging, intrusive agreements (e.g., joint military operations, combined customs teams) that have become routine in the U.S.–Canadian case. Alternatively, the Canadian government could take the initiative to engage Mexico in a joint approach toward the United States, but Mexico's reticence and the "defence against defense" advantages that Canada can gain in bilateral negotiations with the United States would seem to argue otherwise.

Another dynamic that links NAFTA to the security imperative is the expression that on foreign policy and security, Mexico and Canada have "European instincts and North American interests." An implication is that the business, financial, and related interests that most benefit from NAFTA would likely support a policy coalition in favor of extensive security cooperation with the United States. This coalition of interests would encounter a broader and more diverse coalition that is more skeptical of U.S. foreign and security policies. Though difficult, this tension appears to be manageable by skillful politicians whose stock in trade is conflict management. It is unlikely that NAFTA would be jeopardized by debates on security.

A different connection between commerce and security, and one that may drive other dynamics, is the extent to which the Bush administration uses (or is perceived to use) trade policy as a tool of broader U.S. foreign policy. It has been reported that the negotiation of Singapore's trade pact with the United States received favored treatment while

Chile's was delayed. Singapore supported Operation Iraqi Freedom, while Chile did not. U.S. trade representative Robert Zoellick was quoted to the effect that people were disappointed about Chile's stance in UN Security Council debates on Iraq (Blustein 2003). Connecting a top security priority such as policy toward Iraq to routine commercial agreements may be questionable, if understandable. But linking a questionable security issue such as antidrug policy to commerce with the United States' main trade partner sends a troubling signal. In this case, a White House drug policy official reportedly threatened U.S. retaliation if Canada relaxes its laws against marijuana. "[The official] didn't spell out what the American response would be, but he invoked images of tie-ups at border crossings and intense bureaucracy" (CBC News. 2003). To audiences watching the Homeland Security apparatus take shape, such a comment cannot be reassuring.

Regional integration moves at different speeds in different policy areas. For years, the prospect of a free trade agreement between the United States and Mexico seemed remote. The economies were too unequal; a free trade agreement would overwhelm a much smaller Mexican economy. But the coincidence of international context and political leadership brought a remarkable breakthrough in the early 1990s. The hub-and-spokes dynamic in the security arena reinforces a historical pattern, but it does not rule out decisions by future leaders to revisit and resculpt the agencies and programs that were hurriedly invented to respond to problems of the day.

Notes

1. Nor do scholars, evidently; a major recent collection (Chambers and Smith 2002) devotes 15 chapters and more than 500 pages to NAFTA, with nothing substantial on national security, or on public security for that matter. To the extent that NAFTA increases commercial dependency on the U.S. market, some Mexicans and Canadians may view NAFTA as a security threat.

2. I use "deepening" in the sense of adding organizational complexity to NAFTA's governance or of moving up the ladder from free trade to customs union and common market. It stands in contrast to "broadening," which refers to adding new members to NAFTA.

3. Canadian policymakers recite from memory that 40 percent of Canada's gross national product comes from exports and that 90 percent of those exports go to the United States. Time is often crucial. E.g., an automobile assembly plant in

Detroit places an order for seats to be delivered hours later from Canada, color coordinated to fit the cars as they come off the line.

4. After September 11, the Canadian government promptly set up coordinating arrangements to mirror the U.S. Office of Homeland Security, beefed up investments in intelligence and defense, and passed antiterrorism legislation (Rudner, forthcoming). See also Mirus (2001).

5. "Hub-and-spokes" refers to the U.S. government's negotiation of different bilateral arrangements with Canada and Mexico, rather than pursuing an integrated, trilateral approach.

6. Pastor (2002) gives a useful comparison of the approaches to NAFTA and the European Union.

7. U.S.–Canadian formal security relations are quite dense. A recent parliamentary report notes 80-plus defense agreements, 250 memoranda of understanding between the two defense departments, and 145 bilateral forums in which defense matters are treated. "Approximately 600 Canadian Forces' personnel serve in the U.S., mostly in NORAD related assignments. In addition, Canadian government and industry representatives visit the U.S. 20,000 times on defence related matters each year" (Standing Committee on National Security and Defence 2002, 39). "In the intelligence domain very close cooperation and intelligence sharing takes place between the relevant agencies of the US and Canada. However, these do not take place purely on a bilateral or hemispheric basis. The basis for intelligence cooperation is an alliance that brings together the US, UK, Canada, Australia (and, to a somewhat more limited extent in recent years New Zealand). This core alliance also involves other parties of a limited basis (e.g., Norway, Sweden, Japan, Netherlands, etc.). Since Sept 11 the boundaries of intelligence cooperation have expanded into a broader ranging coalition" (Martin Rudner, personal communication, December 4, 2002).

8. The Bush–Chrétien tie was already strained, due to Canadian ambassador Raymond Chrétien's stated preference in May 2000 for an Al Gore victory in November.

9. Unlike Prime Minister Chrétien, who did not make U.S.–Canadian relations a central concern, newly elected Prime Minister Paul Martin campaigned on improving relations and moved quickly to start the process. President Fox was put on the defensive when the regularization issue lost momentum after September 11; antiwar sentiment and midterm elections in July 2003 further limit his room for maneuvering.

10. The U.S.–Canadian agreement can be found at www.whitehouse.gov/news/releases/2002/09/20020909.html; the U.S.–Mexican agreement can be found at www.whitehouse.gov/infocus/usmborder.

11. "NAFTA-Plus" is understood as free trade with cooperation in other areas (e.g., energy or migration).

12. David Shirk, personal communication, April 6, 2003. I draw here on his comparative analysis of the agreements.

13. Interestingly, nowhere in the action plan does the word "terrorist" or "terrorism" appear, whereas in the U.S.–Canadian agreement the term appears seven times.

14. NEXUS is a special inspection program that allows prescreened low-risk travelers a rapid clearance by U.S. and Canadian border officials. Approved applicants are issued photograph-identification and a proximity card and are entitled to use special NEXUS-dedicated lanes at crossing points. Source: White House news releases.

15. The USA Patriot Act (PL 107-56, 115 Stat. 272, 2001) is the principal statutory response by the federal government to the September 11 attacks. I mention only seven relevant points here. First, it grants additional powers to federal authorities to monitor communications and gather information within the United States to investigate suspected terrorists. Second, it lowers the wall separating foreign intelligence gathering and domestic law enforcement as these are conducted within the United States. Third, it actively encourages information sharing between law enforcement and intelligence officers. Fourth, it strengthens anti-money-laundering sanctions and organizational capacity and adds these to antiterrorist provisions. Fifth, it extends extraterritorial application of U.S. law in several respects, e.g., the serving of warrants related to terrorists crimes or application of sanctions against foreign banks involved in money laundering. Sixth, it substantially enlarges the list of foreign crimes that can lead to money-laundering prosecutions when the proceeds from those crimes are laundered in the United States. Seventh, in recognition that it responds to an emergency, a number of its provisions carry "sunset clauses," i.e., after a specific time period (usually five years) the provision lapses, unless Congress explicitly renews it.

16. These data are from the Center for Immigration Studies, based on a U.S. Census Bureau estimate for 2000.

17. A clear picture of the emerging database architecture is not available. Yet the fragments of information available in the media provide interesting glimpses. E.g., "American law enforcement officials across country will soon have access to data base of 50 million overseas application for US visas, including photos of 20 million applicants; database will provide personal information and will tie together State Dept. computer system linkup, scheduled within next month, [with] intelligence agencies, FBI and police departments . . . . The database, which will become one of the largest offering images to local law enforcement, is maintained by the State Department and typically provides personal information like the applicant's home

address, date of birth and passport number, and the names of relatives" (Lee 2003). A Mexico City daily newspaper reported an Associated Press article to the effect that the U.S. government had purchased from ChoicePoint, a private company, the database of Mexico's national voter registry and the driver's license registry for the Federal District. According to the story, the U.S. government had acquired databases from ten Latin American countries (available at www.reforma.com).

References

Bailey, John, and Sergio Aguayo, eds. 1996. *Strategy and Security in U.S.–Mexican Relations: Beyond the Cold War.* U.S.–Mexico Contemporary Perspectives Series 9. San Diego: Center for U.S.–Mexican Studies at the University of California.

Benitez Manaut, Raúl. 2001. Seguridad y geopolítica en América del Norte: El Tratado de Libro Comercio—regionalismo versus nacionalismo. In *Las relaciones de México con Estados Unidos y Canadá: Una mirada al nuevo milenio,* ed. Rosío Vargas et al. Mexico City: Centro de Investigaciones sobre América del Norte, Universidad Nacional Autónoma de México.

Blustein, Paul. 2003. Trade Accords Become a U.S. Foreign Policy Tool. *Washington Post,* April 29, E1, E4.

Buzan, Barry, Ole Weaver, and Jaap de Wilde. 1998. *Security: A New Framework for Analysis.* Boulder, Colo.: Lynne Rienner.

Camarota, Steven A. 2001. Immigrants in the United States—2000: A Snapshot of America's Foreign Born Population. Center for Immigration Studies. www.cis. org/articles2001/back101.html.

Camp, Roderic Ai. 1999. *Politics in Mexico.* New York: Oxford University Press.

CBC News. 2003. U.S. Warns Canada against Easing Pot Laws. Internet edition, May 2. Available at http://www.cbc.ca/.

Chambers, Edward J., and Peter H. Smith, eds. 2002. *NAFTA in the New Millennium.* San Diego: Center for U.S.–Mexican Studies at the University of California; Edmonton: University of Alberta Press.

Cope, John A. 1996. In Search of Convergence: U.S.–Mexican Military Relations into the Twenty-First Century. In *Strategy and Security in U.S.–Mexican Relations: Beyond the Cold War,* ed. John Bailey and Sergio Aguayo. U.S.–Mexico Contemporary Perspectives Series 9. San Diego: Center for U.S.–Mexican Studies at the University of California.

Edgar, Alistair D. 2002. Let's Get a Continental Defence Market Treaty. *Policy Options / Options Politiques,* April: 50–56.

Fortmann, Michel, and David G. Haglund. 2002. Canada and the Issue of Homeland Security: Does the "Kingston Dispensation" Still Hold? *Canadian Military Journal*, spring: 17–22.

Granatstein, J. L. 2002. A Friendly Agreement in Advance: Canada–U.S. Defense Relations Past, Present and Future. *C. D. Howe Institute Commentary*, no. 166 (June).

Hartlyn, Jonathan, Lars Schoultz, and Augusto Varas. 1992. Introduction. In *The United States and Latin America in the 1990s: Beyond the Cold War*, ed. Jonathan Hartlyn, Lars Schoultz, and Augusto Varas. Chapel Hill: University of North Carolina Press.

Haynal, George. 2002. Interdpendence, Globalization and North American Borders. *Policy Options / Options Politiques*, September: 20–26.

King, David L. 2001. The Canadian–American Defence Relationship: What Next for Canadian Defence Policy? Paper presented at a Canada–United States defense symposium, University of Manitoba, October.

Kitchen, Veronica M. 2003. Re-Thinking the Canada–United States Security Community. Paper presented at an International Studies Association Conference, Portland, Ore., February 26–March 1.

Latell, Brian. 2002. U.S. Foreign Intelligence and Mexico: The Evolving Relationship. In *Transnational Crime and Public Security: Challenges to Mexico and the United States*, ed. John Bailey and Jorge Chabat. San Diego: Center for U.S.–Mexican Studies at the University of California.

Lee, Jennifer. 2003. Threats and Responses: Law Enforcement: State Dept. Link Will Open Visa Database to Police Officers. *New York Times*, February 1.

MacLean, George A. 2002. Refefining Continental Defence: The Hemispheric Multilateral Dimension. *Policy Options / Options Politiques*, April: 46–49.

Mazza, Jaqueline. 2002. *Don't Disturb the Neighbors: The United States and Democracy in Mexico, 1980–1995.* New York: Routledge.

Mirus, Rolf. 2001. After Sept. 11: A Canadian–U.S. Customs Union. *Policy Options / Options Politiques*, November: 50–52.

Pastor, Robert A. 2002. A Regional Development Policy for North America: Adapting the European Union Model. In *NAFTA in the New Millennium*, ed. Edward J. Chambers and Peter H. Smith. San Diego: Center for U.S.–Mexican Studies at the University of California,; Edmonton: University of Alberta Press.

Paz, Maria Emilia. 1997. *Strategy, Security and Spies: Mexico and the U.S. as Allies in World War II.* University Park: Pennsylvania State University Press.

Ridge, Tom. 2003. Securing America's Borders: The Border of the Future. Prepared remarks of the assistant to the president for homeland security, briefing to the U.S. Senate, May 1.

Rudner, Martin. Forthcoming. Challenge and Response: Canada's Intelligence Community and the War on Global Terrorism. In *9/11: The Impact and Aftermath for Canada and Canadians* ed. Jack Jedwab and Hector Mackenzie. Toronto: Butterworth-Heinemann.

Shirk, David A. 2003. Law Enforcement and Public Security Challenges in the U.S.–Mexican Border Region. Paper presented at an International Studies Association Conference, Portland, Ore., February 26–March 1.

Standing Senate Committee on National Security and Defence, Government of Canada. 2002. *Defence of North America: A Canadian Responsibility.* Ottawa: Government of Canada.

PART FIVE

SOCIAL ISSUES

CHAPTER TEN

NAFTA AND MEXICAN MIGRATION TO THE UNITED STATES

Frank D. Bean and B. Lindsay Lowell

After the twin towers of the World Trade Center collapsed on September 11, 2001, it soon became evident that the administration of George W. Bush had reversed its priorities regarding U.S. immigration policy vis-à-vis Mexico. Instead of advocating increases in Mexican migration to the United States, together with the "regularization" of migrants already in the country, positions that reflected both the labor needs of the booming U.S. economy in the late 1990s and President Bush's desire to curry political favor with Latinos, the administration shifted its emphasis to tougher inspections and tighter controls at the border as national security anxieties about threats of additional terrorist attacks trumped all other policy goals. What had seemed a realistic possibility of achieving a historic bilateral migration accord between the United States and Mexico right after Presidents Fox and Bush met in the United States on September 5, 2001, turned into a remote possibility (Castañeda 2003). With the issue of reforming U.S. immigration policy regarding Mexico relegated to a low priority, if not off the policy agenda altogether, migration from Mexico, particularly unauthorized migration and the U.S. policies affecting it, resumed their usual confused, messy, and contradictory status on the country's public policy agenda (Bean and Stevens 2003).

What is significant about this change is that it represented the end of a brief and unusually favorable immigration attitude in the United States, a time notable for the embrace of the idea that the country needed more low-skilled labor migration from Mexico. Ironically, the North American Free Trade Agreement (NAFTA), which many supporters thought would reduce such migration, probably helped to create this view. After NAFTA went into effect in January 1994, but prior to September 11, 2001, both economic circumstances and migration policy discussions steadily moved the views of both the public and policymakers toward a greater appreciation of the role that labor migration was playing in the U.S. economy and of the need to adopt changes that would better institutionalize both its nature and magnitude, not only to better ensure labor supply (a major interest of both U.S. business and the Mexican government) but also to reduce the dangers of illegal border crossings and exploitation (an interest of the Mexican government and human rights groups in both countries) (U.S.–Mexico Migration Panel 2001).

The fact that migration from Mexico, especially unauthorized migration, had increased enormously during the late 1990s was hardly noticed at all, not only because U.S. government statistical agencies were slow to detect and report it, but also because the strength of the U.S. economy was increasingly directing attention to rising labor shortages, not gluts of unskilled workers. The oft-announced hope (or hype) that the passage of NAFTA would reduce unauthorized migration from Mexico seemed completely forgotten. If anything, the benefits of a booming economy, itself perceived to be reinforced, if not caused, by NAFTA-encouraged free trade, had generated a result none of the prognosticators of NAFTA's migration effects had foreseen. There was a growing sentiment that the country needed even more low-skilled labor migrants than the champions of such migration themselves might have advocated. If NAFTA had helped to generate unparalleled prosperity in the country, then so too perhaps might more labor migration from Mexico.

But now such notions seem quaint. The stagnation of the country's economy and the importance of national security issues direct attention elsewhere. In particular, given the loose labor markets in the United States at the moment, they invite a return to the more difficult and vexing questions of the degree to which changes in economic and migration policy actually affect migration patterns. One such question concerns the connections between policy milestones like NAFTA and its effects on migration. If NAFTA was oversold to skeptical legislators as a mechanism for reducing unauthorized Mexican migration, a possibility that seemed contradicted by the robust economic growth and the high migration of the late 1990s, does this mean that NAFTA exerted no such effect on migration? Given the unusual strength of the economy during this time, is it even possible to disentangle NAFTA's migration effects from the influences of other factors affecting migration? Is it possible that there have been no single or simple effects of NAFTA on migration? Perhaps there are multiple effects, some operating positively and some negatively so as to at least partially offset one another?

The purpose of this chapter is to try to shed light on possible responses to such questions, if not to answer them definitively. We organize our effort in the following five topics: (1) the history of Mexican migration to the United States, (2) the often unauthorized nature of Mexican migration, (3) the pre-NAFTA Mexican economic context, (4) the pattern of Mexican migration flows since the Immigration Reform and Control Act (IRCA) and NAFTA, and (5) policy implications and considerations for the future.

MEXICAN MIGRATION BACKGROUND TO NAFTA

The policy importance of Mexico to the United States is reflected in the publication of a raft of books during the late 1990s on United States–Mexico relations and Mexican migration (e.g., Bean et al. 1997; Oppenheimer 1995; Castañeda 1995; Fuentes 1996). It is also illustrated by the high priority the Democratic administration of Bill Clinton gave in 1993 to congressional ratification of NAFTA, an initiative begun in the previous George H. W. Bush administration, and by the loan-guarantee package put together by the Clinton administration to assist the Mexican government through the economic difficulties created by the Mexican peso devaluation of December 1994. As Oppenheimer (1995) has noted: "No single country in the post–Cold War era affects the U.S. national interest in more ways than Mexico" (p. xi). While many observers in the post–September 11 environment might view such statements as exaggerated, there remains little doubt that Mexico is of considerable importance to the United States in numerous ways. The most important, perhaps, involves Mexican migration to the United States.

The volume of Mexican migration to the United States since 1970 has exceeded that coming from any other country. This was especially true during the 1990s (1991–2000), when Mexico accounted for 24.7 percent of all legal entrants to the United States; whereas the Philippines, in second place, provided only 5.6 percent (U.S. Immigration and Naturalization Service 2003). Analysts estimate that Mexicans constitute an even greater presence among unauthorized migrants than among legal migrants (about 55 percent of all unauthorized migrants vs. about 7 percent for the next largest group, El Salvadorans) (U.S. Immigration and Naturalization Service 1999; Passel 1999). To speak of immigration without making a distinction between legal and unauthorized migration is thus to oversimplify substantially the reality of the U.S. immigration picture, and it is not possible to take unauthorized migration to the United States into account without paying special attention to the Mexican case. Thus, the reality in recent years is that Mexican migration to the United States is relatively large and different in kind from the migration flows from other countries.

In considering the policy conundrum of unauthorized migration, it is important to understand the historical background of Mexican emigration to the United States. The high profile of Mexican migration for U.S. policy is relatively new. Until recently, Mexican migration, compared with that from other nations, was not particularly large and, in practice if not always in law, was relatively unrestricted, with exceptions such as the repatriation of large numbers of Mexican migrants in the 1930s and again in 1954 (Freeman and Bean 1997; Laslett 1996). In comparison with the massive immigrations from Europe in the last half of the nineteenth century and the first decades of the twentieth century, Mexican immigration contributed, until recently, only a small part of U.S. population growth. Its pre–World War II peak occurred in the 1920s, when the economic disruptions of the Mexican Revolution (1910–20) and the civil wars that followed led many Mexicans to migrate to the United States in search of jobs. In the 1920s, 459,000 Mexicans were registered as immigrating to the United States, equivalent to 3.2 percent of the total Mexican population in 1921. These numbers of Mexican immigrants were not to be surpassed until the 1970s, but they were not exceptional. Several European countries (Italy, Germany, and the United Kingdom) contributed similar numbers of immigrants, while twice that number of immigrants came from Canada in the 1920s. Even Ireland, long past the peak of its contribution to U.S. population growth, sent a higher proportion of its population as immigrants to the United States than did Mexico in these years. Some 5.2 percent of the Irish population immigrated to the United States in the 1920s, despite the attainment of Irish Independence that removed one of major ostensible causes of Irish emigration.

Not only was Mexican migration not particularly voluminous; much of it was also temporary. Partly as a result, Mexican immigrants have had one of the lowest naturalization rates of any immigrant group (Jasso and Rosenzweig 1990, table 3.1). Census figures also suggest substantial emigration out of the United States by Mexican immigrants (Freeman and Bean 1997). Whereas 728,000 Mexicans are recorded as immigrating to the United States between 1901 and 1930, the numbers of the Mexican-born population in the United States in 1930 amounted to 641,000, and these would have included many who had not documented their immigration. By 1950, the Mexican-born in the census had dropped to 452,000, reflecting not only mortality and the low level of immigration after 1930 but also the forced repatriations of Mexicans in the 1930s. There are no satisfactory estimates of Mexican return migration to Mexico, but it is clear the amount of return migration has been quite high in virtually all years, although it may have declined substantially during the 1990s as a consequence of beefed up enforcement along the border (Bean et al. 1994; Reyes, Johnson, and Van Swearingen 2002; Massey, Durand, and Malone 2002; Mexican Ministry on Foreign Affairs and U.S. Commission on Immigration Reform 1997).

Mexican migrants to the United States until the 1960s were predominantly employed in types of work that were temporary and seasonal in nature. The rapid expansion of Californian agriculture depended on a seasonal labor force. There was not the work in fruit and vegetable production to employ people the year round and, consequently, it was attractive only to the newest entrants into the labor force, immigrant or not, who had no other sources of work. For most workers in California, seasonal work in agriculture was a step toward finding more permanent work either in the rural areas or in the cities. Thus, turnover was high. The difficulties recruiting a labor force from California's resident population made Mexican migrant labor an attractive option for farmers. It was also attractive for the migrants themselves, who could earn much higher wages than in Mexico and could save enough to maintain their families in the villages and, at times, enable them to invest in land or animals. So long as the Mexican migrants wished to return, the arrangement suited both sides. Until the 1970s, most Mexican migrants did wish to return; but in the last three decades of the twentieth century, Mexican immigration not only increased in volume but also increasingly involved permanent immigration (Bean, Edmonston, and Passel 1990; Marcelli and Cornelius 2001).

It was at this juncture that Mexican migration perhaps became a critical, if not always explicit, issue for U.S. immigration policy. Other shifts in the flows of immigrants in the 1970s and 1980s played a part in changing immigration policy in the 1980s, particularly the increases in immigration from Asia. However, the major piece of immigration legislation in the 1980s, the Immigration Reform and Control Act of 1986, and the policy debates around it, were substantially affected by the peculiar challenge posed by Mexican immigration (Bean, Vernez, and Keely 1989). Whereas previous immigration policies toward Mexico had tended to operate on the adage "If it ain't broke, don't fix it," IRCA involved a determined effort to find a solution to what were perceived to be problems raised by Mexican unauthorized migration (Massey, Durand, and Malone 2002). Confronted with the reality of millions of unauthorized Mexicans residing in the United States and the prospects of many more following them, IRCA, through legalization and employer sanctions, recognized the de facto situation of Mexican migrant settlement, while seeking to limit employer demand for further immigration. As various observers have pointed out, NAFTA was, in migration policy terms, a further arm of this strategy (Smith 1997; Weintraub 1997), at least insofar as it might reduce unauthorized migration by increasing job growth in Mexico. What has not been previously emphasized is that IRCA's failure to stem unauthorized migration after the first couple of years probably helped create political conditions favorable to NAFTA's political passage in the United States, meaning that the two pieces of legislation need to be considered together when assessing their migration consequences.

UNAUTHORIZED MEXICAN MIGRATION

During the past three decades, the component of the Mexican-born population in the United States that has attracted the most media attention is the unauthorized migrant population. This group has frequently galvanized public opinion and attracted the attention of U.S. policymakers (U.S. Commission on Immigration Reform 1994; Bean et al. 1997; Espenshade and Belanger 1998), as illustrated by three special governmental initiatives undertaken to address immigration issues. First, in 1981 the Select Commission on Immigration and Refugee Policy released its report, noting that "one issue has emerged as most pressing—the problem of undocumented/illegal migration" (1981, 35). Second, in 1986 Congress passed IRCA in an effort to reduce unauthorized migration. Third, in 1996 Congress passed welfare reform and immigration legislation partly to curtail unauthorized migration by limiting the public benefits available to noncitizen immigrants (Espenshade, Baraka, and Huber 1997; Van Hook and Bean 1999).

An unauthorized migrant is a person who resides in the United States but whose status is not that of a U.S. citizen, permanent resident, or authorized visitor (Van Hook and Bean 1999). Various labels have been applied to what we call here unauthorized migrants, including "undocumenteds," "illegals," "illegal aliens," and "illegal immigrants." Each of these terms has a somewhat different meaning and connotation. We use the term *unauthorized migrant* because it best defines the group to which we are referring. We do not use the term *undocumented* because many unauthorized migrants have documents, although counterfeit ones. Nor do we use the term *illegal* (although in a technical sense these migrants are illegal) because the United States does not systematically enforce laws making it illegal for employers to hire such persons.

It is important to note that unauthorized migrants are heterogeneous with respect to duration of stay. To avoid misunderstanding evidence about migration flows, it is particularly crucial to recall certain distinctions based on duration of stay, such as that between temporary and permanent migrants (or sojourners and settlers, to use the more sociological terms) (Chavez 1988; Espenshade 1995a; Woodrow and Passel 1990). Much of the historical and current debate about unauthorized migration derives from differences in perceptions about whether sojourners or settlers dominate such flows. Insofar as the unauthorized migrant population is made up of sojourners, return migrants represent outflows that help to offset inflows. Outflow is a critical component because, in the case of unauthorized Mexican migrants, the majority of entrances has been offset by exits, at least until recently, as indicated by estimates of repeat entrances (Espenshade 1995b) and net flow (Woodrow and Passel 1990). During the 1970s, many observers mistook substantial numbers of border apprehensions as indicating large net inflows. By failing to account for outflow, such observers greatly exaggerated the rate of growth of the unauthorized migrant population. In effect, the error was to assume that the number of settlers predominated over sojourners, when in fact the opposite was the case.

Given the frequent preoccupation in the United States with unauthorized migration, and given that persons from Mexico, by all accounts, make up more than half of all unauthorized immigrants (Bean, Edmonston, and Passel 1990; U.S. Immigration and Naturalization Service 2000), it is not surprising that many analysts and policymakers focus attention on how many unauthorized Mexican migrants reside in the United States, often ignoring research findings about other aspects of unauthorized migration. For example, in a front-page story about the results of the Mexico–U.S. Binational Migration Study, the *New York Times* (Dillon 1997) emphasized the study's research findings about the size of this population to the exclusion of other results. Similarly, when policymakers consider immigration issues, the question of Mexican *legal* immigration in particular often ends up either ignored altogether or underemphasized. This is illustrated in the focuses of the two major immigration-related studies mounted by the U.S. Commission on Immigration Reform during the 1990s. One of these was conducted by the National Research Council and examined the demographic and economic effects on the United States of *immigration in general* (Smith and Edmonston 1997). The other was carried out by the Mexico–U.S. Binational Migration Study Group and focused predominantly (though not exclusively) on *unauthorized* Mexican migration (Mexican Ministry on Foreign Affairs and U.S. Commission on Immigration Reform 1997). In a similar vein, the U.S. Congress has often focused its *explicit* attention on illegal migration, concentrating its legislative efforts in 1996, for example, on border control and on other efforts to slow unauthorized immigration. The de facto effect of this focus was to emphasize only the unauthorized component of Mexican migration. Perhaps it is not surprising that so many of those members of Congress considering whether to vote for NAFTA convinced themselves that it would help to resolve what was perceived as the country's problem with unauthorized Mexican migration.

THE PRE-NAFTA ECONOMIC CONTEXT IN MEXICO

But if worries about unauthorized migration in the United States, together with the hope that increased free trade might reduce such migration, made supporting the passage of NAFTA more palatable, what conditions in Mexico that led to a desire to adopt NAFTA? For the most part, they revolved around economic rather than migration experiences and issues. Mexico's policies toward economic development went through profound transformations during the 1980s. The earlier model of development, implemented most intensely in the postwar period, involved what was called import-substituting industrialization (ISI), a policy advocated at the time by the Economic Commission for Latin America and the Caribbean and one often typical of Latin American and Caribbean countries generally (Iglesias 1993). In terms of delivering overall economic growth in the Mexican case, the policy succeeded. Gross domestic product increased by about 5 to 6 percent a year for three decades, from the 1950s through the 1970s (Bean, Escobar, and Weintraub 1999). The benefits of the growth were not equitably distributed, and Mexico's income distribution was highly skewed in favor of upper-income families. Emigration from Mexico to the United States was substantial during all of this high-growth period, presumably in part because much poverty persisted, particularly in rural areas, and inadequate opportunities existed for those sharing only marginally in the overall economic growth. The push–pull factors that explain much of the migration from Mexico to the United States were evident (Diaz-Briquets and Weintraub 1991). The migration networks that had been established during the *bracero* program were consolidated during the ISI period.

Although the strong economic growth generated by the substitution policy began to stall during the 1970s, thanks to high oil prices resulting from the 1973–74 Yom Kippur War and easy loans from foreign lenders, Mexico did not encounter major difficulties until 1982 when oil prices declined and U.S. and world interest rates rose sharply (Weintraub 1990). The old development model no longer appeared to work. Other than oil, which in 1982 accounted for 72 percent of the value of Mexican exports, Mexican products were not competitive in export markets. One option available was to default on external loans, but the country chose instead to reschedule them. Alternatively, Mexico could have deepened the ISI model and even expanded the already substantial role of government enterprises in the economy, as some Mexicans advocated. This was rejected because it probably would have had to be accompanied by debt repudiation under conditions imposed by creditors that could not have been met.

The third main option, and the one selected, was to change the model from development from within to building an export economy. In 1986, during the presidency of Miguel de la Madrid (1982–86), Mexico acceded to the General Agreement on Tariffs and Trade, a step explicitly rejected following long negotiations during the previous administration of José López Portillo (1976–82). Improvements in the economic performance came slowly. The Mexican economy grew modestly over the next five years, and hardly at all in per capita terms (Lustig 1992). The minimum wage, which serves as a benchmark for many other wages, fell by about 40 percent in real terms during this period. Evidence indicates that income distribution became marginally more unequal. It was apparent that even in good times in Mexico, at least as measured by the overall growth in gross domestic product (GDP) during the ISI period, emigration to the United States was substantial; it was also clear after 1982, when the economy worsened, that emigration accelerated.

The new export-led recovery model required a reduction in the cost of imported goods, particularly intermediate products which make up the bulk of Mexican merchandise imports, so as not to unduly burden exporters. By the time the negotiations took place for Mexico's participation in NAFTA, the trade-weighted Mexican import tariff averaged 11 percent (Gonzalez-Baker et al. 1998). Even more significantly, import licensing was reduced and then eliminated in NAFTA, which was signed by the three North American governments in late 1992. In addition, Mexico agreed in NAFTA to eliminate domestic-content requirements (although with a lag in the automotive industry). This freed producers to purchase intermediate products from the United States and did not tie them to higher-priced products from Mexico.

This policy of free trade under NAFTA formally went into operation on January 1, 1994. During early 1994, inflation in Mexico was declining, foreign reserves were high (in excess of $25 billion), and GDP growth was anticipated at about 4 percent, not remarkable but acceptable (Gonzalez-Baker et al. 1998). However, the deficit in the balance of payments current account had been growing to dangerously high levels—reaching 8 percent of GDP in 1994—and political turmoil, involving disquiet and rebellion in Chiapas, and assassinations of important political leaders, was generating an uneasy investment climate. Shortly after December 20, when Mexico decided to devalue the peso by about 15 percent, investors realized that the amount of outstanding Mexican dollar-indexed, short-term Treasury obligations called *tesobonos* were several times greater than Mexico's foreign reserves. While denominated in pesos, the dollar indexation made these bonds equivalent to dollar instruments whose attractiveness to investors had been in part that they constituted a hedge against devaluation. The economic consequences were severe, and the Mexican authorities were forced to devote most of their activities in 1995 to dealing with the financial and economic fallout. GDP in 1995 fell by 6.9 percent. Real wages declined by about 15 percent, and urban unemployment rose by about 2 million persons.

By early 1996, the financial situation seemed to have stabilized. The peso was steady, the stock market was high, and Mexico was able to borrow on world money markets. Inflation reached 52 percent in 1995, but it declined substantially in 1996, and even further thereafter. Led by the export sector, the Mexican economy performed quite well, with overall growth rates in GDP of about 5 percent a year, in considerable measure because of the strength of the U.S. economy that made up the market for much of Mexico's exports. Thus, after a rocky start, Mexico seems to have made a successful transition to a new economic growth model, though the global economic slowdown starting in 2001 and lasting until this writing is placing strains on the country's economy. In any case, the economic difficulties that led to NAFTA can be said to have been followed by a period of fairly strong economic growth, thus raising the question of whether this NAFTA-induced growth resulted in any reduction in unauthorized migration to the United States, as so many observers thought (or hoped) it might? It is this question to which we now turn our attention. But in addressing this question, it is first necessary to ask whether IRCA had achieved its purpose in slowing Mexican migration to the United States.

IMMIGRATION RESPONSES TO IRCA AND NAFTA

U.S. responses to the perceived costs and benefits of Mexican migration, as manifested in various kinds of U.S. immigration and immigrant policies, constitute another set of factors that influence Mexican emigration dynamics. Historically, these responses have included early labor recruitment drives on the part of U.S. entrepreneurs that, because the U.S. government condoned them, amount to de facto pro-immigration policies (Cardoso 1980). The classic post–World War II case was the *bracero* program, which legalized specified annual amounts of contract agricultural and manufacturing employment of migrants, running from the beginning of the war until 1964 when the program was terminated (Bean, Vernez, and Keely 1989). The initiative was the first programmatic effort to "control the flow" while at the same time providing for cheap labor in the U.S. economy. The U.S. Immigration and Naturalization Service did little to curtail the illegal entry of workers who came outside the numbers allowed by the program, an apparently contradictory policy, but one that in reality served to meet the needs of two constituencies at once, namely, the employers interested in inexpensive labor on the one hand and others who were concerned about the illegality of such migration on the other hand (Calavita 1992).

IRCA's Influence

The major post–World War II legislative initiative to curtail illegal migration to the United States (including that from Mexico) was IRCA, which was passed in 1986 (Bean, Vernez, and Keely 1989). A principal objective of IRCA was to reduce the number of illegal immigrants coming to and residing in the United States. The law attempted to accomplish this through (1) the legalization of many unauthorized immigrants already residing in the United States; (2) the prohibition of the hiring of undocumented workers and the enforcement of this prohibition; and (3) the authorization and appropriation of increased resources for enforcement of activities by the border patrol.

One of the major criteria by which the effectiveness of IRCA can be judged is the extent to which the flow of illegal immigrants into the country was actually reduced and the extent to which the size of the resident illegal alien population was diminished (beyond the reduction brought about by the legalization programs). Certainly IRCA reduced the number of illegal residents by virtue of its legalization program. A Seasonal Agricultural Workers program also legalized substantial numbers of temporary migrants. Thus, a major question is, apart from changes in the size of the undocumented population already living here, and apart from legalizing a group of temporary circular migrants, did IRCA otherwise reduce the numbers of illegal entrants coming to the United States, especially in the years immediately after its passage?

Some indication of an answer to this question can be provided by examining apprehensions data, one of the most frequently cited sources of information about undocumented immigration to the United States. Apprehensions statistics come from monthly tallies of the number of times persons entering the country illegally are apprehended by the U.S. border patrol or by other INS enforcement personnel. More than 90 percent of apprehensions (92 percent in fiscal 1986 and 1988) are made by the Border Patrol, and of these, more than 99 percent consist of persons who "enter without inspection" as opposed to visa overstayers, that is, persons who enter on tourist, student, or work visas and then overstay the term of the visa. Apprehensions of unauthorized entrants have averaged over 1 million a year since 1982. These numbers seem to imply an unauthorized population of enormous size in the United States. But not only do such apprehensions include various types of migrants, they also include persons who have been apprehended several times. Also, many persons apprehended during a given year return to Mexico before the end of the year. Thus, the number of apprehensions, which peaked during the 1980s at 1,767,400 in fiscal year 1986 (U.S. Immigration and Naturalization Service 2003), substantially overstates the size of the unauthorized population that enters and remains in the country within any given year. Finally, apprehensions statistics alone could also lead to an understatement of the unauthorized flow of migrants if many entrants go undetected.

Despite the possibility that many entrants go undetected, apprehensions statistics are of considerable value for making assessments of the flow of unauthorized Mexican migrants. Data on apprehensions are particularly useful for gauging changes from one time period to another in the flow of unauthorized entrants. Because almost all apprehensions involve Mexicans (e.g., 92 percent in fiscal 1987), data on apprehensions are virtually the only large-scale database from which to gauge, however roughly, flows from Mexico. In fact, total border patrol apprehensions declined after the passage of IRCA, from 1,767,400 in fiscal 1986 to 1,190,488 in fiscal 1987, to 1,008,145 in fiscal 1988, to 954,253 in fiscal 1989, before starting up again. The data on the number of apprehensions for fiscal 1961 to 2001 encompass five distinct periods. The first is 1977–82, a relative boom for the Mexican economy. During this time, apprehensions were relatively stable, or even declined slightly at times. The second period is 1983–86, after the slowdown in the Mexican economy but before the passage of IRCA. During this time, apprehensions jumped sharply (by almost 46 percent from fiscal 1982 to fiscal 1983). The third period includes 1987–89, the fiscal years immediately after the passage of IRCA. During this time, apprehensions declined through 1989. However, apprehensions did not fall to their 1977–82 levels. As to the extent to which IRCA was responsible for this decline after 1986, it appears that the legislation is associated with some reduction in unauthorized flows after the 1982 decline in the Mexican economy, but this reduction does not drop to earlier levels (those of the 1977–82 period).

The fourth period is the years 1990–93, the "late" IRCA but pre-NAF-TA period. During this time, apprehensions again moved upward, closer to pre-IRCA levels, indicating that the deterrent effects of IRCA had seemingly dissipated. The fifth period is fiscal 1994 to 2000, which is the post-NAFTA and (in the case of 1995) the post-peso devaluation period. It is important to keep in mind during this period that enforcement increases during the period are taking place. As we note in the next section, where such factors are considered, there is reason to think that apparent increases in the flows from Mexico during the 1990s are at least as much the result of economic conditions in the United States as they are the consequence of conditions in Mexico or of legislation.

A consistent pattern emerges from these data and from other research studies (Bean et al. 1990). A clear reduction in the flow of unauthorized immigrants across the United States–Mexico border appears to have occurred in the post-IRCA period. Furthermore, this reduction took place in the presence of increased INS effort, indicated by more line-watch hours and upgraded equipment—factors that would increase apprehensions, not decrease them. The research also suggests that a significant portion of the post-IRCA drop in apprehensions can be attributed to the legalization of large numbers of Mexicans in the general legalization and Seasonal Agricultural Workers programs. Thus IRCA was associated with a reduction in illegal Mexican immigration to the United States during the three years immediately after the legislation was passed. After that, the research suggests that unauthorized migration was again on the rise.

To what extent can the reduction that occurred be attributed explicitly to the deterrent effects of employer sanctions? Though the legalization programs accounted for a substantial part of the reduction, they did not account for all of it, suggesting that sanctions might explain the residual (Bean, Edmonston, and Passel 1990). However, the fact that the implementation of sanctions occurred gradually over a three-year period, with the INS not fully enforcing sanctions compliance until 1989, the third year after the law was passed, suggests that sanctions may *not* have accounted for the decline. The greatest reductions took place in the first and second years of the legislation, not in subsequent years when sanctions were more strongly enforced. Thus, the decreased flows may have owed less to the deterrent effects of sanctions than to generalized patterns of anxiety and rumor, especially in Mexico, about what the effects of the law might turn out to be. Once it was learned that the legislation was not going to lead to draconian outcomes (e.g., unauthorized migrants being thrown in jail), the process of unauthorized labor migration resumed unabated.

NAFTA's Influence

All of the events and actions in Mexico—the policy changes, the adjustments to them, and the economic declines experienced first in 1982 and then in 1995—had significant impacts on migration. They helped bring on much internal migration, as different regions of the country and different sectors had variable experiences; and much emigration out of the country, as economic prospects altered. Because the peso's devaluation raised unemployment in Mexico and increased the peso value of remittances sent back by Mexican workers earning dollars in the United States, it also raised the attractiveness of labor migration to the United States. To what extent did illegal flows actually increase because of economic crisis conditions in Mexico? Although research is still inconclusive, the answer appears to be that Mexican migration flows indeed increased as a result of the peso devaluation, but other factors may have affected the flow even more. The number of gross apprehensions during the first year after the peso devaluation was up nearly 40 percent over 1994. But factors besides the peso devaluation also contributed to this increase: lower overall U.S. unemployment rates (from 6.6 to 5.6 percent over the period), appreciably higher aggregate U.S. unemployment from the beginning of 1994 to early 1995; and more hours devoted to border enforcement. Research by Bean and Cushing (1995) suggests these factors could account for as much as two-thirds of the increase in apprehensions of Mexican migrants during 1995. Thus, conditions in the United States affected emigration changes as much as conditions in Mexico after the peso devaluation in 1994.

This conclusion is buttressed by apprehension statistics. The numbers rise steadily during the latter half of the 1990s, reaching levels that involve new highs. Some of this increase results from increased border enforcement, involving nearly a tripling of the number of Border Patrol officers. However, the growth in the size of the unauthorized Mexican population in the United States during this period indicates that not all of the increase can be due to increased enforcement. This growth was reflected in the results from the 2000 U.S. Census, which analysts have argued show a substantial increase in the size of the Mexican unauthorized population after 1995 (Bean et al. 2001). Some have argued in turn that this growth derives from the increased enforcement causing unauthorized migrants to stay in the United States rather than return to Mexico (Massey, Durand, and Malone 2002). However, though this has clearly occurred to some extent, the dramatic rise in apprehensions suggests that not all of it is due to this factor alone.

Thus, the conclusion that clearly seems warranted is that unauthorized Mexican migration to the United States increased during the 1990s, probably because of the strength of the labor market during this period. Not much basis emerges from the evidence, therefore, to conclude that NAFTA had the often politically expected dampening effect on migration. More likely is that the somewhat improved economy in Mexico during the latter part of the 1990s helped to foster additional migration by making it more affordable for many of the persons predisposed to go to the United States. This has always been the prediction of many economic development scholars (Weintraub 1990; Martin 1997; Portes and Bach 1985). Whatever the case, unauthorized migration continued at as high a pace as ever. And early indications for the first few years of the twenty-first century indicate that it seems not to be slowing down, despite the stagnation of the U.S. economy (Porter 2003).

CONCLUSIONS AND FUTURE CONSIDERATIONS

An important question for the future concerns the degree to which economic growth and declining fertility in Mexico will lead to reduced migration to the United States during the next two or three decades. Birthrates in Mexico have fallen precipitously during the past couple of decades, from an average of about 6.1 children per woman in 1974 to about 2.4 children per woman in 1999 (CONAPO 1999). These drops have been so steep that each of the past six or seven Mexican birth cohorts has been smaller than the one immediately preceding it, reversing the pattern of steady increase that had obtained previously. This means that unless fertility goes back up, the size of the Mexican labor force (by which we mean the number of persons each year looking for employment) could be expected to stop growing and perhaps start to shrink a bit sometime between 2010 and 2015 (Mexican Ministry on Foreign Affairs and U.S. Commission on Immigration Reform 1997). Moreover, if economic growth in Mexico sustained reasonable but not unrealistic levels of about 6 to 7 percent a year, the number of jobs in Mexico could easily within a decade equal the size of the workforce, a circumstance not holding in the country for as long as anyone can remember.

Given this, the question becomes: Would migration to the United States then start to subside? This, of course, can only be answered in a somewhat speculative manner because we cannot be confident that the trends we are assuming will in fact occur. But even if they did, there are reasons to think Mexican migration might not slow down substantially. These reasons have mainly do to with the kinds of forces driving migration. In the Mexican case, two stand out. The first is that so much migration has already occurred that it will continue to spawn more migration (the cumulative causation phenomenon noted by Massey, Durand, and Malone 2002). The second is that there are likely to continue to be economic reasons (e.g., higher wages) and family and household reasons to migrate, even if it becomes easier to find employment in Mexico. Thus, while certain kinds of pressures to migrate might ease under the conditions of the scenario just outlined, other factors driving migration can be expected to continue to exert their influence.

More broadly, the Mexican-origin population has and will continue to have an impact on the ethnic makeup of the United States. Not only will the proportion of the Mexican origin population that is foreign born continue to be large, but also the Mexican origin population in the United States will become an increasingly important component of the overall population, becoming the largest minority ethnic group early in the next century. This growth has implications for the future social, economic, and political conditions of the United States. Its young age structure relative to non-Hispanic whites, for example, means that the Mexican origin population will contribute more to the working-age population, will have a greater stake in the educational system, and may, as a result, become more politically active. In addition, because the Mexican-origin population in the United States seems likely to continue to be made up of a very high proportion of foreign-born individuals, both immigration policy in the United States and U.S. relations with Mexico will continue to retain their important places on the public policy agenda of the United States.

References

Bean, Frank D. 1998. *Migration between Mexico and the United States: Binational Study, Thematic Chapters, Research Reports and Background Materials, Vols. 1, 2, & 3*. Mexico City and Washington, D.C.: Mexican Ministry of Foreign Affairs and U.S. Commission on Immigration Reform.

Bean, Frank D., Roland Chanove, Robert G. Cushing, Rodolfo de la Garza, Gary Freeman, Charles W. Haynes, and David Spener. 1994. *Illegal Mexican Migration and the United States/Mexico Border: The Effects of Operation Hold-the-Line on El Paso and Juárez.* Washington, D.C.: U.S. Commission on Immigration Reform.

Bean, Frank D., Rodolfo Corona, Rodolfo Tuiran, and Karen. Woodrow-Lafield. 1998. The Quantification of Migration between Mexico and the United States. In *Migration between Mexico and the United States: Binational Study, Thematic Chapters, Vol 1.* Mexico City and Washington, DC: Mexican Ministry of Foreign Affairs and U.S. Commission on Immigration Reform.

Bean, Frank D., Rodolfo Corona, Rodolfo Tuiran, Karen A. Woodrow-Lafield, and Jennifer Van Hook. 2001. Circular, Invisible, and Ambiguous Migrants: Components of Difference in Estimates of the Number of Unauthorized Mexican Migrants in the United States *Demography* 38: 411–22.

Bean, Frank D., and Robert G. Cushing. 1995. The Relationship between the Mexican Economic Crisis and Illegal Migration to the United States. *Trade Insights* (Center for the Study of Western Hemispheric Trade, University of Texas) 5 (August): 1–4.

Bean, Frank D., Barry Edmonston, and Jeffrey Passel. 1990. *Undocumented Migration to the United States: IRCA and the Experience of the 1980s.* Washington, D.C.: Urban Institute Press.

Bean, Frank D., Thomas Espenshade, Michael White, and Robert J. Dymowski. 1990. Post-IRCA Changes in the Volume and Composition of Undocumented Migration to the United Sates: An Assessment Based on Apprehensions Data. In *Undocumented Migration to the United States: IRCA and the Experience of the 1980s,* ed. Frank D. Bean, Barry Edmonston, and Jeffrey Passel. Washington, D.C.: Urban Institute Press.

Bean, Frank D., Rodolfo O. de la Garza, Bryan R. Roberts, and Sidney Weintraub, eds. 1997. *At the Crossroads: Mexico and U.S. Immigration Policy.* Lanham, Md.: Rowman and Littlefield.

Bean, Frank D., Augustín Escobar Latapí, and Sidney Weintraub. 1999. *La dinámica de la emigración mexicana.* Mexico City: CIESAS and Porrua.

Bean, Frank D., Elaine Sorensen, Leighton Ku, and Wendy Zimmerman. 1992. *Immigrant Categories and the U.S. Job Market: Do They Make a Difference?* Washington, D.C.: Urban Institute Press.

Bean, Frank D., and Gillian Stevens. 2003. *American's Newcomers: Immigrant Incorporation and the Dynamics of Diversity*. New York: Russell Sage Foundation.

Bean, Frank D., Jennifer Van Hook, and Karen Woodrow-Lafield. 2001. *Estimates of Numbers of Unauthorized Migrants Residing in the United States: The Total, Mexican, and Non-Mexican Central American Unauthorized Populations in Mid-2001*. Pew Hispanic Center Study, Washington, D.C.: www.pew hispanic.org/site/docs/pdf/study_-_frank_bean.pdf.

Bean, Frank D., George Vernez, and Charles B. Keely. 1989. *Opening and Closing the Doors: Evaluating Immigration Reform and Control*. Washington, D.C: Urban Institute Press.

Bureau of Citizenship and Immigration Services. No date. *Statistical Yearbook, 2001*. Washington, D.C.; www.immigration.gov/graphics/aboutus/statistics/ENF2001list.htm.

Calavita, Kitty. 1992. *Inside the State*. New York: Routledge.

Cardoso, Lawrence A. 1980. *Mexican Emigration to the United States: 1897–1931*. Tucson: University of Arizona Press.

Castañeda, Jorge G. 1995. *The Mexican Shock: Its Meaning for the U.S.* New York: New Press.

———. 2003. The Forgotten Relationship. *Foreign Affairs* 82, no. 3: 67–81.

Chavez, Leo. 1988. Settlers and Sojourners: The Case of Mexicans in the United States. *Human Organization* 47, no. 2: 95–107.

CONAPO (Consejo Nacional de Poblacion). 1999. *La Situacion Demografica de Mexico*. Mexico City: CONAPO.

Díaz Briquets, Sergio, and Sidney Weintraub, eds. 1991. *Determinants of Emigration from Mexico, Central America, and the Caribbean*. Boulder, Colo.: Westview Press.

Dillon, Sam. 1997. U.S.–Mexico Study Sees Exaggeration of Migration Data. *New York Times*, August 31, 1.

Espenshade, Thomas J. 1995a. Unauthorized Immigration to the United States. *Annual Review of Sociology* 21:195–216.

———. 1995b. Using INS Border Apprehension Data to Measure the Flow of Undocumented Migrants Crossing the U.S.–Mexico Frontier. *International Migration Review* 29, no. 2: 545–65.

Espenshade Thomas J., Jessica L. Baraka, and Gregory A. Huber. 1997. Implications of the 1996 Welfare and Immigration Reform Acts for U.S. Immigration. *Population and Development Review* 23, no. 4: 769–801.

Espenshade, Thomas J., and M. Belanger. 1998. Immigration and Public Opinion. In *Crossings: Mexican Immigration in Interdisciplinary Perspectives*, ed. Marcelo M. Suarez-Orozco. Cambridge, Mass.: Harvard University Press.

Freeman, Gary P., and Frank D. Bean. 1997. Mexico and U.S. Worldwide Immigration Policy. In *At the Crossroads: Mexico and U.S. Immigration Policy*, ed. Frank D. Bean, Rodolfo O. de la Garza, Bryan R. Roberts, and Sidney Weintraub. Lanham, Md.: Rowman and Littlefield.

Fuentes, Carlos. 1996. *A New Time for Mexico*. New York: Farrar, Straus, and Giroux.

Gonzales-Baker, Susan, Frank D. Bean, Augustin Escobar, and Sidney Weintraub. 1998. International Migration to the United States: The Growing Importance of Mexican Migration In *Crossings: Mexican Immigration in Interdisciplinary Perspectives*, ed. M. Suarez-Orozco. Cambridge, Mass.: Harvard University Press.

Iglesias, Enrique V., ed. 1993. *El legado de Raúl Prebisch*. Washington, D.C.: Inter-American Development Bank.

Jasso, Guillermina, and Mark Rosenzweig. 1990. *The New Chosen People: Immigrants to the United States*. New York: Russell Sage Foundation.

Kurthen, Hermann, Jürgen Fijalkowski, and Gert G. Wagner, eds. *Immigration, Citizenship, and the Welfare State in Germany and the United States: Immigrant Incorporation*. Greenwich, Conn.: JAI Press.

Laslett, John H. M. 1996. Historical Perspectives: Immigration and the Rise of a Distinctive Urban Region, 1900–1970. In *Ethnic Los Angeles*, ed. Roger Waldinger and Mehdi Bozorgmehr. New York: Russell Sage Foundation.

Lofstrom, Magnus, and Frank D. Bean. 2002. Assessing Immigrant Policy Options: Labor Market Conditions and Post-Reform Declines in Immigrants' Receipt of Welfare, *Demography* 39: 617–37.

Lustig, Nora 1992. *Mexico: The Remaking of an Economy*. Washington, D.C.: Brookings Institution Press.

Marcelli, Enrico A., and Wayne A. Cornelius. 2001. The Changing Profile of Mexican Migrants to the United States: New Evidence from California and Mexico. *Latin American Research Review* 36, no. 3: 105–31.

Martin, Philip. 1997. Do Mexican Agricultural Policies Stimulate Emigration? In *At the Crossroads: Mexico and U.S. Immigration Policy*, ed. Frank D. Bean, Rodolfo O. de la Garza, Bryan R. Roberts, and Sidney Weintraub. Lanham, Md.: Rowman and Littlefield.

Massey, Douglas S., Jorge Durand, and Nolan J. Malone. 2002. *Beyond Smoke and Mirrors: Mexican Immigration in an Era of Economic Integration*. New York: Russell Sage Foundation.

Mexican Ministry on Foreign Affairs and U.S. Commission on Immigration Reform. 1997. *A Report of the Binational Study on Migration*. Mexico City and Washington, D.C.: Mexican Ministry on Foreign Affairs and U.S. Commission on Immigration Reform.

Oppenheimer, Andres. 1995. *Bordering on Chaos: Guerillas, Stockbrokers, Politicians, and Mexico's Road to Prosperity.* Boston: Little, Brown.

Passel, Jeffrey S. 1987. Change in the Undocumented Alien Population in the United States, 1979–1983. *International Migration Review* 21, no. 4: 1304–34.

———. 1999. The Number of Undocumented Immigrants in the United States: A Review and New Estimates. In *Illegal Immigration in America: A Reference Handbook*, ed. D. W. Haines and K. E. Rosenblum. Westport, Conn.: Greenwood Press.

Porter, Eduardo. 2003. Immigrants' Population Gains Maintain Speedy 1990s Pace. *Wall Street Journal*, March 10, B2.

Portes, Alejandro, and Robert L. Bach. 1985. *Latin Journey: Cuban and Mexican Immigrants in the United States.* Berkeley: University of California Press.

Reyes, Belinda L., Hans P. Johnson, and Richard Van Swearingen. 2002. *Holding the Line? The Effect of Recent Border Build-up on Unauthorized Immigration.* San Francisco: Public Policy Institute of California; www.ppic.org/main/publication.asp?i=158.

Select Commission on Immigration and Refugee Policy. 1981. *U.S. Immigration Policy and the National Interest.* Washington, D.C.: U.S. Government Printing Office.

Smith, James P., and Barry Edmonston. 1997. *The New Americans: Economic, Demographic, and Fiscal Effects of Immigration.* Washington, D.C.: National Academy Press.

Smith, Peter H. 1997. NAFTA and Mexican Migration. In *At the Crossroads: Mexico and U.S. Immigration Policy*, ed. Frank D. Bean, Rodolfo O. de la Garza, Bryan R. Roberts, and Sidney Weintraub. Lanham, Md.: Rowman and Littlefield.

U.S. Commission on Immigration Reform. 1994. *US. Immigration Policy: Restoring Credibility.* Washington, D.C.: U.S. Commission on Immigration Reform.

U.S. Department of Justice. 1992. *Immigration Reform and Control Act: Report on the Legalized Alien Population.* Washington, D.C.: U.S. Government Printing Office.

U.S. Immigration and Naturalization Service. 1995. *Statistical Yearbook of the U.S. Immigration and Naturalization Service, 1994.* Washington, D.C.: U.S. Government Printing Office.

———. 1999. *Statistical Yearbook of the U.S. Immigration and Naturalization Service, 1998.* Washington, D.C.: U.S. Government Printing Office.

———. 2000. *Statistical Yearbook of the Immigration and Naturalization Service, 1999.* Washington, DC: U.S. Government Printing Office.

———. 2003. *Statistical Yearbook of the U.S. Immigration and Naturalization Service, 2002.* Washington, D.C.: U.S. Government Printing Office.

U.S.–Mexico Migration Panel. 2001. *Mexico-U.S. Migration: A Shared Respinsibility.* Washington, D.C., and Mexico City: Carnegie Endowment for International Peace and Instituto Tecnologico Autonomo de Mexico.

Van Hook, Jennifer, and Frank D. Bean. 1998a. Estimating Unauthorized Mexican Migration to the United States: Issues and Results. In *Migration Between Mexico and the United States, Binational Study, Vol. 2.* Mexico City and Washington, D.C.: Mexican Ministry of Foreign Affairs and U.S. Commission on Immigration Reform.

————. 1998b. Welfare Reform and Supplemental Security Income Receipt among Immigrants in the United States. In *Immigration, Citizenship, and the Welfare State in Germany and the United States: Immigrant Incorporation,* ed. Hermann Kurthen, Jürgen Fijalkowski, and Gert G. Wagner. Greenwich, Conn.: JAI Press.

Weintraub, Sidney. 1990. *A Marriage of Convenience: Relations Between Mexico and the United States.* New York: Oxford University Press.

————. 1997. U.S. Foreign Policy and Mexican Immigration. In *At the Crossroads: Mexico and U.S. Immigration Policy,* ed. Frank D. Bean, Rodolfo O. de la Garza, Bryan R. Roberts, and Sidney Weintraub. Lanham, Md.: Rowman and Littlefield.

Woodrow, Karen A., and Jeffrey S. Passel. 1990. Post-IRCA Undocumented Immigration to the United States: An Assessment Based on the June 1988 CPS. In *Undocumented Migration to the United States: IRCA and the Experience of the 1980s,* ed. Frank D. Bean, Barry Edmonston, and Jeffrey Passel. Washington, D.C.: Urban Institute Press.

CHAPTER ELEVEN

NAFTA AND MEXICAN HIGHER EDUCATION

Carlos Ornelas

Although education was not a direct matter of negotiations for the North American Free Trade Agreement (NAFTA), parallel talks began among high-level public servants, entrepreneurs' representatives, and top administrators of higher education institutions of Canada, Mexico, and the United States. The aim was to step up academic exchanges, provide new research orientations, and devise human resource development strategies.[1] Because of the recognition of huge "asymmetries," the participants expected that some agreements would have consequences on evaluation and accreditation practices, especially in Mexico. This takes place in a context of reform embracing the whole educational system.

This chapter argues that the major implications of NAFTA in Mexican higher education were to accelerate trends already in motion and to contribute to legitimizing the politics of modernization fixed authoritatively by Carlos Salinas de Gortari's administration. Ten years after NAFTA, the trilateral discussions have lost momentum but they have served to improve accreditation mechanisms in Mexico and have led to programs for regional academic mobility and collaborative research projects.

BACKGROUND: EMBARKING ON AN OVERHAUL

The Salinas government began in the midst of a legitimacy crisis due to the low credibility of the 1988 election results. Salinas was categorized as a neoliberal politician who aimed to align Mexico with globalization trends and follow the World Bank's and International Monetary Fund's policies. Neoliberalism was the new ogre of the left and nationalist forces. Salinas did not refute those allegations. Quite the contrary, he later took actions to support them.[2]

First, in the political domain, Salinas—in a kind of blitzkrieg tactic —jailed the "moral leader" of the oil industry workers just 40 days after his inauguration. This was a clear message to all labor bosses that it was time to modernize the corporatist pact between the workers and the state; Salinas wished to reduce the degree of autonomy of the labor union leaders. The launching of the Solidarity program, in addition to being a less bureaucratic path for allocating resources for social projects, was also a means to tame the Institutional Revolutionary Party's (Partido Revolucionario Institucional, PRI) traditional sectors and make them work more closely with the government and support the new policies, even against their will. In the midterm elections of 1991, the PRI recovered control of the Chamber of Deputies and Salinas was thus able to make more drastic changes in legislation.

Second, in economic terms, the aim was to fortify the process of "reducing the state" initiated by the administration of Miguel de la Madrid. In 1986, Mexico joined the General Agreement on Tariffs and Trade and started the privatization of government enterprises. Salinas pressed harder for a more open and market-oriented economy; he reprivatized the banks, sold the state-owned telephone company to private investors, and began to lobby for constitutional revisions to change land tenure, reform the *ejidos*, and allow more private investment in rural areas. The economic reforms also involved more effective tax collection—through centralization—renegotiating the external debt, and joining the Organization for Economic Cooperation and Development (OECD). NAFTA negotiations represented the major initiative in economic and social policies. The United States was no longer the menace to Mexican sovereignty but instead a potential partner in trade—a benevolent partner.

The politics and the rhetoric of the Mexican Revolution ended. It seemed that Mexico had experienced a change of regime without removing the dominant party. Somebody said that it was a perestroika without glasnost. Yet as many polls showed, neoliberal policies and especially NAFTA had heavy popular support. The modernization discourse and government practices supplied legitimacy to Salinas's policies. "Modernization" was the key word in undertaking any policy project. This was also the case in education.

THE MODERNIZATION OF EDUCATION

Salinas was familiar with the human capital theory, and he contended that investments in health and education yield high returns. He argued that without a mass of highly educated and productive citizens, economic reforms will fail. Despite the fact that he praised both teachers and the history of Mexican education, the president expressed strong criticism of the educational system. This was because of its low quality, irrelevant educational content, high inequality, and inefficient administration. Consequently, the modernization of the education program should address those issues in a systematic way (Salinas de Gortari 1989).

Salinas appointed Manuel Bartlett as secretary of public education. Bartlett had been secretary of government (*gobernación*) in the de la Madrid administration, responsible for the organization of the 1988 elections, and he had been accused by the opposition of manufacturing the electoral fraud. Nevertheless, he was also a professional public servant, able to deal with conflict, and a politician who could deliver. The Secretariat of Public Education (SEP) was in turmoil because the government—during the crisis of the 1980s—had reduced funds to public education.

In order to put together *The Educational Modernization Program: 1989–1994* (Federal Executive Power 1990), Bartlett organized a broad consultation, although the goals and projects had Salinas's stamp. The main objective was to elevate the quality of education, to make its content relevant to the needs of people and society and appropriate for the future of Mexico. The program also included a clear goal: to make education more egalitarian and to reach "those most in need." The first target was to decentralize the system to make its management more effective (Federal Executive Power 1990).

THE QUALITY AND FAIRNESS OF EDUCATION REFORM

Even before beginning to speak about NAFTA, the Salinas government launched an education reform program whose main elements persisted during the six-year term of Ernesto Zedillo and reached greater depth in the administration of Vicente Fox. Remarkable advances have been witnessed in the efficiency of basic education, because there are more schooling possibilities for poor groups in the society, although there is no tangible proof that the quality of education is any better.

A more open spirit in educational policy was already observed that subsequently was more visible during the negotiations on behalf of higher education, when the NAFTA spirit was invoked. Although decentralization of basic education had been announced since 1982, the government could not advance toward its complete accomplishment. Economic reforms and their international opening were undertaken with great vigor. Although basic educational reforms preceded many recommendations of UNESCO and the World Bank, they were generally consistent with them. As with the *Jomtien* document, the Mexican government gave priority to questions that related to fairness and quality.[3] For the first time, the Mexican government accepted the advice and took loans from the World Bank for basic education in order to carry out compensatory programs for poor people. This was severely criticized by left-wing academics (cf. Noriega 2000).

Bartlett dealt with grave conflicts within the powerful National Education Workers Union (SNTE), the most powerful such union in Latin America. In March and April 1989, large demonstrations of teachers who were fighting for "trade union democracy and higher salaries" agreed with the government in wanting to change union leadership. That same month, the clique controlling the SNTE was removed, and Salinas appointed Elba Esther Gordillo as the new leader. This opened the way to formulate new contracts.

In January 1992, Salinas appointed Ernesto Zedillo as the new secretary of public education. Zedillo was ready to make concessions to the SNTE that Bartlett opposed. In May 1992, the National Agreement to Modernize Basic Education (the National Agreement) was signed, under which basic and normal education was decentralized. Amendments to article 3 of the Constitution were introduced, and the General Education Law was enacted to legitimize the reforms.[4]

The secretary of public education, the governors of the 31 states, and the leader of the SNTE signed the National Agreement; President Salinas also signed as an honorary witness. The transfer was an impressive affair. In just a few days, the federal government stepped largely aside and gave the states administrative control of the education of more than 14 million preschoolers and secondary and normal students. Labor relations with more than 700,000 teachers, control over more than 100,000 school buildings, and 22 million pesos worth of furnishings and other assets—as well as a greater degree of autonomy (although not as many as one might have expected)—were given to the states to plan the growth and design strategies to provide the necessary educational services (Mancera and Vega 2000, vol. 1, 54). From what it is known from the literature, no other country has experienced a transfer of this magnitude in such a short time. An expert on many decentralization projects around the world called the transfer a "Blitzkrieg" (Hanson 2000, 406). However, the decentralization was more symbolic than real; it became known as *educational federalization*, although decision-making powers continued to be in the hands of the central government. States are merely administrators.[5]

One of the aims of the National Agreement and the program was to improve national results. However, one can judge the reality of quality improvement because the national government keeps secret the standardized tests in primary education, even in the government of Vicente Fox. On the basis of international comparisons, Mexico occupies a rather poor place in mathematics, sciences, and languages.[6] Perhaps national tests to more up to secondary education (10th–12th, high school grades), are a measure of overall basic education (kindergarten–9th grade). This test, known as Exani-I, is not compulsory, although its application is increasing; it is designed and organized by the National Center for the Evaluation of Higher Education (Ceneval). In 1994, it was used for slightly more than 360 thousand students in the metropolitan area of Mexico City; in 2001 it was compulsory for more than four million students, equally divided between boys and girls, throughout the whole country. Table 11.1 shows the results of the examinations, as well as those of the Exani-II (similar to the Scholastic Aptitude Test of the United States) for slightly more than 1.3 million students in 2001.

The main fact that stands out in these results is that there is a big division between male and female students that persists over the years. The second observation is that although certain progress is evident in grades kindergarten through nine, the percentage of correct answers is very low; students do not respond to half of what it is assumed they should know from the curriculum.[7] The results, however, are consistent with international tests. The measurements of students wishing to enter institutions of higher learning are even poorer.

Public and private institutions have their own admission rules, although they depend more on the Exani to select their students. Each institution establishes a low limit for who will be admitted, although I suspect that prestigious private universities demand higher marks.

Table 11.1. Grade Point Average (Scale 0–100)

Exani-I: After completion of grades K–9

	1994	1995	1996	1997	1998	1999	2000	2001
Male	40.7	43.8	44.0	49.0	50.0	50.0	49.2	48.7
Female	38.8	41.7	42.7	47.2	47.8	47.8	47.3	46.5

Exani-II: After completion of grades 10–12

	1994	1995	1996	1997	1998	1999	2000	2001
Male	42.5	38.0	36.8	38.5	37.2	37.3	36.8	38.3
Female	39.2	34.3	33.2	36.0	34.7	35.2	35.3	36.5

Source: Author's use of data in tables from Centro Nacional de Evaluación para la Educación Superior (2002).

Note: Exani-I and Exani-II are aptitutde tests.

Large federal universities, such as the Autonomous National University of Mexico (UNAM), and the Autonomous Metropolitan University (UAM), do not use such tests. UNAM practices automatic passing; that is, those having successfully passed their high school exams can enter the university directly, which is approximately 70 percent of those graduating each year.

The conclusion is that in spite of the impetus from NAFTA, high school is of relatively lower quality, its graduates are not well prepared, institutions of higher education do not have demanding entry requirements, and automatic passing it is a populist throwback that persists today in at least 15 of the largest universities. Mexico has a long way to go to reach standards of a quality similar to those of its commercial partners.

The educational modernization policy has had more success in searching for fairness and in reducing the educational backlog. Another aim of the reform was to reduce the gap between rich and poor states. Table 11.2 shows that these asymmetries in primary education are being gradually reduced while indicators of the efficiency of primary education are improving.

Table 11.2. Efficiency Indicators, Selected Mexican States and Years

Nation or State	Year	Repetition rate	Dropout rate	Terminal efficiency[a]	Enrollments in junior high[b]
National	1982	11.1	6.9	61.7	86.8
	1992	9.8	4.1	71.6	82.9
	2002	5.6	1.7	87.7	93.4
Nuevo León	1982	6.2	2.9	77.6	95.5
	1992	5.1	3.5	85.1	92.1
	2002	2.5	0.7	94.3	98.5
Oaxaca	1982	17.7	8.8	49.9	71.0
	1992	17.1	5.9	58.4	70.9
	2002	9.8	2.2	82.9	91.9

Source: Secretaría de Educación Pública (2002, anexo estadístico).

[a] Percentage of students who finish the course work in six years.
[b] Percentage of students who finished primary education and enroll in junior high school (seventh to ninth grades).

In Nuevo León, for example, the richest state, the student repetition index went down from 5.1 percent in 1992 (the last year before decentralization) to 2.5 percent in 2002, an improvement of 2.6 percentage points; only Mexico City has better indicators. In Oaxaca, the reduction was from 17.1 to 9.8 percent, an improvement of 7.3 points. Retention of students has increased throughout the system, as can be seen in table 11.2's column showing dropouts; Oaxaca is the state where this progress is most noticeable. The result is that final efficiency (for many the strongest fairness indicator) increased more rapidly in poor states, in part because the starting point was lower. Furthermore, registration in secondary institutions increased quite rapidly because of constitutional changes that made secondary education compulsory, but also because of the depreciation of the Primary Certificate and rising social aspirations. This index grew by 6.4 percent nationally, by 3.0 percent in

Figure 11.1. Gap in Terminal Educational Efficiency, Selected States of Mexico

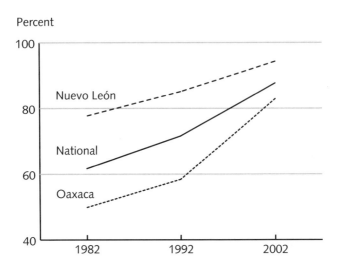

Nuevo León, and by more than 20 percent in Oaxaca. Figures 11.1 and 11.2 illustrate gap reductions between poorer and richer states.

A more reasonable explanation to account for these increases has to do with compensatory programs. Not only because of internal pressures, and pressure from international agencies, chapter 3 of the General Law of Education is devoted to promoting fairness and equality in opportunities for economically depressed social groups. The government established the National Council for Educational Promotion (Consejo Nacional de Fomento Educativo, or CONAFE) in 1972, but its mission, was then marginal: It offered compensatory programs and administered educational programs in remote areas, where formal schooling was scarce or did not exist. CONAFE is today a vigorous institution fulfilling a crucial role in reducing the gap that exists between rich northern states and poor states in the south. For example, its activity in Nuevo León is insignificant, whereas in Oaxaca in 1988 it offered school services to more than 45,000 Indian children in more than 20 languages (CONAFE 1999).

In 1992, SEP, with the support of the World Bank, introduced more ambitious compensatory programs in economically deprived areas. The most important of these was the Program to Reduce the Educa-

Figure 11.2. Enrollments in Junior High School, Selected States of Mexico

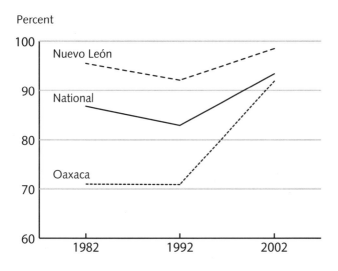

Percent

tional Backlog (PARE, by its Spanish initials). This program began in the four poorest states—Chiapas, Oaxaca, Guerrero, and Hidalgo—and subsequently was expanded to 10 other states. In 2003, although under different names, PARE offered services in 24 states. This program provides incentives to teachers to work in remote and poor areas, as well in indigenous school areas. It also provides funds to build schoolrooms and other installations; it prints books and other material in Indian languages and provides funds and scholarships to underprivileged children to attend junior high school far from their own communities. And what is perhaps most important—through the Solidarity Program; later, Programa de Educación, Salud y Alimentación (PROGRESA); and today Contigo (the government and the population working together)—the federal government is supplying money for scholarships and foodstuffs to poor children who live in depressed areas. This is an important incentive for families to send their children to school instead of putting them to work. PARE is the most important component of these programs.

Mexico has recorded important advances in educational fairness. Nevertheless, these compensatory programs have not been sufficient to end to the gap between rich and poor states, not even in 25 or 30 years. And the programs have done even less to eliminate Mexico's asymmetries with its associates in NAFTA. The trinational cooperation among the three countries in elementary and secondary education may be impossible. This, however, is not the case for higher learning. There, international influence is considerable, even though the government has promoted the institutional change required in universities only since 1989.

GOODBYE TO TRADITIONAL UNIVERSITY AUTONOMY

Chapter 7 of the Modernization of Education Program was devoted to higher education. It followed almost literally the strategies established in 1985 by the semiautonomous National Association of Universities (ANUIES). The emphasis of this chapter was on how to assure reaching the goals of quality, relevance, equity, and efficient management in public institutions, especially in the autonomous universities. Words seldom used in autonomous universities emerged as watchwords for educational development: cooperation, linkages to industry and services, research oriented to economic development, new sources for financing, and above all evaluation and accreditation. Public universities, and all public institutions, were to be held accountable. University autonomy, said Secretary Bartlett, stands neither for independence from the state nor alienation from society.[8]

Although the aim in basic education was to decentralize management, in higher education the target was to establish uniform criteria and establish more government control over a loose set of public universities. Evaluation was the key word. New institutions to carry out evaluation of higher education emerged early in the administration, and their development was sped up when NAFTA was announced as a possibility.

This evaluation of education procedures in Mexico in the 1990s may seem strange to foreign observers. However, Mexican autonomous universities and institutions of higher education run by the government were not accountable to anyone. They were establishments centered in themselves, without linkages, bonds, or even dialogue with industry or society overall. University autonomy was a plus during the years of strong authoritarianism; those institutions were sanctuaries for dissent and centers for resistance to the state's cultural dominance. Nevertheless, autonomy also isolated the universities and permitted the government to be careless about their development.

INTERNAL POLITICS, EXTERNAL INFLUENCES

The Salinas administration's strategy to deal with the issue was a leap toward the future rather than reliance on careful evolution. Even before NAFTA, the secretary of public education brought to the attention of rectors of universities the need to have quality equal to international standards, to have universities open to the scrutiny of society, and to strengthen collaboration with other countries. In meetings with ANUIES, the secretary and the rectors engaged in long discussions about university autonomy and the limits of government intervention. The rectors resisted the administration's proposals and preferred unilateral evaluation procedures, and a policy based on compromises ensued. This policy was for the government to help the universities set up peer review committees to carry out the evaluation of programs and institutions, and for SEP to ask international teams to evaluate Mexican higher education.[9]

A frantic pace of evaluation of Mexican higher education followed. Everything and everyone was evaluated in few years—institutions, programs, professors, and students. SEP created a special Fund to Modernize Higher Education (FOMES). Public universities competed for resources of this fund through "modernization" projects to improve management and later for funding large research projects. ANUIES and the government established the National Commission for the Evaluation of Higher Education, the Interinstitutional Committees for the Evaluation of Higher Education or peer reviews committees, and in 1994 Ceneval.

The evaluation of the system was done in 1990 by a team from the International Council for Educational Development, which was headed by the renowned educator Philip H. Coombs. His report, in addition to legitimating the government initiatives, provided momentum for international cooperation (Coombs 1991).

Some suggestions of that report became routine in the following years: accreditation under international standards; student mobility and exchanges; faculty development; institutional competition; and collaboration with productive sectors.

These activities were modified a few years later after recommendations to the Mexican authorities by the OECD (1997). Most important, because the members of the Coombs team were welcomed at every institution they visited, resistance to the changes was largely limited to left-wing militants and university labor unions.

The U.S. and Mexican governments established the Bi-National Commission for Educational and Cultural Exchange in 1990. Bartlett championed that initiative south of the border. In Mexico, the traditional grant programs are called Fulbright–Garcia Robles, to symbolize the bonds between the two nations. Together with SEP and the Secretariat for External Relations, this commission was key in launching the Mexican Association for International Education, an institution founded by rectors and administrators of international exchange programs.[10]

When Bartlett was replaced by Ernesto Zedillo as secretary of public education, it was time to explore trilateral cooperation. In the official view, Mexican higher education needed a cathartic move, and NAFTA provided the umbrella.

WINGSPREAD: THE GROUNDWORK

Under the spirit of NAFTA, but without clear-cut linkages to it, the U.S. government invited Mexican and Canadian counterparts to begin discussions to explore the benefits of close North American collaboration in higher education. Government representatives of the three countries met in Washington in February 1992, and then in March in Ottawa. They established a steering committee to organize a first encounter to discuss trilateral collaboration in higher education. The meeting was held in Racine, Wisconsin, from September 12 to 15, 1992, at the Wingspread Conference Center.

Under the institutional leadership of the U.S. Information Agency (USIA) for the U.S. government, the Secretariat of Public Education for Mexico, and the Ministry of External Affairs and International Trade for the Canadian central government, a group of public servants, rectors and presidents of universities, and business and foundation representatives engaged in discussions to outline an *Agenda for North American Higher Education Cooperation*. The conference concluded with basic agreements and set up strategic initiatives. A report on the conference stated: "While the impending NAFTA was a clear and positive reference point for much of their discussion, educational leaders and official representatives all underscored the necessity and urgency to broaden dialogue to a much wider context across-the-board for continental cooperation and collaboration" (Johnson Foundation 1993, 4).

The agreements stressed the symbolic shifts occurring in the three countries, especially in Mexico, where a nationalist ideology had an anti–United States history. The rhetoric was constructed to avoid bitter debates among the negotiators and confrontations with other political forces within their respective countries. Phrases like "internationalization of higher education is key to the quality of higher education and research" were used. Other phrases included these: "Better understanding and acceptance of our distinctive realities are essential components of stronger partnership." "Enhanced trilateral collaboration in higher education built upon existing relationships and benefits for the three countries." Collaboration also "provides additional impetus to greater cooperation within our respective countries and supports bilateral relations."

The essential initiatives were of practical orientation aiming at constructing institutional means to collaborate. A task force was established to draft the agenda and propose new and ample meetings following what became known as the Wingspread Statement. This group focused on means to reinforce national efforts in support of innovation and human resource development. The task force identified five issues of common interest:

1. mobility of students and faculty,
2. networking and the impact of information management technologies on human resource development,
3. strategic partnerships,
4. faculty and institutional development, and
5. leveraging of resources.

The asymmetries among the three countries were part of the discussions but not recognized in the statement. The imbalances were also evident in the caliber of the representatives of each country. Those who attended from Mexico were the rectors of the most important public and private universities, the under secretary for higher education, and the head of a big corporation, whereas the attendees from the United States and Canada were officers of medium-sized colleges and universities, foundation representatives, and public servants at the level of director general (assistant secretary).

The meeting at Racine was not open to observers or the press. It was the first gathering, and no one was sure whether agreements would be reached. The following assemblies were also designed to propagate the partnerships to come. The rector of the University of Guadalajara organized the First Conference of University Presidents of North America to give visibility to the discussions and attain support from other orga-nizations, as well as to forestall criticism from the left-wing press and academics.[11]

The task force and a few advisers met in Ixtapa and Quebec to prepare the Vancouver Symposium, which was held in September 1993. In order to provide more substance to the deliberations, papers were commis-sioned to determine the numbers and kinds of United States–Canada–Mexico academic linkages. The first drafts of those inventories provided surprises, particularly in Mexico. Even before protection by NAFTA's umbrella existed, 34 institutions of higher education had more than 200 collaborative projects with U.S. and Canadian institutions. The major ones involved faculty and student exchanges, but there were also collab-orative research projects. Some of these were well funded and had mea-surable results.[12]

VANCOUVER: THE LEAP FORWARD

The meeting at Vancouver had more senior representation and stressed the asymmetries. Whereas for Mexico this was of transcendent impor-tance, for other delegates the higher education collaboration initiative was seen as an addendum to NAFTA. The leadership of Mexico's higher education structure, headed by secretary of public education Ernesto Zedillo, attended the conference. This symbolized the great impor-tance Mexico assigned to these gatherings. For some unexplained rea-son, the minister of defense of Canada, Thomas E. Siddon, opened the symposium.

Few people really believed that the "underlying aim" of these meet-ings was to begin a process of cultural integration of the peoples of North America, as proposed by Joseph Duffy, director of the USIA and head of the U.S. delegation. According to him, "Economic integration, without a deepening commitment to the education and cultural di-mensions of the relationship, poses unacceptable risks." He suggested that the three countries pay closer attention to a North America cul-tural identity. The importance of the Vancouver meeting was in the policies agreed to by the three groups (Inter-American Organization for Higher Education and the Open Learning Agency 1993, 7).

The concrete conclusions pointed toward expanding higher educa-tional research and training among the three countries to meet world-wide economic competition. Six conclusions were for immediate un-dertaking, and three were for the future. Although they overlap in minor aspects, they are worth summarizing because they had practical implications.

These were the recommendations for immediate action:

1. Establishment of a North American Distance Education and Research Network as a consortium to simplify access to information and to support education research and training among participating institutions.

2. Formation of an enterprise/education trilateral mechanism to examine issues relating to mobility, portability, and the certification of skills.

3. Establishment of programs to enable the faculty and administrators from all three countries to meet with colleagues to explore and develop trilateral higher education collaborative activities in priority areas of concern.

4. Establishment of an electronic information base in each of the three countries with coordinated sharing of information on initiatives and resources relevant to trilateral cooperation.

5. Strengthening and expanding North American studies programs to promote trilateral linkages in support of research and curriculum development.

6. Establishment of a program to support intensive trilateral exchange, research, and training for students.

These were the recommendations for longer-term implementation:

1. Establishment of a North American Cooperative Higher Education Council comprising representatives of the communities incorporated into higher education in the three countries.

2. Development and implementation of a consortium to broker access to recognized graduate distance education and to develop mechanisms for awarding degrees.

3. Continuing and enhancing support by research granting agencies, foundations, and other partners for trilateral collaborative research programs and research networks.

All these recommendations had significance in the three countries, but mostly in Mexico. Its system of higher education was underdeveloped both in terms of economic resources and preparation of its faculty. Mexicans stressed the asymmetries on matters of finance, but their partners had a broader view. They also emphasized practices and impediments to academic mobility and credit recognition. The agreements reached on higher education under the influence of the NAFTA conversations gave new impetus to the proposals for the modernization of education programs, and the suggestion of the Coombs team. This impulse went beyond Salinas's term.

BACK TO THE INTERNAL FRONT: OVERCOMING BARRIERS

NAFTA, together with the two parallel agreements on environment and labor introduced by Bill Clinton's administration, came into force on January 1, 1994. That year was one of tremendous social conflict in Mexico: the uprising of the Zapatista movement, a virulent electoral campaign, political assassinations, internal strife in the Salinas government, and, at the end of the year, a devaluation of the peso. The first year of the Zedillo administration was centered on economic negotiations to recover from the crisis and on preparing government plans for the rest of his *sexenio*.

Because Zedillo had been secretary of public education, the *Program for Educational Development: 1995–2000* had practically the same goals as the Salinas modernization program. The main objectives in higher education were to consolidate the institutions created, strengthen faculty development, and move forward from evaluation to accreditation. This process is still ongoing in the Fox government (see Federal Executive Power 2001, part 3, chap. 3).

For North American students and professionals, the absence of a regional system of cooperation in evaluating and recognizing educational preparation and professional ability constituted an obstacle to academic mobility. Neither Mexico nor Canada has voluntary accrediting bodies similar to those in the United States. Some private institutions of higher learning in Mexico, like the Monterrey Technological Institute and the University of the Americas, resolved the credit transfer problem with the U.S. universities by applying for their own accreditation with the Southern Association of Colleges and Schools. But because U.S. accreditation is not a process that can be exported easily to other countries, the Mexican government worked on other models based on the young institutions created at the outset of the 1990s.

Earlier, licensing was done bureaucratically within SEP. This was based on an act of faith in the credentials universities provided, not in the evaluation of the individual's competence. Therefore, the government gradually transferred the evaluation and recognition of pro-grams to semiofficial institutions like Ceneval, and to peer committees at the undergraduate level. The National Council for Science and Technology (Consejo Nacional de Ciencia y Tecnología, CONACYT) was charged with the evaluation of graduate programs (cf. Ornelas 1996).

In addition, the government worked to create a context favoring professional associations (under the control of Ceneval) for professional accreditations resembling the U.S. pattern. Moreover, these steps were taken while looking at trilateral relations generally, and at labor issues. Three segments were of particular concern to Mexico. First, there are differences between the three countries for licensing and professional enhancement. Second, there are administrative barriers to the recognition of diplomas and short-course studies issued by the other countries. Third, the differences between professional competencies and university degrees are still unresolved (Didou 2000).

Such a movement in Mexican higher education was resisted in several ways. Left-wing parties and academics criticized the evaluation and accreditation institutions; the Ceneval professional examinations were the major target of criticism. Some rectors fought because university autonomy was being terminated by the government initiatives. University labor unions argued that salary negotiations, the new schemes for professorial advancement (peer review), and productivity incentives for the faculty were all impositions of NAFTA or the World Bank.[13] At UNAM during the 10-month strike of 1999–2000, one demand of the radical students was that UNAM should break relations with Ceneval; the strikers won on that point. Nevertheless, government efforts continue. In 2002, for the first time in Mexican history, the public universities were audited by the Federal Congress, and the Supreme Court established that the universities must be accountable at all times.[14] In fact, university autonomy as conceived during the time of the Mexican Revolution is now history.

TRILATERAL COOPERATION

Although collaboration between Mexican universities has not advanced at a good pace, the evaluation and accreditation of institutions have contributed to lowering barriers to more healthy trilateral cooperation in North America. Not all the agreements of the Vancouver communiqué were implemented, and the objective of creating a North American higher education system is far from being accomplished.

Nevertheless, after 10 years of NAFTA, academic exchanges of faculty and students and also collaborative research programs have grown. Consortia of diverse sizes and nature now exist with regular funding mechanisms and follow-up meetings.

More than 10 years have passed from the North American Regional Academic Mobility Program, a three-year pilot project started in 1992, to the Consortium for North American Higher Education Collaboration (CONAHEC). The pilot project began with the participation of 15 universities, 5 in each country, and in only three fields of study: business, engineering, and the environment (IIE 1994). CONAHEC is made up of 18 institutions from Canada, 60 from Mexico, and 55 from the United States; in addition, major associations of colleges and universities of the three countries take part. They promote more than 20 study programs and have a collaborative research agenda.

The most visible and dynamic accomplishment is the Program for Student Mobility. This works as a sort of specific consortium and is managed by the Fund for the Improvement of Post Secondary Education of the U.S. Department of Education, the Human Development Fund of Canada, and SEP in Mexico. In capturing the spirit of NAFTA, this program is designed to improve the development of human resources for work in any of the three countries. It emphasizes the transfer of academic credits, mutual recognition of academic programs among participant institutions, and the development of joint or uniform curricula. It also works on foreign language training and on the study of the cultures of the three countries.

The program began in 1995. At its most recent meeting, held in Toluca, Mexico, in November 2002, it reported than more than 50 consortia, and more than 330 institutions from North America took part. Faculty exchanges are still weak, but participating institutions have high expectations for improvement. As far as Mexico is concerned, the most important relationship still is with the United States. Growth in the movement of Mexican students to American universities in 10 years has been almost 100 percent. From 6,450 students at the beginning of 1992, the number grew to 12,518 by the end of 2002 (IIE 2003, 8.).

It is almost impossible to give the number of binational or trilateral research projects funded by the three governments, foundations, participating institutions, and private firms. However, in the inner circles of the various consortia, everyone speaks of the considerable work-in-progress in many fields. UNAM transformed its Center for the Study of the United States into the Center for North American Studies. Other institutions—such as El Colegio de Mexico, Colegio de la Frontera Norte, and the University of Guadalajara—created centers to study North American issues and cultural development.[15] ANUIES is surveying Mexican universities to update the inventories of collaborative exchange and research projects.

CONCLUSION

As government officers point out, propensities to modernize higher education were already in place when NAFTA came into being. However, estimating what would have taken place without NAFTA's impulse is difficult. It is unlikely that the accreditation and accountability of public institutions would have been as vigorous as they are now. Although opposition to international influences still exists, and new fears of academic privatization are of concern to many, it appears that the path to the increasing integration of higher education is clearly laid out.[16]

The Mexican government chose to face the globalization challenges that the country faces in cooperating with its two powerful allies. The asymmetries among the three countries will long persist, development will remain unequal, and there are risks and dangers ahead given these realities. Yet it is better to walk in good company than to hit the road in isolation.

Notes

1. Only chapter 12 of NAFTA, pertaining to marketing services in the three countries, makes reference to professional exchanges. Articles 1201 through 1204 provide that citizens of the other two countries will receive national treatment. Article 1205 prohibits a residence requirement for a citizen of one of the other two countries in order to provide a professional service. Article 1210 suggests the creation of standard criteria for recognition of professional credentials. Cf. Secretaría de Economía, *Tratado de Libre Comercio de América del Norte*, www.economía.gob.mx.

2. I base this and following points on Cornelius and Craig (1991); and Roett (1995).

3. *Jomtien* set the pace for reaching the UNESCO objective of "education for all." See International Consultative Forum on Education for All (1991) for a comparison of the international agenda and the modernization program of Salinas. The main issues are practically the same.

4. This section is based on a book I am preparing, *El federalismo y la descentralización de la educación* (Federalism and decentralization of education; Ornelas 2004).

5. I wrote a broader explanation about this thesis and its political consequences. Cf. Ornelas (2000).

6. The government of Ernesto Zedillo did not permit the publication of the results of Mexico from the Third International Mathematics and Sciences Study (TIMSS) of 1993, measuring the progress in mathematics and sciences of students in basic and medium education (K-12). The newspaper *Reforma* (October 15, 2001) published the results, and this gave raise to a political scandal. Mexico took the 4 last places and 2 last but 1 among 42 countries participating. In language, Mexico was, next to last, ahead only of Brazil. Cf. OECD (2001).

7. The scale Ceneval uses—which is not published in its documents—runs from 700 to 1,300. I made the conversion to the 0–100 scale to measure percentages of correct answers.

8. Manuel Bartlett Díaz, "Speech Closing the International Seminary on Evaluation of Higher Education." Due to the fact that when the conference proceedings were printed he was no longer the secretary, his speech was not published.

9. There is a detailed analysis in Ornelas (1996).

10. This new association has its own journal, *Educación global.*

11. The meetings were open to the press and to every professor who wished to attend. Interestingly enough, even though the organizers expected some degree of opposition or public protests, nobody did so. The papers of that conference were published in Gacel, Adelman and Van Der Donckt (1993).

12. The Mexican inventory was in charge of ANUIES; cf. Marúm, Marroquin, and Didou (1993). The inventories in the United States and Canada include more than 80 institutions and partnerships with Mexican correspondents; cf. IIE (1993, appendix 5).

13. Cf. Aboites (1997); for him, the only aim of NAFTA is to promote privatization and market-driven higher education in Mexico.

14. See *Reforma*, "Limita la Corte Autonomía" (*sic*), first page note, September 5, 2002 .

15. Even the University of Guadalajara, the second-largest public university in Mexico, is planning to open a campus in Los Angeles; see *Reforma*, March 9, 2003, 12-A. I do not know of any evaluation regarding the quality of those programs.

16. The fears now proceed from the growing importance and powers of the World Trade Organization in promoting trade liberalization. Of particular interest to radical academics in relation to education is the General Agreement on Trade in Services. Cf. Robertson, Bonal, and Dale (2002). Mexican scholars have cited this paper in recent debates in conferences held in Mexico City. There are a few

newspaper notes in *Reforma* and in "Campus," a specialized supplement of *Milenio*, March–April 2003.

References

Aboites, Hugo. 1997. *Viento del norte: TLC y privatización de la educación superior en México*. Mexico City: Universidad Autónoma Metropolitana and Plaza y Valdés.

Ceneval (Centro Nacional de Evaluación para la Educación Superior). 2002. *La primera etapa: 1994–2001*. Mexico City: Ceneval.

CONAFE (Consejo Nacional de Fomento Educativo). 1999. *Programas compensatorios*. México City: CONAFE.

Coombs, Philip H., ed. 1991. *A Strategy to Improve the Quality of Mexican Higher Education*. Mexico City: Secretariat of Public Education and Fondo de Cultura Económica.

Cornelius, Wayne A., and Ann L. Craig. 1991. *The Mexican Political System in Transition*. San Diego: Center for U.S.–Mexican Studies at the University of California.

Didou, Sylvio. 2000. Macrorregionalización y políticas de educación superior: México Ante el TLCAN. *Revista de la educación superior* 115 (July–September). Available at www.anuies.mx.

Federal Executive Power. 1990. *The Educational Modernization Program: 1989–1994*. Mexico City: Secretariat of Public Education.

———. 2001. *Programa nacional de educación: 2001–2006*. Mexico City: Secretaría de Educación Pública.

Gacel, Jocelyne, Alan Adelman, and Pierre Van Der Donckt. 1993. *Educación superior e integración regional en América del Norte: Primera conferencia de rectores de América del Norte*. Guadalajara: Universidad de Guadalajara.

Hanson, Mark. 2000. Educational Decentralization around the Pacific Rim. *Journal of Educational Administration* 38, no. 5 (October): 406–11.

IIE (Institute of International Education). 1993. *North American Higher Education Cooperation: An Inventory of Canada–U.S.–Mexico Academic Linkages*. New York: IIE.

———. 1994. *North American RAMP: Regional Academic Mobility Program*. New York: IIE.

———. 2003. *Open Doors: 2002*. New York: IIE.

Inter-American Organization for Higher Education and the Open Learning Agency. 1993. *North American Higher Education Cooperation: Implementing the Agenda—Report on the International Symposium on Higher Education and*

Strategic Partnerships Vancouver. Mississauga, Ont.: Inter-American Organization for Higher Education and the Open Learning Agency.

International Consultative Forum on Education for All. 1991. *Final Report.* Paris: UNESCO.

Johnson Foundation. 1993. *North American Higher Education Cooperation: Identifying the Agenda.* Racine, Wis.: Johnson Foundation.

Mancera, Carlos, and Luis Vega. 2000. Oportunidades y retos del federalismo educativo: El camino recorrido 1992–2000. In *Memoria del quehacer educativo: 1995–2000,* ed. Secretaría de Educación Pública. Mexico City: Secretaría de Educación Pública.

Marúm, Elia, Ermilo Marroquín, and Sylvie Didou. 1993. Acuerdos y convenios entre instituciones mexicanas de educación superior y sus contrapartes en los Estados Unidos y Canadá. *Revista de la educación superior* 87 (July–September): 159–87.

Noriega, Margarita. 2000. *Las reformas educativas y su financiamiento en el contexto de la globalización: El caso de México, 1982–1994.* Mexico City: Universidad Pedagógica Nacional and Plaza y Valdés.

OECD (Organization for Economic Cooperation and Development). 1997. *Exámenes de las políticas de educación superior: México, educación superior.* Paris: OECD.

———. 2001. *Knowledge and Skills for Life: First Results from PISA 2000.* Paris: OECD.

Ornelas, Carlos. 1996. Evaluación y conflicto en las universidades públicas mexicanas. *Reforma y Utopía* 15 (summer): 5–34.

———. 2000. The Politics of the Educational Decentralization in Mexico. *Journal of Educational Administration* 38, no. 5 (October): 426–41.

———. 2004. *El federalismo y la descentralización de la educación* (Federalism and decentralization of education). Mexico City: Taurus, forthcoming.

Robertson, Susan L., Xavier Bonal, and Roger Dale. 2002. GATS and the Education Service Industry: The Politics of Scale and Global Reterritorialization. *Comparative Education Review* 46 (November): 472–96.

Roett, Riordan, ed. 1995. *The Challenge of Institutional Reform in Mexico.* Boulder, Colo.: Lynne Rienner.

Salinas de Gortari, Carlos. 1989. Discurso en el edificio sede de la SEP. *Boletín informativo de la Secretaría de Educación Pública,* January 16.

Secretaría de Educación Pública. 2002. *Segundo informe del labores.* Mexico City: Secretaría de Educación Pública.

CHAPTER TWELVE

POVERTY AND INEQUALITY

John Scott

On a relevant measure of strengthening the North American *Community*—economic convergence between and within countries—the evidence available so far for the first decade of the North American Free Trade Agreement (NAFTA) is not especially encouraging. Economic convergence between Mexico and the United States has been as elusive after NAFTA as before, and within Mexico the post-NAFTA period has been characterized by regional (north–south), sectoral (urban–rural) and even intrasectoral polarization, and increasing income inequality at the household level. Why has the accelerated convergence predicted by traditional growth and trade theory between the poorer and richer parties (countries, regions, sectors, households) within the North American community failed to materialize so far?

The short answer is that poorer regions and households in Mexico have entered NAFTA severely underequipped to reap the benefits of free trade in two principal areas: (1) human capital and (2) integration to international markets (physical access as well as capacity to adapt to new market conditions). The obstacle to equitable development in this period has thus not been the opening of the market but the (pre-NAFTA) distribution of the conditions necessary to participate in the productive opportunities offered by it. The good news is that these conditions can be overcome through fairly obvious policy instruments: (1) investing in the education of future workers in poorer households; (2) building communications and transport infrastructure to connect the poorer southern regions to the northern market; and (3) deregulating factor markets and providing the necessary transitional support programs to allow migration from traditional low-yield activities, notably corn and bean production, to more productive jobs within or outside agriculture. The bad news is that the first two are long-term instruments, which should have been in place well before NAFTA to allow a more equal access to its benefits within the trade agreement's first decade. Second, though some notable structural reforms and support programs were introduced with NAFTA to facilitate this transition for the poorest and most vulnerable sectors, the expected structural transformation of the Mexican agriculture sector has as yet failed to occur.

The rest of the chapter is structured as follows. The second section reviews the evidence on the evolution of poverty and inequality in Mexico before and after the initiation of NAFTA. The third section considers the principal underlying causes explaining these trends, focusing on limited growth and the concentration of productive assets. The fourth section considers the role of the state and political institutions in accounting for these trends, and the fifth and sixth sections review government failures in social policy and agricultural policy accounting for low and inequitable levels of human and physical capital, and thus for the limited capacity on the part of the poor to exploit the opportunities for growth opened up by NAFTA. The seventh section concludes with a brief note on the prospects for equitable development in Mexico beyond NAFTA's first decade.

A WEAKENING COMMUNITY?

To set in context the evolution of inequality and poverty in Mexico before and after the introduction of NAFTA, we must consider the evolution of the Mexican economy during this period and note two factors hampering any attempt to isolate the causality of NAFTA in these trends. First, (unilateral) trade liberalization in Mexico began when the country joined the General Agreement on Tariffs and Trade (GATT) in 1986, and it was well advanced by the time NAFTA came into force. Between 1985 and 1988, the proportion of national products covered by import permits was reduced from 92 to 23 percent and the average tariff dropped from 23.5 to 11 percent.[1] Second, any process of economic convergence in North America that might have been associated with this liberalization was interrupted by two big shocks to Mexico's economy during the past two decades—the 1983 debt crisis and the 1995 "tequila" crisis.

Having noted this, the impact of NAFTA on trade, foreign direct investment (FDI) flows, economic growth, and employment is quite

Figure 12.1 Real Gross Domestic Product per Capita in Relation to Leading Regional Economy

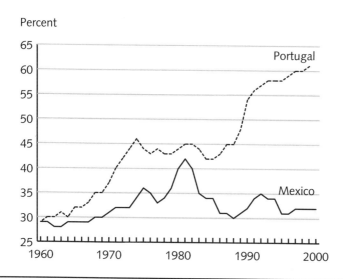

Source: Data from World Bank, Global Development Network Database. Leading economy for Mexico: United States; for Portugal: United Kingdom–Germany–France average.

evident (USTR 2002). Mexico's exports to the United States and Canada, already accounting for three-quarters of Mexican exports in 1993, increased by 225 percent (93 percent for the rest of the world) from 1993 to 2001 (to $139 billion), and average yearly FDI flows to Mexico jumped threefold from the period 1987–93 to 1994–2000 (to $11.7 billion). The growth in exports accounts for more than half of the increase in Mexico's gross domestic product (GDP) in the period 1993–2001, and more than half of the jobs created in the period 1994–2000, paying salaries almost 40 percent higher than in nonexport manufacturing.

Have these benefits been sufficient for convergence between Mexico and the United States, despite the 1995 crisis? Have they been distributed equally within Mexico, and, in particular, have they reached poor people? The evidence for the 1990s suggests a negative answer to the first question.[2] It is interesting to compare Mexico's experience with that of Portugal (figure 12.1), which became a member of the European Economic Community (EEC) precisely when Mexico entered the GATT, in 1986. In that year, the two countries also had almost exactly the same

GDP per capita in real (purchasing power parity) terms. Between 1960 and 1980, both had been converging toward their respective leading regional economies, having started from a similar distance from them, but in the last two decades their paths differ sharply. After entering the EEC, Portugal set into a rapid path of convergence, while newly liberalized Mexico stalled around a postcrisis level close to what had been achieved in the early 1970s.

On the second question, the evidence available so far suggests a similarly pessimistic answer. First, in terms of economic sectors, during the period 1993–99 manufacturing exports grew 190 percent while agricultural exports expanded only 60 percent. Within these sectors, the bulk of exports have concentrated in maquiladoras and large and foreign-owned firms in the case of manufacturing, and in high-value-added fruits and vegetable production in the case of agriculture (López-Córdova 2001).

Second, regional inequalities have deepened, even when controlling for differences in economic structure (Esquivel et al. 2002). The share of national GDP contributed by the three poorest states in Mexico (Chiapas, Guerrero, and Oaxaca), accounting for 10.6 percent of the population, was 5.33 percent in 1993, shrinking further by 7.3 percent by 1999, and their share in national manufacturing output (2.03 percent in 1993) dropped by 17.2 percent in the same period.

Third, consider income inequality and poverty at the household level. Given the extent of trade liberalization achieved prior to NAFTA, as noted above, the distributive effects associated with the opening of the Mexican economy should be expected to appear well before 1994. Bracketing out the 1995 crisis (1994–96), we observe a trend of increasing income inequality between 1984 and 2000 (figures 12.2 and 12.3). The bulk of the increase in inequality occurred in the pre-NAFTA phase of liberalization (1984–89).

The evolution of poverty in this period is less clear, because it is sensitive to methodological variations in the measurement of poverty. Figure 12.2 reports three estimates of trends in poverty rates, based on the same household income and expenditure surveys and the same food basket to anchor the poverty line, but differing (among other) in the following aspects: (1) Lustig and Székely (1997) use *income adjusted* for underreporting by households to ensure consistency with aggregate household income as reported in the national accounts; (2) Cortez and others (2002) use *unadjusted income*, following the methodological

Figure 12.2. Poverty and Inequality, 1984–2000 (percent)

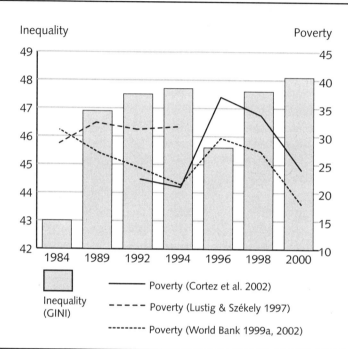

Sources: Data from Corbacho and Schwartz (2002); World Bank (1999a, 2002); Lustig and Székely (1997); Cortez et al. (2002).

parameters recently proposed by an independent academic committee and adopted by the federal government as the official national poverty measure for Mexico; and (3) the World Bank (1999a, 2002) uses *unadjusted consumption.* Each of these series of measures has complementary advantages and limitations: the first reflects *aggregate economic growth* (though it allocates this growth more or less arbitrarily to different income groups); the second reflects *current income,* as reported by households; and the third reflects *permanent income* and is thus less sensitive to short-term income shocks. In the first two conceptions, we observe slightly *increasing* trends in the poverty rate. If we adopt the third as the relevant standard, however, the poverty rate shows a continuous decline over the period, only interrupted by the 1995 crisis, from 31 to 18 percent (or from 22.6 to 17.6 million persons).

In the last case, it is interesting that poverty and inequality appear to be *negatively* correlated, contrary to what might be assumed. This is

Figure 12.3. Growth, Changes in Inequality, and Poverty Reduction (average annual change)

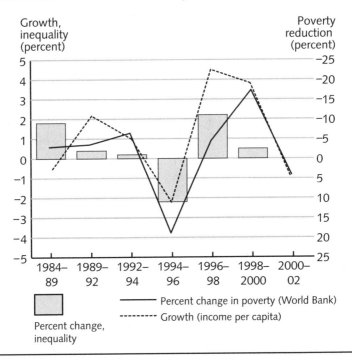

Sources: Data for growth, Instituto Nacional de Estadistica, Geografia e Informática; for poverty in 2002, projected applying income elasticity of poverty observed in 1998–2000; see sources for figure 12.2.

explained by the contrasting effect of economic growth on these distributive measures (figure 12.3): Growth is naturally associated with poverty reduction, but it also appears to be associated with increasing inequality in this period. The latter may suggest that Mexico still finds itself in the left side of its Kuznets curve and has thus yet to reach its point of maximum inequality. As we will see in the next section, however, this rise in inequality has little to do with Kuznets's hypothesis, and much with the effect of economic liberalization in the context of a highly unequal distribution of productive assets. In the case of the 1995 crisis, the momentary decline in inequality despite a sharp increase in poverty suggests that the negative impact on nonpoor people was even deeper—though also more transient.

Table 12.1. Decomposition of Change in Poverty between Growth and Distributive Effects

Period	Growth (percent)	Distributive Change (percent)
1984–89	26	74
1989–94	54	46
1992–96	100	0
1996–2000	88	12

Sources: Lustig and Székely (1997); Cortez et al. (2002).

LIMITS TO EQUITABLE GROWTH

That "growth is good for the poor"[3] is both evident enough as a general empirical fact and not especially interesting for understanding poverty in a highly (and chronically) unequal society, like Mexico. A growth-based strategy for poverty reduction can be more or less effective depending on the prospects for growth and the distributive changes accompanying growth, so a more relevant question might be: Is growth *as good as it could be* for the poor? This could hardly be answered in the affirmative in the case of Mexico in the period under consideration (1984–2000), when the impact of growth on the poor was *doubly* disappointing: (1) the annual growth rate achieved in this period was obviously disappointing, at 1 percent on average, and (2) the effectiveness of this modest growth in reducing poverty was further hampered by the accompanying rise in inequality.

Table 12.1 presents decompositions of the change in poverty in growth and distribution effects reported in Lustig and Székely (1997) and Cortez and others (2002). We can see that the change in poverty estimated by the former in the period 1984–89 was due mainly to the notable rise in inequality in this period, while the evolution of poverty in the 1990s estimated in the latter source was explained mainly by the evolution of average incomes.[4] During the 1984–2000 period, the effect of the modest growth in average income was almost completely canceled out for the poorest third of the population by the concurrent decline in their income share (by 0.9 percent per year in average), implying a "lost decade and a half" in average real income at this end of the distribution.

Adding the 2000–2 recession (see figure 12.3) to the latter trends, the question cannot be eluded: Why was the opening of the Mexican economy followed by poor growth and increasing inequality, in contrast to what might be expected from traditional growth and trade theory? Because we are interested in the long-term growth and distributive prospects of NAFTA in the light of the first decade, it will be useful to distinguish between *proximate* causes, contingent on transitory events, and *ultimate* causes, associated with more stable structural characteristics of the Mexican economy (and polity).

The proximate causes underlying the three periods of negative growth accounting for the low growth rate over the whole period (figure 12.3) are well known: the 1983 debt crisis, the 1995 exchange rate crisis, and the recent downturn in the U.S. economy. Though these shocks were independent of the opening up of the Mexican economy, NAFTA has certainly deepened the dependence of the Mexican economy on the U.S. economy, in good as well as bad times. Conversely, the proximate causes of the trend of increasing inequality seem closely associated with the process of trade liberalization and economic integration with the North, though the ultimate causes are to be found in the historical distribution of productive assets in Mexico.

First, at a regional level, the divergence we have documented above between northern and southern states is consistent with recent models of international trade emphasizing geography (transport and communication costs) and external economies. In these models, physical access to large markets of goods and factors can become a more important determinant for the location of firms than low labor costs. Given the existing distribution of rail and road infrastructure in Mexico, radiating from Mexico City and failing to connect the southern states to international markets in the north, the probable effect of NAFTA is to reduce the comparative advantage of the south relative to the north (Dávila, Kessel, and Levy 2002). The principal gains in employment and wages so far have been achieved in large (formal sector) manufacturing firms and maquiladoras close to the northern border, while extreme poverty in Mexico is still concentrated in the primary sector (especially subsistence corn farmers), and in the south.

Second, at the individual level, the principal single factor limiting the ability of the poor to benefit from free trade appears to be education. In general, changes in the distribution of personal income may be viewed as a function of changes in three underlying factors: (1) the distribution of productive assets (e.g., human capital), (2) the price of these assets (e.g. returns to education), and (3) their rate of use (e.g., participation in the labor market). The principal causes of the increase in earnings inequality between 1984 and 1994 are changes in schooling and in the returns to schooling during this period.[5] The more important factor here has been the widening returns to education (skills), which have declined over the period at lower to medium schooling levels and increased at higher education levels. This phenomenon has been observed in many other countries, and is partly due to the rising demand for skilled labor in the increasingly globalized and technology-intensive markets. It is thus clearly associated with trade liberalization.

Contrary to what might be expected, protection in Mexico prior to 1986 favored goods intensive in low-skill labor, and liberalization has therefore increased the relative wages of skilled workers (Hanson and Harrison 1995). Given the size of the educational gap between Mexico and the other NAFTA members—the average schooling of the adult population in Mexico is only 60 and 50 percent of what it is in the United States and Canada, respectively—low-skilled industries in the latter are skilled-intensive in relation to Mexico.

The polarizing impact of increasing returns to education could in principle have been (over)compensated by equalizing trends in either of the two other relevant variables—the distribution of educational assets and participation rates—and this has indeed been observed in other countries where income inequality has *decreased* during recent decades despite open markets.[6] In the case of Mexico, however, the distribution of schooling has unfortunately contributed to aggravate the polarizing price effect in the 1984–94 period, despite the fact that this distribution has not worsened significantly (table 12.2).[7] This happened because, as can bee seen in the table, the largest gains in schooling were achieved in the middle of the distribution and, though the percentage change for the poorest and richest quintile were comparable in 1984–94, the widening gap in returns to education implied considerably higher income gains at the top end.

The further rise in inequality observed after 1996 may be similarly explained. As was noted above, the massive NAFTA-induced increase in FDI flows since 1994 has increased demand for skilled labor. The distribution of schooling in Mexico in the middle 1990s was among the

Table 12.2. Distribution of Schooling, 1984–2000 (25–65 year olds)

Quintile	Average Schooling			Change (percent)	
	1984	1994	2000	1984–94	1994–2000
1	2.2	2.8	3.3	26.6	18.7
2	3.0	3.9	5.3	30.0	36.5
3	3.9	5.1	6.5	32.2	27.6
4	5.6	6.7	7.8	19.7	17.3
5	7.9	9.9	10.8	24.8	9.6
Gini[a]	0.3453	0.3473	0.3001	0.6	−13.6

Source: Author's calculations using data from Instituto Nacional de Estadística, Geografía e Informática, Encuesta Nacional de Ingreso y Gasto de los Hogares 1984, 1994, 2000.

[a] Gini coefficient of the distribution of schooling years among 25–65 year olds.

most polarized in Latin America (IDB 1998). Though schooling inequality has somewhat declined since then (mostly in favor of lower-middle-income groups), it is unlikely that this has been sufficient to counteract the price effect. To this we must add the NAFTA-induced regional divergence noted above. The fact that income inequality has increased only marginally in 1994–2000 despite this additional factor, suggests that we may finally have reached the turning point in the increasing trend of income inequality in Mexico.

THE ROLE OF THE STATE

In the absence of credible democratic institutions, the claim to legitimacy of the governments of Mexico for most of the twentieth century was based on the redistributive ideals emanating from the Mexican Revolution, within a stable political and economic environment, ensuring adequate levels of long-term economic growth. The end of this stability in the past two decades of the twentieth century,[8] and the persistence of high levels of income and asset inequality throughout this period,[9] may therefore also be interpreted as a *policy failure* of the postrevolutionary regime. In the following sections, we consider the two most relevant redistributive instruments used in this period: social and agricultural policy. We will see that some notable policy initiatives were undertaken in the past decade to correct these failures, representing relevant (if belated) efforts to allow the most vulnerable and poorest populations to benefit from economic liberalization.

At a more fundamental level, limited state institutions, limited growth, and persistent inequality may have been closely interlinked in Mexico. Easterly, Fiess, and Lederman (2002) argue that an important part of the income gap between Mexico and the United States may be explained by the institutional gaps between the two countries in terms of accountability, political stability, government effectiveness, regulatory quality, the rule of law, and control of corruption. On a longer historical perspective, Engerman and Sokoloff (2002) relate the continuous trend of economic divergence between Mexico and the United States during the past three centuries to the diverging paths of institutional development in the two countries,[10] which in turn is explained by contrasting patterns in the original distribution of land between the two countries. Even the 1983 debt crisis initiating the period of stagnation and increasing inequality was ultimately an effect of Mexico's chronically limited fiscal capacity, which may again be explained by the highly concentrated distribution of income.

Considering specific policies in the face of NAFTA, the analysis of the previous section suggests two principal demands:

- augmenting the general level and reducing the concentration of human capital, especially education (but also health and nutrition), as well as other assets; and

- investing in transport and communication infrastructure connecting the economic periphery (south) with the northern market.

Before proceeding to the first issue in the next sections, it is useful to briefly comment on transport infrastructure. But this chapter has nothing to say about another area of intervention commonly demanded in the face of trade liberalization—industrial policy—for the simple reason that this had been absent from the public policy agenda in Mexico well before NAFTA.

As I have noted in the previous section, the geographic distribution of economic activities within Mexico plays a significant role in explaining diverging regional growth patterns after the introduction of NAFTA. The poorest states in the southeast (Chiapas, Oaxaca, and Guerrero) face particular restrictions in their capacity to integrate to the more dynamic poles of development. First, their populations are exceptionally dispersed: The percentage of the population living in relatively isolated localities of fewer than 500 inhabitants (at five or more kilometers from larger localities) in these states is more than double the average for the rest of the country (Dávila, Kessel, and Levy 2002). Second, the radial structure of the mayor train and road connections in Mexico means that these states face exceptional transport costs in bringing their merchandise to the largest internal and external markets. An investment program to build the required transport infrastructure planned at the beginning of the Ernesto Zedillo administration had to be shelved following the 1995 crisis. The Vicente Fox administration has launched a broad project—the Plan Puebla-Panama—aiming to integrate the south beyond Mexico with the rest of the Mexican and North American markets.

HUMAN DEVELOPMENT AND SOCIAL POLICY

Despite significant progress in education and health achievements during the second half of the twentieth century, Mexico's human development record is generally bellow expectations given its per capita income level. Infant mortality is above average for upper-middle-income countries (World Bank 1999b), comparable to China, not much lower than Vietnam, and higher than Sri Lanka, despite the distance between Mexico and these countries in per capita income and public spending (table 12.3), and literacy and secondary enrollment rates are similarly disappointing. Despite exceptional progress in average schooling over the past four decades, from 2.8 to 7.7 years, the latter still represents a two-year schooling deficit given Mexico's per capita income (Londoño 1996).

This record is aggravated by the distribution of these achievements, as we saw in the case of schooling in the previous section. By one estimate, the schooling gap between the richest 20 percent and poorest 40 percent of the population in Mexico was the widest in Latin America in the past decade, and the average schooling for the poorest 10 percent of the adult population was approximately equivalent to, half of, and a third of the level achieved by the corresponding decile in Honduras, Peru, and Chile, respectively.[11] Complete primary education, which in Argentina, Chile, and Uruguay is achieved even by those in the poorest decile, is not achieved until the seventh decile in the case of Mexico.

Table 12.3. Human Development and Economic Resources

Indicator		Mexico	Chile	Vietnam	China	Sri Lanka
GDP per capita (purchasing power parity dollars)	1999	7,719	8,370	1,755	3,291	3,056
Gini coefficient	1990s	53.7	56.5	36.1	40.3	34.4
Life expectancy (years)	1998	72	75	68.5	70	73.5
Infant mortality (percentage of live births)	1998	3	1	3.4	3.1	1.6
Illiteracy (percentage of adult population)	1998	9	4.5	7	17	9
Secondary enrollment (percentage of age group)	1997	66	85	55	70	76

Sources: World Bank (1999b, 2000b).

An important part of the explanation for Mexico's modest and highly unequal human development record lies in the distribution of income, which severely limits the access of poorer households to private health and education services, as well as to goods and assets complementary to these in the production of health and educational achievements. But the distribution of income is in turn largely explained by the prevailing distribution of assets, especially, at the lower end of the distribution, schooling. Given the distribution of private spending capacity on health and education services in Mexico, the educational and health opportunities open to the poor depend to a large extent on their access to publicly provided services.

Historically, the equalizing impact of public education and health spending in Mexico has faced four principal constraints: (1) chronically restricted fiscal capacity has limited the amount of public resources available for these services; (2) urban bias, centralization, and high

Table 12.4. Public Social Expenditures

Period	Percentage of Gross Domestic Product	Percentage of Public Expenditures
1971–76	6.7	31.2
1977–82	8.5	32.9
1983–88	6.6	30.1
1989–94	7.7	45.2
1995–2000	8.8	55.8

Source: Government of Mexico (2000).

Note: Public expenditures are considered net of debt payments and state revenue shares.

opportunity costs (especially in education) have limited the access by the poor to public services; (3) social spending patterns have been biased in favor of the most regressive services (tertiary education and health services for the insured); and (4) a general lack of transparency and accountability, explained in part by powerful teacher and health worker unions, has limited the quality of these services.

In the four decades between the early 1940s and 1982, social spending in Mexico grew from less than 2 percent to more than 9 percent of GDP. This growth reflected the creation and expanding coverage of social security in the 1940s and 1950s,[12] and a rapid expansion of public education in the 1970s. In the aftermath of the 1983 crisis, social spending was cut back and only regained its 1982 level—as a proportion of GDP as well as in real per capita terms—by the end of the 1990s. In contrast to the earlier peak, financed by high levels of public expenditure, the latter has been achieved by almost doubling the share of social spending in the public budget during the 1990s (table 12.4).

Considering the distribution of public spending on education, following the 1968 student revolt, in the 1970s the share allocated to upper-secondary and tertiary education jumped from 20 to 42 percent, despite an expansion in enrollment in public basic education from 9.7 to 16.5 million students. The impact on spending per student in basic education was aggravated in the 1983–88 adjustment period, because the latter level absorbed a disproportionate share of the budgetary

Table 12.5. Public Spending per Student in Primary Education, Mexico versus Regional Averages, 1960–90

Country, Region, or Group	Purchasing Power Parity Dollars (1985)	GDP per Capita (percent)	School Hours per Year
Mexico	175	4	780
Latin America and Caribbean	256	9.1	952
East Asia and Pacific	295	9.3	1097
Organization for Economic Co-operation and Development	1,656	15.7	974

Source: Barro and Lee (1996) data set.

cuts. To put these figures in perspective, table 12.5 compares spending per student in primary education in Mexico during the 1960–90 period with averages for three relevant regions. These notable spending gaps are reflected in comparatively limited schooling hours, and more important, in the quality of education. Unfortunately, systematic comparable information on the quality of education in Mexico has been scarce until recently. Though Mexico participated in a mayor international evaluation of language and mathematical achievements in basic education in 1995,[13] the government administration at the time (Zedillo) was the only one of all participating countries vetoing the publication of its results. Today we know that Mexico was placed at the lower ranks, as it has in a more recent evaluation conducted by the Organization for Economic Cooperation and Development. An autonomous body responsible for the evaluation of basic education in Mexico was only set up in 2003.

Two important policy shifts in the 1990s improved the equity of public education spending significantly. First, public spending per student in primary education increased six times in real terms in the two previous administrations (1988–2000), as a result of various factors: the recovery of pre-1983 levels of education spending as well as of the budget share allocated to primary education (from 33 percent in the 1983-1988 administration to 40 percent in the 1990s),[14] in the context of a stagnating number of students in public education at this level (from 13.9 million in 1980 to 13.5 in 1990 and 13.7 in 2000). The latter is explained in part by the decline in population growth, and by the fact that by 1980 public primary education had already reached a coverage of 85 percent of the relevant age group; but a slight decline to 83 percent by 1990 suggests other demand factors. Those who can afford it may be opting out of public education in favor of higher-quality private services. More disturbingly, there is evidence that poorer households had to opt out of a complete basic education for their children altogether, in favor of earlier incorporation to working activities—effectively dissaving in terms of their children's potential human capital—as a survival strategy following the 1983 and 1995 crises.[15]

The second relevant policy change, partly in response to the latter problem, was the introduction by the Zedillo administration in 1997 of the Programa de Educación, Salud y Alimentación (PROGRESA), an innovative antipoverty program offering direct monetary transfers to poor rural households conditional on participation in basic education (for the relevant age group) and health services. This program set a new standard for social policy in Mexico in multiple respects, contrasting with the Programa Nacional de Solidaridad (PRONASOL), the ambitious but unaccountable and politically tainted anti-poverty program of the Carlos Salinas de Gortari administration.

First, perhaps surprisingly, it is the first social program in Mexico to apply transparent targeting mechanisms, effectively identifying the poorest rural localities and households, using, at the latter level, proxy-means tests based on a full census of socioeconomic characteristics and economic assets within these localities. Second, it exploits synergies among education, health, nutrition, and monetary transfers in the production of human capital, offering its beneficiaries a long-term chance to escape chronic (intergenerational) poverty on a permanent basis, as well as short-term income support. Third, this is the first social program in Mexico to have been subject to a rigorous impact evaluation, with a baseline and panel of treatment and control groups, planned from the conception of the program.[16]

Fourth, due to the positive result of the latter, the program is also notable in having survived not only to a change of administration (in contrast to all the mayor antipoverty initiatives over the last two decades), but to the first change in 70 years of the party in power. It is to the credit of the Fox administration that, recognizing the merits of the previous administration's flagship program, it resisted the temptation to reinvent, expanding instead PROGRESA's coverage from 2.3 to 4.2 million households, from basic to postsecondary education, and from rural to the semiurban and urban localities, under a new brand name—Opportunidades.

Fifth, it complements traditional supply-side spending in health and education (still representing 95 percent of public spending in these areas) with demand-side subsidies. In addition to empowering the users rather than providers of these services, this strategy targets directly the principal restriction we have noted for the rural poor to access postprimary education. In its educational component PROGRESA offers scholarships of increasing value at higher grades (differentiated in favor of girls after primary education),[17] designed to cover the opportunity cost of attending school for children and youngsters in these communities.

To appreciate the apparent effect of the latter on the demand for education among the poor, as well as the remaining inequities and the effect of the 1995 crisis, figure 12.4 presents the participation in public education by income-ordered population deciles between 1992 and 2000. In the case of basic education, we observe a trend of increasing progressivity between 1992 and 1994, interrupted (primary level) or reversed (secondary level) by the 1995 crisis (1994–96), and resumed between 1998 and 2000. The effect of the crisis as well as the post-1996 recuperation with PROGRESA and the resumption of economic growth for the poorest 20 percent is especially notable in the case of secondary education.

It can also be observed, however, that the coverage of tertiary education is extremely regressive, and the gains in coverage over the decade have been limited to the upper half of the income distribution. Taking into account the noted shift in the educational budget in favor of basic education, the distribution of total public spending has converged toward neutrality, from a regressive pattern at the start of the decade. PROGRESA's food aid component, which absorbs the other half of the program's monetary and in kind transfers,[18] and is conditioned on the use of health services, has had an even more dramatic effect on the distribution of food subsidies in Mexico (as well as the use of health services), as we will see in the next section.

Figure 12.4. Distribution of Students and Spending in Public Education by Income Deciles, 1992–2000

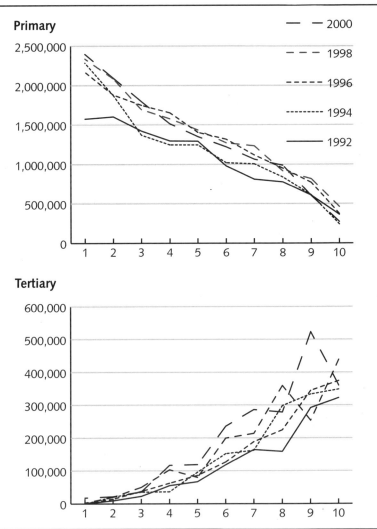

Source: Data from Scott (2002b). Population deciles have been ordered by income per capita.

RURAL AND AGRICULTURAL POLICY

After a prolonged conflict, the Fox administration and the principal peasant organizations have signed the Acuerdo Nacional para el Campo (April 2003) involving a substantial increase and reallocation of

Figure 12.4 *(continued)*

Lower Secondary

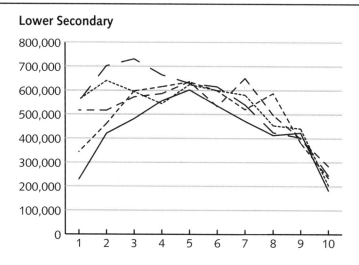

Total public education spending

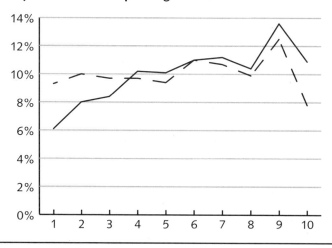

public funds in this sector, and committing the government to the negotiation of parallel agreements protecting the most sensitive crops—
corn and beans—through managed import quotas. NAFTA was
negotiated and initiated under a single-party, corporativist regime, with
significant control over organized producer groups. It is therefore per-

haps not surprising that the first major organized opposition to NAF-TA since the 1994 Zapatista uprising has emerged in the newly democratic context following the 2000 election.

This movement—headed by the main peasant organizations inherited from the old regime, and backed by increasingly anti-NAFTA opposition parties (including the Institutional Revolutionary Party) — demanded the repeal of NAFTA's agricultural chapter, or at least countervailing actions and compensation policies consistent with NAFTA. Under this trade agreement, the liberalization of agricultural products has been phased over a 15-year period, with an important batch of products facing full international competition by January 2003, and corn and beans five years later. To indicate the significance of the latter for producers and consumers in Mexico, note that domestic corn and bean productivity per hectare has been, on average over the past three decades, just 25 percent and 50 percent of U.S. productivity, respectively.

Policies to improve the distribution of the gains from NAFTA are thus important for reasons of political economy as well as distributive justice. The two objectives must be carefully distinguished, however. As usual in the political economy of policy reform, the most vocal opposition is representative of entrenched interest groups that were the traditional beneficiaries of trade and agricultural policies in the past, rather than the groups most in need of such support—the poorest and most vulnerable producers. To understand the distributive implications of NAFTA in the agricultural sector, it is thus important to consider the dual structure of this sector in Mexico (subsistence vs. commercial agriculture), the impact of pre-NAFTA policies within this structure, and the structural reforms implemented simultaneously with trade liberalization to accelerate the transition to a modern competitive agricultural sector.

Although 75 percent of Mexico's population is urban, extreme poverty is still largely a rural problem (table 12.6). The 1995 crisis temporarily increased the urban share in extreme poverty, but the period of liberalization overall has been characterized by an increasing trend in the rural share.

Seventy years after the Mexican Revolution, the poorest among the poor are still landless agricultural workers and subsistence farmers. This is so despite a massive process of land redistribution prolonged over more than six decades (until 1992) and expensive agricultural sup-

Table 12.6. Extreme Poverty in the Rural Sector (percent)

Year	Poverty Rate	Participation in Total Poor Population
1992	35.6	66.2
1994	36.8	72.8
1996	52.4	57.0
1998	52.1	61.6
2000	42.4	68.4

Source: Cortez et al. (2002).

Note: The rural sector includes localities with fewer then 15,000 inhabitants.

port and pricing policies sustained for most of this period. The failure of land reform to set the basis for equitable development in Mexico, as it has in many Asian countries, may be explained by (1) the small size and low quality of the allocated plots, principally used for corn and bean crops; (2) the limited individual property rights entailed by the *ejido* system; and (3) government pricing policies. The first two elements led to a large number of farmers with insufficient land to generate a marketable surplus of production, and often insufficient even to sustain the household without off-farm economic activities. The 1991 agricultural census reported 2.2 million farm-households owning fewer than 5 hectares, 1.3 million of them with fewer than 2.

Pricing policies in agriculture benefited *surplus* producers of basic crops (especially corn and beans) through minimum guaranteed prices, while the real income of urban consumers was protected through a costly untargeted subsidy on these products and their derivatives, principally the tortilla. The final incidence of these policies between 1965 and 1982 appears to have favored the latter group, implying a net *tax* on agriculture in the context of an overvalued exchange rate in most years in this period.[19] With the severe fiscal cuts following the 1983 crisis, the generalized food subsidies to consumers became unsustainable.

By the early 1990s, the internal price of corn was 70 percent above international prices (Levy and Wijnbergen 1992), and the generalized tortilla subsidy was insufficient to compensate urban consumers for this differential. The latter was gradually reduced after the middle 1980s (though only eliminated by 1998), in favor of targeted subsidies, principally milk (LICONSA) and tortilla rations (Tortibonos). Unfortunately, the latter were costly in their operation and badly mistargeted: they were concentrated in the urban sector, principally in Mexico City, and the criteria to select beneficiaries lacked transparency end targeting efficiency.[20]

The big losers of these policies have been subsistence farmers and landless rural workers, first by being net *buyers* of corn and thus *taxed* by these pricing policies even in the latter period, and second by missing out on the consumption subsidies. Corn and coffee pricing policies in the 1980s and early 1990s have been estimated to impose implicit taxes on small agricultural producers in the poorest regions of 15 to 30 percent, redistributing the proceeds to large farmers in richer regions (Deininger and Heinegg 1995). To this it must be added that most other support instruments—irrigation, electricity subsidies, credits, and technical assistance—have tended to benefit mostly the larger and richer producers, mostly located in the north of the country.

Against this historical background, it should be clear that the rural poor had little to lose, and potentially much to gain, from the profound policy reforms initiated in the 1990s in this sector. These included, in parallel to the elimination of protectionist pricing policies on basic crops under NAFTA, a number of complementary initiatives designed to facilitate the transition from traditional, low-productivity rural activities to competitive economic opportunities within or outside agriculture: (1) a constitutional reform deregulating *ejido* property to allow the selling and use as collateral of individual plots; (2) a transitional income support program for agricultural producers, the Programa de Apoyos Directos al Campo (PROCAMPO); (3) a broad agricultural investment program designed to increase agricultural productivity through matched grants and support services (Alianza para el Campo), and (4) the reallocation of food subsidies to the rural poor, as part of PROGRESA's broader effort to promote human capital investment in these communities.

The opening up of basic crops (corn and beans) under NAFTA will of course in the short run affect commercial producers of these crops, but it will also benefit subsistence producers—two-thirds of all corn producers in Mexico—as it will all (net) consumers of these products. Deregulation of the *ejido* sector can only increase the economic opportunities available to producers in this sector, and the evidence thus far indicates increasing integration of *ejido* households to nonfarm and non-*ejido* farm activities, which "will ultimately erode differential returns to land, labor and capital across the sectors and reduce rural poverty in Mexico" (World Bank 2000a).

PROCAMPO is an agricultural income support program offering fixed monetary payments per (cultivated) hectare, with eligibility determined by total hectares producing nine traditional crops in the three years *prior* to the program's initiation (in 1994). The program covers about 3 million agricultural producers and 90 percent of Mexico's cultivated area, and it is set to operate only during NAFTA's transitional phase to 2008. By offering a uniform payment per hectare independent of yield and marketed output, in contrast to pre-NAFTA price support policies, the benefits from this program reach subsistence farmers: 45 percent of the area covered belongs to small farmers with 5 or fewer hectares. Thus, though very large farmers at the top income decile obtain a disproportionate share, the transfer is progressive below the seventh decile, and 50 percent reaches the poorest third of the income distribution (figure 12.5). For the poorer *ejidatarios*, the PROCAMPO transfer represents up to 40 percent of their income (Cord and Wodon 1999).

Alianza para el Campo, conversely, has a smaller coverage among poor farmers,[21] and because it involves a more modest scale of resources, it is unlikely to have an important impact on the poor. Though this may suggest that poor farmers in the critical NAFTA transition period are only obtaining short-term consumption benefits, there is evidence that PROCAMPO transfers have an important multiplier effect, associated with a net increase in investment, an increased capacity to enter riskier and higher-yield activities, and a local Keynsian consumption multiplier.

Finally, the substitution of established consumption food subsidies by PROGRESA's nutrition component, at present accounting for two-thirds of all public spending on food subsidies, has implied a radical reallocation from Mexico City to the southern and central states—consistent with the distribution of undernourished children in Mexico (figure 12.6). The share of these resources received by the poorest decile thus *quadrupled* between 1994 and 2000, from 8 percent to 33 percent (figure 12.5). To this direct transfer effect of PROGRESA's food component must be added the indirect effect on the use of health services on

Figure 12.5. Redistribution of Food Subsidies, PROCAMPO (percent) and Health Services for the Uninsured (millions of users) by income deciles, 1994–2000

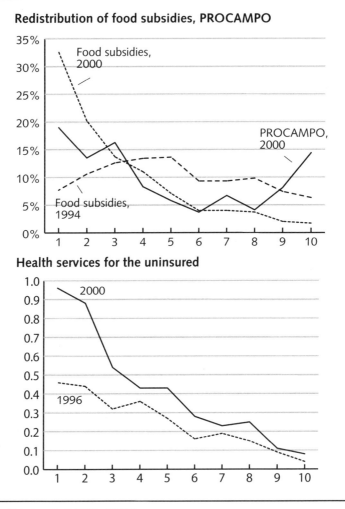

Redistribution of food subsidies, PROCAMPO

Health services for the uninsured

Sources: Data from Scott (2002a, 2002b).

Note: PROCAMPO = Programa de Apoyos Directos al Campo. For food subsidies: *household* deciles ordered by income per capita. For users of health services: *population* deciles ordered by income per capita.

which these transfers are conditioned. Figure 12.5 also shows that the use of health services for the uninsured by the poorest households *doubled* between 1996 and 2000.[22]

Figure 12.6. Regional Distribution of Food Aid and Undernourished Children, 1988 and 1999

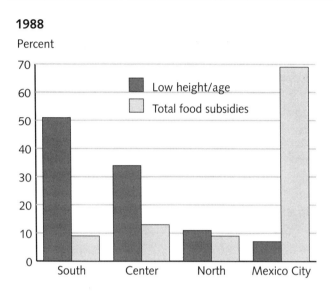

1988

Percent

Legend: Low height/age; Total food subsidies

(South, Center, North, Mexico City)

1999

Percent

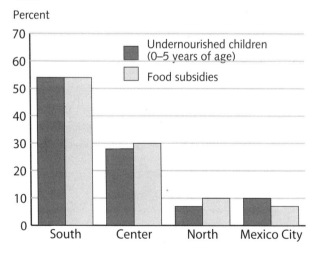

Legend: Undernourished children (0–5 years of age); Food subsidies

(South, Center, North, Mexico City)

Source: Data from Scott (2002a).

FUTURE PROSPECTS AND THE SHADOW OF THE PAST

Speculating on the future distributive implications of NAFTA is a risky business. Analysts in the early 1990s confidently predicted a massive NAFTA-induced exodus from traditional subsistence farming, with hundreds of thousands of rural households forced to migrate into an uncertain economic future. This exodus has yet to happen, because subsistence farmers have proven surprisingly resilient to change. This may reflect in part the combined effect of PROCAMPO and PROGRESA, which, perhaps for the first time in Mexico's postrevolutionary history, targeted public resources effectively to this population. But it is probably principally explained by the degree of poverty and vulnerability of these households, lacking the necessary resources to ensure a successful transition from traditional economic activities, and making such a transition too risky to try. Whether the long-term investment incentives integrated in the latter programs,[23] along with the deregulation of land and labor markets, will ultimately succeed in allowing these households to transit more gradually and less uncertainly to better economic activities (assuming such activities will indeed be available in sufficient scale and quality to absorb the displaced workers) is a question that we will only be able to answer with any certainty during NAFTA's *second* decade.

This uncertainty is the unfortunate consequence of the reforms reviewed in the last section—being, though certainly welcomed, in a sense too late, too little. They are too late because spending in basic education before the past decade implied a substantial underinvestment on the *present* workforce, eight years into NAFTA, in relation to our trading partners and competitors. The first generations of poor rural children having had the opportunity to acquire a postprimary education thanks to PROGRESA will be joining the workforce only by NAFTA's second decade. The same applies to the Plan Puebla-Panama initiative to integrate the south, which has yet to report its first results. They are too little because the quantity of public spending on human and physical capital in Mexico's is still curtailed by a chronically low fiscal capacity, and the quality of this spending is still limited by a general lack of accountability on the part of the providers of these services.

Adding to this pessimistic prognosis, it is impossible to ignore the contrast between the success of the past two administrations of the old regime in conceiving and implementing the radical reforms of the 1990s—starting with the negotiation, signing, and implementation of

NAFTA itself—and the failure of the first democratic administration to implement significant policy initiatives, from the construction of a new airport for Mexico City, to the most basic and urgent structural reforms (tax and energy). If the former administrations benefited from a unique and brief window of autonomy, with already weakened corporativist ties but not yet facing the full power of electoral competition, the latter has been hampered by intensive party competition with limited negotiating experience and weak institutions. Finally, though this administration has been more successful in the first half of its term in increasing Mexico's international political activism, it is not clear in the post–September 11, 2001, world order that this has been useful for its stated bilateral agenda of deepening NAFTA toward a European Union–style North American Economic Community.

Notes

1. I.e., average tariff pondered by trade flows (Lustig 1992).

2. See Easterly, Fiess, and Lederman (2002) for a detailed econometric analysis.

3. See Dollar and Kraay (2002), who use this statement as their title.

4. World Bank (1999a) estimates that poverty in 1996 would have been 4 percentage points lower in relation to 1984 had there been no growth in average incomes in this period, but 5 points lower had there been no increase in inequality, or alternatively stated, "one-fourth of the potential poverty reduction from growth may be lost due to rising inequality."

5. Legovini, Bouillon, and Lustig (2001) find that these factors account for 41 percent of the increase in inequality in this period.

6. See Kanbur and Lustig (1999) for a contrast among Mexico, Brazil, and Taiwan in this regard.

7. Legovini, Bouillon, and Lustig (2001) measure a *decrease* in educational inequality during this period, in contrast to the observation in the present chapter of a very slight *increase*, which may be due to our restriction to the 25-to-65-year-old population. Note, however, that the absolute gap in average schooling between the poorest and richest quintile grew from 5.7 to 7.1 years between 1984 and 1994, expanding further to 7.5 by 2000.

8. The 1940–80 period of sustained economic growth came to a halt with the 1982 debt crisis, and the even longer record of political stability was interrupted in 1994 by the Zapatista uprising and the political assassinations of the presidential candidate and general secretary of the ruling party.

9. Estimates of the Gini coefficient for Mexico exist from 1950, though comparability is limited prior to 1984. Most acceptable estimates for the 1950s, 1960s,

and 1970s range over values above 0.50; see Deininger and Squire (1996) database and Széckely (1998, table 1.1).

10. From an estimated 90 percent of income per capita in the British colonies that were to become the founding states of the United States, Mexico's GDP per capita in real terms declined to 50 percent of the U.S. figures in 1800, stagnating at about 30 percent during the twentieth century (Engerman and Sokoloff 2002, table 5).

11. The data are from IDB (1998), appendix table 1.2.III, for 25-year-olds. Filmer and Pritchett (1998) present a broader set, where only the Indian subcontinent and Morocco appear be more unequal than Mexico.

12. The two principal institutions of social security, the Instituto Mexicano del Seguro Social and the Instituto de Seguridad y Servicios Sociales de los Trabajadores del Estado, were created in 1944 and 1959, respectively.

13. This was the Third International Mathematics and Science Study.

14. This turnabout may be explained in part by the incorporation of Pedro Aspe as finance minister in the Salinas cabinet, coauthor of a mayor study identifying the noted inequities in educational spending in the 1970s and early 1980s (Aspe and Beristáin 1984).

15. Observe the absolute stagnation and absolute decline in the participation in primary and lower secondary education, respectively, in the poorest quintile between 1994 and 1996, in figure 12.4.

16. See www.ifpri.prg for the principal evaluation results.

17. These range from $9 per month in third-grade primary education, to $54 and $62 in the last year of high school for boys and girls, respectively.

18. This involves a fixed monetary transfer per beneficiary household and food supplements for infants and pregnant or lactating mothers.

19. Lustig (1989, 108). See also Levy and Wijnbergen (1992); Friedman and Legovini (1995).

20. A total of 62 percent of the beneficiaries of the targeted milk food subsidy (44 percent for tortillas), are in the six richer deciles of the income distribution (Scott 2003).

21. The 1997 *ejido* survey reports 10 percent of *ejidatarios* benefiting from Alianza, and 84 percent benefiting from PROCAMPO.

22. This cannot be attributed to PROGRESA's demand-inducing effect exclusively; it also reflects the extension in the coverage of these services through other programs of the Health Ministry, probably in coordination with PROGRESA.

23. This is implicitly in the case of PROCAMPO, by the announced transitional horizon of the program.

References

Aspe, P. and J. Beristáin. 1984. Distribution of Educative and Health Services. In *The Political Economy of Income Distribution in Mexico,* ed. P. Aspe and P. E. Sigmund. New York: Holmes & Meier.

Barro, R., and J.W. Lee. 1996. International Measures of Schooling Years and Schooling Quality. *American Economic Review Papers and Proceedings* 86, no. 2: 218–23.

Corbacho, A., and G. Schwartz. 2002. *Mexico: Experiences with Pro-Poor Expenditure Policies.* IMF Staff Working Paper WP/02/12. Washington, D.C.: International Monetary Fund.

Cord, L., and Q. Wodon. 2001. *Do Mexico's Agricultural Programs Alleviate Poverty? Evidence from the Ejido Sector.* Washington, D.C.: World Bank.

Cortez, F., D. Hernández, E. Hernández-Laos, M. Székely, and H. Llamas. 2002. *Evolución y características de la pobreza en México en la última década del siglo XX.* Documentos de Investigación 2. Mexico City: Secretaría de Desarrollo Social.

Dávila, E., G. Kessel, and S. Levy. 2002. *El sur también existe: Un ensayo sobre el desarrollo regional de México.* Mexico City: Economía Mexicana.

Deininger, K., and A. Heinegg. 1995. *Rural poverty in Mexico.* Washington, D.C.: World Bank.

Deininger, K., and L. Squire. 1996. Measuring Income Inequality: A New Data-Base. *World Bank Economic Review* 10, no. 3: 565–91.

Dollar, D., and A. Kraay. 2002. Growth Is Good for the Poor. *Journal of Economic Growth* 7, no. 3: 195–225.

Easterly, W., N. Fiess, and D. Lederman. 2002. NAFTA and Convergence in North America: High Expectations, Big Events, Little Time. Unpublished manuscript, World Bank, Washington, D.C.

Engerman, S.L., and K.L. Sokoloff. 2002. *Factor Endowments, Inequality, and Paths of Development among New World Economies.* NBER Working Paper 9259. Cambridge, Mass.: National Bureau of Economic Research.

Esquivel, G., D. Lederman, M. Messmacher, and R. Villoro. 2002. Why NAFTA Did Not Reach the South. Unpublished manuscript, World Bank, Washington, D.C.

Filmer, D., and L.H. Pritchett. 1998. *The Effect of Household Wealth on Education Attainment around the World: Demographic and Health Survey Evidence.* World Bank Working Paper. Washington, D.C.: World Bank.

Friedman, Lustig, and A. Legovini. 1995. Mexico: Social Spending and Food Subsidies during Adjustment in the 1980s. In *Coping with Austerity,* ed. N. Lustig. Washington, D.C.: Brookings Institution Press.

Government of Mexico. 2000. *Informe de gobierno, poder ejecutivo federal, Gobierno de México.* Mexico City: Government of Mexico.

Hanson, Gordon H., and Ann Harrison. 1995. *Trade, Technology and Wage Inequality in Mexico.* NBER Working Paper 5110. Cambridge, Mass.: National Bureau of Economic Research,

IDB (Inter-American Development Bank). 1998. Facing Up to Inequality in Latin America. IDB Annual Report. Washington, D.C.: IDB.

Kanbur, R., and N. Lustig. 1999. *Why Is Inequality Back on the Agenda?* Working Paper WP 99-14, Department of Agricultural, Resource, and Managerial Economics. Ithaca, N.Y.: Cornell University.

Legovini, A., C. Bouillon, and N. Lustig. 2001. Can Education Explain Changes in Income Inequality in Mexico? Unpublished manuscript, Inter-American Development Bank, Washington, D.C.

Levy, S., and S. Wijnbergen. 1992. Maize and the Free Trade Agreement between Mexico and the United States. *World Bank Economic Review* 6, no. 3: 481–502.

Londoño, J.L. 1996. *Poverty, Inequality, and Human Capital in Latin America, 1950–2025.* Latin American and Caribbean Studies, Viewpoints Series. Washington, D.C.: World Bank.

López-Córdova, J.E. 2001. *NAFTA and the Mexican Economy: Analytical Issues and Lessons for the FTAA, INTAL-ITD-STA.* Occasional Paper 9. Washington, D.C.: Inter-American Development Bank.

Lustig, N. 1989. Magnitud e impacto del gasto público en el desarrollo social de México. *Investigación económica 187.*

———. 1992. *Mexico: The Remaking of the Mexican Economy.* Washington, D.C.: Brookings Institution Press.

Lustig, N., and M. Székely. 1997. *México: Evolución económica, pobreza y desigualdad.* Washington, D.C.: Inter-American Development Bank.

Scott, J. 2002a. *Distribución de la ayuda alimentaria en México: La revolución de los noventa.* CIDE Working Paper DE-240. Mexico City: Centro de Investigación y Docencia Económicas.

———. 2002b. *Public Spending and Inequality of Opportunities in Mexico.* CIDE Working Paper DE-235. Mexico City: Centro de Investigación y Docencia Económicas.

———. 2003. Public Spending and Inequality of Opportunities in Mexico: 1992–2000. In *Public Spending and Poverty in Latin America,* ed. Q. Wodon. Stanford, Calif.: Stanford University Press.

Székely, M. 1998. *The Economics of Poverty and Wealth Accumulation in Mexico.* London: Macmillan.

USTR (Office of the U.S. Trade Representative). 2002. *Annual Report of the President of United States on the Trade Agreements Program.* Washington, D.C.: USTR.

World Bank. 1999a. *Government Programs and Poverty in Mexico.* Report 19214. Washington, D.C.: World Bank.

———. 1999b. *World Development Report 1999.* New York: Oxford University Press.

———. 2000a. Mexico Ejido Reform: Avenues of Adjustment—Five Years Later. Unpublished manuscript, World Bank, Washington, D.C.

———. 2000b., *World Development Report 2000.* New York: Oxford University Press.

———. 2002. *Country Assistance Strategy: Mexico.* Report 23843-ME. Washington, D.C.: World Bank.

PART SIX

POLITICAL ISSUES

CHAPTER THIRTEEN

NAFTA AND SOVEREIGNTY

James Robinson

Trade agreements rarely elicit more than casual indifference from the general public, but link an agreement to sovereignty and passions fly. As the North American Free Trade Agreement (NAFTA) negotiations began, supporters of the agreement used arguments that NAFTA would strengthen collective sovereignty in North America, and the opponents asserted the trade pact would weaken sovereignty. Because NAFTA touched on many sensitive issues, sovereignty was often utilized to stir national support, but mainly opposition, to the agreement. Sovereignty became linked to "economic sovereignty," "cultural sovereignty," "territorial sovereignty," "agricultural sovereignty," "environmental sovereignty," "security sovereignty," "financial sovereignty," and "electoral sovereignty," to cite only a few examples. This loose use of the concept of sovereignty was apparent not only in popular debates, but also in academic and intergovernmental discussions.

The fact that sovereignty was used, more often than not, incorrectly in these discussions, does not diminish its importance in the debates. In politics, (mis)perceptions can be just as important as reality. However, if sovereignty is simply identified with a state's functional tasks, the provision of public goods, or power capabilities, then everything the state does, domestically and internationally, affects its sovereignty; and if that were the case, the concept of sovereignty would be meaningless. For this reason, sovereignty must be distinguished from functional responsibilities or state capacities, especially if the impact of NAFTA on its members' sovereignty is to be properly assessed.

This chapter begins by examining the meaning of sovereignty—that is, as the concept is currently understood by legal and political scholars.

The chapter then summarizes the three countries' positions on sovereignty in terms of NAFTA. Finally, attention turns to how NAFTA, as a form of regional integration, has affected the sovereignty of its members. While debate in the NAFTA countries continues over the effects of the trade pact on their sovereignty, this chapter argues that important changes to sovereignty have occurred only in Mexico. Canadian and U.S. sovereignty have been relatively untouched by NAFTA, essentially because the trade agreement embodied the institutional interests of their sovereignties. But because NAFTA did not reflect the characteristics of Mexico's sovereign institutions, NAFTA helped create domestic and international pressures on the Mexican state to make its sovereign institutions more democratic, more transparent, and more accountable. This change in the nature of Mexican sovereignty represents a radical departure from its past.

Given the confusion in the NAFTA–sovereignty debate, it is worth emphasizing that trade, like capitalism generally, is a process of Schumpeterian "creative destruction" that can contribute to technological innovation, sectoral transformation, the collapse of firms, and even the rise and decline of states. The point is that change inevitably follows trade. If change did not come with trade, there would be no point in engaging in trade in the first place. But change does not necessarily mean sovereignty is being undermined, enhanced, or modified. The question that must be asked is what kind of change is a result of this trade, or trade agreement, and does that change affect state sovereignty? It is essential therefore to begin with a proper understanding of sovereignty before considering whether, and in what way, changes produced by NAFTA affected the sovereignty of its members.

SOVEREIGNTY AS LEGITIMATE AUTHORITY

Sovereignty is often defined in terms of control, specifically state control over national decisions pertaining to activities within its territorial borders. Confusion arises as to whether control refers merely to the legal right to make decisions or also includes control over outcomes of such decisions. The idea that sovereignty includes control over outcomes was apparent when one U.S. official, commenting on Mexico's decision to sign NAFTA, declared: "Conceding sovereignty is the price of leaving poverty; prosperity has its costs."[1] If sovereignty were simply about control, then states would be giving up part of their sovereignty every time they signed an international agreement. However, negotiating and signing international agreements is a sovereign right and does not necessarily entail a lessening or loss of sovereignty. Sovereignty is, in essence, a form of legitimate authority, an authority that gives a sovereign state the legal right to exercise control over decisions regarding its domestic affairs. Sovereignty also includes the right to enter into international activities, organizations, and regimes. But basically, sovereignty "is a matter of political authority and not of political power" (Middleton 1969, 133). Political authority refers to a legal right to make decisions, not to control outcomes.

Sovereignty is also associated with territoriality, although territoriality is primarily important for sovereignty in that it delimits the geographic domain of sovereign authority. Territoriality does not define or constitute sovereignty. When analysts note how territorial borders are no longer tightly controlled, with global flows of investment, trade, drugs, pollution, migration, and information going largely unregulated, they sometimes refer to the de-territorialization of the state or impermanence of state boundaries. They often conclude this necessarily entails a loss of sovereignty. However, others maintain such flows are possible only because of the strength invested in a sovereign authority. Clearly territory is important for sovereignty, but its relationship to sovereignty is ambiguous. If Mexico loses half of its territory to the United States or Quebec secedes from Canada, Mexico and Canada are still sovereign entities, albeit their domains of legal authority have changed. If border controls are weakened, then the ability of the state to exercise its sovereignty is made more difficult, but the state still retains its legal authority.

Given these confusions, it is useful to distinguish between "de jure" and "de facto" sovereignty, the former referring to legal rights and the latter to the capacity to exercise those rights (Jackson 1990). When politicians speak of a diminution or increase in sovereignty, they are usually referring to a loss or gain in the capabilities of a sovereign state, not to its legal authority. The existence of sufficient capabilities for the state to exercise its sovereign rights may be a precondition for sovereign recognition, but the amount of capabilities a state has does not change the amount of sovereignty (Fowler and Bunck 1995). The United States has more capabilities than Canada or Mexico, but Canada and Mexico would be the first to assert this does not mean the United States has more sovereignty. By its nature, sovereignty necessarily implies sovereign (legal) equality.

Confusion surrounding sovereignty may also be due to the importance given to the rights of self-determination and nonintervention for a sovereign state, as these rights are also linked with control, autonomy, and self-defense (Krasner 1999a, 34–52). Sovereign states have a right of self-determination, but that does not mean sovereign authorities have the right to adopt any policy they choose, even if the policy is strictly domestic. Sovereign states are bound by laws and any sovereign state that claimed it was not bound by law could hardly expect its citizens to be legally bound to obey its commands (Middleton 1969, 152). There are legal limits to what the sovereign may choose as a policy, so sovereign rights are never absolute. If a state's sovereignty were absolute and unconditional, then, as Kelsen noted, "only the sovereignty of one state could be presupposed and the sovereignty of this state would exclude the sovereignty of all other states" (Kelsen 1969, 121) The idea that sovereignty is unlimited legal supremacy is a self-contradiction, for any sovereign "who claims to possess legal authority admits by doing so that there is some legal justification for his rule, and accordingly that there must be some limit to what he is entitled to do" (Middleton 1969, 147).

Moreover, if sovereignty corresponded to absolute authority, then any state entering into an international agreement with other sovereign states could never claim the terms of the treaty were binding on the other states, because to do so would be to deny the sovereignty of the other states (Middleton 1969, 152–53). Absoluteness only refers to "the scope of affairs over which a sovereign body governs" (Philpott 1999, 571). Clearly "absoluteness" cannot mean absolute and unconditional authority. As one legal scholar put it: "Sovereignty is internal self-determination and independence from any superior power. It is not, however, independence from international law" (Wildhaber 1983, 437).

National and international law define the standards for legitimate authority for the sovereign state. Yet there remains the issue of whether national law takes precedence over international law. As Kelsen pointed out, the primacy of national law cannot be asserted if the principle of sovereign equality is to exist (1969, 122). The relationship between national and international law for sovereignty is complicated, and there is no universal consensus on exactly what this relationship entails. But the prevailing position can be defined as follows.

The idea that the sovereignty of the state, that is, the state as a supreme power, is not in conflict with international law because international law is valid for the state only if recognized by this state, and hence is not superior to the state, is quite compatible with the fact that a state, in recognizing international law by virtue of its sovereignty, and thus making it part of its own (national) law, restricts its sovereignty, that is to say, restricts its freedom of action or competence by accepting the obligations established by general international law and by treaties concluded by itself (Kelsen 1969, 127).

The limitations imposed by international law on the freedom to make decisions and carry out actions by the sovereign state do not correspond to a diminution or loss of sovereignty so long as the sovereign state has chosen to enter into an international agreement of its own accord. In fact, "the right of entering into international engagements is an attribute of state sovereignty" (Middleton 1969, 153). Without international law, sovereign rights and responsibilities lose all meaning. Thus, a recognized sovereign state has the "positive freedom" or legal authority to determine what its domestic and international policies will be (i.e., self-determination), in addition to "negative freedom," meaning the right to be protected from external control (i.e., the right of nonintervention; Middleton 1969, 149–50). But ultimately the sovereign state's "negative freedom" remains valid only so long as the exercise of "positive freedom" is consistent with domestic and international law. To argue that sovereignty entails absolute and unconditional authority is to accept "the strange conclusion that law can confer on a man the right to act as if law did not exist" (Middleton 1969, 147). Sovereignty requires the acceptance of international and domestic law for sovereignty to have any legal and coherent meaning.

Is it possible that a state might give up or lose part of its sovereignty by entering into a legal obligation that restricts the exercise of its sovereign rights? Indeed, it may be possible for a state to surrender all or part of its sovereignty by entering into a legal agreement but to enter into an international agreement that legally restricts the freedom or capacity of a sovereign state is not the same as entering into an agreement where the state surrenders part or all of its legal sovereign authority. The Hague Court clarified this point in the case of *Wimbledon* when it concluded that an international obligation may restrict the sovereign rights of a state, but its sovereignty remains because "entering into international engagements is an attribute of State sovereignty" (as cited in Middleton 1969, 153). Though domestic polities and government officials may think entering into an international treaty, especially one with heavy obligations, involves a surrender or compromise of sovereignty, this is only the case if the state is surrendering its legal authority. A state that signs an international treaty is simply making itself "bound to conduct itself in accordance with that law or obligation. No question of control by any external authority is involved" (Middleton 1969, 154). If the state retains its legal right of independence and legitimate authority, the state retains its legal sovereignty.

Because sovereignty refers to legal authority over domestic and foreign policies, two standards of legitimacy exist. Domestic standards correspond to national law and reflect a legal relationship between state and society. International standards are negotiated between states as members of the international community. These two standards are referred to as the "internal" and "external" dimensions of sovereignty. The exact content of national and international law has historically evolved, so the "internal" and "external" nature of sovereignty has changed considerably since its acceptance at the Treaty of Westphalia in 1648. Not only have the "internal" and "external" dimensions of sovereignty developed over centuries, but so too has the relationship between these two dimensions, so that the relative importance of domestic and international standards in defining sovereign practices has not remained the same (Murphy 1996, 81–120; Barkin and Cronin 1994, 107–30). In the nineteenth century, the domestic was more important while the underlying principle that justified its significance was based on positive law and the emergence of nation-state. The twentieth century, especially after World War II, saw a revival of natural law and increasing weight given to the standards of international law, particularly in the areas of human rights and democracy (Lyons and Mastanduno 1995). Internal and external standards of legitimacy are not fixed and depend on historical contingencies as well as the evolving interests of states, societies, and the international community.

With changes in the internal and external dimensions of sovereignty, and the relationship between them, there is always variation in sovereignty across international systems. But there is also variation within systems in that the sovereignties of different states are not identical at any given time. A useful distinction here is between states that embody "national sovereignty" and those that incorporate "constitutional sovereignty" (Shinoda 2000). In national sovereignty, states are conceived of as organic entities, as the ultimate expression of power and authority. Nationalism and imperialism of the nineteenth century gave concrete expression to this idea. In effect, in national sovereignty the will of a nation has priority over formal legal rules.

By contrast, constitutional sovereignty refers to the idea that state power and authority should always be constrained by domestic and international law. There is not only a rule of law, but laws also rule over sovereigns. National and constitutional sovereignty are two "ideal types," and most states embody elements of both. However, democracies like Canada and the United States tend to be far more constitutional sovereignties, although the United States does have its moments of nationalistic excess.[2] Historically, Mexico has always been a national sovereignty, despite the existence of a constitution and the presence of legal institutions. But with NAFTA, that has begun to change, and in the past 10 years Mexico has made significant strides toward becoming a "constitutional sovereignty" that accepts the importance of the rule of law.

U.S. SOVEREIGNTY AND NAFTA

The United States has always been a "constitutional sovereignty." Drawing on the liberal principles of John Locke, the Founding Fathers crafted a constitution that ensured the sovereign, and its representatives, would be subject to the rule of law, even if sovereignty were located in "the people" (Deudney 1995, 197–200). Unquestionably, the United States has also at times pursued national goals in a manner that violated domestic and international law, including the sovereignty of other states.[3] In the late nineteenth century, the U.S. secretary of state, Richard Olney, proclaimed that "the United States is practically sovereign" in Latin America (cited in Knight 1992, 20). Such sentiments have not completely disappeared, as evident from President George H.W. Bush's assertion that the United States has the right to kidnap foreigners in their own countries.[4]

Yet for much its history, the United States conducted itself as a "constitutional sovereignty" and demonstrated a commitment to legal principles. But the United States has also chosen to interpret those legal principles in a highly nationalistic fashion.[5] In a democratic society, this tends to result in hotly contested debates about the efficacy of tying U.S. interests to international commitments. Failure to support the Havana Charter and, more recently, the Kyoto Protocol reflects a historic pattern of U.S. reluctance to back international initiatives that might in any way "compromise" or "lessen" its sovereignty. This schizophrenia has been evident in U.S. trade policy that, after World War II, promoted an unconditional interpretation of the most-favored-nation clause in the General Agreement on Trade and Tariffs (GATT), but by the 1970s began incorporating an "aggressive reciprocity" with Section 301 of the 1974 Trade Act and later "Super 301" in 1988. Nationalism and unilateral initiatives have also been evident in other U.S. strategies, such as the Helms-Burton legislation, the latter being in apparent contradiction with NAFTA investment rules.[6] Such contradictions are the inevitable result of decisionmaking processes in an open "constitutional sovereignty."

The fact that the United States is a "constitutional sovereignty" meant there would be considerable debate about NAFTA, and this debate revealed considerable opposition in the United States. The NAFTA debate in the United States reflected many concerns and produced a strange coalition opposed to the trade pact. Some opponents, like Ross Perot and Patrick Buchanan, based their arguments on the dangers of such an agreement to U.S. sovereignty. Virtually all of these arguments were concerned, however, with issues of capabilities or control, rather than legal authority. A few, like Ralph Nader, did raise concerns that NAFTA might force the United States to accept international standards in, for example, environment and labor that would legally limit U.S. sovereign autonomy. For some, the question was whether the United States would be part of a "race to the bottom" in terms of lax standards or whether U.S. standards, such as in labor rights, would have to improve to meet Mexico's extensive labor laws.

For others, the parallel agreements in environment and labor offered a means of "enhancing" U.S. sovereignty, because harmonization of standards impinge more directly on domestic policy, rather than trade, and this would help undercut some of Mexico's comparative advantages (Gruben and Welch 1994, 182, 194–95). Such contradictory arguments reflected confusion over what NAFTA integration entailed and what enforcement mechanisms would be included in the final agreement. Of more immediate relevance is the fact that the type of "constitutional sovereignty" in the United States allowed for debates, public pressures, and, ultimately, the need for Bill Clinton's administration to add supplementary agreements to NAFTA deal with the environment, labor issues, and retraining for displaced workers, agreements which Canada and Mexico initially opposed because of concerns about their sovereignty (Sánchez 1994, 100). But while the agreements, essentially about standards-related measures (SRMs), were included in NAFTA, there was room for sovereigns to opt out of these legal constraints.

The constitutional nature of U.S. sovereignty also allowed the United States to gain bargaining advantages over Mexico (Carranza 2002, 149). The United States could point out that any NAFTA agreement would have to be ratified by the U.S. Congress, whereas the Mexican legislature would rubber-stamp any agreement the president presented to it. U.S. negotiators could use this legal constraint to extract concessions from Mexico (Putnam 1988; Avery 1998; Mayer 1998). Moreover, Mexico needed the agreement more than the United States or Canada, due to economic problems and the need to enhance its international credibility and domestic legitimacy. It is worth noting the Mexican government devoted far more resources to lobbying the U.S. Congress to pass NAFTA than it did on its own Congress.

By contrast, Canada could be a tougher bargainer with the United States and did gain important concessions.[7] Canada also had the luxury of knowing that it could fall back on the Canada–U.S. Free Trade Agreement (CUFTA) if NAFTA negotiations failed. With respect to public concerns that U.S. sovereignty would be threatened or diminished by the agreement, this has not been the case, although the degree of U.S. control over its environment, employment, trade flows, and investment has altered with NAFTA. Ultimately these changes do not have to do with a change in the legal authority of the U.S. sovereign so much as control over outcomes in U.S. markets.

Nonetheless, some NAFTA opponents took this to mean a lose of U.S. economic sovereignty, whether it was in jobs, investment flows, or control over production. But in the early twenty-first century, most foreign direct investment, international production, and trade are undertaken by multinational corporations (MNCs), a fact that is relevant in assessing their importance for sovereignty. As Reich observed, it is no longer meaningful to refer to most MNCs as having a clear national identity such as "American," "Canadian," or "Mexican" (Reich 1991). Therefore, linking economic transactions with national identities and sovereign authorities remains problematic. Moreover, because MNCs are, at least in the North American context, private-sector actors further divorces their activities from sovereign states. Finally, most international trade is now intraindustry and intrafirm (Weintraub 1997, 35), so the consequences of trade are more likely to affect companies rather than states (Krugman 1994; *Foreign Affairs* 1994). Whether these activities have contributed to a transfer of legal authority from sovereign states to MNCs is doubtful, although they have affected sovereign capabilities and power.

Has the NAFTA actually affected U.S. sovereignty? Clearly, NAFTA has heightened American sensitivities about sovereignty, but no one has demonstrated that NAFTA has diminished (or increased) U.S. legal authority. Given the fact that trade and investment have grown significantly between the United States and its NAFTA partners, one could make the case NAFTA has increased the United States' sovereign capabilities. The freedom NAFTA gave to MNCs may have constituted a threat of sorts by potentially lowering environment and labor standards, but as the supplementary agreements lack real enforcement mechanisms means governments have little to fear in sovereign losses from this source. In terms of the U.S. sovereign authority, the obvious conclusion is "the national power to make decisions in these [NAFTA related] fields is not removed by NAFTA" (Weintraub 1996, 149).

CANADIAN SOVEREIGNTY AND NAFTA

NAFTA, for Canada, was to a large extent about making sure that the 1989 CUFTA was not watered down. Moreover, because Mexico represented only 1 percent of Canadian trade, while the United States represented 75 percent, Canada saw NAFTA as a modification of CUFTA. Because of Mexico's limited relationship with Canada as well as the reality of U.S. economic power, NAFTA for Canada meant focusing on U.S.–Canadian issues. Canadian sensitivities regarding sovereignty were however quite evident prior to NAFTA. If the 1988 elections were any indication, the fact that almost 60 percent of the populace voted against Brian Mulroney's government and CUFTA indicated that most Canadians were opposed to a free trade pact with the United States. In 1992, an opinion poll by Angus Reid–Southam revealed 66 percent of Canadians were against the agreement.[8] Despite this opposition, Canada saw in NAFTA an opportunity to lock the United States into a multilateral trade regime that would limit U.S. arbitrariness and unilateralism. Although Canada was eager to negotiate trade rules in a wide range of areas, two closely related problems were of importance to the Canadians in terms of sovereignty: "cultural sovereignty" and "national treatment."[9]

The Canadian position on "cultural sovereignty" has no clear parallel in the United States or Mexico. Cultural identity has always been an important concern of Canadians as long as the United States has had a culture industry to export. Culture here refers specifically to "popular" or "mass culture," and Canadian culture is that produced by Canadian culture industries, such as Canadian newspapers, television, radio, magazines, and videos. Canadians have been concerned about protecting and promoting Canada's "cultural industries" at least since the mid–nineteenth century (Robert 2000, 47). But what does "cultural sovereignty" mean to Canadians? According to one Canadian analyst, "cultural sovereignty is the power of a sovereign government to control the operation of cultural industries" (Thompson 1992, 270). As this same individual points out, "given an anthropological definition of culture, cultural sovereignty would be absurd" (p. 270 n. 6). Whether it is absurd or not, cultural sovereignty has been a major issue in Canada, especially during trade negotiations with the United States. By contrast, concerns about cultural sovereignty in the United States and Mexico have been largely nonexistent. That does not mean that there have not been occasional doubts about cultural assimilation in Mexico or in the United States in terms of culture as an export business, where cultural exports generate roughly a $4 billion trade surplus (Robert 2000, 93).

But only in Canada has the issue of culture been tied to sovereignty, and even as distinguished a figure as John Kenneth Galbraith warned in 1968 that "the critical issues in sovereignty were not economic but cultural" (Thompson 1992, 277). Once Canada obtained a cultural exemption in the CUFTA, its position with regard to the NAFTA was that the exemption was nonnegotiable. For the most part, Canada achieved this objective in the NAFTA, although the United States did retain the right to retaliate if Canada invoked this exemption (Robert 2000, 95; Thompson 1992, 280). The United States gained another important concession in that Canada accepted the U.S. position of culture as a business (Thompson 1992, 282).

Have NAFTA provisions ensured the establishment of "cultural sovereignty"? It is doubtful, but it also depends on what is meant by "cultural sovereignty." If this refers to the government's legal power to control its cultural industries, then NAFTA simply reinforced CUFTA, which already provided legal protection. But because sovereignty refers to legitimate authority, rather than the power to control outcomes,

NAFTA has undoubtedly increased the flows of American culture into Canada. Some might say this threatens Canada's "cultural sovereignty," but sovereignty is a legal right and has nothing to do with the efficiency or survival of different sectors of a country's economy, unless the survival threatens the existence of the country. Whether Canadian culture survives or not, albeit important to Canadians, is not an issue that affects the legal rights of the Canadian sovereign to make authoritative decisions regarding national affairs.

A related concern for Canadians was the principle of "national treatment." National treatment refers to the right of the host country to apply its rules when, for example, a foreign firms wish to engage in business in that country (Rugman 1994, 111–13). Canada feared U.S. economic power, and it preferred to have a trade agreement based on national treatment rather than reciprocity, because the latter would contribute to a harmonization of national standards and practices. Making uniform the standards and practices of the three countries might diminish Canadian and Mexican control over their economies because they would give up more than the United States, because of the United States' greater bargaining power.

Even if the United States gave up less, however, anything it gave up would also reflect a lessening of control over its domestic economy, despite the fact that this might be accompanied by greater influence in the Canadian and Mexican markets. Maintaining the principle of national treatment ensured that this would not happen in any of the countries. Accordingly, "national treatment is a safeguard for Canadian sovereignty" (Rugman 1994, 114). While national treatment covers a variety of issues, it is primarily reflected in standards, technical regulations, and conformity assessments that are dealt with in chapter 9 of NAFTA. Yet standards are not mandatory under NAFTA and are usually determined by private standardizing bodies, rather than the state. While NAFTA does include SRMs, these obligations provide governments with the opportunity to opt out if they are concerned about their sovereignty. Even if NAFTA had incorporated a principle of reciprocity, and this had resulted in an extension of U.S. standards and practices, it would not mean that Canada or Mexico had lost any of their sovereignty as they had freely entered into the agreement and accepted the principle of reciprocity. In other words, their legal right of self-determination would not be infringed upon by an acceptance of reciprocity, even though reciprocity might restrict the exercise of sovereign rights.

In 1996, a Canadian expert concluded that while economic integration was surely occurring with NAFTA, "this economic integration is not leading down a slippery slope of surrender of sovereignty by Canadian governments" (Smith 1996, 66). No doubt that conclusion would remain valid today, but then NAFTA never was about a surrender of Canadian sovereignty. Trade disagreements between the United States and Canada will occur despite (or because of) NAFTA, but disagreements are essentially about interests. "The fact that the players involved include two sovereign states is almost incidental" (Stairs 1996, 30).

MEXICAN SOVEREIGNTY AND NAFTA

Unlike the United States and Canada, which are "constitutional sovereignties," Mexico's sovereignty has long been a "national sovereignty." In a sense, the differences in the nature of the three countries' sovereignties reflect their fundamental differences in political cultures, legal frameworks, as well as levels of development. Theoretically, the concept of "national sovereignty" refers to sovereignty defined as the state's control over activities within its national territory. The emphasis is on control, with little attention given to the issue of legal right or legitimate authority. Dating from independence, "the sovereignty issue [for Mexico] became subsumed in the quest for a secure state and a legitimate government to succeed the Castilian monarchy. Political order took precedence over political right" (Knight 1992, 17; also see Sikkink 1997, 101–19; and Meyer 1998, 79–98). Mexico does have a constitution that locates sovereignty in the people, but before NAFTA, the existence of "popular sovereignty" in Mexico was nothing more than a fiction to legitimize state power and national control. Mexican sovereignty has historically been highly nationalistic, defensive, and insular, especially vis-à-vis the United States, to which it lost roughly half its national territory in the nineteenth century and from whom it continued to suffer numerous illegal interventions in the twentieth century. "National sovereignty" not only served to protect the state from foreign interference but also shielded economic elites from foreign competition and political elites from international scrutiny. Part of this defensive stance meant having a foreign policy that was always "contrary to American interests," which represented "a sort of shield for Mexico" (Pastor and Castañeda 1988, 192). It was for this reason that Mexico rejected the Alliance of Progress, being one of the few Latin American countries to do so (Pastor 1993, 66). Mexico also declined to join the GATT in th·

early 1980s and turned down tentative proposals by the Reagan administration for the creation of a North American Common Market.

Mexican sovereignty was not only defensive in its outward stance toward the world; it was also authoritarian in its control over its domestic population. This required a "permanently strong state" that, from the late 1920s to the 1990s, was to be maintained by the Mexican president, who came from only one political party. However, the economic crises of the 1980s forced government officials to turn to new strategies of "opening" the Mexican market, which included signing NAFTA;[10] and this economic reorientation required a radically new conception of sovereignty. The Salinas administration, therefore, made the argument that a permanently "strong state" was not necessary for Mexico's sovereignty (Salinas de Gortari 1988, 123–28). In his first state of the nation report in 1989, Salinas attacked "the outmoded view that confuses being progressive with being statist. . . . In Mexico, a larger state has resulted in less capacity to respond to societal demands" (Salinas de Gortari 1989, 13, 18). Rather, sovereignty required "perpetual economic competitiveness" in world markets. As Salinas summed up: "Mexico will be able to strengthen its sovereignty through a stronger economy" (cited in Pastor 1990, 19).

Salinas and his team of technocrats believed that state-led capitalism, long the Mexican model of development, was no longer viable. State interventionism was in fact codified in articles 25 and 26 of the Mexican Constitution, and thus Mexico's "national sovereignty" prescribed a distinctive role and conception for the state. Given the historical and deeply entrenched Mexican view of national sovereignty, the initiatives taken by Salinas to internationalize the economy were nothing short of a historical watershed for the country. NAFTA was to be the centerpiece in a new strategy of developing a stronger Mexican economy and presumably a "stronger" sovereignty. Naturally, opponents to Salinas's economic policies, such as Cuauhtémoc Cárdenas, claimed that NAFTA and the economic opening amounted to a "renunciation by Mexico of its sovereign rights" (Cárdenas 1990, 117). In turn, Salinas characterized the *cárdenistas* as allies of those who seek to weaken national sovereignty (Salinas de Gortari 1990, 9–14). Still others argued that by constraining flows of information and free speech and by attacking NAFTA opponents as traitors to Mexico, Salinas was reasserting the tradition of presidential authoritarianism (Aguilar Zinser 1994, 124).

Salinas's radical redefinition of Mexican sovereignty was not really about sovereignty so much as sovereign capabilities. If the Mexican economy became stronger, through whatever policies, this was not increasing the legal authority of the sovereign state. However, it was increasing the resources of the state and thereby enhancing its ability to carry out functional tasks over which the sovereign state had authority. Thus, the economic strategies of the Salinas administration did not alter the legal basis on which Mexican sovereignty rested. But in the minds of Mexicans, sovereignty remained at the forefront of their concerns. "Concerns range from the denunciation that Mexico is surrendering its oil resources to U.S. interests, that the country is giving up its regulatory powers necessary to design development, industrial and agricultural policies, to the outright conviction that Mexico is, by virtue of NAFTA, falling under the political and strategic influence of Washington" (Aguilar Zinser 1994, 123).

However, the liberal foundations of NAFTA, in defining a minimal economic role for the state, did violate "the spirit though not necessarily the letter of the Mexican constitution." It did so "by calling into question the state's interventionist role in the economy and much of the state's regulatory authority over commerce, property rights, and investment" (Erfani 1995, 177). NAFTA extended U.S.-style property rights to Mexico in terms of investment, services, and intellectual property, which represented a significant departure from article 27 of the Constitution that authorized the sovereign state to be the final arbiter of property rights (Schlefer 1990; cited in Erfani 1995, 178). By altering its legal domain of authority, NAFTA modified the range of issue areas over which the state had legal control but did not lessen its sovereignty.

Beyond NAFTA's legal technicalities, it also contributed to unleashing more subtle and powerful forces of political and social change. As experts now recognize, trade policy inevitably influences domestic politics and sometimes even a state's political system. Salinas sought to introduce radical economic reforms without political change, but this treacherous path was made more daunting by the fact that he had won the 1988 presidential under highly questionable circumstances, so that when his administration came into office it was already confronted with problems of legitimacy. Such problems carried over into NAFTA negotiations, which were largely conducted by the government's "inner circle" ("La Comision Inter-Secretarial") and a few important sectors ("El Consejo Asesor del TLC") (Rubio 1992; Bulmer-Thomas, Craske, and Serrano 1994b, 209–11).

The rigidity of Mexico's political system and the government's failure to allow serious debate about NAFTA provided fuel for NAFTA opponents to push more vigorously for democratization, government accountability, and institutional openness (Aguilar Zinser 1994, 119). Economic opening often contributes to political liberalization, and, in the case of Mexico, with NAFTA came closer scrutiny of Salinas's political practices and increased pressures for institutional reforms (Delal Baer 1991). Salinas was banking on economic growth to ensure his legitimacy, but NAFTA was also creating more international attention on Mexican elections and human rights practices, which may have led the government to "allow" a few opposition victories in the early 1990s.

However, the 1988 elections, which nearly resulted in the victory of a leftist government, had also caught the attention of the United States, which recognized the importance of promoting economic stability and encouraging the process of political liberalization in Mexico. Mexico also edged closer to the United States by muting its criticism of the George H.W. Bush administration's invasion of Panama and pledging its support for the 1991 Gulf War, which was remarkable given Mexico's long-standing understanding with the United States that the two countries would "agree to disagree" (Ojeda 1976; Bulmer-Thomas, Craske, and Serrano 1994b, 221–22). Such radical changes in Mexico's traditional policies galvanized society to pressure Salinas to legitimize his new "openness" and alignment with the United States.

Salinas's redefinition of sovereignty, along with his historic shift toward the United States and commitment to NAFTA, initially generated only lukewarm support in Mexico. In 1992, 42 percent of Mexicans thought the free trade pact would benefit the country, but by 1995 support had declined to 20 percent.[11] Four years later, public opinion in Mexico was still declining, with more than 43 percent convinced that their parents had had a better standard of living 30 years before.[12] It had been a given that Mexico would have high adjustment costs after NAFTA went into effect,[13] but the events that followed the signing of NAFTA could not possibly have been foreseen. Still, it was not a coincidence that on the day NAFTA went into effect the Zapatista movement in Chiapas launched its uprising. The Zapatistas claimed the liberalization of trade under NAFTA, along with the revision of article 27 of the Constitution (which protected communally held "*ejidal*" lands), constituted a "death sentence for the indigenous people."

Political assassinations followed, along with massive capital flight, which left the country on the brink of disaster by the beginning of 1995. NAFTA had linked the United States and Mexico closer together, and the Clinton administration, along with the International Monetary Fund (IMF), went to great lengths to piece together a rescue package to save the Mexican peso and NAFTA. It has been suggested that because Clinton felt the need to bail out Mexico, NAFTA had compromised U.S. sovereignty. NAFTA had increased the interdependence between the two countries, but this had not affected U.S. legal authority, that is its sovereignty. Conversely, in 1995, Mexican public opinion polls showed that more than 60 percent of the population believed accepting financial aid from the United States endangered Mexico's national sovereignty.[14] Again, this was not really the case, although the substantial "conditionality" attached to IMF and U.S. loans did narrow the range of Mexico's sovereign authority, but Mexico clearly remained a sovereign state.

By "opening" its domestic economy under NAFTA, Salinas had also opened Mexican society to nongovernmental organizations (NGOs), MNCs, and international organizations, which brought information, new political values, and support for the domestic polity.[15] Salinas had aimed to implement "perestroika without glasnost," but his government soon discovered it is "much harder to maintain a political wall when the social and economic walls are coming down" (Pastor 1993, 24). Mexico's civil society had been slowly developing from the late 1960s, but with NAFTA and the changes of the early 1990s, its civil society began to become a viable and coherent force for the first time in history (Bilello 1996; Fox and Hernandez 1992). Through increasing international contacts, Mexico's civil society and international NGOs began pressing the state for serious political reforms related to environment, human rights, and democratic elections. As the international community was also paying close attention to Mexico's internal affairs after NAFTA, Salinas, and his successor Ernesto Zedillo, could no longer ignore such pressures. The Mexican state had to begin redefining its standards of legitimacy, so that its sovereignty was being transformed from a "national sovereignty" to a "constitutional sovereignty," even if Salinas and Zedillo did not recognize this process.

The most striking example of this change can be seen in Mexico's adoption of democratic reforms. Before NAFTA, the government of

Mexico refused to accept any type of international interference into Mexico, or from any other country, especially with respect to its political system. When the Inter-American Commission on Human Rights (IACHR) ruled that Mexico had to reform its electoral practices, the Mexican representative responded if a state allowed an international body to rule on the legality of its electoral procedures, "[that] state would cease to be sovereign." He added that by passing judgment on electoral processes, the IACHR was intervening in the state's sovereign affairs (OAS 1990, especially 543–61). Nonetheless, the IACHR ruled the Mexican government had ratified without reservation the treaties of the American Convention on Human Rights, which established the right to vote, and thus the Mexican government was responsible for the protection of these rights.[16] Growing concern about Mexico's human rights situation had also led Salinas in June 1990 to establish the National Commission on Human Rights, which happened to be just days before Salinas was to meet with George H. W. Bush to discuss NAFTA (Lutz 1993).[17]

Domestic NGO groups in Mexico pressed for democratic reforms as well as revisions to NAFTA.[18] Environmental groups pressured the Mexican government to adopt stricter codes,[19] while democratic organizations began to assert themselves effectively through a broad coalition known as the Alianza Cívica (Aguayo Quezada 1995). In essence, Mexican society, with help from the international community (Millett 1994; Chand 1997), was becoming an important actor in its own right and was forcing the state to redefine the terms of sovereign legitimacy. President Zedillo gave rhetorical support to Mexico's traditional "national sovereignty," citing that democracy cannot be imposed from outside.[20] But responding to external and internal pressures, Zedillo's electoral reforms allowed for much cleaner elections in 1997 and 2000, which enabled an opposition candidate to win the presidency for the first time in more than 70 years. By undermining its "imperial presidency" and invigorating domestic society (and linkages to the international community), NAFTA had helped to create the conditions for the possibly of an "electoral democracy" in Mexico, and in the process it had contributed to the first significant steps in the transformation of Mexican sovereignty.

INTEGRATION, INSTITUTIONALIZATION, AND SOVEREIGNTY

According to Salinas, NAFTA was about "economic, not political integration" (cited in Pastor 1993, 53), and to a certain extent he was correct. However, integration cannot occur without some minimal level of institutionalization, and this is necessarily political and relates to questions of sovereign authority. As Robert Pastor has noted, "The problem is how to relate sovereignty to integration, to unite the logic of politics with that of economics" (Pastor 1993, 105). NAFTA provides a legal framework to facilitate trade and investment, but as forms of integration go, NAFTA is minimalist. That is, NAFTA is a "free trade area" that involves the removal of tariff barriers.

By contrast, the European Union is an "economic union" where members have common standards and highly compatible economic and social policies, such as fiscal, industrial, regional, and monetary policies, the latter having led to the adoption of a common currency (Keohane and Hoffmann 1991; Peterson 1997). If the EU evolves into a "political union" which theoretically is the intent, it will be impossible to speak of its members as being sovereign for they will have common policies in areas like foreign policy and defense, which will have meant delegating their sovereign authority to supranational institutions. As a form of integration, NAFTA in no way compares with the EU. But then, the circumstances in North America differ from those in Europe. NAFTA is a work in progress and "deepening" or 'broadening' of NAFTA may eventually occur. Deepening would mean, for example, adopting common standards in areas like health, labor, and environment, and could theoretically entail an altering of sovereign rights in these functional areas. Broadening would involve an expansion of the NAFTA in terms of the areas to be covered in the agreement or in its membership. In neither case does this lessen the sovereign authority of its members.

Ultimately, how NAFTA affects state sovereignty depends on the legal authority of its institutions or "regulatory regimes." For example, the dispute settlement mechanism in NAFTA (chapter 19) represents a redistribution of regulatory functions (not redistribution of legitimate authority) defined in terms of a set of rules that apply equally to the three countries. Admittedly, how chapter 19 affects specific state institutions and domestic practices may vary in each of the countries,[21] and even though NAFTA allows, for example, for a majority of non-U.S. arbitrators to rule against the United States, the NAFTA mechanism does not require the United States to implement the decision (Abbott 1995, 185).

The three North American countries created NAFTA as a free trade agreement, with little or no interest in developing a political union, which would have required establishing regional institutions with extensive authority including effective enforcement mechanisms. NAFTA members wanted clear and precise rules to facilitate trade and investment but minimal authority in the regional institutions. Because of strong political sensitivities about sovereignty in each country, none would have considered the creation of a strong regional judicial body, for example, as exists in Europe, and if they had attempted to do so this would have raised important constitutional issues in each country (Abbott 2000, 519). The United States is particularly averse to the creation of a supranational authority, but Mexico also has opposed the establishment of such regional institutions (Abbott 1992, 931–32; Zamora 1997, 53–71).

Given that NAFTA was concerned primarily with trade and investment among private actors (multinationals), NAFTA's regulatory regimes were precise and transparent in order to reassure potential investors and traders in the three countries. Also demanded was precision in NAFTA rules by the national legislative bodies of Canada and the United States, because they were accountable to their private sectors. NGOs also exerted pressure on the two legislative bodies for transparent and precise rules. Canada's and the U.S. "constitutional sovereignties" influenced the nature and type of NAFTA rules and regulations that were adopted, clearly because of their need to respond to domestic polities.

The level of obligation created by NAFTA is also distinctive. As the United States was able to gain concessions from Canada and Mexico, it had an interest in ensuring a fairly high level of obligation to NAFTA's precise rules and terms of agreement, which would also serve to protect the interests of U.S. investors. Similarly, Canada and Mexico sought to limit U.S. nationalistic excesses by ensuring that the level of obligation to NAFTA would be high. But the level of obligation to NAFTA is lower than the in the EU, where "member states have arguably entered into an arrangement from which they are not entitled to withdraw" (Abbott 2000, 534). By contrast, NAFTA allows members to withdraw from the agreement, which reflects its creators' intent not to infringe on members' sovereignties.

Such flexibility in NAFTA, reflecting the sovereign sensitivities of its members, has resulted in a lack of "regional governance," which may ultimately prevent the development of regional political institutions or possibly the expansion of the accord to other countries (Pastor 2001). Given the strong sovereign identities of its members, as well as the lack of political motivation, it is hard to imagine NAFTA progressing very far in terms of political integration or high levels of delegation of political authority to regional institutions. The United States seemingly prefers to have, in effect, two bilateral relationships within NAFTA. This "institutional deficit" in the North American community may well protect the sovereignty of its members, but it creates problems of regulating and controlling cross-border flows between its members, be they in trade, investment, migration, drugs, guns, or pollution. In time, unregulated flows may contribute to the development of new regional mechanisms of regulation, which might result in a "multilayered institutional authority" like that in Europe. The presence of several semiregulatory institutions along the U.S.–Mexican and U.S.–Canadian borders indicates that some form of "multi-layered institutional authority" may already be emerging (Blatter 2001). If such an authority is not developed, not only may the economic benefits of NAFTA be jeopardized but there could be high social and political costs as well (Sánchez 1994, 112).

CONCLUSION

Although sovereignty is often linked to debates about the importance of NAFTA, much of this discussion mistakes sovereignty for national control or state capabilities. Sovereignty refers to a legal right, or legitimate authority, to make decisions governing the internal and externals affairs of a state. This legitimate authority has both domestic and international dimensions, which interact with each other and evolve over time.

With NAFTA, the three North American states significantly modified their relationships with each other: Border controls were relaxed; trade and investment rules were tightened; and guidelines on environment, labor, and retraining programs were prescribed. All three states gave up some degree of control over their domestic markets in addition to lessening the effectiveness of their policy tools, yet this is always the case when countries sign trade agreements. But increased interdependence does not mean a loss or gain in sovereignty. To suggest that the

United States, Canada, and Mexico are "more" or "less" sovereign than they were before NAFTA is to misunderstand the meaning of sovereignty as a set of legal rights. The sovereignties of the United States and Canada have not been affected by NAFTA. No binding legal rules were introduced in NAFTA that diminishes or enhances the sovereign authority of its members. NAFTA has, however, had an important effect on Mexican sovereignty in helping to transform the country's domestic standards of legitimacy and to increase the importance of international standards. Yet even this represents a change in the nature of Mexico's sovereignty, but does not entail an increase or diminution of sovereignty. For Mexico, this change can be described as a transformation from "national sovereignty" to "constitutional sovereignty."

Whether Mexico can sustain this process of constitutionalism remains to be seen. NAFTA has generated substantial benefits for all its members, but it has produced adjustment costs as well. This has affected migration, crime, and hardship on both sides of the U.S.–Mexican border. The lack of a defined supranational authority in NAFTA ensures that the three sovereignties will continue to maintain their traditional legal authority, but the "institutional deficit" also means it will be more difficult to address common problems, especially along the borders. The absence of a permanent mechanism of consultation for the three governments is a weakness in NAFTA (Carranza 2002),[22] but the priority of its members has been to protect their sovereignties, and they have managed to do so effectively. Sovereign sensitivities were important in the development of NAFTA and will play an important role in the evolution of NAFTA. Whether NAFTA's "institutional deficit" will be eventually corrected will depend upon whether its members continue to value sovereignty more highly than solutions to shared problems, problems they will continue to face in the coming years.

Notes

1. The quotation is from Elliot Abrams and is cited in Smith (1992, 19).

2. "Constitutional sovereignties" are often federal systems, but this does not contradict sovereignty, because states' rights are an embodiment of the principle of self-determination of a free people. For further discussion, see Wildhaber (1983, 432–35).

3. Krasner (1999b); for a critique of Krasner's position, see Philpott (2001).

4. This was after the United States kidnapped Humberto Alvarez Machain from Mexico in order to bring him to trial for alleged involvement in the 1985

murder of an agent of the U.S. Drug Enforcement Administration.

5. The U.S. position on international law is reflected in its attitude toward the International Court of Justice (ICJ). After helping to create the Court and gain acceptance by Congress of compulsory jurisdiction of the ICJ, the Senate added the Connally Reservation, which permits the United States to decide for itself which disputes fall under its domestic jurisdiction. See Keohane, Moravcsik, and Slaughter (2000, 473).

6. The Helms-Burton legislation punishes foreign firms that deal with Cuba. Helms-Burton is an egregious example of the extraterritorial application of U.S. law and was challenged by the European Union in the World Trade Organization. On this dispute, see Lowenfeld (1996).

7. Mexico also gained some concessions, e.g., on oil and finance, but these were more the result of the skill of Mexico's negotiators than the institutional form of its sovereignty.

8. These data are cited in Rugman (1994, 113).

9. Some Canadians also expressed concerns about "agricultural sovereignty," "political sovereignty," and "economic sovereignty," but these debates essentially echoed arguments made in the United States and Mexico. See Smith (1996, 39–68); Stairs (1996, 1–38); and Wonnacott (1994, 163–75).

10. The strategy of internationalizing its domestic market also led Mexico to join the Organization of Economic and Cooperative Development, the General Agreement on Trade and Tariffs, and the Asia-Pacific Economic Cooperation forum.

11. "TLC: Un balance en la opinión pública," *Este País*, no. 58, 1996, 29; cited in Dresser (1998, 252).

12. This figure is taken from a 1999 *Wall Street Journal* poll, cited in Conger (2001, 62).

13. Many of Mexico's adjustment problems are analyzed in Poitras (2002).

14. *Reforma*, January 30, 1995; cited in Hoebing, Weintraub, and Delal Baer (1996, 81).

15. E.g., in 1984 there were 4 human rights organizations in Mexico, but by 1991 there were 60 and by 1993 there were approximately 200; see Sikkink (1993, 430) and Lutz (1993, 79).

16. Franck (1992, 46); and Fox and Roth (2001). The ratification of the treaties was also, as Mexico's former ambassador to the OAS, Santiago Onate, stated in Cerna (1997, 208), an exercise in Mexico's sovereign prerogatives.

17. The U.S. Congress began hearings on human rights in Mexico, and there was concern among Mexicans the hearings might derail NAFTA. See also Chabat (1991).

18. Societal groups wanting to renegotiate NAFTA formed the Red Mexicana de Accion Frente al Comercio. See Kingsover (2001, especially chap. 4).

19. The environmental groups included Grupo de los Cien, Asociación de Grupos Ambientalistas, Red Fronteriza de Salud Ambiental, and Red Mexicana de Acción Frente al Tratado de Libre Comercio. See Sánchez (1994, 98).

20. See the Zedillo quotes in Gonzalez and Haggard (1998, 316–17).

21. The binational panels created by chapter 19 has changed how the United States determines unfair trading practices that merit countervailing duties. Chapter 19 has also contributed to domestic judicial reform in Mexico because of competition from international tribunals. Both of these examples are cited in Goldstein et al. (2000, 391).

22. NAFTA institutions can also be faulted for their absence of democratic accountability. On this point, see Stein (2001).

References

Abbott, Frederick M. 1992. Integration without Institutions: The NAFTA Mutation of the EC Model and the Future of the GATT Regime. *American Journal of Comparative Law* 40: 917–48.

———. 1995. *Law and Policy of Regional Integration: The NAFTA and Western Hemispheric Integration in the World Trade Organization System.* London: Martinus Nijhoff.

———. 2000. NAFTA and the Legalization of World Politics: A Case Study. *International Organization* 54, no 3: 519–47.

Aguayo Quezada, Sergio. 1995. A Mexican Milestone. *Journal of Democracy* 6, no. 2: 157–67.

Aguilar Zinser, Adolfo. 1994. Is There an Alternative? The Political Constraints on NAFTA. In *Mexico and the North American Free Trade Agreement: Who Will Benefit?* ed. Victor Bulmer-Thomas, Nikki Craske, and Mónica Serrano. New York: St. Martin's Press.

Avery, William P. 1998. Domestic Interests in NAFTA Bargaining. *Political Science Quarterly* 113, no. 2: 282–305.

Barkin, J. Samuel, and Bruce Cronin. 1994. The State and the Nation: Changing Norms and the Rules of Sovereignty in International Relations. *International Organization* 48, no. 107: 107–30.

Bilello, Suzanne. 1996. Mexico: The Rise of Civil Society. *Current History* 95, no. 598: 82–87.

Blatter, Joachim. 2001. Debordering the World of States: Towards a Multi-Level System in Europe and a Multi-Polity System in North America? Insights from the Border Regions. *European Journal of International Relations* 7, no. 2: 175–210.

Bulmer-Thomas, Victor, Nikki Craske, and Mónica Serrano, eds. 1994a. *Mexico and the North American Free Trade Agreement: Who Will Benefit?* New York: St. Martin's Press.

———. 1994b. Who Will Benefit? In *Mexico and the North American Free Trade Agreement: Who Will Benefit?* ed. Victor Bulmer-Thomas, Nikki Craske, and Mónica Serrano. New York: St. Martin's Press.

Cárdenas, Cuauhtémoc. 1990. Misunderstanding Mexico. *Foreign Policy* 78 (spring): 113–30.

Carranza, Mario. 2002. Neighbors or Partners? NAFTA and the Politics of Regional Economic Integration in North America. *Latin American Politics and Society* 44, no. 3: 141–57.

Cerna, Christine M. 1997. International Law and the Protection of Human Rights in the Inter-American System: Rethinking Sovereignty in an Age of Regional Integration (in Spanish). In *El papel del derecho internacional en América: La soberanía nacional en la era de la integración regional.* Mexico City: Autonomous National University of Mexico and American Society of International Law.

Chabat, Jorge. 1991. Mexican Foreign Policy in 1990: Electoral Sovereignty and Integration with the United States. *Journal of Interamerican Studies and World Affairs* 33, no. 4: 1–25.

Chand, Vikram K. 1997. Democratisation from the Outside In: NGOs and International Efforts to Promote Open Elections. *Third World Quarterly* 18, no. 3: 543–61.

Conger, Lucy. 2001. Mexico's Long March to Democracy. *Current History* 100: 58–64.

Delal Baer, M. 1991. North American Free-Trade. *Foreign Affairs* 70, no. 4: 132–49.

Delal Baer, M., and Sidney Weintraub, eds. 1994. *The NAFTA Debate: Grappling with Unconventional Trade Issues.* Boulder, Colo.: Lynne Rienner.

Deudney, Daniel H. 1995. The Philadelphia System: Sovereignty, Arms, Control, and the Balance of Power in the American States-Union, Circa 1787–1861. *International Organization* 49, no. 2: 191–228.

Dresser, Denise. 1998. Post-NAFTA Politics in Mexico: Uneasy, Uncertain, Unpredictable. In *The Post-NAFTA Political Economy: Mexico and the Western Hemisphere,* ed. Carol Wise. University Park: Pennsylvania State University Press.

Erfani, Julie A. 1995. *The Paradox of the Mexican State: Rereading Sovereignty from Independence to NAFTA*. Boulder, Colo.: Lynne Rienner.

Foreign Affairs. 1994. Responses: "The Fight over Competitiveness." *Foreign Affairs* 73, no. 4: 186–203.

Fowler, Michael Ross, and Julie Marie Bunck. 1995. *Law, Power, and the Sovereign State*. University Park: Pennsylvania State University Press.

Fox, Gregory H., and Brad R. Roth. 2001. Democracy and International Law. *Review of International Studies* 27, no. 3: 327–52.

Fox, Jonathan, and Luis Hernandez. 1992. Mexico's Difficult Democracy: Grassroots Movements, NGOs, and Local Government. *Alternatives* 17, no. 2: 165–208.

Franck, Thomas M. 1992. The Emerging Right to Democratic Governance. *American Journal of International Law* 86: 46–91.

Goldstein, Judith, Miles Kahler, Robert O. Keohane, and Anne-Marie Slaughter. 2000. Introduction: Legalization and World Politics. *International Organization* 54, no. 3: 385–99.

Gonzalez, Guadalupe, and Stephan Haggard. 1998. The United States and Mexico: A Pluralistic Security Community? In *Security Communities*, ed. Emmanuel Adler and Michael Barnett. New York: Cambridge University Press.

Gruben, William C., and John Welch. 1994. Is NAFTA More Than a Free Trade Agreement: A View from the United States. In *Mexico and the North American Free Trade Agreement: Who Will Benefit?* ed. Victor Bulmer-Thomas, Nikki Craske, and Mónica Serrano. New York: St. Martin's Press.

Hoebing, Joyce, Sidney Weintraub, and M. Delal Baer, eds. 1996. *NAFTA and Sovereignty: Trade-Offs for Canada, Mexico, and the United States*. Washington, D.C.: CSIS.

Jackson, Robert H. 1990. *Quasi States, Sovereignty, International Relations, and the Third World*. Cambridge: Cambridge University Press.

Kelsen, Hans. 1969. Sovereignty and International Law. In *In Defense of Sovereignty*, ed. W. J. Stankiewicz. New York: Oxford University Press.

Keohane, Robert O., and Stanley Hoffmann, eds. 1991. *The New European Community: Decision-Making and Institutional Change*. Boulder, Colo.: Westview Press.

Keohane, Robert O., Andrew Moravcsik, and Anne-Marie Slaughter. 2000. Legalized Dispute Resolution: Interstate and Transnational. *International Organization* 54, no. 3: 457–88.

Kingsover, Ann E. 2001. *NAFTA Stories: Fears and Hopes in Mexico and the United States*. Boulder, Colo.: Lynne Rienner.

Knight, Franklin W. 1992. The State of Sovereignty and the Sovereignty of States. In *Americas: New Interpretative Essays*, ed. Alfred Stepan. New York: Oxford University Press.

Krasner, Stephen D. 1999a. Globalization and Sovereignty. In *States and Sovereignty in the Global Economy*, ed. David A. Smith, Dorothy J. Solinger, and Steven C. Topik. New York: Routledge.

———. 1999b. *Sovereignty: Organized Hypocrisy.* Princeton, N.J.: Princeton University Press.

Krugman, Paul. 1994. Competitiveness: A Dangerous Obsession. *Foreign Affairs* 73, no. 2: 28–44.

Lowenfeld, Andreas F. 1996. Agora: The Cuban Liberty and Democratic Solidarity (Libertad) Act, Congress, and Cuba: The Helms-Burton Act. *American Journal of International Law* 90: 419–34.

Lutz, Ellen L. 1993. Human Rights in Mexico: A Cause for Continuing Concern. *Current History* 92, no. 571: 78–82.

Lyons, Gene M., and Michael Mastanduno, eds. 1995. *Beyond Westphalia? State Sovereignty and International Intervention.* Baltimore: Johns Hopkins University Press.

Mayer, Frederick W. 1998. *Interpreting NAFTA.* New York: Columbia University Press.

Meyer, Lorenzo. 1998. La Construccion Histórica de la Soberanía y del Nacionalismo Mexicanos. In *México ante el Fin de la Guerra Fría*, ed. Ilán Bizberg. Mexico City: El Colegio de México.

Middleton, K. W. B. 1969. Sovereignty in Theory and Practice. In *In Defense of Sovereignty*, ed. W. J. Stankiewicz. New York: Oxford University Press.

Millett, Richard. 1994. Beyond Sovereignty: International Efforts to Support Latin American Democracy. *Journal of Interamerican Studies and World Affairs* 36, no. 3: 1–23.

Murphy, Alexander B. 1996. The Sovereign State as Political-Territorial Ideal. In *State Sovereignty as Social Construct*, ed. Thomas J. Biersteker and Cynthia Weber. Cambridge: Cambridge University Press.

OAS (Organization of American States). 1990. *Annual Report of the Inter-American Commission on Human Rights 1989–1990.* Washington, D.C.: OAS General Secretariat.

Ojeda, Maro. 1976. *Alcances y límites de la política exterior de México.* Mexico City: El Colegio de México.

Pastor, Robert A. 1990. Post-Revolutionary Mexico: The Salinas Opening. *Journal of Interamerican Studies and World Affairs* 32 (fall): 1–22.

———. 1993. *Integration with Mexico: Options for U.S. Policy.* New York: Twentieth Century Fund.

———. 2001. *Toward a North American Community: Lessons from the Old World for the New.* Washington, D.C.: Institute for International Economics.

Pastor, Robert A., and Jorge G. Castañeda. 1988. *Limits to Friendship: The United States and Mexico.* New York: Alfred A. Knopf.

Peterson, John. 1997. The European Union: Pooled Sovereignty, Divided Accountability. *Political Studies* 45: 559–78.

Philpott, Daniel. 1999. Westphalia, Authority, and International Society. *Political Studies* 47: 566–89.

———. 2001. Usurping the Sovereignty of Sovereignty. *World Politics* 53, no. 2: 297–324.

Poitras, Guy. 2002. *Inventing North America: Canada, Mexico, and the United States.* Boulder, Colo.: Lynne Rienner.

Putnam, Robert. 1988. Diplomacy and Domestic Politics: The Logic of Two-Level Games. *International Organization* 42, no. 3: 427–60.

Reich, Robert. 1991. *The Work of Nations.* New York: Alfred A. Knopf.

Robert, Maryse. 2000. *Negotiating NAFTA: Explaining the Outcome in Culture, Textiles, Autos, and Pharmaceuticals.* Toronto: University of Toronto Press.

Rubio, Luis. 1992. *¿Cómo va a afectar a México el Tratado del Libre Comercio?* Mexico City: Fondo de Cultura Económica.

Rugman, Alan M. 1994. North American Economic Integration and Canadian Sovereignty. In *The NAFTA Debate: Grappling with Unconventional Trade Issues,* ed. M. Delal Baer and Sidney Weintraub. Boulder, Colo.: Lynne Rienner.

Salinas de Gortari, Carlos. 1988. *Ideas y compromisos.* Mexico City: National Executive Committee of the Institutional Revolutionary Party.

———. 1989. *Primer informe de gobierno 1989.* Mexico City: Presidencia de la Republica.

———. 1990. *Segundo informe de gobierno 1990.* Mexico City: Presidencia de la Republica.

Sánchez, Roberto. 1994. NAFTA and the Environment. In *Mexico and the North American Free Trade Agreement: Who Will Benefit?* ed. Victor Bulmer-Thomas, Nikki Craske, and Mónica Serrano. New York: St. Martin's Press.

Schlefer, Jonathan. 1990. History Counsels "No" on NAFTA. *New York Times,* June 12, F11.

Shinoda, Hideaki. 2000. *Re-Examining Sovereignty: From Classical Theory to the Global Age.* New York: Palgrave.

Sikkink, Kathryn. 1993. Human Rights, Principled Issue-Networks, and Sovereignty in Latin America. *International Organization* 47, no. 3: 633–59.

———. 1997. Reconceptualizing Sovereignty in the Americas: Historical Precursors and Current Practices (in Spanish). In *El papel del derecho internacional en América: La soberanía nacional en la era de la integración regional.* Mexico City: Autonomous National University of Mexico and American Society of International Law.

Smith, Murray G. 1996. Canada and Economic Sovereignty. In *NAFTA and Sovereignty: Trade-Offs for Canada, Mexico, and the United States,* ed. Joyce Hoebing, Sidney Weintraub, and M. Delal Baer. Washington, D.C.: CSIS.

Smith, Peter. 1992. The Political Impact of Free Trade on Mexico. *Journal of Interamerican Studies and World Affairs* 34, no. 1: 1–26.

Stairs, Denis. 1996. The Canadian Dilemma in North America. In *NAFTA and Sovereignty: Trade-Offs for Canada, Mexico, and the United States,* ed. Joyce Hoebing, Sidney Weintraub, and M. Delal Baer. Washington, D.C.: CSIS.

Stein, Eric. 2001. International Integration and Democracy. *American Journal of International Law* 95, no. 3: 489–534.

Thompson, John H. 1992. Canada's Quest for Cultural Sovereignty. In *North America without Borders? Integrating Canada, the United States, and Mexico ,* ed. Stephen J. Randall. Calgary: University of Calgary Press.

Weintraub, Sidney. 1996. NAFTA and U.S. Economic Sovereignty. In *NAFTA and Sovereignty: Trade-Offs for Canada, Mexico, and the United States,* ed. Joyce Hoebing, Sidney Weintraub, and M. Delal Baer. Washington, D.C.: CSIS.

———. 1997. *NAFTA at Three: A Progress Report.* Washington, D.C.: CSIS.

Wildhaber, Luzius. 1983. Sovereignty and International Law. In *The Structure and Process of International Law ,* ed. R. St. J. MacDonald and Douglas M. Johnston. Amsterdam: Matinus Nijhoff.

Wonnacott, Ronald J. 1994. Canada's Role in NAFTA: To What Degree Has it Been Defensive? In *Mexico and the North American Free Trade Agreement: Who Will Benefit?* ed. Victor Bulmer-Thomas, Nikki Craske, and Mónica Serrano. New York: St. Martin's Press.

Zamora, Stephen. 1997. Allocating Legislative Competence in the Americas: Early Experience under NAFTA and the Challenge of Hemispheric Integration (in Spanish). In *El papel del derecho internacional en América: La soberanía nacional en la era de la integración regional.* Mexico City: Autonomous National University of Mexico and American Society of International Law.

CHAPTER FOURTEEN

DEMOCRACY IN MEXICO

José Woldenberg Karakowsky

The past 10 years in Mexico's political life can be summarized as a series of political and legal transformations that have laid the groundwork, actually generated over several decades, to gradually alter the monochromatic authoritarian regime inherited from the Mexican Revolution to a pluralistic, fully democratic one. The process culminated in 1996 in the construction of the institutional and legal structure that had begun following the 1977 political reform. Thanks to the vision of the government and the parties represented in the Congress, the norms to guarantee transparent elections and respect for the right to vote established in the Constitution have promoted the development of political plurality, balanced political contests, and strengthened the party system in support of democratic competition.

Because of those innovations, the 1997 elections, which took place under the protection of the new laws, brought about substantive changes in both the political map and the operation of the institutions of the republic: the right of the citizens to elect the chief of government of Mexico City was recognized—this person previously was appointed by the president of the republic—and this resulted in the election of a candidate of the opposition Party of the Democratic Revolution (Partido de la Revolución Democrática, PRD) to lead the most important city in the country. Because of the correlation of forces in 1997, the official Institutional Revolutionary Party lost its absolute majority in the chamber of deputies for the first time in the history of modern Mexico.

The dizzying changes of the past decade had their corollary in the elections of 2000, which not only confirmed the advances of many earlier local elections but also saw a candidate from the opposition win the majority in the presidential election without generating conflict or pos-telectoral instability, even though neither he nor his party obtained sufficient votes to count on a majority in the Congress.

The new design of the political map had immediate consequences on the general operation of the state as it accentuated the division of powers and the legislative branch came to be the counterweight to the executive, as formally contemplated in the Constitution of 1917, and even in that of 1857. Together with clean elections and a high turnout, Mexico showed what it was: a diverse, pluralist country, and that federalism had not been in vain.

Even if these are the most visible results of a political process that began with the 1977 political opening, it is pertinent to point out that the democratic transition is not isolated in time from other important social and economic changes that contributed to redesigning the country as a whole. Decades of modernization and recurrent crises, and significant transformations in policy, demography, and culture, combined to make outdated the model of government that arose from the Mexican Revolution, bringing the need to construct an open economy and a democratic political system whose validity is not in doubt today. The peculiarity of the Mexican transition lies precisely in the fact that both strategic reforms took place within a continuum of modernization and via an extremely complex process without creating a constitutional crisis. On the contrary, the changes were accomplished in an evolutionary manner and without infringing on the rule of law, despite resistance to the path of modernization. That empirically verifiable reality goes against the determinist hypothesis that democratization is the product of the advancement of an economic model that does not take into account the historical analysis of the political situation.

CONDITIONS FOR THE DEMOCRATIZATION OF MEXICO

By virtue of the peculiarities of the dominant political regime in Mexico in the twentieth century, democratizing efforts were primarily concentrated in giving validity to citizens' votes deposited in the voting urns and in creating and improving the rules of electoral institutions capable of representing and producing legitimate pluralities in a society in the process of modernization and growth. Unlike what happened during the 1980s and 1990s in a majority of cases throughout Latin America, where democracy appears as a restoration, a return to earlier political and social experiences, Mexico took a different course. To some extent, Mexico's transition resembles more the transitions of Eastern Europe where the democratic process leads to the creation of a political reality that had not been experienced before. Nevertheless, there was one distinctive and crucial difference in the Mexican transition: Mexico had the historical advantage of having a republican and constitutional framework that had been in effect since 1917, and even earlier.

However, the missing element to attain democracy in Mexico was to reform all aspects of the electoral process: organization, legal framework, and regulatory institutions. The initial objective was to eradicate fraudulent practices that annulled or distorted the popular vote of the citizenry by creating a legal framework, enabling the emergence of the nation's true political plurality without artificial restrictions.

Another important difference in the Mexican case is that the presence of strong parties with national influence was, in large measure, a creation of that very transition. It is true that the party that grew out of the Mexican Revolution—the Institutional Revolutionary Party (Partido Revolucionario Institucional, PRI)—was present, but the remaining parties, specifically Partido de Acción Nacional (PAN), had a weak following in many parts of the country. An eloquent example of the absence of electoral competition and an illustration that the Mexican political system did not reflect the actual political life of the country was the presidential election of 1976, in which only one candidate was registered, that of the PRI, who won the contest unopposed with 100 percent of the votes cast, although this happened in a country in political turmoil. The 1970s in Mexico were preceded by the student movement of 1968, which was violently suppressed by the government, and was followed by an increasing and new social mobilization embracing trade unions, agrarian organizations, universities and institutions of higher learning, and cultural centers, as well as by the eruption of urban and rural guerrilla warfare. To a great extent, this guerrilla activity stemmed from the 1968 repression, and a conviction that political change could take place only by violent means. It is important, therefore, to emphasize the contrast with 1976, when the country was affected by a growing climate of confrontation, convulsion, and agitation, and the presidential election was little more than a formality.

It can be said that for decades the Mexican electoral structure did not represent political realities. Diverse groups and movements, dissidents or nonconformists, did not have a national voice, and there was neither coherence nor coordination; true national political parties did not exist.

The weakness of electoral life was a product of the absence of parties and national organizations able to present an alternative and a real challenge to the governing coalition. As Pereyra (1990, 132) has written, one of the symptoms, perhaps "the main symptom of PRI hegemony lies in the nonexistence of national parties that may have grown outside the main trunk of the Mexican revolution."

Ideology, mechanisms, and the laws associated with their operation had made it possible for the PRI to embrace almost all aspects of Mexican life: institutions and political forces; business groups; middle-class organizations; and farm organizations—including diverse and even conflicting popular trends deriving from *cardenismo*, such as revolutionary nationalism, or from segments inclined to capitalist and market-driven modernization. Within this enormous coalition, fundamental politics were practiced by appointing the right people to the right positions at all levels (federal, state, or municipal); and deciding who assumed legislative posts. That was the modus operandi of the hegemonic party, with the president in the vortex of the pyramid.

Because of this, democratic transition in Mexico had to solve two basic and complementary questions: consolidating the development of political parties and giving them national reach; and creating of laws and institutions to regulate their application. The first objective consisted of creating a framework to enable new parties to operate without obstacles or artificial restrictions. The second was to eliminate all fraudulent practices that were used to render the popular vote useless.

The revolutionary state, heir of the armed movement, modernizer, embracer, and hegemonic, operated on the basis of two premises: absence of competing parties; and nonexistence of open electoral rules. That reality began to change drastically in 1977. That year began what can be called the "structure of change" that was to come, starting with an initiative of political reform, which opened the gates to the free development of organized parties and their participation in the electoral world. The reform permitted the incorporation of political parties with conditional registry into the electoral arena, including the more significant political forces of the Mexican left wing, which until then had been alienated. Political parties were defined in the Constitution as "entities of public interest" that permitted recognition of their legal rights as integral parts of the state. The reform created deputies elected under proportional representation, thereby injecting pluralism into the Chamber of Deputies and providing representation in other federal entities; and parties acquired a voice in the media and access to public funds, having established that national political parties would be entitled to take part in local and municipal elections. This allowed constitutionally protected and legitimate alternatives to be represented throughout the country.

This would be the basis upon which the democratizing process would be developed. The reform was a protective umbrella with a very important characteristic—it was devoted not only to players who already occupied a place within the legal system but also to those who had never been inside. When enacted, these changes provoked an enormous debate, resistance, and had a great public impact. The intention behind the reform was very simple: On the one hand, it aimed to strengthen existing organizational options, but on the other it allowed the entry of new forces that had been traditionally excluded from the electoral process.

Thanks to this initial opening, diverse groups with diverging ideologies, previously closed off from electoral life, were gradually incorporated into mainstream political life. Electoral competition became the focal point of political life of the country. Starting in 1977, a democratizing process that would become unstoppable took shape by strengthening the parties and inspiring new leaps of democratic expansion, which crystallized in successive changes in the electoral system.

Between 1977 and 1996, Mexico went through a broad cycle of electoral reforms, which dealt with six large topics: (1) party leadership, (2) strengthening the legislative process, (3) electoral institutions, (4) the electoral rule of law, (5) rules for electoral competition, and (6) political reform in the country's capital. The construction of an electoral framework with the support of the main political parties on these points made it possible for Mexico to attain its aspiration of becoming a true political democracy.

THE STAGE OF INTENSE DEMOCRATIZATION

It is impossible to comprehend the dynamic of the change that took place in the past decade without going back to the 1988 elections, which marked a definite eruption of pluralism and the decline of single-party rule. Two circumstances came together to underscore the significance of those elections: the economic crisis of the so-called lost decade with its deplorable effects on the living conditions of the population; and a split in the PRI, the "official party," the greatest it had suffered since

1952. The immediate effects were felt when Cuauhtémoc Cárdenas, propelled by the National Democratic Front (Frente Democrático Nacional, FDN), a broad center–left coalition, received 30 percent of the popular vote in the 1988 presidential election.

Under these conditions, the voting results in 1988 produced these innovations in the political system, despite the justified questioning of the transparency of the electoral process: a new partisan electoral framework with three large competitive parties; entry into the Senate of the first four senators not supported by the PRI (senators for Micho-acán and the Federal District were backed by the FDN); and a new composition of the Chamber of Deputies—260 from the PRI and 240 from opposition parties. However, a questionable electoral process and the lack of confidence in its transparency, which later would extend to federal elections, demonstrated the need to undertake a redesign of the electoral framework to make it possible for a baseline to be reestablished to ensure a level playing field and a minimum climate of confidence and coexistence among the parties. And precisely because this found its expression at a time of political plurality, it was a task that the government could neither undertake nor put into effect unilaterally.

Notwithstanding the tense atmosphere that existed among the principal political forces of the country (PRI, PAN, and FDN), and particularly between the FDN and president-elect Carlos Salinas de Gortari, there was a consensus to move toward an electoral reform that would expand guarantees of transparency in the electoral process and, with it, resolve differences through a legal and nonviolent channel. There can be no doubt that this was one of the fundamental aspects to assure the advancement of the democratizing process in the coming years.

At the beginning of the 1990s, the task to construct a new electoral framework was begun. Thus, in 1990, the Federal Electoral Institute (Instituto Federal Electorai, IFE) was created, whose main political function was to remove the lack of confidence in the electoral process and instead give it credibility, and to install the IFE as the sole legitimate method to resolve political disputes for government and legislative positions.

With the new electoral authority, the elections of 1991 contrasted positively with those of three year earlier. The large participation of the citizenry (about 70 percent of the electorate) was accomplished in an environment of transparency and electoral legitimacy. At the federal level, the PRI experienced a remarkable recovery, and PAN became the second political force. The Party of the Democratic Revolution, in which the leaders of the FDN and the Mexican Socialist Party converged, competed in its first election; the result was worse than what had been attained by the coalition of five organizations three years earlier.

With this new advantage in the polls, the government initiated one of the most significant operational changes of the decade when President Salinas de Gortari proposed ambitious changes in the Constitution that would radically modify the country's political and social panorama. Mexico was entering a stage of accelerated economic reform that had been initiated in 1985 by President Miguel de la Madrid.

The proposed economic reform, nevertheless, had profound political implications. Whether desired or not, it was also a change in negotiating guidelines and political stability that had been based on a hegemonic presidential regime. The change then appeared on all fronts—from the top, obtaining support from the executive branch; in a market-oriented system, which paradoxically undermined the basis of support that typified presidential power; and from many other flanks, including a society that had grown weary of a clientalistic status quo and corporatist policy.

It should be remembered that just 10 years ago, when NAFTA was approved (by a Congress with a PRI majority), the great subject still pending in Mexico was the use and abuse of presidential power and the absence of competitive parties enabling the Congress to act as a counterweight to the executive power, and that federalism had become a reality. In the electoral field, it was still necessary to demonstrate that the elections were to choose who should govern; it was necessary to instill confidence in the fundamental democratic method.

THE POLITICAL ANSWER TO THE ECONOMIC CRISIS AND VIOLENCE, 1994–1996

In 1994, the political situation required an extraordinary effort by all parties to strengthen and validate laws, institutions, and the viability of electoral functions in an atmosphere filled with violence, and which culminated in the uprising of the Zapatista army on January 1 of that year, the day on which NAFTA came into existence. In July, the main political parties signed a series of agreements and undertook commitments that were seen as a "contribution to the peace process" and which could be validated only by impartial elections accepted by all.

Basically, the parties agreed to support the independence of the electoral authority. They agreed to give up their vote in the decisionmaking institutions and instead to incorporate "citizen counselors" with voice and vote. A series of legal amendments were fashioned to increase the reliability of the electoral process by strengthening guarantees of transparency, giving equal access to the media by the parties, and preventing the use of public resources and programs to favor a given party or candidate. The ominous signs of violence in the country increased with the assassination of the PRI candidate for the presidency, magnifying risks of violence and underscoring the responsibility of the different political actors to maintain the electoral contest within peaceful channels.

Thanks to legal guarantees, the behavior of the political parties, and the positive response of the electorate, voting day in 1994 passed with absolute normality. The 1994 elections were a crucial event for modern Mexico: On August 21, 1994, 78 percent of registered citizens, 35 million Mexicans, exercised their right to vote. The PRI won the presidential election with 50.1 percent of the vote, PAN came in second with 26.6 percent, and the PRD was third with 17 percent.

The 1994 elections demonstrated that agreements among the three large national political parties were possible, and that their national leaders could offer positive results to their supporters following the exhausting multilateral negotiations that had taken place. The elections also demonstrated that the three large political parties were able to withstand a tense political atmosphere, and the citizenry demonstrated by their enthusiasm that they supported the democratic reforms. An extraordinarily active and strong multiparty system came into existence and began to guide future Mexican political life. However, what was most important is that the 1994 electoral changes responded to what could have been an ominous and confrontational outcome, with great potential for future violence. The crisis was averted, due largely to the operation of the parties, and no one should forget their contribution to the peaceful coexistence within the country.

Just a few weeks after it came into power, the new government had to confront a drastic devaluation of the national currency, which revealed inadequacies and contradictions of the economic policy followed during the previous decade, and that macroeconomic balances did not correspond to the microeconomic dynamics of the country's productive activity. The 1995 economic contraction was even more severe than the one that occurred in 1983, when the debt crisis erupted; unemployment reached unprecedented levels, and private debt (due to an increase in interest rates) put the Mexican financial system at risk.

Despite the urgent measures adopted to contain and deal with the crisis, the government continued to move forward on electoral reform in such a way as to fulfill the "double mandate" that Octavio Paz alluded to in the 1994 elections for "change and stability. One lesson of these elections was to show the spirit of the majority was for priority for democratic reforms" (Paz 1994, 302).

In 1996, the political parties agreed to vast reforms in institutions and electoral laws in Mexico following one of the most prolonged and intense political negotiations of recent years. It was a difficult and long process that did not end with the hoped-for consensus but nevertheless did produce an array of fundamental amendments to advance Mexico's democratic consolidation. There can be no doubt that these changes were the basis for legal, fair, and transparent elections.[1]

There were six topics around which consensus of the parties was forged in 1996. First, the total autonomy of electoral entities was institutionalized, and since then the electoral authority has enjoyed full independence from the government. The eight electoral counselors and the president of the council, the only members with a vote in the supreme organ of the IFE, were elected by consensus of the political parties in the Chamber of Deputies. There was a double arrangement: The government removed itself from the electoral organization, passing it to persons enjoying the confidence of all political parties; and each political party and each parliamentary faction in the Congress had a nonvoting representative in the highest organ of the electoral directorate so that that each could follow, step by step, all the work of the electoral authority.

Second, the electoral tribunal, the organization in charge of settling legal controversies, underwent important modifications. The nomination of magistrates by the president of the republic with consent of the Senate was abandoned, and instead the Senate voted on the appointment of magistrates after they were proposed by the Supreme Court of Justice.

Conversely, the tribunal was no longer limited to dealing only with federal problems but could be appealed to in cases the local conflicts; its control, in other words, was extended to the oversight of the constitutionality of state electoral authorities. Electoral qualification became fully jurisdictional.[2] Finally, the law added new defense procedures, new channels for electoral or political appeals both for citizens and political parties.

Third, the electoral reform changed the legal regime of political parties. The requirement to be represented in the Congress was increased (only those parties with a vote greater than 2 percent were entitled to enter the Chamber of Deputies), and a new way was created for organizing different factions through political groupings. This is a two-way system in that it permits access for new political options, and an exit vote for those proposals that do attain minimum citizen support.

Fourth, the formulas for representation in the Congress were adjusted to better balance the relationship between votes and seats. The formula in the Chamber of Deputies, in which there are 500 legislators (300 elected in single districts by relative majority, and 200 by proportional representation) was altered to assure that no party could have a number of deputies elected under both systems more than 8 percent greater than its national voting percentage.

Greater pluralism was injected into the Senate. It has a total of 128 members. In each of the 32 entities, two senators are elected under the principle of relative majority and a third is assigned to the first minority. The remaining 32 senators are elected by proportional representation by a vote at the national level.

Fifth, electoral competition was opened in Mexico City by means of the direct election of its chief of government, and the powers of the Federal District legislative assembly was expanded based on the 16 political delegations into which the capital is divided.

Sixth, competitive electoral conditions were improved. Public financial resources to the parties were sharply increased, as was their access to electronic media. In addition, the resources were distributed more equitably. The electoral authority had better instruments to investigate, audit, and check party campaign expenditures. Improvements of competitive conditions in 1996 were perhaps the most visible and decisive of the reforms, in effect closing the lengthy cycle of legal and constitutional changes in search of a more competitive system of government.

The new electoral structure was the stage that, in 1997, led to a democratic contest producing a political reality unheard of until then: a Chamber of Deputies without a majority, becoming a counterweight to the executive power. Clearly, this is an example of how changes in the electoral system affected other spheres and generated other changes in the system of government.

The federal elections of July 2, 2000, took place on the same legal basis. Thanks to the confidence in the electoral structure and transparency, a succession of groundbreaking democratic firsts occurred on that day in a country with an authoritarian tradition. For the first time in more than seven decades, a candidate who had not been sponsored by the governing party was victorious; for the second time, the president of the republic and his party did not attain an absolute majority in the Chamber of Deputies, and, as a result, each law was a new calculation and was the outcome of agreement between at least two of the three main political parties. Nor did the Senate elected in 2000, to remain until 2006, have an absolute majority.

Mexico's political transformation is highly significant. The reforms provide recognition of parties as entities of public interest that are engaged in electoral competition that has gradually gained strength and has made the electoral process the compulsory arena for all relevant political forces in the country. From those developments, there was a new turn in reinforcing the rights of the parties; from absolute distrust to the creation of credible and legitimate institutions; from a single party to a legitimate plurality of political parties; from isolated victories of parties not affiliated with the government to effective and systematic alternation in hundreds of municipalities and federal entities; from a qualified majority in all parliamentary activities to counterweights and balances coming from divided governments in many states and then at the federal level; and, the culmination, in the alternation of the federal executive, thus redesigning the map of political representation in the republic.

More than a reform confined to electoral procedures, or a "liberalization" that does not change the arrangement of power, Mexico was able during the past two and one-half decades to modify the sensitive wellsprings of national life (see Becerra, Salazar, and Woldenberg 2000). Thanks to that history of gradual and agreed legal changes, Mexico today is a democracy—nothing more but nothing less.

DEMOCRATIC CONSOLIDATION

The issue is not to recognize and celebrate what has been achieved, because in history there are no final destinations. However, I believe that it is indispensable not to lose sight of unquestionable characteristics of Mexico's political life in order to assess the present and future of the Mexican democracy. Just to mention some of the most outstanding current realities: We have pluralism in Mexico today; parties with solid roots; a participatory citizenry; real electoral competition; credible elections; alternation of power at all levels; separation of powers; expanding federalism; and an active supervision of public life by the media and civil society.

At the final stages of its democratic transition, Mexico does not have to face the task of creating a new constitutional order to give meaning to the changes already accomplished—as the countries of Eastern Europe had to do more than a decade ago. However, there is a need to make a series of adjustments to renovate political practices and to grease the operation of institutions in order to improve their day-to-day efficiency, and to achieve better performance by political actors, especially the parties, the legislature, and the government. In other words, there is a new agenda on the table that derives directly from democratic reality, and not from lack of accomplishment.

It is time to recognize that though many in Mexico, in academia and the parties, worked to revamp the electoral process, little attention was given to examining the requirements for efficient government in an open economy and with a new institutional and democratic foundation. The democratizing emphasis was understandable, but it is now clear that to speak of Mexico's future implies speaking of matters pertaining to the exercise of government power. To put it in terms used by Camou (2001), the time has come to discuss openly the points of equilibrium necessary to establish stability and the maintenance of democracy, that is, between stability and change, liberty and order, expansion of political participation and efficiency in decisionmaking, and government obligations and civic responsibility.

These elements are not exclusive, but they must be judged and placed in an institutionally coherent and functional design for guarantees of democracy to work in their two dimensions—on the one hand, to ensure the functioning of institutions; and on the other, to ensure that these institutions meet the needs of society, especially in overcoming poverty and inequality. Both sides of the equation translate into "good government," and there are great challenges on both sides. I take the liberty in the following comments to outline my view of some of the requirements relevant to the quality of Mexican democracy.

The State of Law

The first requirement that arises refers to the state of law. It can be stated with confidence that none of the problems that must be addressed in the consolidation of democracy in Mexico is as profound as the absence or nonapplication of the law in many areas fundamental for the harmonious existence of a society. Alarming levels of insecurity, corruption, and impunity persist to this day; the authorities hesitate to apply the law, and citizens resist complying with it. This is an enormous shortcoming that one can identify daily and that could undermine living together democratically.

The nature of the problem that Mexico faces in this matter exceeds the mere judicial or legal sphere because the use of legalism is transmitted by compliance with the contents of the law. In other words, it is necessary to understand that establishing an authentic democratic state unquestionably requires reforming the judicial power and other institutions of preventive and procurement justice. In reality, we are dealing with a problem of a social and general nature that transcends mere legal dimensions and should be considered in its political dimension as a matter essential to the reform of the state and the renewal of the ethical standards upon which political culture rests.

During the past few years, a true "juridical transition" has taken place, which has been accompanied by a strengthening of the judicial power and greater public awareness of the importance of law and civil rights, and that has also been accompanied by the creation of autonomous representatives of human rights, as well as greater public sensitivity to different abuses of rights and freedoms of citizens. But reality categorically confirms that we are still very far from having compliance with the law as a constant. It is not a question of weaknesses of a code or the errors of those in charge of administering the law, or the concentration of corruption or impunity, but rather to underscore the bad general situation of what some experts call "the state of legality."

If a state of laws finds its legitimacy in complying with the laws and in the existence of institutional mechanisms to prevent some agents from enjoying exceptional privileges and advantages compared with the rest of society, it is obvious that we are still very far for this state of affairs in most spheres of our social life. In other words, even with democratic advances, the absence of a true state of law gives rise to what scholars have called a "low-intensity" citizenship. The theme of a state of law revolves, in good part, around the possibility that in Mexico citizenship can be fully expressed and, with that, that there are guarantees of social and civilized standards for living together.

Citizenship and Democratic Political Culture

The proper functioning of a democratic regime requires as an axis a new policy that establishes order in the activity of the state and requires the education of citizens so that they can play an active role in society. In other words, in a democracy, policy must be an activity that is eminently of the people and not the exclusive responsibility of a minority that takes on the role of "representative" of the people; that is, it is necessary for the citizen to recognize himself or herself as the subject of policy and not as the passive object of acts of the government.

On this point, there is a deficit that should not be underestimated. Data from opinion polls about citizenship culture and civic education taken by IFE and the Government Secretariat (Secetaría de Gobernación) reveal that there are serious problems in the perceptions citizens have about values, institutions, and democratic legitimacy (Flores and Meyenbereg 2002; Secetaría de Gobernación 2002). An authoritarian and intolerant idea of social relationships is often prevalent, as well as extremely low levels of knowledge about politics. There is a tendency to value the attributes of a "strong leader" more than those who know and always apply the laws. High proportions of citizens questioned do not read newspapers and do not listen to radio or television news, but they summarily judge the negative qualifications of the Congress, parties, and politics in general. The public dimension generally appears to be like an alien universe and unreliable. As a result, there is a sort of antagonism between the effective electoral participation of the citizenry proved in elections and their basic notions about democracy that seems to be paradoxical or, at least, not irrelevant and meriting attention.

The presence of those traits in the national political culture shows that political change does not produce linear or uniform modifications in the perception of the public, and that there is nothing automatic in the formation of a favorable consciousness of institutions and of the subject of democracy itself. For this reason, parties, the electoral authority, the media, the government, and above all, the educational structure must help to strengthen democratic values.

The self-renewal of democratic habits is possible in countries with long democratic traditions and popular participation, but in the case of a recent democracy, such as the Mexican one, it would be unjustifiable to assimilate the fragility of the democratic culture as the expression of a nonexistent electoral routine or to the disenchantment with the representative model. Precisely because Mexico is a heterogeneous, diverse, and underdeveloped country, where modern forms of political organization coexist or combine with community democracy, democratic tradition, and an authoritarian heritage, it is indispensable not to give up the task of raising the level of an appropriately democratic civic culture so that all citizens can participate, having full knowledge of the process. Indeed, the disposition of citizens to participate is negatively correlated with their evaluation of the propriety of political activity; hence the more politics is discredited, the more it is seen as inherently corrupt and mean spirited, and the less fertile the soil is for roots of the democratic system to take hold.

The Responsibilities of Political Parties

Mexico had parties that knew how to channel and promote democratization, and as a result the country needs its parties to be capable of taking charge of a complex democratic life. Democratic consolidation will not progress unless it is by the disposition and work of the political parties themselves. In a democracy, the parties, as legitimate representatives of society, must be in the vanguard to put in place the visions of the government and country that will be decided finally by the citizens. But there is no construction that deserves or merits adoption without diagnosis or projects, without serious and rigorous proposals about the country and its problems and its opportunities. Seen in the proper light, democratic quality depends on the quality of the parties and its politicians, and the legislative and governmental programs. A political life without ideas can generate only an empty and vulnerable democracy. Parties have in their hands the privilege and responsibility to support democracy through their proposals and daily actions.

Parties are the main political protagonists, and like it or not, they are the ultimate mentors of democracy and civic education. That is why it is not only a task of the parties to start a productive dialogue and to maintain civilized and respectful interaction but also to look beyond the momentary electoral calculation to agree on the reforms they have diagnosed as fundamental for the institutional and economic development of the country. For example, political parties in Mexico as a whole share the idea that broad fiscal reform is necessary to strengthen public finances because the country has a weak tax collection system—fiscal pressure, that is, tax collection as a percentage of gross domestic product is hardly half the average for countries belonging to the Organization for Economic Cooperation and Development (OECD 2001)—and nevertheless the political parties have not managed to agree on the design of this reform.

Other topics that political parties have identified as fundamental to the country's development and that are part of the so-called structural reforms are energy reform, for which the discussion is about to take place as to how to expand investments, especially in the electricity sector; and labor reform, to introduce flexibility into the labor market while guaranteeing labor rights. These are just some examples of an agenda for which the programmatic elaboration is at the disposition of the parties in order to translate interparty agreements into laws.

The present and future of democracy, and with it the millions of people making up Mexican society, are in the hands of those who are directly responsible for the Mexican state and the political parties. Therefore, they have, as do few other institutions, an irreplaceable role, and therefore the behavior of the parties cannot be seen as an academic exercise but rather as a permanent task of strong pulling together to generate a rigorous virtuous circle with a higher quality of partisanship.

The Responsibility of the Media

The question of the media has a universal dimension and is present in the deliberations of all modern democracies. Because of this, the role of the media is not a random or secondary topic in the Mexican agenda. In fact, because there is nothing in modern democratic politics that does not pass through the mass media, the media have an indispensable task in consolidating changes attained and improving democratic existence. The media are not a substitute for schools in their educational function, but the media exert influence on the civic culture of the citizenry, who ultimately embody democratic values.

In the strictly political field, the current challenge lies in consolidating democracy; not in showing that alternation is possible. Rather than guaranteeing plurality, the media face the challenge of ensuring high-quality professionalism. It would be desirable if the constitutional obligation that guided the work of the electoral authority to ensure clean and credible elections could also orient the work of the media to ensure the certainty of legality, independence, impartiality, and objectivity.

Government Management

One of the greatest expectations of democracy is to create efficient and able governments, ready to listen and attend to the needs of society and to set a course supported by the broadest possible consensus, and always in touch with the legislative power that is the counterweight and the necessary collaborator of the executive branch. That is not the starting point of Mexican democracy, but it is today one of the pending tasks that we must begin to tackle.

As stated at the beginning of this chapter, the transition coincided in time with structural adjustments, and it was conditioned by the country's modernization during the second half of the twentieth century, a period replete with economic crises as well as deep structural reforms that reshaped political relationships between society and the state. By virtue of that dialectic, the old rules of political contest were disrupted, creating imbalances and new needs in society, the economy, politics, law, the world of labor and agriculture, which process ended by eroding the arrangements based on presidential government and a singular political culture that had prevailed for many years without leading to serious setbacks. That process also modified the government's operating logic, and the emergence of a democratic order modified the government's relations with the citizenry and disrupted the way in which governmental political decisions were made and implemented.

The consolidation of democracy implies the end of discretional options in dealing with the country's affairs. The presence of a Congress fully autonomous from the executive power and the existence of an opposition make it impossible to use the old formula to govern. The issue is not only a question of banishing authoritarianism but also of how to perform public duties efficiently and effectively.

It seems evident that Mexico must fill the gap left by presidential economics with new practices and laws that go beyond the need to stimulate genuine administrative reform and more transparent governing techniques. The key probably lies in assuming that there is a need not only to develop a series of new government policies but also to end uncertainty and to ensure government efficiency. It is necessary to construct a lasting national coalition in support of consistent policies for the state that go beyond changes in the management of the country that democracy already guarantees in Mexico.

Notes

1. A detailed revision of constitutional changes and the 1996 electoral law may found in Becerra, Salazar, and Woldenberg (1997).

2. By virtue of the content of this book, it is pertinent to point out for a better understanding by a reader more familiar with the United States system than with the Mexican system, that there are three large original differences between the two electoral systems, which in principle determine the evolution and their present form. The first and more evident of these differences has to do with the method of electing the president in each country; whereas Mexico has adopted the direct way, the United States since 1787 has an system of indirect election through an electoral college. Even though it is possible to deliberate about the validity of a system such as the American in modern societies, the fact is that for over 200 years this has been demonstrated to be functional and useful for North American society, and it is obvious that the political forces of that country continue to support it.

The second great difference between the two models lies in the historical confidence factor. Elections in Mexico evolved on the basis of a lack of confidence in the process, in the authorities, and between adversaries, to the point of producing a complex law with many safety devices to check discretional decisions in electoral processes. The Unites States, until now, has been able to handle the political competition based on the confidence of the electorate, the protagonists, and the authorities, and this has produced flexible laws giving the authorities room to maneuver.

The third difference has to do with the legal design of the system. Mexico has opted for centralizing norms and electoral contest in a code and in a federal organ, such that IFE organizes federal elections on the basis of rules that are identical for all states and municipalities in the country. In the United Sates, the electoral organization is decentralized and states, and in many cases even counties, determine their own rules respecting such sensitive issues as registration of voters and even the design of the ballots themselves.

References

Aguilar Camín, Héctor. 2000. *México: La ceniza y la semilla.* Mexico City: Cal y Arena.

Becerra, R., P. Salazar, and J. Woldenberg. 1997. *La reforma electoral de 1996.* Mexico City: Fondo de Cultura Económica.

———. 2000. *La mecánica del cambio político en México.* Mexico City: Cal y Arena.

Camou, Antonio. 2001. Gobernabilidad y democracia. In *Cuadernos de divulgación y cultura democrática.* Número 6. Mexico City: Instituto Federal Electoral.

Cordera, Rolando. 2000. *Crónicas de la adversidad.* Mexico City: Cal y Arena.

Flores, J., and Y. Meyenberg. 2002. *Ciudadanos y cultura de la democracia, encuesta nacional.* Mexico City: Instituto Federal Electoral and Universidad Nacional Metropolitana.

Gómez Tagle, S., and M. E. Valdés. 2001. *La geografía del poder y las elecciones en México.* Mexico City: Instituto Federal Electoral.

Lujambio, A. 2000. *El poder compartido: Un ensayo sobre la democracia mexicana.* Mexico City: Océano.

Molinar Horcasitas, J. 1991. *El tiempo de la legitimidad: Elecciones, autoritarismo y democracia en México.* Mexico City: Cal y Arena.

OECD (Organization for Economic Cooperation and Development). 2001. *Tax Burdens in OCDE Countries.* Paris: OECD.

Pascual Moncayo, Pablo. 1995. *Las elecciones federales de 1994.* Mexico City: Cal y Arena.

Paz, Octavio. 1994. Las elecciones: Doble mandato. *Vuelta*, no. 215, October.

Pereyra, Carlos. 1990. *Sobre la democracia.* Mexico City: Cal y Arena.

Salazar, Luis. 1998. *1997: Elecciones y transición a la democracia en México.* Mexico City: Cal y Arena.

———, ed. 2001. *México 2000: Alternancia y transición a la democracia.* Mexico City: Cal y Arena.

Secretaría de Gobernación. 2002. *Encuesta sobre ciudadanía y prácticas democráticas.* Mexico City: Secretaría de Gobernación.

Silva Herzog-Márquez, Jesús. 1999. *El antiguo régimen y la transición en México.* Mexico City: Planeta Joaquín Mortiz.

Woldenberg, José. 2002. *La construcción de la democracia.* Mexico City: Plaza y Janés.

CHAPTER FIFTEEN

NORTH AMERICAN INTEGRATION

A SPONTANEOUS PROCESS OR
A DRIVEN ENTERPRISE?

Jesús F. Reyes-Heroles

The concept of North America has gradually evolved during the past decade and now carries much more than a geographical reference. Today, the mention of North America immediately elicits thoughts of an economic subregion of the world, of a sizable market, and of three countries embedded in a process of growing integration.

A key element of the relevant issues is to determine the nature and trends of the underlying (structural) transformations that have driven and will drive the process of integration in the future. One can reasonably claim that, up to now, the benefits of free trade, investment, and migration flows, all derived from the demographic "complementarity" among the three societies, have been the dominant forces driving the process.

However, other factors have emerged and are rapidly acquiring increasing importance in shaping North American integration. The power of technological change and the transformations it endlessly introduces in transportation, communications, and the information industries is the best example of these new forces. Another is regional security, especially after the terrorist attacks of September 11, 2001.

A distinct but critically important issue is the adequacy, in terms of responsiveness and speed, of institutional change to support and even foster integration. Is ongoing institutional change keeping pace with structural integration? Have we devised sufficient tools to deal with the inevitable sources of conflict? And most important, have we made enough progress in building an understanding of the North American

The author thanks Alejandro Hope for his invaluable input during the writing of this chapter.

reality, in making public opinion understand the issues, and in shaping a shared view about the joint future of the three countries?

Finally, the discussion about North American integration frequently lacks a sense of purpose. Does attention to these matters respond to an intellectual interest to understand them? Or is this attention an actual policy debate likely to generate positive momentum? As long as integration is considered a means to accelerate economic growth, and by doing so reduce disparities between incomes of citizens in the three countries, the interest in North American integration will respond to the need to view it as an instrument for promoting regional prosperity. This chapter considers the questions of the terms, nature, pace, and prospects of this process, with the view that further integration will occur to the benefit of the three economies and that institutions will need to speed up their adjustment.

THE DOMINANT FACTORS

Every day, it becomes more evident that the pace, scope, and direction of North American integration responds to the evolution of a set of strong "structural" variables that underlie and determine the medium-term trend of the process. Government policies and institutional reform follow, after changes already have taken place. Like it or not, in matters of North American integration, real transformations lead and governments follow.

If trade issues are considered, it is useful to remember that in 1990, three years before the North American Free Trade Agreement was enacted, a high trade concentration (between the three signatory countries) did already exist. Of their total exports that year, 65.6 percent of Canada's and 68.8 percent of Mexico's had the United States as their destination. On the U.S. side of the equation, the situation was similar; considering total U.S. imports, 14.8 percent were from Canada and 6.1 percent from Mexico.

Foreign direct investment (FDI) followed a similar pattern. In 1990, more than 15.8 percent of U.S. FDI went to Canada and 2.2 percent to Mexico. Still, the United Kingdom received more U.S. investment than the two NAFTA partners. Of the total assets of foreign companies in Mexico in 1990, more than 72 percent of the total were owned by U.S. companies. The United States was also the leading investor in Canada.

With regard to migration, reality has also been leading institutional development. In 1990, there were 0.8 million persons born in Canada and 6.5 million born in Mexico living in the United States. This means that of the persons born in Canada and Mexico, 2.7 percent and 7.9 percent lived in the United States even before NAFTA. If the descendants of these persons are considered, they add up to a significant proportion of the total U.S. population.[1] This number was increasing during the early 1990s, when the yearly flow of Mexicans migrating to the United States was on the order of 300,000 in net terms. Today, the Mexican-born population is 12.4 million, and the population of Mexican origin is 20.6 million.[2]

Traditionally, financial transactions among the three countries have been substantial. This is also a good example about how reality precedes institutional development. The most obvious example is the remittances of Mexicans. In 1990, these remittances represented 4.4 percent of the total inflows in Mexico's current account. This share increased to 5.2 percent in 2002 and amounted to about 17.3 percent of Mexican oil exports. Despite the relative magnitude of these transfers, it was not until 1999 that actions were taken to reduce the substantial charges that were charged for these transactions.[3] And it was not until 2003 that a joint United States–Mexico initiative to reduce these abusive practices came into being.[4]

The degree of interconnection between the U.S. economy and the Canadian and Mexican economies was already very strong in the pre-NAFTA era. Figure 15.1 shows the very strong correlation between the growth of the U.S. gross domestic product (GDP) and GDP growth in Canada and Mexico. Actually, NAFTA contributed to the increase in these correlations. In the case of Canada, the changes was from 0.98 pre-NAFTA to 0.99 percent for the period starting in January 1994.

For Mexico, the correlation increased from 0.76 to 0.94. It is evident that this summary measure captures an ample array of business interconnections and networks in North America, which were very substantial even before NAFTA formally encouraged trade and investment relationships.

In energy, there has been little progress since the late 1970s, when Mexico became an important supplier of crude oil to the United States (in 1981, Mexico was the largest supplier to the United States). The direct interconnection of the Mexican grid with the U.S. grid is not significant except for the Baja California–California region, and it has not advanced substantially over the past decade. Some developments are worth mentioning. First, a growing share of electricity is generated in

Figure 15.1. Correlation of Canadian GDP Growth to U.S. Growth (percent)

Pre-NAFTA

Percent

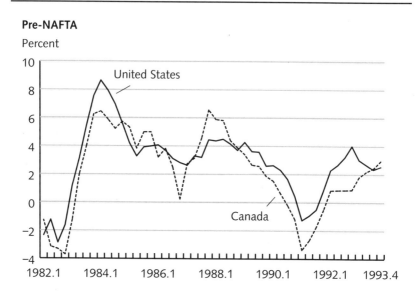

Post-NAFTA

Percent

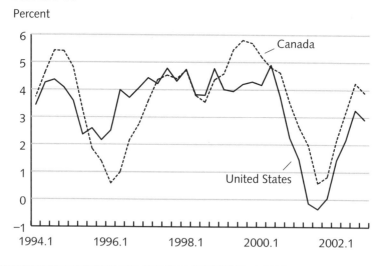

Source: Estimated by Grupo de Economistas y Asociados on the basis of data from U.S. Bureau of the Census and Statistics Canada.

Note: 1982.1 = first quarter of 1982, etc.

Mexico by private companies in total generation (28 percent). U.S. (and Canadian) corporations have been taking part in this process. Second, there is an increasing number of pipeline interconnections between the United States–Canada system and that of Mexico. This made possible growing north–south flows of natural gas; Mexico's imports of natural gas reached $3,260 million in 2002 (figure 15.2).

THE EFFECTS OF NAFTA

NAFTA represents the historically single most important institutional development in the relationships among Canada, Mexico, and the United States. It fostered trade and investment relationships, it introduced side agreements on labor and the environment, and it brought about an ample array of noneconomic benefits.

Although the roots for these relationships among the three countries were already there before NAFTA, the agreement provided a framework that made their growth easier. However, it is a fact that the agreement left some critical issues out, such as the movement of people and the natural integration of the regional labor markets, as well as oil (on the Mexico–United States front), and cultural goods and services (on the Canada–United States side). It also did not consider allocating funds to develop infrastructure in the most backward regions of North America, a feature that has been underscored by its critics, especially in Mexico. In justice, probably NAFTA would not be there if any one of the three countries had pressed more on any one of those issues.

Despite these shortcomings, NAFTA clearly sped up two key interactions: trade and investment. Bilateral trade among the three countries expanded substantially. Exports from Canada and Mexico to the United States increased from 65.6 and 68.8 percent of total exports to 87.4 and 89.1 percent (table 15.1).

NAFTA's effect on migration is unclear. Its impact on increasing FDI may have helped mitigate migration to the United States. However, during the initial stage of adjustment, when some firms closed down as a result of the 1994–95 financial crisis and because they could not compete, some economic activities were damaged and layoffs occurred, and this might have added pressure to migration flows. Probably the most significant effect on migration came a few years later, when NAFTA's impact on the Mexican agricultural sector materialized. As a result of depressed international prices of grains, as well as of increased imports

Figure 15.2. Correlation of Mexican GDP Growth to U.S. Growth (percent)

Pre-NAFTA

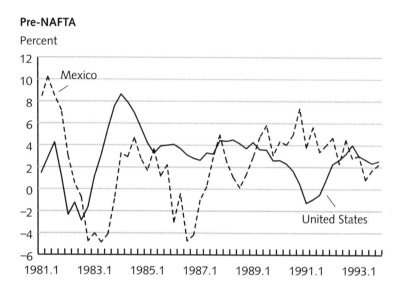

Post-NAFTA

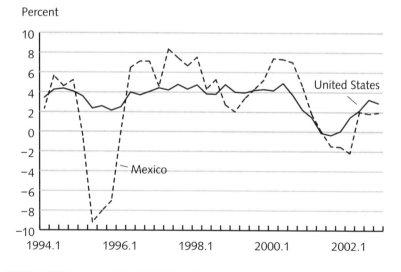

Sources: Data from U.S. Bureau of the Census and Instituto Nacional de Estadística, Geografía e Informática.

Note: 1981.1 = first quarter of 1981, etc.

Table 15.1. Key Pre- and Post-NAFTA Indicators

Indicator	Pre-NAFTA (1990)	NAFTA (2002)
Exports to United States as percentage of total exports		
Canada	65.6	87.4
Mexico	68.8	89.1
U.S. imports as percentage of total imports from		
Canada	14.8	18.2
Mexico	6.1	11.6
Imports from United States as percentage of total imports		
Canada	66.1	62.6
Mexico	65.6	63.4
U.S. foreign direct investment as percentage of total		
In Canada	16.1	8.3
In Mexico	2.4	6.1
Mexican-born persons living in United States		
Absolute (thousands)	4,300	12,360
As percentage of Mexico's population	5.3	12.7
Canadian-born persons living in United States		
Absolute (thousands)	745	678
As percentage of Canadian population	3.0	2.1

Sources: Banamex; Instituto Nacional de Estadística, Geografía e Informática; Bureau of Economic Analysis; U.S. Bureau of the Census; Statistics Canada.

of corn, beans, and wheat, the incomes of farmers declined sharply, thus exerting pressure on rural–urban–U.S. migration (table 15.2).

This sharp decline in prices, in the context of a lack of effective programs to support peasants and farmers' incomes in Mexico, and in the context of an economic slowdown, explains why the exodus of Mexicans to the United States continued under NAFTA during the 1994–2003 period. Migratory flows have continued as a result of a lack of sufficient jobs and low incomes in the communities that traditionally

Table 15.2. Price of Basic Grains, 1993 and 2002 (dollars per bushel)

Grain	1993	2002	Percent change
Corn	3.04	2.33	−23.36
Beans	6.98	5.66	−18.91
Wheat	3.92	5.08	29.59

Source: U.S. Department of Agriculture.

expel migrants. In addition, during this decade new flows emerged, as in the cases of Oaxaca and Veracruz. Mexican GDP per capita increased only 3.8 percent a year during the period of 1994–2002. The implementation of two key government programs to ameliorate rural poverty, Procampo and Alianza para el Campo, did not receive enough financial resources, and the productive reconversion of agriculture was limited.

So many factors intervene in shaping migratory flows that there is no compelling evidence about the net effect of NAFTA on Mexican migration. The bottom line is that yearly net migration showed a slight tendency to increase during the decade and that now two out of three migrants are from urban areas. NAFTA and the mix of Mexican policies have not reduced migration.

NAFTA also produced good results in two other fronts: macroeconomic convergence and "cementing" market reforms in Mexico. With regard to macroeconomic convergence, locking the prices of domestic goods to international prices provided a favorable context for prudent fiscal and monetary policies (table 15.3).

A recent development of great relevance for the future of energy markets in North America is the increase of Mexico's imports of natural gas, due to insufficient investment in Mexico and the substantial increase in demand as a result of the gradual development of distribution infrastructure and, more important, the shift to gas-burning thermoelectrical plants for environmental reasons. It is estimated that in 2006 of the total electricity generated in Mexico, 47.9 percent will be based in natural gas (as compared with only 17.6 percent in 1996), most of it imported from Canada through the United States (table 15.4).

Table 15.3. Macroeconomic Convergence

Measure	1993			2003		
	Canada	Mexico	U.S.	Canada	Mexico	U.S.
Fiscal deficit (percentage of GDP)	−5.9	−0.7	−3.8	−0.9	−0.5	−1.0
Inflation (percent change in consumer price index)	1.8	8.0	2.7	2.9	4.4	2.3
Interest rate (percentage of one-month Treasury bill)	4.8	15.5	3.0	3.3	7.3	1.3
Exchange rate (yearly percentage depreciation)	5.8	4.6	n.s.	−10.2	3.2	n.s.
Monetary expansion	8.2	7.3	10.2	7.7	11.5	8.0

Sources: Grupo de Economistas y Asociados, based on data from Instituto Nacional de Estadística, Geografía e Informática; U.S. Bureau of the Census; and Statistics Canada.

Note: n.s. = not significant.

In addition to the direct and obvious economic benefits deriving from free trade, there are other noneconomic advantages. First, there is a correlation, somewhat contested but nevertheless significant, between the opening of markets and the development of democratic regimes. This has been a clear trend over the past decade, both in Eastern Europe and Latin America. In theory, free trade and free markets stimulate market forces, enhance economic opportunities, increase available information to society, constrain bureaucratic discretion in decisionmaking, and make politicians and officials more accountable to domestic and international actors. By doing these things, free trade should contribute to democratic practices. Free trade is not the main driving force behind democratization. But under certain circumstances, it does facilitate and stimulate the process of democratic change and consolidation.

Table 15.4. Fuels Used for Electricity Generation

Type of Fuel	1996 TJ/day	%	2002 TJ/day	%	2006 TJ/day	%	2011 TJ/day	%
Fuel oil	1,910.9	65.9	2,184	50.9	1,565	33.1	1,069	17.3
Natural gas	508.7	17.6	1,420	33.1	2,260	47.9	3,656	59.1
Diesel	25.3	0.9	27	0.6	27	0.6	35	0.6
Coal	453.3	15.6	662	15.4	870	18.4	1,425	23.0
Total	2,898	100.0	4,293	100.0	4,722	100.0	6,184	100.0

Source: Ministry of Energy (SENER).

Note: TJ = terajoule.

To an extent, global trade stimulates accountability and therefore can contribute to the reduction of one of the most damaging problems for economic growth and public morale: corruption. The interconnection of markets and enhanced transparency, which comes with trade liberalization, can become critical elements for reducing discretionary powers and economic rent seeking, both of which are well-known sources of corruption.

Free trade has also contributed directly to a lessening of corruption. As multiple firms from various nations compete to get access to domestic markets, both for investment opportunities and trade deals, free trade contributes to make the procedures of international transactions more transparent and homogeneous. The room for bribery and corruption can diminish to a certain extent when traders do not have to obtain import licenses or to negotiate the terms of FDI with government officials.

For years, political scientists and economists have argued that free markets can, in some contexts, stimulate democratic change. However, the link between free trade and enhanced transparency has been less evident. The Mexican case is a good example of how deregulation reduces the scope for discretionary decisions. Privatization helps to eliminate economic rents for the bureaucracy. Policies that encourage

competition can diminish the scope for monopolistic profits and practices, which in turn reduces the risk for a takeover of the regulatory authorities.

Democratization, which can flourish when markets are opened,
translates into a more balanced division of powers, an increased capacity of the legislative branch to oversee the executive branch, and into
stronger demands on the judiciary to enforce the law. Freedom of the
press, sometimes enhanced by globalization, can become another
source of oversight for the behavior of economic and political agents.

No doubt, free trade has implied some costs as well, at least in the
short run. Adjustments are needed both in specific sectors and firms.
Sometimes they are concentrated in a particular region that endures
the pain of economic restructuring. Because gains for consumers and
producers are scattered around and the costs of adjustments usually
fall on a few firms and activities, benefits are difficult to portray while
the costs become an easy story for special interest groups and the media. The mobilization of Mexican peasants and farmers early this year is
a prime example. One should not be discouraged by these natural difficulties but instead transform them into an item on the agenda.

Since Mexico entered the General Agreement on Tariffs and Trade in
1986, engaged in a unilateral opening of import markets until 1993
and, finally, the onset of NAFTA in 1994, the country has been the recipient of the economic and noneconomic benefits of trade liberalization. Yet the costs should not be taken lightly: The difficult adjustment
faced by many sectors in Mexico has led to a barrage of bad press directed at NAFTA and NAFTA-related policies, like privatization, and has
transformed North American integration into a lightning rod for every form of discontent. Over the long run, these problems can produce
a gradual erosion of the pro-NAFTA consensus in all three countries
and, in a worst-case scenario, derail the enterprise.

THE FUTURE

The set of underlying forces behind North America's integration
evolves over time. Some of the factors continue acting, although with
different intensities and modalities, while new ones emerge or become
more relevant.

Forces leading to further economic integration are still strong.
There are multiple opportunities for increased trade. The degree of
openness of the three economies can continue to rise, especially in the

Table 15.5. Trade Openness, 2002 (percent)

Country	Imports/GDP	Exports/GDP	Total trade/GDP
Canada	36.6	40.9	77.6
Mexico	26.5	25.2	51.7
United States	13.3	9.3	22.6

Sources: Instituto Nacional de Estadística, Geografía e Informática; Banco de México; U.S. Bureau of the Census; Canadian Department of Foreign Affairs and International Trade.

United States (table 15.5). The margin for further import penetration may be exhausted in some markets (e.g., the case of blue jeans in the United States), but in others there is room for further trade expansion among the three economies. The institutional framework established by NAFTA will continue to allow for this. However, caution needs to be exerted to prevent some reversals; the case of the Mexican grain markets is probably the best example in this regard. For those cases, more effective programs to support reconversions are needed and should receive special attention.

With regard to investment flows, most of the opportunities still lie ahead. The relative scarcity of capital in Canada and especially in Mexico, as compared with the United States, is a reality. In Mexico, the ratio of capital to worker is still a fraction of the equivalent number in its two NAFTA partners. In addition, yearly gross capital formation per worker in Mexico is a fraction of that in its two NAFTA partners. For example, in 2001 Canada added $36,267 per worker and the United States added $54,916, while Mexico only added $3,058 (table 15.6). Yearly flows of $12 to $15 billion in FDI to Mexico are insufficient to reduce these differences during the next two decades. Even the goal of the Vicente Fox administration of $20 billion per year seems too low. However, the experience of the past few years indicates that more domestic reforms are needed to attract the volume of FDI required to have a significant impact on capital deepening and growth. This is an issue for which more decisive and effective action is needed.

Even if the idea of constituting trilateral funds to finance programs of infrastructure development resembling the model followed by the European Union is discarded, creative thinking is needed to find a

Table 15.6. Gross Capital Formation per Worker

Year	Canada	Mexico	United States
1990	39,077	1,479	33,706
1995	31,523	1,254	40,717
2000	37,381	3,126	56,160
2001	36,267	3,058	54,916

Sources: Grupo de Economistas y Asociados, based on data from Organization for Economic Cooperation and Development; Instituto Nacional de Estadística, Geografía e Informática; U.S. Bureau of the Census; and Statistics Canada.

North American version to increase investment in infrastructure that could work in the North American political and institutional environment. The need for substantial transfers is so strong that sooner or latter the three countries will face the need to find a solution to this. An expansion of the mandate and resources of the North American Development Bank would be a move in the right direction.

Obviously, if sufficient capital (private or governmental) does not flow to Mexico, South–North income differences will endure and migration will continue or even increase. The forces arising from the demographic complementarity between Mexico and the United States are so strong that it is hard to imagine institutional arrangements capable of deterring migration without exacerbating tension in the Southern border of the United States, which in turn would contaminate the overall process of integration (figure 15.3).

In the medium term, with a growing U.S. economy, the number and skills of the U.S. population will not match the jobs needed. More young and relatively unskilled workers will be needed. In addition, only a continuous and rapid expansion of the U.S. economy will generate the resources to sustain the pensions of the baby boomers.

The United States needs more young people to support its aging population. At the same time, with current investment levels, Mexico cannot provide well-paid jobs to its population. However, this will gradually change over time, as birth rates decrease even more in Mexico and there is a surge in better-paying jobs as a result of higher FDI.

Figure 15.3. Mexico–United States Demographic Complementarity

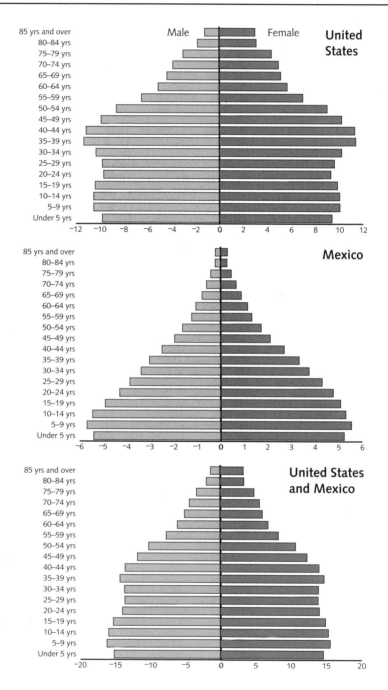

Under what modality and at what pace can labor markets be incorporated into the integration process? A lesson gained under duress is that a comprehensive and far-reaching strategy, such as the one proposed by the Mexican government in early 2001, is doomed to fail. Even under conditions when the U.S. economy has the capacity to absorb more immigrants into productive jobs, the willingness of U.S. society to absorb them might not exist. The capacity of any community to incorporate newcomers with different cultural backgrounds depends on several noneconomic factors, such as concentration of the newcomers in certain areas, the relative size of the new community versus the old, the pace of newcomer growth, and the attitude of newcomers toward integration in the community (language, values, traits, etc.). It is one thing to place migration issues at the top of the bilateral agenda, and another to try to deal with this complex issue with one simple stroke.

Probably the most promising road would be to work for piecemeal reforms that can reduce the overall numbers of undocumented migrants who cross the border every day. For instance, it might be possible to recognize the complementarity of U.S. and Mexican labor markets in some sectors and then to create the mechanisms needed to allow (via special visa categories) to respond to needs for qualified Mexican workers in specific industries. One way to prove that there is a real political will to address migration in North America in a privileged manner would be to establish exceptional status for Canada and Mexico, setting up a "NAFTA regime."

Without neglecting its political and social relevance, from an economic point of view, the issue of amnesty for the population of foreign origin living in the United States is of secondary importance. It has more to do with the rule of law and a deterrent for undocumented migrations in the future than with the number and nature of current migrants.

In addition to the more traditional issues, such as trade, FDI, and migration, other recent developments clearly show the uncontainable nature of North American integration and underscore institutional slackness. The case of electronic commerce deserves mentioning. It is estimated that in 2002 the total value of electronic trade transactions originated in Mexico with destination in the United States amounted to $280 million. Despite some general provisions included in NAFTA, it was not until 2001 that Mexico introduced specific domestic regulation to deal with this issue.

Trinational cooperation on tax issues seems less than adequate. Current agreements concentrate on avoiding double taxation, which is clearly needed, but not on helping participating countries to institute more effective tax collection. The total revenues of the three countries' federal governments are too different. The low levels of tax collection in Mexico should be a source of concern. It is estimated that in 2003 Mexican tax collection was equivalent to about 12 percent of GDP. This is clearly insufficient to support the minimal requirements of the government of a country in North America, and it translates into a structural inability of the Mexican government to respond to infrastructure development and, more important, to expand a social safety net that gradually converges with its NAFTA counterparts.

Ultimately, the tax-collection capacity of the Mexican state must be enhanced if it is to improve the country's public welfare. This can only happen if tax revenues in Mexico increase, an issue where trinational cooperation would be welcomed and highly positive. Cooperation on this front could take the form of information sharing on financial transactions and asset holdings of nationals of other NAFTA countries. This could help improve the capacity of all three governments to properly assess taxable income and eventually increase tax receipts.

Competition between the financial institutions of the three countries for the funds of citizens of the other two countries has been there for decades. There is also growing consciousness of the competition with third countries (non-NAFTA) to attract the resources of NAFTA-country citizens. U.S. Federal Reserve statistics indicate that in 1990 Mexicans (both persons and corporations) had $16.6 billion in assets invested in the U.S. financial system. These amounts represented 46.5 percent of the total liabilities of the Mexican financial system. If labor income, interest, and dividends are considered together, it indicates that cross-country income generation is significant and growing, and that the tax authorities of the three governments do not know how to deal with this growing phenomenon.

The most relevant of the recent developments in North America is the change in policies derived from the terrorist attacks of September 11, 2001. This tragic event, and its aftermath including the war in Iraq, have modified the perception, vision, and policies related to U.S. "homeland security" and the participation of its two neighbors in the actions to assure that security. Canada and Mexico reacted speedily to beef up security measures. The concept of a North American "security perimeter" became one way to understand the new context in which integration could proceed. The basic question was: Do Canada and Mexico want to be "within" or "without" the security perimeter? The answer of both countries was an unambiguous "within"—up to a point—as shown by the rapid development of the "smart borders" concept by Canada and Mexico. In any case, the United States has not responded with enthusiasm, and the concept of a North American security perimeter is still under scrutiny. The qualified Canadian and Mexican answer of "up to a point" is due to the fact that if the idea of a common security perimeter were to develop, so too would the concepts of increased homogeneity of customs policies and practices, as well as a special immigration policy for North American nationals.

In addition, in the case of Mexico, it is not clear how far the Fox administration is willing or able to move in the direction of further cooperation on the security front. The disagreement over the U.S. actions in Iraq made it dramatically evident that Mexico and the United States do not necessarily see eye-to-eye on the nagging question of the war against terrorism and that national interests are still apt to clash from time to time. Furthermore, the strong undercurrent of Mexican nationalism will prevent the country from becoming a NATO-like partner of the United States on security matters in the foreseeable future.

LOOKING AHEAD

What does this new context mean in terms of the actions and policies that the three countries have to implement vis-à-vis each other? Do Canada and Mexico have the financial, material, human, and institutional resources to cope with the new challenge?

Should actions of this new stage follow a comprehensive approach with centralized coordination, or can the necessary actions be undertaken on the basis of a decentralized scheme? Is the United States ready to act with the aim of fostering the development of its neighbors, especially Mexico, as a means to strengthen its "homeland security"?

The answers to these questions are in the making. However, at least four ideas are worth underscoring. First, the process of North American integration will continue anyway; hence, it is preferable to tackle it in an orderly manner than in a disorderly way. Second, further integration and the regional prosperity that should be associated with it becomes essential to lock in desirable policies and to strengthen the governability of the three neighbors. Third, further integration can become a catalyst for additional reforms, which in turn could strengthen governability. Fourth, more attention is needed to envisage a program to craft more effective social policies, especially in Mexico, to make a reality of the promise that integration will lead to increased welfare for the population.

The proposals for a comprehensive and centralized approach have been facing much resistance, especially in the United States.[5] The main arguments of those who reject them is that it is not feasible in the North American context. However, they do not explain why nor propose alternative solutions to address these issues.

An explanation for this lack of vision about future stages of NAFTA is the slow pace at which the citizens of the three countries have advanced in their understanding of North America. There is no question that knowledge about each other has improved since NAFTA came into existence. There is no doubt that, in the Mexico–United States case, the presence in the United States of more than 12 million Mexican-born persons has had a major effect in improving the two countries' understanding of each other. However, our understanding of North America, as a complex socioeconomic and political reality, is clearly wanting and therefore insufficient to overcome much resistance to further integration. Misperceptions about the NAFTA neighbors endure. In addition, new resistance against globalization and modernization have emerged. In Mexico, for example, "privatization" has become a bad word, and actions to foster the restructuring of existing state-owned enterprises encounter strong resistance.

In this context, the task of educating people in the three countries about North America becomes essential, as well as a prerequisite to shaping a vision for the future of the region. An issue that has to be underscored is the change in the world's conditions between 1994 and 2003. When NAFTA was signed 10 years ago, China was only emerging. Today it has become the United States' second largest trading partner after Canada, displacing Mexico from that position.

The structural forces pushing for further integration exist and are strong. However, it is imperative to keep moving ahead. If education about NAFTA and institutional development do not catch up soon with the reality on the ground, the potential dislocations and misunderstandings will continue to grow unabated. The anti-NAFTA forces are still strong in all three countries, as the recent wave of peasant mobilization in Mexico made abundantly clear.

Ten years of NAFTA have made it clear that NAFTA alone is not sufficient to promote shared prosperity throughout the region. NAFTA must once again be seen and defended not as an end in itself but as a necessary instrument to achieving a more ambitious goal: peaceful and harmonious coexistence among three prosperous and self-confident countries. That vision should guide the process and provide it with a political logic that has been lacking in recent times. In its absence, all discussions of specific policy issues will be marred by divisive political debates stemming from the idea that further integration is incompatible with the preservation of national self-determination. This would transform a largely spontaneous process into a disjointed enterprise.

Notes

1. The migratory flows from the United States to Canada and Mexico should not be overlooked. E.g., it is estimated that 350,000 U.S. citizens spend most of each year in Mexico, becoming semi-immigrants.

2. See chapter 10 of this book for an in-depth analysis of these trends.

3. During 1999 and 2000, two relevant actions occurred. Mexican consulates in the United States started disclosing information about the charges of the companies operating remittances, with the help of the Consumer Protection Agency (Profeco), and two class-auction suits were brought against Western Union.

4. In March 2003, Bansefi announced its participation in the remittances market, which in turn is expected to reduce costs.

5. Probably the best example of this kind of proposal is found in Pastor (2001).

References

Andere, Eduardo, and Georgina Kessel, eds. 1992. *México y El Tratado Trilateral de Libre Comercio: Impacto sectorial.* Mexico City: Instituto Tecnológico Autónomo de México and McGraw-Hill.

Asociación Mexicana de Estudios sobre Canadá. 2001. *Revista mexicana de estudios canadienses.* Nueva época, núm. 1. Mexico City: Asociación Mexicana de Estudios sobre Canadá.

———. 2002. *Revista mexicana de estudios canadienses.* Nueva época, núm. 3. Mexico City: Asociación Mexicana de Estudios sobre Canadá.

Coalition for Secure and Trade-Efficient Borders. 2001. *Rethinking Our Borders: A Plan for Action.* Ottawa: Coalition for Secure and Trade-Efficient Borders.

Comisión sobre el Futuro de las Relaciones México–Estados Unidos. 1988. *El desafío de la interdependencia: México y Estados Unidos.* Mexico City: Fondo de Cultura Económica.

Cook, Philip S., ed. 1991. *Winners and Losers: Readjustment Mechanisms in a North American Free Trade Agreement.* Santa Fe, N.M.: North American Institute.

Dobell, Rodney, and Michael Neufeld, eds. 1993. *Beyond NAFTA: The Western Hemisphere Interface.* Compilation of a forum organized by the North American Institute in Querétaro, Mexico. Lantzville, B.C.: Oolichan Books.

Feinberg, Richard E., John Echeverri-Gent, and Friedemann Müller, eds. 1990. *Economic Reform in Three Giants.* U.S.–Third World Policy Perspectives 14. New Brunswick, N.J.: Transaction Books.

Gilbreath, Jan, and David Hurlbut. 1992. *Free Trade with Mexico: What's in It for Texas?* Austin: University of Texas Press.

Hart, Michael. 1990. *A North American Free Trade Agreement: The Strategic Implications for Canada.* South Halifax: Institute for Research on Public Policy.

Instituto Politécnico Nacional. 1991. *Historia y porvenir de México ante el Tratado de Libre Comercio.* Mexico City: Instituto Politécnico Nacional.

Kiy, Richard, and John D. Wirth. 1998. *Environmental Management on North America's Borders.* College Station: Texas A&M University Press.

Knepper, William E., ed. 1991. *Harmonizing Economic Competitiveness with Environmental Quality: A North American Challenge.* Santa Fe, N.M.: North American Institute.

Margain, Eduardo. 1995. *El TLC y la crisis del neoliberalismo mexicano.* Mexico City: Centro de Investigaciones sobre América del Norte, Universidad Nacional Autónoma de México.

North American Institute (NAMI). 1993. *The North American Environment: Opportunities for Trinational Cooperation by Canada, the United States, and Mexico.* Santa Fe, N.M.: NAMI.

Pastor, Robert A. 2001. *Toward a North American Community: Lessons from the Old World for the New.* Washington, D.C.: Institute for International Economics.

Reynolds, Clark W., Leonard Wavermen, and Gerardo Bueno. 1991. *The Dynamics of North American Trade and Investment.* Stanford, Calif.: Stanford University Press.

Roett, Riordan, ed. 1989. *México y Estados Unidos: El manejo de la relación.* Mexico City: Siglo Veintiuno Editores.

Sistema de Información Empresarial Mexicano (SECOFI). 1992. *Tratado de Libre Comercio en América del Norte.* Monografías. 2 vols. Mexico City: SECOFI.

U.S.–Mexico Binational Council. 2001. *New Horizons in U.S.-Mexico Relations. Recommendations for Policymakers.* Washington, D.C.: CSIS.

INDEX

Page numbers followed by the letters n *and* t *refer to notes and tables, respectively.*

Abrego, García, 223–224
AC. *See* Andean Community
Accreditation, transnational standards for, 300–301
Acuerdo Nacional para el Campo, 324–325
Afghanistan, U.S. war in, 246
AFI. *See* Agencia Federal de Investigación
AFL-CIO: and fast-track authority, 137, 139; FTAA and, 142–143; NAALC and, 132, 135; NAFTA and, 137, 138, 140, 142; transnational cooperation, 143–144
Agencia Federal de Investigación (AFI), 218, 219
Agenda for North American Higher Education Cooperation, 296
Agreement on Cooperation in Combating Narcotics Trafficking and Drug Dependency (1989), 214
Agricultural chapter(s): of NAFTA, 326; in regional trade agreements, 28t–29t
Agricultural tariffs, within NAFTA, 55
Agricultural trade agreements: disputes, *xiv,* 10–11, 12, 16, 17; negotiation of, 11, 19n

Agriculture: Mexican migration and, 267; Mexican policy on, 324–330; NAFTA impact on, 326–330, 332, 395–397, 398t, 402; water supply for, 111, 116. *See also* Mexican agriculture
Al Qaeda, 246. *See also* September 11 terrorist attacks
Alanís, Gustavo, 102
Alianza Cívica, 196–197, 358
Alianza para el Campo program, 329, 398
Alliance of Progress, 353
American Convention on Human Rights, 358
Americas: recession in, 54, 60; regional trade agreements in, 21, 22t–23t. *See also* North America
Andean Community (AC): intraregional export shares, 47, 48t; regional trade agreements, 22t, 23t; trade intensity index, 47, 48t
Andean Group, success of, 25
Andean Pact, characteristics of, 21
Anti-bullionists, 69
Anti-Drug Abuse Act (U.S. 1986), 221, 230n–231n

Antidumping and countervailing duties: complaints against Mexico for, 165; elimination of, 60*n*; NAFTA group on, 167, 167*t*, 168*t*; in regional trade agreements, 28*t*–29*t*; in sugar trade dispute, 12; U.S. policy on, 55, 56

Antigua and Barbuda, trade agreements, 22*t*

ANUIES. *See* National Association of Universities

Arellano Félix, Benjamin, 226

Argentina: education in, 318; exchange rate depreciation, 37, 38; trade agreements, 22*t*, 26

Armed forces. *See* Canadian military; Mexican military

ASEAN. *See* Asian Free Trade Area

Asia: education spending, 321*t*; foreign direct investment in, 41, 42*f*; industry relocation to, 85

Asian Free Trade Area (ASEAN): intraregional export shares, 48*t*; trade intensity index, 48*t*

Asia-Pacific Economic Cooperation: intraregional export shares, 48*t*; trade intensity index, 48*t*

Australia, trade agreements, 48*t*

Auto Pact (1965), 25, 53, 61*n*

Automotive industry: competition in, 17; impact of NAFTA on, 52–53; intraindustry trade, 9, 19*n*; just-in-time inventory model, 9, 10, 17, 59, 247, 255*n*–256*n*; in regional trade agreements, 28*t*–29*t*

Autonomous Metropolitan University (UAM), 290

Autonomous National University of Mexico (UNAM), 290, 301, 302–303

Bahamas, trade agreements, 22*t*

Banamex. *See* Banco Nacional de México

Banco Nacional de México (Banamex), 13

Bank of England, 69

Bank of Mexico, 74, 75, 79, 80–81, 85, 88*n*

Barbados, trade agreements, 22*t*

Bartlett, Manuel, 287, 288, 294, 296

BECC. *See* Border Environment Cooperation Commission

Belize, trade agreements, 22*t*

Bilateral investment treaties (BITs): growth in, 27; policy options for, 57–59

Bilateral tax treaties (BTTs): growth in, 27; policy options for, 57–59

Bilateral trade agreements: as complicating factor, 38, 57; and foreign direct investment, 27

Binational Commission, 174–175, 179, 181

Bi-National Commission for Educational and Cultural Exchange, 296

Binational Study: Migration between Mexico and the United States, 18

BITs. *See* Bilateral investment treaties

Bolivia, trade agreements, 22*t*, 28*t*, 38

Border(s). *See* Canadian border; Mexican border; United States border

Border Environment Cooperation Commission (BECC), 96, 97, 112

Bracero program, 273–278

Brazil: antidumping and countervailing duties proceedings, 168*t*; Argentinean peso crisis and, 38; deforestation, 114; exchange rate depreciation, 37; and FTAA talks, 57; as regional hegemon, 24; regional trade agreements, 22*t*, 23*t*, 26

Bretton Woods system, 76–77

BTTs. *See* Bilateral tax treaties

Buchanan, Patrick, 348

Bullionists, 69

Bush, George H.W.: foreign policy, 178; and free trade, *xii–xiii,* 3, 164;

invasion of Panama, 356; Mexican relations, 173, 175, 215; NAFTA negotiations, 358; on sovereignty, 347

Bush, George W.: antiterrorism policies, 176–177, 246; election of, 178; fast-track trade authority, 139; on free trade, 54; immigration policy, 238, 263; labor unions and, 127; Mexican relations, 176–177, 178; and North American cooperation, 246; trade policies, 254–255

Buy America initiative, 58

Byrd Amendment (U.S., 2000), 55

CACM. *See* Central American Common Market

California: environmental standards, 110; investor complaints against, 110; water resources, 112

Camarena, Enrique, 209–210

Canada: assistance to Mexico, *xiv*; economic policies, 74, 76, 83; effective exchange rate, 83*t*; expectations for NAFTA, 3, 4, 14; and foreign direct investment, 39–42, 44*t*–45*t*, 46, 49, 50–51, 52, 58, 392; FTAA negotiations and, 143; impact of NAFTA on, 143, 393; investor complaints against, 110; labor costs, 83*t*; migration to U.S., 392–393; and NAFTA institutional structure, 161–162, 163; NAFTA negotiations, 349; new policy directions, 3; reaction to terrorism, 236–237, 406–407; view of free trade, *xiii, xiv,* 3, 4, 24. *See also entries under* Canadian

Canada–United States Free Trade Agreement (CUSFTA), 22*t*; and antidumping/countervailing duties, 60*n*; Canadian culture exemption, 351; Canadian experience of, *xiv*; and foreign direct investment,

41–42, 44*t*–45*t*, 51, 53; impact of, 114–115; NAFTA negotiations and, 349, 350; opposition to, *xiii*, 3, 24; provisions of, 25; tariffs in, 21

Canada-U.S. Record of Understanding (1988), 55

Canadian Action Network, 135, 139

Canadian border: crossing procedures, 17, 59; security of, 237–238; Smart Border agreements, 17, 59, 240, 247–250, 252–253, 407

Canadian economy: capital formation per worker, 402, 403*t*; capital shortage in, 402; dependence on U.S. economy, 5, 47–48; employment, 83*t*, 125; GDP, 393, 394*f*; inflation, 83*t*, 84, 84*f*; interest rates, 83–84, 83*t*; manufacturing sector, 125–126; performance *vs.* North America, 82*t*–83*t*, 83–86; regional integration of, 393–395, 394*f*, 396*f*, 399*t*; wages, 125–126, 147*n*

Canadian education, intra-NAFTA cooperation, 296–303

Canadian environmental protection: agreements, 94, 95, 105–106; complaints against, 100, 115, 118*n*; enforcement, 108; policies, 99; pollution, 114–115; resource depletion, 114–115

Canadian foreign policy: anti-American tilt in, 254; tensions with U.S., 243–245; U.S. national security and, 235

Canadian Labor Congress (CLC), 135–136, 139, 140, 142, 143

Canadian labor protections: complaint mechanisms, 129; complaints against, 130–131, 132–133, 133*t*. *See also* North American Agreement on Labor Cooperation

Canadian labor unions: activism, 135–136, 139–140; policies, 137; power of, 126, 145

Canadian military: NAFTA and, 238–239; strength of, 244, 246
Canadian national security policy: North American cooperation, 240–242, 245, 246–247, 247–248, 251–253, 253–255, 256n; security measures, 252, 256n
Canadian NGOs: influence of, 97; and NAFTA negotiations, 360
Canadian population, in U.S., 251, 253, 397t
Canadian public opinion: on NAFTA, 350, 408; on U.S. policy, 247
Canadian sovereignty: concerns, 348; cultural sovereignty, 350–352; NAFTA and, 350–353, 362; national treatment, 350, 352
Canadian trade: agricultural tariffs, 55; agricultural trade agreements, 11, 19n; antidumping and countervailing duties proceedings, 168t; automotive industry, 9, 10, 17, 255n–256n; disputes, 55, 61n; exports, 83t, 238, 392, 395, 397t; extra-NAFTA exports, 5, 6t, 7f, 8t; free trade agreements, 25, 105–106, 144; intraindustry trade, 19n; intra-NAFTA exports, xi, 5, 6t, 7f, 8t, 47–48, 58, 398; intra-NAFTA imports, 309; manufactured goods exports, 10; NAFTA impact on, 395, 397t; openness, 401–402, 402t; regional trade agreements, 22t, 23t, 29t, 38, 57; rules of origin, 57; trade negotiations, 60n
Canadian-U.S. relations: Canadian military and, 246; Cold War and, 248; history of, xiv; terrorism and, 246, 406–407; U.S. war on drugs and, 255
Capital formation per worker, 402, 403t
Capital mobility, labor unions and, 143
Capitalism, as creative destruction, 342
Cárdenas, Cuauhtémoc, 192, 354, 376

Cárdenas, Lázaro, 242
Cardinal Posadas Ocampo, Juan Jesús, 213
Caribbean: education spending, 321t; foreign direct investment in, 54; investment diversion and, 32
Caribbean Community (CARICOM), trade agreements, 22t, 23t, 25, 29t
CARICOM. See Caribbean Community
Carter, Jimmy, 173
Castañeda, Jorge, 74, 172, 177, 180
CEC. See North American Commission for Environmental Cooperation
CENDRO. See National Drug Control Center
Ceneval, 295, 301
Center for Immigration Studies, 251
Center for North American Studies, 302–303
Center for the Study of the United States, 302–303
Central America: cheap labor in, 9, 16; economic integration in, 117; trade agreements, 16, 54, 95, 104–105
Central American Common Market (CACM), 22t–23t, 25
Centro de Investigación y Seguridad Nacional (CISEN), 212
Centro Mexicano de Derecho Ambiental, AC, 101, 102
Centro Nacional de Comunicación Social, 191
CER: intraregional export shares, 48t; trade intensity index, 48t
Cervantes, Enrique, 226
Chiapas: economy of, 310, 317–318; education in, 293
Chile: economic data, 319t; education in, 318; free trade agreements, 16, 105–106, 106–107, 117, 144, 254–255; human development data, 319t; NAFTA membership, 56, 57,

105; regional trade agreements, 22*t*, 23*t*, 27, 29*t*, 38, 54, 56, 57, 95
China: antidumping and countervailing duties proceedings, 168*t*; economic data, 319*t*; human development data, 318, 319*t*; industry relocation to, 9, 16; labor rights in, 145; regional trade agreements, 23*t*; U.S. trade with, 5, 408
Chrétien, Jean, 237, 246, 256*n*
Citibank, 13
Citizen complaint mechanisms: environment, 96, 99, 100, 106, 107, 108, 117; labor, 129, 142
Civic Alliance. *See* Alianza Cívica
Civil society: definition of, 187; in Mexico, 187
CLC. *See* Canadian Labor Congress
Clean Air Act Amendments (1990), 110
Clinton, Bill: drug policies, 219; fast-track trade authority and, 38, 138–139; free trade and, 164; Mexican financial rescue, 265; Mexican relations, 173, 175; NAFTA environmental provisions and, 348; NAFTA labor provisions and, 127, 131, 137, 140, 348; NAFTA ratification and, 265, 300
Cold War, and North American national defense policy, 240–241, 242–243, 248
Colegio de la Frontera Norte, 303
Colombia, trade agreements, 22*t*, 27, 38
Colosio, Luis Donaldo, 216
Comité para la Protección de los Recursos Naturales, AC, 101
Common Borders forum (1989), 139–140
Compensation for free trade losers, *xii*, 125, 326
Competition: in attracting FDI, 58; benefits of, *xii*, 10; from outside NAFTA, 17; policy in regional trade agreements, 28*t*–29*t*

CONAFE. *See* National Council for Educational Promotion
CONAHEC. *See* Consortium for North American Higher Education Collaboration
Confederación de Trabajadores de México (CTM), 132, 140, 144
Congreso de Trabajo (LC), 132, 140, 141
Consejo Nacional de Ciencia y Tecnologia. *See* National Council for Science and Technology
Consortium for North American Higher Education Collaboration (CONAHEC), 302
Consumers, benefits from free trade, *xii*
Contigo, 293
Continental Social Alliance, 142, 143
Convergencia de Organizaciones Civicas para la Democracia, 193
Coombs, Philip H., 295
Corruption: free trade and, 400; in Mexican political system, 210, 211, 213, 218, 226, 228–229, 244, 383, 400
Costa Rica: foreign direct investment in, 53; trade agreements, 22*t*, 23*t*, 38, 105–106
Cross-Border Crime Forum, Canadian-U.S., 249
CTM. *See* Confederación de Trabajadores de México
Cuba, North American policy on, 243–244
Cuban missile crisis, 243, 244
CUFTA [CUSFTA]. *See* Canada–United States Free Trade Agreement
CUSFTA. *See* Canada–United States Free Trade Agreement
Customs unions: antidumping and countervailing duties, 60*n*; characteristics of, 21, 55; deepening NAFTA into, 56; regional trade agreements and, 30

Davis, Gray, 110
De la Madrid, Miguel: drug policies, 209, 210, 212, 214; economic policies, 271, 286; reform and, 377; U.S. relations, 170, 175
Decree on Rules for the Temporary Stay of Foreign Agencies Representatives, 215
Defensive import-substituting investment, in regional trade agreements, 36
Deforestation, 114, 115
Democracy, free trade and, 399–401
Democracy in Mexico: conditions required for, 372–375; consequences of, 372; current state of, 381–382; development of, *xiii*, 371–372, 375–381, 382–387; education of citizens for, 384–385; NAFTA and, *xiii*, 342, 356, 357–358, 377; NGOs and, 188–189, 194–195, 196–201, 202; and political parties, 373–375, 378, 385–386
Denmark, 74
Department of Education, U.S., 302
Department of Homeland Security, U.S.: creation of, 235; fear of, 255; and NAFTA, 239–240
Derbez, Luis Ernesto, 177
Developing nations: foreign direct investment in, 50; investment protections in, 33
DFS. *See* Dirección Federal de Seguridad
Diaz Ordaz, Gustavo, 243
Diefenbaker, John, 244
Dirección Federal de Seguridad (DFS), 212
DISEN. *See* General Directorate of Investigation and National Security
Dispute resolution. *See* Investor dispute settlement provisions; Labor dispute resolution; Trade dispute resolution
Domestic firms, in regional trade agreements, 35–36

Domestic policy, and foreign direct investment, 46, 58
Dominica, trade agreements, 22*t*
Dominican Republic, trade agreements, 23*t*, 29*t*
Drug trafficking: NAFTA impact on, *xiii*, 229; and U.S.-Mexican relations, 176, 209–212, 214–215, 219–222, 226–230, 244. *See also* Mexican drug policies; United States drug policies
Duffy, Joseph, 298
Dynamic gains from trade, in trade agreements, 31–33

East Asian tigers, lessons of, 26
Economic Commission for Latin America and the Caribbean, 39, 271
Economic Complementarity Agreement (1943), 166
Economic convergence within NAFTA: avenues for achieving, 307–308, 317; monetary convergence, 75–82, 86–88; NAFTA impact on, 307, 309–310, 398, 399*t*; obstacles to, 314–316, 317–318
Economic effects of regional trade agreements, 30–34
Economic instability, vulnerability to, 31
Economic integration: advantages of, 52; and environmental protection, 116–117; intraindustry trade, 9–10, 19*n*; in Latin America, 117; motives for, 10; NAFTA impact on, 398, 399*t*; and vulnerability to instability, 31. *See also* Free trade agreements
Ecuador, trade agreements, 22*t*, 23*t*, 38
Education: and direct foreign investment, 58–59; of public about NAFTA, 408–409. *See also* Canadian education; Mexican education; United States education
The Educational Modernization Program: 1989–1994, 287, 294

EEC. *See* European Economic Community
EFTA. *See* European Free Trade Area
El Colegio de Mexico, 303
El Salvador: foreign direct investment in, 53; trade agreements, 22t, 23t
Employment: Canada, 83t, 125; Mexico, 83t, 124–126, 308–309; United States, 82t, 125
Energy products: electricity demand projections, 115; fuels for electricity generation, 400t; and North American relations, 247; trade in, 393–395, 398; U.S. national security and, 238. *See also* Oil
Entrepreneurial investment, in Mexico, 13
Environmental agreements: Canada, 94, 95, 105–106; Latin America, 95, 96, 104–107; Mexico, 94, 95, 96; proliferation of, 94; transparency in, 97–99, 100–101, 104; United States, 94, 95, 96, 106–107
Environmental protection: challenges for North America in, 107–115; citizen empowerment, 98–99, 106, 107, 108, 117; complaint mechanisms, 96, 99, 100, 106, 107, 108–111, 117; environmental review of trade agreements, 95; future directions, 116–117; importance to trade, 97, 117; investor dispute settlement provisions and, 107, 108–111; NAFTA impact on, *xiii*; pollution, 93, 94, 102, 111, 113–115; in regional trade agreements, 28t–29t; resource depletion, 111–115. *See also* Canadian environmental protection; Mexican environmental protection; North American Agreement on Environmental Cooperation; United States environmental protection
Environmental Protection Agency (EPA), 103

EPA. *See* Environmental Protection Agency
Espinosa de los Reyes, Jorge, 170
Ethyl Corporation, 110
Europe, foreign direct investment by, 51
European Community: EC1992 program, 26; trade agreements, 26
European Economic Community (EEC), 309–310
European Exchange Rate Mechanism, 73, 88n
European Free Trade Area (EFTA): intraregional export shares, 48t; trade agreements, 22t; trade intensity index, 47, 48t
European Union: characteristics of, 359; currency, 74; foreign direct investment in, 41, 42f; goal of, 359; history of, 4; as integration model, 142, 402; intraregional export shares, 47, 48t; labor protections, 136; purpose of, 161; regional trade agreements, 22t, 23t, 38, 56; right of withdrawal from, 360; trade intensity index, 47, 48t
Exani-I and II, 289, 290t
Exchange rate: fixed: dangers of, 71, 72, 73, 75; as transition to dollarization, 79–80, 80–81; floating: as accepted standard, 72, 74–75, 87; Mexican economy and, 79–80, 82, 87; NAFTA and, 75–76; short-term disruptions under, 75; and foreign direct investment, 47; nominal targets for, 76–77; and trade volume, 74, 75

Factor costs and availability, and foreign direct investment, 46
Farm Bill (U.S., 2002), 55
Fast-track trade authority, 38, 54, 137, 138–139, 139, 171
FAT. *See* Frente Auténtico del Trabajo
FBI. *See* Federal Bureau of Investigation

FDI. *See* foreign direct investment

FDN. *See* National Democratic Front

FEADS. *See* Office of the Special Prosecutor for Crimes against Health

Federación de Sindicatos de Empresas de Bienes y Servicios (FESEBS), 135, 140, 141

Federal Bureau of Investigation (FBI), 217, 249

Federal Electoral Institute (IFE), 376, 384

Federal Judicial Police (FJP), 213, 214, 219

Federal Preventive Police (PFP), 216, 226

FESEBS. *See* Federación de Sindicatos de Empresas de Bienes y Servicios

First Conference of University Presidents of North America, 297–298

FJP. *See* Federal Judicial Police

Foreign Assistance Act (U.S.), 221

Foreign direct investment (FDI): attracting, 58–59; bilateral trade agreements and, 27; Canada and, 39–42, 44t–45t, 46, 49, 50–51, 52, 58, 392; corporate motivations for, 33–34, 35f; data sources and problems, 39–41; decline in, 54; in developing nations, 50; factors affecting, 43–47; horizontal, 34, 51–53; impact of regional trade agreements on, 21–24, 27–54, 30f, 35f; intra-NAFTA, 50–51, 53; Mexican law on, 37; by Mexico, 49, 70; in Mexico, 4, 13–14, 13f, 41–42, 43, 44t–45t, 46, 50–51, 52, 61n, 73, 116, 308–309, 392, 402; NAFTA and, 41–42, 43, 44t–45t, 395, 397t; NAFTA impact on, 52–53; recent patterns in, 41–42, 42f; by region, 41–42, 44t–45t; sectoral differences in, 52–53; by United States, 46, 49,

51, 52, 53, 116, 392; in United States, 41–42, 44t–45t, 46; vertical, 34, 51–53

Foreign direct investment agreements, policy options for, 57–59

Foreign Investment in Latin America and the Caribbean, 39

Fox, Vincente: agricultural policy, 324–325; antipoverty programs, 323; drug policies, 219, 225–226; on economic integration, 117; economic policies, 74, 318, 402; education policies, 287, 289, 300; election victory, 197; environmental protection and, 100–101, 104; foreign policy, 241, 407; free trade proposal, 164; and governmental transparency, 100–101; migration policies, 180, 238, 263; and NAFTA-Plus, 18, 246–247, 247–248; September 11 attacks and, 237, 246; U.S. relations, 164–165, 172, 174t, 176–177, 178, 246, 256n; on water supply, 113

Free trade: assessing benefits of, *xi–xii*; democracy and, 399–401; neoliberal institutionalism on, 162–163; non-economic impact, *xii–xiii*

Free trade agreements (FTAs): antidumping and countervailing duties, 60n; characteristics of, 21; environmental review of, 95; goals of, 108; motivations for, 26; opposition to, 137; proliferation, *xi*, 21. *See also* Agricultural trade agreements; Bilateral trade agreements; Economic integration; Regional trade agreements; *specific agreements*

Free Trade Area of the Americas (FTAA): agricultural trade in, 10; alternatives to, 142; goals for, 57; impact of, 16–17; negotiations,

23*t*, 24–25, 106, 109, 124, 136; prospects for, 239; significance of, 60; union demands for, 142–143; and U.S. policy, 54
Free Trade Commission, 166
Freedom of Information Mexico AC (LIMAC), 199–201
Frente Auténtico del Trabajo (FAT), 132, 134, 140–141, 142, 150*n*
Frente Democrático Nacional. *See* National Democratic Front
FTAA. *See* Free Trade Area of the Americas
FTAs. *See* Free trade agreements
Fugitive Identification and Alert Program, 224
Fulbright-Garcia Robles grants, 296
Fund for the Improvement of Post Secondary Education, 302
Fund to Modernize Higher Education, 295

G-3. *See* Group of Three (G-3)
Galbraith, John Kenneth, 351
Garment industry: foreign direct investment by, 53; investment diversion in, 32
GCAN Insurance Company, 176
General Agreement on Tariffs and Trade (GATT): agricultural trade in, 10; extension of principles in, 27; Generalized System of Preferences, 26; labor provisions in, 135; Mexico and, 166, 245, 271, 286, 308, 309–310, 353–354, 401; Uruguay Round, 171; U.S. trade policy and, 348; violations of, 55
General Directorate of Investigation and National Security (DISEN), 212
General Directorate of Political and Social Investigation, 212
General Education Law (1992), 288, 292

Gordillo, Elba Esther, 288
Government procurement provisions, in regional trade agreements, 28*t*–29*t*
Gravity model of regional trade agreement impact, 43
Grenada, trade agreements, 22*t*
Group of Three (G-3), 22*t*, 27, 28*t*
Growth, economic: in Mexico, *xv*, 11, 14, 15*f*, 18, 70, 270–273, 278–279, 308–309, 309*f*, 313–316; NAFTA and, *xiv*; in U.S., 5
Grupo de los Cien Internacional, AC, 101
Guatemala: foreign direct investment in, 53; trade agreements, 22*t*, 23*t*
Guerrero: economy of, 310, 317–318; education in, 293

Hague Court, 345
Hang Young Co., 131
Havana Charter, 347
Helms-Burton Act, 348
HFCS. *See* High-fructose corn syrup
Hidalgo, education in, 293
High-fructose corn syrup (HFCS), trade disputes, 12, 17
High-Level Contact Group for Drug Control (HLCGDC), 176, 219, 228, 245
Hills, Carla, 171
HLCGDC. *See* High-Level Contact Group for Drug Control
Honduras: education in, 318; foreign direct investment in, 53; trade agreements, 22*t*, 23*t*
Horizontal foreign direct investment, 34
Hub-and-spoke agreements: costs of, 38–39, 57; future of, 246–247
Human Development Fund of Canada, 302

Human rights: NAFTA impact on, *xiii*. *See also* Mexican human rights

IACHR. *See* Inter-American Commission on Human Rights

ICSID. *See* International Center for Settlement of Investment Disputes

IFE. *See* Federal Electoral Institute

ILO. *See* International Labor Organization

IME. *See* Institute of Mexicans Abroad

IMF. *See* International Monetary Fund

Immigration and Naturalization Service, U.S. (INS), 251, 273, 276

Immigration Reform and Control Act (1986) [IRCA], 268, 274–277

Import-substitution industrialization (ISI), 25, 271

INCD. *See* National Institute for Controlling Drugs

Income inequality in Mexico, 310–312, 311*f*, 312*f*; avenues for remedying, 307–308, 317; causes of, 314–316, 317; and education, 290–294, 291*t*, 292*f*, 293*f*, 318–319; redistribution efforts, 316–317, 319–320, 326–327, 329–330, 330*f*, 332

Inflation: in Canada, 83*t*, 84, 84*f*; impact of, 84–85; in Mexico, 71, 72, 83*t*, 84–86, 84*f*, 85*f*, 273; in United States, 82*t*, 84, 84*f*, 85*f*

Infrastructure: and direct foreign investment, 58–59; and economic convergence, 307, 314, 317–318; NAFTA provisions for, 395, 402–403; protection of, 249; and resource protection, 112–113, 116–117; on U.S.-Mexican border, 179

INS. *See* Immigration and Naturalization Service, U.S.

Insider firms, in regional trade agreements, 34–36, 53

Institute for Labor Studies, 144

Institute of Mexicans Abroad (IME), 180

Institutional Revolutionary Party (PRI): assassinations, 215–216; corruption in, 244; democratization and, 371, 374, 375–376, 378; foreign policy, 242; hegemony of, 191, 192, 196, 197, 286, 373–374; labor unions and, 141; NAFTA and, 326; NGOs and, 189

Institutional structure: regional integration and, 391–392, 405; types of, 162–163. *See also* NAFTA institutional structure

Instituto de Estudios del Trabajo, 144

Instituto Federal Electoral. *See* Federal Electoral Institute

Integrated National Security Enforcement Teams, 249

Intellectual property provisions, in regional trade agreements, 28*t*–29*t*

Inter-American Commission on Human Rights (IACHR), 358

Inter-American Development Bank, 55

Inter-American Treaty of Reciprocal Assistance (Rio Treaty; TIAR), 237, 239, 242

Interest rates: Canada, 83–84, 83*t*; Mexico, 83*t*, 84, 85–86, 86*f*; U.S., 82*t*, 83–84, 85–86, 86*f*

Interinstitutional Committees for the Evaluation of Higher Education, 295

International Center for Settlement of Investment Disputes (ICSID), 109

International Conference about Social Dimensions (1995), 136

International Council for Educational Development, 295

International Court of Justice, U.S. sovereignty and, 363*n*

International Labor Organization (ILO), 134, 136

International law, and sovereignty, 343, 344–346, 358
International Military Education and Training (MET) programs, 227
International Monetary Fund (IMF), 285; and foreign direct investment reporting, 39; and Latin American debt crisis, 26
Intrafirm trade, in regional trade agreements, 34
Intraindustry trade, 9–10, 19n
Intraregional trade, regional trade agreements' impact on, 47–50, 48t
Investment creation, in regional trade agreements, 32
Investment diversion, in regional trade agreements, 32
Investment provisions, in regional trade agreements, 28t–29t, 32–33
Investor dispute settlement provisions: in regional trade agreements, 28t–29t; undermining of environmental protection by, 107, 108–111
Iraq War (2003): impact on NAFTA, 146; and North American relations, 165, 246, 247, 407; and U.S. trade policy, 254–255
IRCA. See Immigration Reform and Control Act
ISI. See Import-substitution industrialization
Israel, trade agreements, 22t, 38
Italy, antidumping and countervailing duties proceedings, 168t

Jamaica, trade agreements, 22t
Japan: antidumping and countervailing duties proceedings, 168t; trade agreements, 23t; trade disputes, 61n
Joint Defense Commission, 242
Just-in-time inventory model, 9, 10, 17, 59, 247, 255n–256n

Kennedy, John F., 244
Keohane, Robert, 162–163
Kingston Dispensation, 242
Knowledge-capital model of regional trade agreement impact, 43
Kyoto Protocol, 347

Labor, cheap: as Mexican advantage, 16; sources of, 9, 16
Labor dispute resolution, mechanisms for, 128, 129–131, 134
Labor market, regional integration of, 405
Labor protections: activism, 131–132, 133–134, 135–136, 137–144; convergence of, 124; NAFTA impact on, xiii; in regional trade agreements, 28t–29t. See also North American Agreement on Labor Cooperation
Labor unions: activism, 131–132, 133–134, 135–136, 137–144; demands for FTAA, 142–143; fast-track authority and, 137, 139, 171; impact of NAALC on, 123–124, 128, 131–132; impact of NAFTA on, 146; importance to NAFTA success, 145–146; NAALC enforcement and, 130; NAALC negotiations and, 127; need to strengthen, 135; opposition to, 143, 146, 148n–149n; transnational cooperation, 143–144. See also Canadian labor unions; Mexican labor unions; United States labor unions
Latin America: debt crisis in, 26; economic integration in, 117; education spending, 321t; environmental agreements, 95, 96, 104–107; foreign direct investment in, 54, 59; import-substitution industrialization in, 25; industry relocation to, 85; policy reform in, 27; regional trade agreements in, 22t–23t, 24–25, 25–27

Latin American Free Trade Area, 25
Law. *See* International law; Rule of law
Law enforcement, 253, 257*n*; border
    security, 237–238, 251–252; data-
    bases, 253, 257*n*–258*n*; North
    American cooperation, 238, 249–
    250; USA Patriot Act and, 235, 253,
    257*n*. *See also* Mexican drug policies;
    Rule of law; United States drug
    policies
Law of International Extradition, 223
LC. *See* Congreso de Trabajo
Ley Federal Contra la Delicuencia
    Organizada (1996) [LFCDO],
    217–218
LFCDO. *See* Ley Federal Contra la
    Delicuencia Organizada
Liberal Party (Canada), on NAFTA,
    xiii, 3, 4
Lichtinger, Victor, 94, 101–102, 113–
    114
LIMAC. *See* Freedom of Information
    Mexico AC
Locke, John, 347
Lomé Convention, 26
Lopez Mateos, Adolfo, 243
López Portillo, José, economic poli-
    cies, 271
Los Trabajadores/as contra el Área de
    Libre Comercio de las Américas,
    142

Macedo de la Concha, Rafael, 226
Machain, Alvarez, 214
MacLarty, Thomas, 173
Malherbe de León, Oscar, 223
Maquiladoras: direct foreign invest-
    ment and, 9–10, 13; economic
    growth and, 310, 314; labor rights
    in, 148*n*; pregnancy test require-
    ments, 131; rise and decline of, 9,
    16, 85, 124, 125; wages in, 125–126
Martin, Edwin, 243

Martin, Paul, 246, 256*n*
Media: definition of, 190; Mexican
    NGOs and, 191, 196, 199; in Mexi-
    co, 191, 195, 386; oversight function,
    401; perceptions of Mexico, 194;
    power of, 190–191
Mercosur. *See* Southern Cone Com-
    mon Market
MET programs. *See* International
    Military Education and Training
    (MET) programs
Metalclad Corporation, 110, 111
Methanex Corporation, 110
Mexican Academy of Human Rights,
    192
Mexican agriculture: NAFTA impact
    on, 326–330, 332; policy reforms,
    307–308, 328–329; productivity of,
    326
Mexican Association for Internation-
    al Education, 296
Mexican border: Border 2012 plan,
    113; crossing procedures, 17, 59;
    and future of NAFTA, 179; milita-
    rization of, 214, 225; money laun-
    dering on, 220–221; resource
    depletion at, 111; security of, 237–
    238; Smart Border agreements, 17,
    59, 240, 247–250, 252–253, 407
Mexican Constitution: on law enforce-
    ment, 217; political parties in, 374;
    property rights in, 356; proposed
    changes to, 377; right to informa-
    tion in, 197; role of state in, 354, 355;
    social democracy in, 188–190
Mexican drug policies: corruption
    and, 210, 211, 213, 218, 226, 228–
    229; under de la Madrid, 209, 210,
    212, 214; effectiveness of, 228–229;
    enforcement programs, 210, 211,
    212–214, 216–221, 223–224, 225–
    228, 228–229; extradition, 222–
    224; under Fox, 219, 225–226;

human rights violations, 213, 218; under Salinas, 209, 211–216, 225; U.S. certification and, 221–222; and U.S. relations, 176, 209–212, 214–215, 219–222, 226–230, 244; under Zedillo, 216–222, 225–226

Mexican economy: agriculture sector reforms, 307–308, 328–329; capital formation per worker, 402, 403t; capital shortage in, 402; challenges facing, 18, 403; crises, xiii, 14–15, 37–38, 70, 71–72, 75, 78, 124, 164, 173, 209, 222, 265, 271, 272–273, 277, 300, 308, 314, 317, 323, 326, 354, 375, 378–379, 395; dependence on U.S. economy, 5, 47–48, 72–73, 124; dollarization and, 74, 77–79; employment, xii, 83t, 124–126, 308–309; expansion of, 145; fiscal reform, 114; GDP, 309–310, 309f, 319t, 334n, 393, 396f, 398t; Gini coefficient, 319t, 333n–334n; growth, xv, 11, 14, 15f, 18, 70, 270–273, 278–279, 308–309, 309f, 313–316; impact of NAFTA on, 14–15, 308–309, 314–316; income distribution, 271, 272; inflation, 71, 72, 83t, 84–86, 84f, 85f, 273; interest rates, 83t, 84, 85–86, 86f; market reforms, 398; performance vs. North America, 82t–83t, 83–86; privatization of, 286; problems in, 11, 14–15; recession, 178–179; redistribution in, 316–317, 319–320, 326–327, 329–330, 330f, 332; regional integration of, 393–395, 394f, 396f, 399t; strength of, xiii; wages, 125–126. See also Economic convergence within NAFTA; Income inequality in Mexico

Mexican education: accreditation, 300–301; average vs. U.S. and Canada, 315; civic, 384; and economic convergence, 307, 314–316, 316t;

fairness of, 290–294, 291t, 292f, 293f, 318–319, 321–323, 324f–325f; higher education reform, 294–296; intra-NAFTA cooperation, 296–303; NAFTA impact on, 285, 288, 290, 301; primary and secondary, 287–294; quality of, 289–290, 299–300, 318, 319t, 321, 332; resistance to reform, 288, 295, 298, 301, 303; spending on, 320–323, 321t, 324f–325f

Mexican environmental protection: agencies, 103, 104; complaints against, 100–102, 108; environmental agreements, 94, 95, 96; Federal Office of Environmental Attorney General, 103; hazardous waste disposal, 109; history of, 93–94, 102–103; policies, 99, 100–102, 102–104, 116–117; pollution, 93, 94, 102, 111, 113–114; post-NAFTA improvement in, 94, 95, 96, 101–102; resource depletion, 111–114, 116–117

Mexican Environmental Secretariat, 104

Mexican foreign policy: anti-American tilt in, 239, 242, 245, 254, 353–354, 356; independence of, 242; tensions with U.S., 243–245; U.S. antiterrorism campaign and, 235

Mexican health service use, 329–330, 330f

Mexican human rights: increased awareness of, 383–384; pressure to improve, 192–193, 357, 358; U.S. exemptions for, 242–243; war on drugs and, 213, 218

Mexican labor protections: complaint mechanisms, 129; complaints against, 129–130, 130, 133t, 135; impact on U.S. and Canada, 143; model for, 147n–148n; negotiations, 134, 139; policies, 131. See also North American Agreement on Labor Cooperation

Mexican labor unions, 140–141; activism, 132, 135, 140–141; education
reform and, 288, 301; impact of
NAALC on, 144–145; need to
strengthen, 135; policies, 137; power
of, 126, 145; and public services,
320; taming of, 286; transnational
cooperation, 144
Mexican migration. See Migration
from Mexico
Mexican military: growth of, 245–
246; training and aid for, 217, 218,
220, 226–227; in war on drugs,
210, 212–213, 216–219, 224–228,
246
Mexican national security policy:
anti-NATO tilt in, 239; North
American cooperation, 240–242,
245, 246–247, 247–248, 252–253,
254–255; U.S. national security
and, 240
Mexican NGOs: emergence of, 187–
193; future challenges for, 201–
204; legal status of, 202–203; media
and, 191, 196, 199; under NAFTA,
193–195, 357; political impact of,
196–201; political role of, 200–201,
201–202; pressure exerted by, 358;
rising influence of, 97–98, 101–102,
102–103, 357; transnational cooperation, 195; transparency and, 193–
194, 195, 198–199, 201, 202
Mexican political system: characteristics of, 388n; corruption in, 210,
211, 213, 218, 226, 228–229, 244,
383, 400; history of, 172–173, 353–
354, 358, 371–381; and income
inequality, 317; legitimacy in, 316;
NAFTA's impact on, 355–356, 377;
prisoner torture scandal, 192;
public cynicism about, 200; reforms in, 80, 88, 97, 135, 382–387,
408; responsiveness of, 387; and
rule of law, 383–384; unrest in, 300,

326, 333n, 356–357, 373, 377–378.
See also Democracy in Mexico
Mexican population: demographic
complementarity with U.S., 403,
404f; in U.S., 177–178, 267, 277,
279, 393, 397t
Mexican poverty: antipoverty programs, 322–323, 328–330, 330f,
331f; causes of, 11, 326–327; impact of growth on, 313–314, 313t;
impact of NAFTA on, 310–312,
311f, 312f, 313t. See also Economic
convergence within NAFTA
Mexican public opinion: environmental expectations, 98, 102; on
NAFTA, 14, 15–16, 24, 237, 354,
356, 408; political education of,
384; on security cooperation, 254;
on sovereignty, 355; on U.S., 247,
286, 296–297
Mexican reforms: agricultural policy,
307–308, 328–329; education, 288,
294–296, 295, 298, 301, 303; fiscal
reform, 114; market reforms, 398;
in political system, 80, 88, 97, 135,
382–387, 408
Mexican sovereignty: characteristics
of, 347, 353–354, 357–358; concerns, 348; NAFTA and, 286, 341,
347, 353–358, 360; and U.S. war on
drugs, 210, 211–212, 214–215, 217,
218, 219, 220–221
Mexican trade: agricultural imports
vs. exports, 11; agricultural tariffs,
55; agricultural trade agreements,
11–12, 19n; agricultural trade
disputes, 12, 16, 17; antidumping
and countervailing duties proceedings, 168t; automotive industry, 9; basis of success in, 16–17;
bilateral trade agreements, 46;
bureaucracy, 167–169, 171–172;
disputes, 55; in energy products,
398; exports, 70–71, 83t, 238, 271,

309, 310, 392, 395, 397*t*, 405; extra-NAFTA exports, 5, 6*t*, 8*f*, 8*t*; free trade agreements, 71, 166, 174; free trade proposal, *xii*, 3, 25; intra-NAFTA exports, *xi*, 5, 6*t*, 8*f*, 8*t*, 47–48, 58; intra-NAFTA imports, 398; manufactured goods exports, 10; NAFTA impact on, 393–395, 397*t*; openness, 401–402, 402*t*; regional trade agreements, 22*t*, 23*t*, 27, 29*t*, 38, 56, 57. *See also* Maquiladoras

Mexican-U.S. relations: history of, *xii–xiii, xiv*, 146, 164–165, 165–166, 170–171, 173, 177–179, 224–225; migration and, 18, 165, 172, 176–177, 180, 403; NAFTA and, 3–4, 170–171, 171–172, 174–176, 177–178, 229; terrorism and, 164–165, 176–177, 246, 406–407; war on drugs and, 176, 209–212, 214–215, 219–222, 226–230, 244

Mexico: agricultural policies, 324–330; antipoverty programs, 322–323, 328–330, 330*f*, 331*f*; birthrate, 278; Canadian assistance to, *xiv*; compensating impacted workers, *xii*, 326; earthquake of 1985, 192; economic cooperation with U.S., 71–72; economic policies, 14–16, 18, 46, 71–72, 74–82, 83, 85–86, 87–88, 270–272, 285–286; effective exchange rate, 83*t*; expectations for NAFTA, 14, 270; expropriation of U.S. oil companies, 241, 242; foreign direct investment by, 49, 70; foreign direct investment data for, 39–41; foreign direct investment in, 4, 13–14, 13*f*, 41–42, 43, 44*t*–45*t*, 46, 50–51, 52, 61*n*, 73, 116, 308–309, 392, 402; foreign direct investment laws, 37; and GATT, 166, 245, 271, 286, 308, 309–310, 353–354, 401; government transparency in, 97–99, 100–101, 104,

320, 376, 387; impact of NAFTA on, 14–15, 37, 47, 72, 87, 102, 124–126, 272–273, 362, 393, 401, 402; indigenous people of, 356; infant mortality rate, 318, 319*t*; investment diversion and, 32; investment in U.S., 406; investor complaints against, 109, 110, 111, 165; labor costs, 83*t*, 85; labor policies, 144–145; life expectancy, 319*t*; media in, 191, 195, 386; motives for NAFTA, 4; and NAFTA institutional structure, 161–162, 163; NAFTA negotiations, 349, 355–356; national debt, 73; new policy directions, 3; OECD membership, 94; perceptions of, 194; property rights in, 355; protectionist acts, 17; reaction to terrorism, 236–237, 406–407; regional disparities within, *xii*, 15, 271, 290–294, 291*t*, 292*f*, 293*f*, 307, 310, 314, 317–318; risks of NAFTA for, 4; rules of origin, 57; social welfare spending, 320–323, 321*t*, 324*f*–325*f*, 332; taxation in, 286, 327–328, 386, 406. *See also entries under* Mexican

Mexico City: air pollution in, 93, 94, 102; crime in, 216; earthquake of 1985, 192; government of, 371; water supply, 113

Mexico-U.S. Binational Migration Study Group, 270

Miami Summit (1994), 138

Migration: freedom of transit, 135, 138, 297, 299, 300, 395; Smart Border agreements and, 248–249; and U.S. national security, 238, 250–253; volume of, 251

Migration from Mexico: eliminating need for, 18, 245, 264, 279, 405; history of, 264, 265–268, 271, 272, 274–278; NAFTA impact on, *xiii*, 264–265, 277–278, 395–398, 397*t*,

Migration from Mexico *(continued)*
403; NAFTA-Plus and, 18; projected
trends in, 278–279; U.S. views on,
263–264, 270, 273, 405; and U.S.
national security, 238, 250–253; and
U.S.-Mexican relations, 18, 165, 172,
176–177, 180, 403; volume of, 251,
253, 269–270, 274–276, 277, 392–
393. *See also* United States immigration policy
Migratory Birds Convention Act
(Canada), 115
Military forces. *See* Canadian military; Mexican military
Ministry of Commerce and Industrial Promotion (SECOEI), 167–168
Ministry of External Affairs and
International Trade, 296
Ministry of the Economy (Mexico),
167–168
Monetarists, 70
Monetary policy: conditions for
coordination of, 70; in Mexico,
71–72, 74–82, 85–86, 87–88
Monetary theory: history of, 69–70;
importance of agreement in, 70
Monserrat, trade agreements, 22t
Monterrey Technological Institute,
300
Mulroney, Brian, *xiii,* 350
Multilateral Agreement on Investment, 57
Multinational corporations (MNCs):
fear of, 24; motivations for foreign
direct investment, 33–34, 35f;
public opinion of, 60; response to
NAFTA, 51; response to regional
trade agreements, 33–37, 35f, 51–53;
and sovereignty, 349–350; U.S. *vs.*
others, 52; vertical integration, 51–53
Mutual Legal Assistance Treaty
(1991), 214
Myers, S. D., 110

NAAEC. *See* North American Agreement
on Environmental Cooperation
NAALC. *See* North American Agreement on Labor Cooperation
NAD Bank. *See* North American Development Bank
Nader, Ralph, 348
NAFTA: and antidumping/counter-
vailing duties, 55, 56, 60n; Chilean
membership, 56, 57, 105; deepening of, 55–57, 239–240, 359; dispute settlement in, 12, 161–162,
359–360; educating public about,
408–409; environmental institutions, 93, 96, 97, 162, 163; expansion of, 143–144; and foreign
direct investment, 41–42, 43, 44t–
45t, 50–51, 53, 395, 397t; history
of, *xii,* 3, 25; inclusiveness, *xi;*
intraregional export shares, 47, 48t;
investor-state disputes under, 107,
108–111; labor side agreements,
123, 162, 163; migration provisions, 250; monetary cooperation
in, 75–82; monetary integration of,
73, 74; negotiation and ratification, 102, 127, 139–140, 140, 222,
254, 265, 325–326, 332–333, 341,
349, 355, 358; opposition to, 3, 4,
24, 55, 127, 136, 137–144, 172, 193,
325–326, 341, 350, 354; problems
faced by, 179–181; provisions of,
24, 26, 27, 28t; public perception
of, 237; purpose of, 14, 43; reaction
to September 11 attacks, 236–237,
406–407; right of withdrawal
from, 360; studies on, 159–160;
success of, *xiv;* tariffs in, 21; taxation in, 57; trade intensity index,
47, 48t; and transaction costs, 163,
165–167; Transitional Adjustment
Assistance Program, 125; U.S.
national security and, 239–240;

value of unions in, 145–146. *See also* North American Agreement on Environmental Cooperation; North American Agreement on Labor Cooperation

NAFTA impact: on agriculture, 326–330, 332, 395–397, 398*t*, 402; on automotive industry, 52–53; on Canada, 143, 393; on Canadian sovereignty, 350–353, 362; on economic convergence, 307, 309–310, 398, 399*t*; evaluation of, *xi–xii*, 163–169; on foreign direct investment, 52–53; on labor unions, 146; on Mexican economy, 14–15, 308–309, 314–316; on Mexican education, 285, 288, 290, 301; on Mexican NGOs, 193–195, 357; on Mexican politics, 355–356, 377; on Mexican poverty, 310–312, 311*f*, 312*f*, 313*t*; on Mexican sovereignty, 286, 341, 347, 353–358, 360; on Mexican-U.S. relations, 3–4, 170–171, 171–172, 174–176, 177–178, 229; on Mexico, 14–15, 37, 47, 72, 87, 102, 124–126, 272–273, 362, 393, 401, 402; on migration from Mexico, *xiii*, 264–265, 277–278, 395–398, 397*t*, 403; significance, *xii–xiii, xiv*; on trade, 47, 48*f*, 393–395, 397*t*; on U.S., 47, 126, 143, 362, 393; on U.S. economy, 126; on U.S. sovereignty, 348–350, 359–360, 362; on workers, 144–145, 401. *See also* Canadian-U.S. relations; Mexican-U.S. relations

NAFTA institutional structure, 162; Antidumping and Countervailing Duties Group, 167, 167*t*, 168*t*; Committee on Measures Relating to Normalization, 167; committees and working groups, 166–167; erosion of, 169; Free Trade Com-

mission, 166; government bureaucracies, 163, 167–169; limitations of, 165, 178–179, 236, 361, 362, 402; philosophy underlying, 160–163; sovereignty and, 161–162, 359–361; value of, 166–167; Working Group on Rules of Origin, 167

NAFTA-Plus, 18, 246–247, 247–248

National Action Party (PAN), 141, 197, 220, 373, 376–377, 378

National Agreement to Modernize Basic Education (1992), 288–289

National Association of State Congresses, 201

National Association of Universities (ANUIES), 294, 295

National Commission for the Evaluation of Higher Education, 295

National Commission on Human Rights, 358

National Confederation of Popular Organizations, 189

National Council for Educational Promotion (CONAFE), 292

National Council for Science and Technology (CONACYT), 16, 301

National Democratic Front (FDN), 192, 376

National Drug Control Center (CENDRO), 213, 218, 226

National Education Workers Union (SNTE), 288

National Institute for Controlling Drugs (INCD), 213, 218, 226

National Network of Civil Organizations for Human Rights: Full Rights for All, 193

National Research Council, 270

National security: defined, 235–236. *See also* Canadian national security policy; Mexican national security policy; United States national security policy

National Trade Union Confederation, 136
National Union of Farm Workers, 143
National Union of Workers (UNT), 141, 144
National Wildlife Foundation, 107
National Workers Union, 135
NATO: Canadian contingent, 244; Mexico and, 237; and U.S.-Canada relations, 248
Neoliberal institutionalism, on free trade, 162–163
New Democratic Party (Canada), 139
New York Times, 270
New Zealand, trade agreements, 48t
NEXUS, 252, 257n
NGOs. *See* nongovernmental organizations
Nicaragua: and San José Accord, 244; trade agreements, 22t, 27, 29t, 38
Nongovernmental organizations (NGOs): environmental activism, 94, 97–99, 101, 102–103, 117; FTAA negotiations and, 143; impact of NAALC on, 123–124, 128, 131–132; and investor dispute resolution procedures, 109; labor activism, 131–132, 135–136, 140; NAFTA impact on, *xiii*; political role of, 197–198; rising influence of, 94, 97–99, 101, 102–103; transnational cooperation, 195, 202. *See also* Canadian NGOs; Mexican NGOs; United States NGOs
NORAD, 248, 256n
North, Douglas, 162
North America: foreign direct investment in, 41, 42f, 54; policy-making venues for, 236–237; regional trade agreements in, 25. *See also* Regional integration in North America
North American Agreement on Environmental Cooperation

(NAAEC): complaint mechanisms, 96, 99; goals of, 99; impact of, 93–94, 97–99, 348; Joint Public Advisory Committee, 98; as model, 104–105, 117; purposes of, 96; secretariat location, 163
North American Agreement on Labor Cooperation (NAALC): dispute resolution mechanisms, 128, 129–131, 134; enforcement, 127, 134; impact of, 123, 124–126, 127–128, 131–132, 144–145, 348; Labor Cooperation Commission, 143; limitations of, 127, 129–130, 131; negotiations, 127, 140; opposition to, 142, 144; proposals for changes in, 134–136; secretariat location, 163
North American Commission for Environmental Cooperation (CEC): complaints investigated by, 100; enforcement by, 108, 110, 115, 118n; establishment of, 97; host country, 95; role of, 98, 115
North American Common Market, proposal for, 354
North American Cooperative Higher Education Council, 299
North American Development Bank (NAD Bank), 112–113, 116, 403
North American Economic Community, proposal for, 164
North American Regional Academic Mobility Program, 302
Northern Border Response Force, 214, 218
Northern Triangle, trade agreements, 23t, 29t
Nuevo León, education in, 291–292, 291t, 292f, 293f

OAS. *See* Organization of American States
Oaxaca: economy of, 310, 317–318; education in, 291–293, 291t, 292f, 293f

Oaxaca Group, 199
OECD. *See* Organization for Economic Cooperation and Development
Offensive import substitution, in regional trade agreements, 36
Office of the Special Prosecutor for Crimes against Health (FEADS), 218, 226
Office of the U.S. Trade Representative, 117
Oil: for electricity generation, 400*t*; Mexican economy and, 271; NAFTA and, 395; U.S.-Mexican relations and, 180, 393
Olney, Richard, 347
Operación Halcón, 214
Operation Casablanca, 220–221
Opportunidades, 323
Opposition: to CUSFTA, *xiii*, 3, 24; to free trade, 137; to NAALC, 142, 144; to NAFTA, 3, 4, 24, 55, 127, 136, 137–144, 172, 193, 325–326, 341, 350, 354; to regional integration, 408
Organización Regional Interamericana, 142
Organization for Economic Cooperation and Development (OECD): education and, 295, 321*t*; FDI data and, 39; foreign direct investment in, 41–42, 44*t*–45*t*; investment protections in, 33; Mexico in, 94, 286; taxation in, 386
Organization of American States (OAS), 221
Outsider firms, in regional trade agreements, 34–36, 53

Páez, Arturo Everardo, 223
PAN. *See* National Action Party
Panama, trade agreements, 23*t*
Paraguay, trade agreements, 22*t*, 26
PARE. *See* Program to Reduce the Educational Backlog

Partido de Acción Nacional (PAN). *See* National Action Party
Partido de la Revolución Democrática (PRD). *See* Party of the Democratic Revolution
Partido Revolucionario Institucional (PRI). *See* Institutional Revolutionary Party
Party of the Democratic Revolution (PRD), 371, 377, 378
Pastor, Robert, 359
Paz, Octavio, 379
Pemex. *See* Petróleos Mexicanos
Permanent Joint Board on Defense, 242
Perot, Ross, 4, 24, 348
Perry, William J., 226
Peru: education in, 318; trade agreements, 22*t*, 23*t*
Petróleos Mexicanos (Pemex), 15, 81–82
PFP. *See* Federal Preventive Police
PGR. *See* Procuradoria Geral de la República
Plan Puebla-Panama, 117, 318, 332
Plenary Group on Law Enforcement, 219
Pollution: Canada, 114–115; Mexico, 93, 94, 102, 111, 113–114; United States, 114–115
Portugal, GDP, 309–310, 309*f*
Posadas, Cardinal, 215
PRD. *See* Party of the Democratic Revolution
PRI. *See* Institutional Revolutionary Party
PROCAMPO. *See* Programa de Apoyos Directos al Campo
Procuradoria Geral de la República (PGR), 213, 218
Professional accreditation, 301
Program for Educational Development: 1995–2000, 300

Program for Mexican Communities Abroad, 180
Program for Student Mobility, 302
Program to Reduce the Educational Backlog (PARE), 292–293
Programa de Apoyos Directos al Campo (PROCAMPO), 328–329, 330*f*, 332, 398
Programa de Educación, Salud y Alimentación (PROGRESA), 293, 322–323, 329, 332
Programa Nacional de Solidaridad (PRONASOL), 322
PROGRESA. *See* Programa de Educación, Salud y Alimentación
PRONASOL. *See* Programa Nacional de Solidaridad
Public opinion: Media power over, 190–191; on NAFTA, 14, 15–16, 24, 237, 350, 354, 356, 408; on regional trade agreements, 59–60. *See also* Canadian public opinion; Mexican public opinion
Public security: defined, 236; North American measures, 241

Quebec Coalition, 136
Quebec Education Central, 136
Quebec Network, 136
Quebec Workers Federation, 136

Rationalization investment, in regional trade agreements, 36
Reagan, Ronald W.: free trade proposals, 354; Mexican relations, 173, 175; war on drugs, 210
Rebollo, Gutiérrez, 218
Red Mexicana de Accion Frente al Comercio (RMALC), 134, 142, 150*n*
Regional integration in North America: educating public about, 408–409; forces driving, 391, 392,

401–402; future challenges and directions, *xiii*, 54–59, 74, 401–409; as goal, 408, 409; impact of terrorism on, 391, 406–407; inevitability of, 405, 407; and institutional structure, 391–392, 405; of labor market, 405; monetary convergence, 75–82, 86–88; opposition to, 408; pre-NAFTA, 392; progress of, 255; purpose of, 392; in taxation, 406. *See also* NAFTA-Plus
Regional trade agreements (RTAs): in Americas, 21, 22*t*–23*t*; complicating factors in, 36–41; depth of integration, 26–27, 28*t*–29*t*; economic effects of, 30–34; economists' view of, 21–24; future policy directions, 54–60; history of, 21; hub-and-spoke pattern, 38–39, 57, 246–247; impact on foreign direct investment, 21–24, 27–54, 30*f*, 35*f*; impact on member countries, 33; impact on trade, 47–50, 48*t*; investment provisions in, 28*t*–29*t*, 32–33; in Latin America, 22*t*–23*t*, 24–25, 25–27; modeling of economic impact, 43–47; in North America, 25; public opinion on, 59–60; response of multinational corporations to, 33–37, 35*f*
Reorganization investment, in regional trade agreements, 36
Ricardo, David, 69
Rio Treaty. *See* Inter-American Treaty of Reciprocal Assistance
RMALC. *See* Red Mexicana de Accion Frente al Comercio
Royal Canadian Mounted Police, 249
RTAs. *See* Regional trade agreements
Ruiz Massieu, Francisco, 215
Rule of law: Mexican political system and, 383–384; and sovereignty, 344–346. *See also* Law enforcement

Rules of origin provisions: in regional trade agreements, 28t–29t; removal of, 56, 57
Russia, trade agreements, 23t
St. Kitts and Nevis, trade agreements, 22t
St. Lucia, trade agreements, 22t
St. Vincent and the Grenadines, trade agreements, 22t
Salinas de Gortari, Carlos: antipoverty programs, 322; democratization and, 376; drug policies, 209, 211–216, 225; economic policies, 285–286, 354–355, 357; education policies, 287–288, 295, 300; environmental protection under, 103; foreign policy, 356; free trade proposal, xii, 3, 164; legitimacy crisis, 285, 355; NAFTA and, 4, 14, 358, 359; political strategy, 356; political unrest and, 300; reform and, 357, 358, 377; on sovereignty, 354–355; U.S. relations, 171, 174–175, 174t, 180, 182n, 209, 214–215, 224–225, 229
San José Accord, 244
Sanitary provisions, in regional trade agreements, 28t–29t
SECOEI. See Ministry of Commerce and Industrial Promotion
Secretariat of Public Education (SEP), 287, 292–293, 296, 300, 302
Secure Electronic Network for Traveler's Rapid Inspection, 252
Security: national security defined, 235–236; public security, 236, 241; use of force and, 236. See also Canadian national security policy; Mexican national security policy; United States national security policy
Select Commission on Immigration and Refugee Policy, 268

SEP. See Secretariat of Public Education
September 11 terrorist attacks: impact on border crossings, 17, 59, 60, 179, 247; impact on NAFTA, 146, 169, 236–237; impact on North American relations, 164–165, 176–177, 246, 406–407; impact on regional integration, 391, 406–407; impact on U.S. immigration policy, 250–251, 263; impact on U.S. politics, 139; impact on U.S. security measures, 235
Services provisions, in regional trade agreements, 28t–29t
Siddon, Thomas E., 298
Sindicatos de Telefonistas de la República Mexicana (STRM), 132, 140
Singapore, trade agreements, 54, 254–255
Sistema de Información Empresarial Mexicano. See Ministry of Commerce and Industrial Promotion
Smart Border agreements, 17, 59, 240, 247–250, 252–253, 407
SNTE. See National Education Workers Union
Social welfare reforms, need for, 408
Solidarity Program, 293
Sony labor case, 148n
South Korea: antidumping and countervailing duties proceedings, 168t; trade agreements, 23t
Southern Cone Common Market (Mercosur): characteristics of, 21, 27; impact on trade, 47, 48f; intraregional export shares, 47, 48t; limited depth of, 55; members, 38; provisions of, 24, 28t; regional trade agreements, 22t, 23t, 28t–29t; tensions within, 37; trade intensity index, 47, 48t; trade patterns in, 26

Sovereignty: constitutional, 346–347, 347–348; cultural, 350–352; de facto *vs.* de jure, 343; definition and types of, 341, 342–347, 361–362; internal *vs.* external, 346; multinational corporations and, 349–350; and NAFTA institutional structure, 161–162, 359–361; national, 346–347, 353–354; rule of law and, 344–346. *See also* Canadian sovereignty; Mexican sovereignty; United States sovereignty
Soviet Union, collapse of, 26
Spaghetti Bowl Effect, 38–39
Special and differential treatment provisions, in regional trade agreements, 28*t*–29*t*
Special Anti-Money-Laundering Unit (UECLD), 218
Special Organized Crime Unit (UEDO), 218
Sprint labor case, 148*n*–149*n*
Sri Lanka: economic data, 319*t*; human development data, 318, 319*t*
Standards, reconciliation of, 17
Static gains from trade, in regional trade agreements, 30–31, 33
STRM. *See* Sindicatos de Telefonistas de la República Mexicana
Sugar industry, trade disputes, 12, 17
Super 301, 348
Sweden, European Union and, 74
Sweeney, John, 144

Taiwan, antidumping and countervailing duties proceedings, 168*t*
Taliban, 246
Tariff(s): elimination in regional trade agreements, 28*t*–29*t*; harmonization of, 56–57
TATs. *See* Transnational arbitration treaties
Taxation: corporate income tax, 58; in Mexico, 286, 327–328, 386, 406;

NAFTA withholding taxes, 57; regional integration in, 406. *See also* Bilateral tax treaties; Tariff(s)
Technical barriers to trade provisions, in regional trade agreements, 28*t*–29*t*
Temporary entry provisions, in regional trade agreements, 28*t*–29*t*
Terrorism: law enforcement efforts, 238, 249–250; and Mexican-U.S. relations, 164–165, 176–177, 246, 406–407; and USA Patriot Act, 235, 253, 257*n*. *See also* September 11 terrorist attacks; United States national security policy
Texas, water resources, 112
TIAR. *See* Inter-American Treaty of Reciprocal Assistance
Trade: automotive industry, 9; change inherent in, 342, 355, 356; in energy products, 393–395; exchange rate and, 74, 75; extra-NAFTA exports, 5, 6*t*, 7*f*, 8*f*, 8*t*; importance of environment policies to, 97, 117; Intra-NAFTA, *xi*, 5, 6*t*, 7*f*, 8*f*, 8*t*, 42*f*, 47–48, 49, 58, 309, 398, 405; methods of analyzing, 4–5; NAFTA creation of, *xi, xii, xv*, 4–10, 395, 397*t*; regional trade agreements' impact on, 47–50, 48*t*. *See also* Canadian trade; Mexican trade; United States trade
Trade Act (1974), 348
Trade agreements. *See* Agricultural trade agreements; Bilateral trade agreements; Free trade agreements; Regional trade agreements; *specific agreements*
Trade creation, in regional trade agreements, 30–31
Trade dispute(s): agricultural, *xv*, 10–11, 12, 16, 17; NAFTA and, *xiii–xiv*; WTO arbitration of, 12, 55,

61*n*. *See also* Antidumping and countervailing duties

Trade dispute resolution: environmental disputes, 96, 99, 100, 106, 107, 108–111, 117; importance of, 17; investor disputes, 28*t*–29*t*, 107, 108–111; labor disputes, 128, 129–131, 134; in NAFTA, 12, 161–162, 359–360; in regional trade agreements, 28*t*–29*t*, 32; WTO panel, 12

Trade diversion effects, in regional trade agreements, 30–31

Trade intensity indices (TIIs), for regional trade agreements, 47, 48*f*

Trade remedy laws, national, 55–56

Trade unions. *See* Labor unions

Transaction costs, NAFTA impact on, 163, 165–167

Transitional costs, in regional trade agreements, 31

Transnational arbitration treaties (TATs), growth in, 27

Transparency, in NAFTA regulations, 360

Transparency and Access to Public Information Law (Mexico), 203

Transparency in government: environmental agreements, 97–99, 100–101, 104; free trade and, 400–401; freedom of information laws, 104, 197; media power and, 191; Mexican NGOs and, 193–194, 195, 198–199, 201, 202; in Mexico, 97–99, 100–101, 104, 320, 376, 387

Treaty of Guadalupe Hidalgo (1848), 4, 170

Treaty of Westphalia (1648), 346

Trinidad and Tobago, trade agreements, 22*t*, 23*t*

Trudeau, Pierre Elliott, 244

Turner, John, 4

UAM. *See* Autonomous Metropolitan University

UECLD. *See* Special Anti-Money-Laundering Unit

UEDO. *See* Special Organized Crime Unit

UNAM. *See* Autonomous National University of Mexico

UNCTAD. *See* United Nations Conference on Trade and Development

Unemployment: compensating impacted workers, *xii*, 125; NAFTA's impact of, *xiv*, 14; rate, by nation, 82*t*–83*t*

UNESCO, 288

United Electrical (UE), 130

United Kingdom: European Exchange Rate Mechanism and, 73, 88*n*; European Union and, 74; foreign direct investment in, 392

United Nations, 242

United Nations Conference on Trade and Development (UNCTAD), 39

United States: agricultural subsidies, 55; compensating impacted workers, *xii*, 125; economic cooperation with Mexico, 71–72; economic policies, 74, 83; effective exchange rate, 82*t*; expectations for NAFTA, 4, 14, 245, 263, 268, 270; FDI incentives programs, 58; foreign direct investment by, 46, 49, 51, 52, 53, 116, 392; foreign direct investment data for, 39–41; foreign direct investment in, 41–42, 44*t*–45*t*, 46; impact of NAFTA on, 47, 126, 143, 362, 393; investor complaints against, 110; labor costs, 82*t*; Mexican financial rescue, 71–72, 124, 164, 173, 222, 265; Mexican investment in, 406; motives for NAFTA, 3–4; and NAFTA institutional structure, 161–162, 163; NAFTA negotiations, 349; new policy directions, 3; protectionist acts, 17; public opinion of free trade, 24,

United States *(continued)*
408; as regional hegemon, 24; regional trade agreements, 22*t*, 23*t*,
29*t*, 38, 54, 57, 96; rules of origin, 57
United States border: Border 2012
plan, 113; crossing procedures, 17,
59; and future of NAFTA, 179;
militarization of, 225; money laundering on, 220–221; resource depletion at, 111; security of, 237–238,
251–252; September 11 attacks and,
17, 59, 60, 179, 247; Smart Border
agreements, 17, 59, 240, 247–250,
252–253, 407. *See also* United States
immigration policy
United States Commission on Immigration Reform, 270
United States drug policies: and
Canadian relations, 255; certification program, 221–222; effectiveness of, 228–229; enforcement
within Mexico, 210, 211–212, 214–
215, 217, 218, 219, 220–221; extradition, 222–224; and Mexican
relations, 176, 209–212, 214–215,
219–222, 226–230, 244
United States economy: capital formation per worker, 402, 403*t*;
dominance of, 5, 47–49, 72–73,
124; employment, *xiv*, 14, 82*t*, 125;
future challenges, 403; growth, 5;
impact of NAFTA on, 126; infla-
tion, 82*t*, 84, 84*f*, 85*f*; interest rates,
82*t*, 83–84, 85–86, 86*f*; manufacturing sector, 125–126; performance *vs.* North America, 82*t*–83*t*,
83–86; recession, 54, 60, 124, 125,
146, 178–179, 264, 314; regional
integration of, 393–395, 394*f*, 396*f*,
399*t*; wages, 125–126
United States education, intra-NAF-
TA cooperation, 296–303
United States environmental protection: agreements, 94, 95, 96, 106–

107; complaints against, 100, 115;
pollution, 114–115; resource depletion, 111–113, 114–115
United States foreign policy: tensions
with Mexico and Canada, 243–245;
trade policy integration with, 254–
255, 347–348; unilateralism in, 247,
348, 350
United States Foreign Terrorist Tracking Task Force, 249
United States immigration policy:
effectiveness of, 276–277; history of,
263, 267–268, 273–278; impact of
September 11 attacks on, 250–251,
263
United States Information Agency
(USIA), 296, 408
United States labor protections: complaint mechanisms, 129; complaints against, 130, 132–133, 133*t*;
model for, 147*n*–148*n*; negotiations, 134; weakness of, 133, 145,
149*n*. *See also* North American
Agreement on Labor Cooperation
United States labor unions: activism,
132, 137–139; policies, 137; power
of, 126, 139, 145; transnational
cooperation, 143–144
United States national security policy: antiterrorism campaign, 235,
253; Canadian views on, 247; and
future of NAFTA, 239–240; issues
and challenges, 237–239; Mexican
views on, 247; migration and,
250–253; North American cooperation, 240–242, 245, 246–247, 247–
248, 251–253, 253–255, 256*n*
United States NGOs: influence of, 97;
and NAFTA negotiations, 360
United States politics, Hispanic population and, 177–178, 180, 279
United States population: demographic complementarity with
Mexico, 403, 404*f*; Mexicans/His-

panics in, 177–178, 267, 277, 279, 393, 397*t*
United States President, fast-track trade authority, 38, 54, 137, 138–139, 139, 171
United States sovereignty: history of, 347–348; and International Court of Justice, 363*n*; NAFTA and, 348–350, 359–360, 362
United States trade: agricultural tariffs, 55; agricultural trade agreements, 11–12, 19*n*; antidumping and countervailing duties complaints, 55, 56; automotive industry, 9; bilateral trade agreements, 46; bureaucracy, 169; with China, 5, 408; disputes, 12, 17, 55; exports, 82*t*, 392; extra-NAFTA exports, 5, 6*t*, 7*f*, 8*t*; free trade agreements, 16–17, 25, 27, 104–105, 106–107, 117, 166, 174; intra-NAFTA exports, *xi*, 5, 6*t*, 7*f*, 8*t*, 49, 398; intra-NAFTA imports, 309, 405; Mexican exports to, 70–71; NAFTA impact on, 393–395, 397*t*; openness, 401–402, 402*t*
United States trade policy: on antidumping and countervailing duties, 55, 56; foreign policy and, 254–255, 347–348
United States v. *Alvarez Machain,* 214
United States welfare programs, Mexican immigration and, 268–269
United States–Canada relations: Canadian military and, 246; Cold War and, 248; history of, *xiv*; impact of September 11 attacks on, 246; terrorism and, 406–407; war on drugs and, 255
United States-Mexican Extradition Treaty, 223
United States-Mexican relations: history of, *xii–xiii, xiv,* 146, 164–165, 165–166, 170–171, 173, 177–179, 224–225; impact of NAFTA on, 3–4, 170–171, 171–172, 174–176, 177–178, 229; migration and, 18, 165, 172, 176–177, 180, 403; terrorism and, 164–165, 176–177, 246, 406–407; war on drugs and, 176, 209–212, 214–215, 219–222, 226–230, 244
United States-Mexico Alliance Against Drugs, 219
University of Guadalajara, 303
University of the Americas, 300
UNT. *See* National Union of Workers
Uruguay: education in, 318; trade agreements, 22*t,* 23*t,* 26
USA Patriot Act, 235, 253, 257*n*
USIA. *See* United States Information Agency

Van Putten, Mark, 107
Vancouver Symposium, 298–300
Velázquez, Fidel, 141
Venezuela: and San José Accord, 244; trade agreements, 22*t,* 27
Vertical foreign direct investment, 34
Vietnam: economic data, 319*t*; human development data, 318, 319*t*
Vogelsang SupWald test, 50

Wages: in Canada, 147*n*; education and, 307, 314–316; NAFTA and, 125–126. *See also* Income inequality in Mexico
Waste Management Inc., 110
Water resources: depletion of, 111–113, 116–117; and North American relations, 247; and U.S. national security, 238
Weintraub, Sidney, 161
Western Hemisphere, proliferation of free trade agreements, *xi*
Wimbledon case, 345

Wingspread conference, 296–298
Wingspread statement, 297
Workers: compensation for free trade
  impact, *xii*, 125, 326; freedom of
  transit for, 135, 138, 395; impact of
  NAFTA on, 144–145, 401; migrant,
  131, 144; resistance to regional
  integration, 408
Workers Against NAFTA, 142
World Bank: education and, 292; on
  hazardous waste disposal, 109;
  International Center for Settlement of Investment Disputes, 109;
  and Latin American debt crisis, 26;
  Mexican reforms and, 285, 288,
  301; poverty measure, 311
World Investment Report (UNCTAD),
  39
World Trade Organization (WTO):
  agricultural trade and, 10; Cancún

meeting, 10; Doha round, 10, 56;
  fear of, 304*n*; regional trade agreements and, 21; trade dispute settlement, 12, 55, 61*n*; and U.S. policy,
  54
Wright, Jim, 170–171
WTO. *See* World Trade Organization

Zapatista movement, 300, 326, 333*n*,
  356–357, 377
Zedillo, Ernesto: antipoverty programs, 322–323; drug policies, 216–
  222, 225–226; economic policies,
  318; education policies, 287; environmental policies, 102; reforms,
  357, 358; as secretary of public
  education, 288, 296, 300, 304*n*, 408;
  on sovereignty, 358; U.S. relations,
  174*t*, 220–221
Zoellick, Robert, 117, 164, 173, 255

ABOUT THE AUTHORS

John Bailey is professor of government and foreign service at Georgetown University, where he has taught since 1970. He has edited several recent books on U.S.–Mexican relations, including *Organized Crime and Democratic Governability: Mexico and the U.S.–Mexican Borderlands* (University of Pittsburgh Press, 2001; coedited with Roy Godson).

Frank D. Bean is professor of sociology and codirector of the Center for Research on Immigration, Population, and Public Policy at the University of California, Irvine. He has published numerous research articles in such scholarly journals as *Demography, Population and Development Review, the American Sociological Review,* and *Social Forces,* as well as written for the *New York Times* and the *Houston Chronicle.* He is the author or editor of 16 books and papers, including *The Hispanic Population of the United States* (with Marta Tienda; Russell Sage Foundation, 1987) and, most recently, "Mexican-Origin Fertility: New Patterns and Interpretations" (*Social Science Quarterly* [2000] 81: 404–20).

Graciela Bensusán is a full-time professor at the Universidad Autonoma Metropolitana and since 1989 has been a part-time professor at the Facultad Latinoamericana de Ciencias Sociales in Mexico City. Her last publication was *El modelo mexicano de regulación laboral* (The Mexican model of labor regulation; Plaza y Valdés Editores, 2000).

Lorraine Eden is professor of management and university faculty fellow at Texas A&M University in College Station, where she teaches courses on multinational enterprises (MNEs) and the economics of international business. Her research focuses on the political economy of MNEs, specializing in transfer pricing, international taxation, and regional integration. She has published almost 100 scholarly papers and books.

Rafael Fernández de Castro is the founder and head of the Department of International Studies at the Instituto Tecnológico Autónomo de México. He is also the director of *Foreign Affairs en Español*. His most recent publications are *México en el mundo: Los desafíos para México en 2001 México* (ITAM, 2002); *Cambio y continuidad en la política exterior de México* (Ariel-Planeta, 2002); and *En la frontera del imperio* (Planeta Mexicana, 2003).

Janine Ferretti is the chief of the Environment Division at the Inter-American Development Bank, which she joined in 2003 after she completed her term as the executive director of the North American Commission for Environmental Cooperation.

Jan Gilbreath is an environmental policy specialist at the U.S. Environmental Protection Agency who focuses her work on issues related to developing countries. She is a former senior associate at the Center for Strategic and International Studies. Her most recent book is *Environment and Development in Mexico: Recommendations for Reconciliation* (CSIS, 2003).

Dan Li is a doctoral student of strategy and international business at the Mays Business School, Texas A&M University. Her research interests focus on strategic management of multinational enterprises, with a particular focus on corporate governance, internal and external networks of multinational firms, and strategic transfer pricing. Her research has been published, or accepted for publication, in *Management International Review*, *Southwest Review of International Business Research*, *Group and Organization Management*, and *Journal of Mathematical Sociology*.

B. Lindsay Lowell is director of policy studies for the Institute for the Study of International Migration at Georgetown University. He was previously director of research for the congressionally appointed Commission on Immigration Reform, where he was also assistant director for the Mexico–U.S. Binational Study on Migration. He recently coedited *Sending Money Home: Hispanic Remittances and Community Development* (Rowman and Littlefield, 2002; with Rodolfo O. de la Garza); and he has published more than 100 articles and reports on his research interests in immigration policy, labor force, economic development, and the global mobility of the highly skilled.

Carlos Ornelas is professor of education and communications at the Metropolitan University in Mexico City. He is the author of 5 books, 24 chapters in other volumes, more than 50 articles, and 20 unpublished policy and research reports. He received the W.G. Walker Best Paper Award (given by the MCB University Press) for his article "The Politics of Educational Decentralization in Mexico," which was published in the *Journal of Educational Administration* (vol. 38, no. 5, 2000).

Rogelio Ramírez de la O is president of Ecanal, a private economic research company that publishes, analyzes, and advises large international firms with interest in Mexico. He publishes monthly and quarterly economic reports for his clients and frequently publishes ad hoc pieces for international think tanks and academic institutions.

Jesús F. Reyes-Heroles is the president of Structura, a Mexican consulting firm. He is the cofounder and executive president of the Grupo de Economistas y Asociados. He was the ambassador of Mexico to the United States from October 1997 to November 2000. Before that, he was secretary of energy in President Ernesto Zedillo's cabinet.

James Robinson is professor of international relations and U.S. foreign policy at the Instituto Tecnologico Autonomo de Mexico. He has published articles on sovereignty, globalization, and U.S. foreign policy. He is now completing a book titled *Globalization and the Reconstitution of Mexican Sovereignty*.

John Scott is a researcher and former director of the Economics Division at the Centro de Investigación y Docencia Económicas in Mexico City. His principal research areas include the study of poverty, social policy, welfare economics, and the philosophy of economics. He has undertaken evaluation studies of the principal antipoverty programs implemented in Mexico in recent years.

María Celia Toro is professor-researcher of international relations at El Colégio de México (Colmex) and was the director of the Centro de Estudio Internacionales from 1997 to 2002 at Colmex. She has served as editor of the international relations quarterly *Foro internacional*, and she is the author of *Mexico's War on Drugs: Causes and Consequences* (Lynne Rienner, 1995) and *Transnational Organized Crime and International Security: Business as Usual?* (Lynne Rienner, 2002).

Ernesto Villanueva is a professor at Universidad Iberoamericana, where he also coordinates the Programa Iberoamericano de Derecho de la Información. His most recent publications include *Etica de la radio y la televisión* (Universidad Iberoamericana–Unesco, 2000) and *Derecho mexicano de la información* (Oxford University Press, 2000).

Sidney Weintraub holds the William E. Simon Chair in Political Economy at the Center for Strategic and International Studies and is simultaneously director of the Americas Program at the center. His most recent publications are *Financial Decision-Making in Mexico: To Bet a Nation* (University of Pittsburgh Press, 2000) and *Constructive Irreverence: Issues in International Political Economy* (CSIS, 2004).

José Woldenberg Karakowsky was the president of the Instituto Federal Electoral from 1994 to 2003. He is now a professor at the School of Political Science at the Universidad Nacional Metropolitana and a member of the National System of Researchers. He was also the president of the Instituto de Estudios para la Transicion Democratica. His recent publications include *Memória de la izquierda* (Cal y Arena, 1998) and *La construccion de la democracia* (Plaza y Janés, 2000).